国家卫生健康委员会"十四五"规划教材配

全国高等学校配套教材

供基础、临床、预防、口腔医学类专业用

基础化学实验
（中英文对照版）

Experiment in Basic Chemistry

第 **5** 版

主　编　李雪华　陈志琼

副主编　苟宝迪　林　毅　于　昆

编　委　（以姓氏笔画为序）

于　昆	大连医科大学	陈志琼	重庆医科大学
王金玲	山西医药学院	武世奎	内蒙古医科大学
王英骥	哈尔滨医科大学	苟宝迪	北京大学
尹计秋	大连医科大学	林　毅	武汉大学
白天语	大连医科大学	周昊霏	内蒙古医科大学
乔秀文	新疆第二医学院	周春艳	广西医科大学
吕雅娟	山西医药学院	赵全芹	山东大学
刘国杰	中国医科大学	秦向阳	空军军医大学
李　蓉	贵州医科大学	梁洪文	重庆医科大学
李振泉	济宁医学院	康　凯	河北医科大学
李雪华	广西医科大学	黄　静	广西医科大学
李献锐	河北医科大学	傅　迎	大连医科大学
李福森	广西医科大学	赖泽锋	广西医科大学
别子俊	蚌埠医科大学	廖传安	广西医科大学
宋　慧	广西医科大学		

编写秘书　周春艳　（兼）

人民卫生出版社
·北京·

图书在版编目（CIP）数据

基础化学实验 / 李雪华，陈志琼主编. -- 5 版.
北京 ：人民卫生出版社，2025. 8. --（全国高等学校
五年制本科临床医学专业第十轮规划教材配套教材）.
ISBN 978-7-117-38292-2

Ⅰ. O6-3

中国国家版本馆 CIP 数据核字第 20251FM919 号

人卫智网	www.ipmph.com	医学教育、学术、考试、健康，购书智慧智能综合服务平台
人卫官网	www.pmph.com	人卫官方资讯发布平台

基础化学实验
Jichu Huaxue Shiyan
第 5 版

主　　编：李雪华　陈志琼
出版发行：人民卫生出版社（中继线 010-59780011）
地　　址：北京市朝阳区潘家园南里 19 号
邮　　编：100021
E - mail：pmph @ pmph.com
购书热线：010-59787592　010-59787584　010-65264830
印　　刷：人卫印务（北京）有限公司
经　　销：新华书店
开　　本：787×1092　1/16　　印张：18
字　　数：472 千字
版　　次：2005 年 2 月第 1 版　　2025 年 8 月第 5 版
印　　次：2025 年 8 月第 1 次印刷
标准书号：ISBN 978-7-117-38292-2
定　　价：55.00 元

打击盗版举报电话：010-59787491　E-mail：WQ @ pmph.com
质量问题联系电话：010-59787234　E-mail：zhiliang @ pmph.com
数字融合服务电话：4001118166　E-mail：zengzhi @ pmph.com

前言

　　《基础化学实验》(第5版)是国家卫生健康委员会"十四五"规划教材《基础化学》(第10版)的配套教材,供高等医学院校五年制基础、临床、预防、口腔医学类和临床药学等专业使用。

　　教材的编写宗旨是以学生自主学习为导向,为学生综合实验技能、创新能力的培养提供策略与手段。注重体现素质教育、创新能力与实践能力的培养,为学生知识、能力、素质协调发展创造条件。

　　本教材自2004年第1版教材出版以来,受到使用单位的欢迎。经过19年的使用,在认真听取使用单位的意见建议后,融合全国多所高等医学院校基础化学教学改革的成果,汲取国内外优秀教材的先进经验,在编写内容和编写方法上进行创新,并在结合实验教学改革所取得新的进展的基础上,修订编写成《基础化学实验》(第5版)。

　　本教材以基础化学实验教学作为培养学生综合实验技能的载体,从教学主体、教学内容、教学手段、教学设计等多方面考虑,将全新教育理念融入教材中,构建有效培养学生自主学习、发现问题、分析问题、解决问题能力的教学体系。在实施实验教学的过程中,学生的角色准确定位,在完成《基础化学实验》课程的学习过程中逐渐获得和完善自主学习能力、创新思维能力和批判性思维等综合素质。

　　本教材是一本综合性基础实验教材,包含了无机化学、分析化学及物理化学等课程的实验内容。教材编排上分为"基础化学实验基本知识"和"基础化学实验课题"两个部分;基础化学实验课题部分,按基本操作训练实验、滴定分析实验、分光光度法实验、化学原理实验、无机化合物制备实验、综合及研究性实验和开放设计性实验7个课题共22个实验进行编写。22个实验根据内容或方法的不同可包含多个相互渗透的子课题。我们希望编排分类清楚、目的明确,便于学生逐级从纵、深两维度掌握实验技能。

　　本教材内容用中、英文编写,内容基本一一对应,以加强学生外语能力的培养,便于全英语教学和双语教学。

　　新修订的教材凸显了以下特点:

　　1. 更新教学和人才培养模式的观念,注重教材的启发性,合理设置实验的编写内容,从实验目的、实验预习作业、实验步骤、数据记录及结果分析到思考题,多方面强化学生的自主学习能力,培养学生综合实验技能。

　　2. 更新调整了实验预习作业方式,通过经典实验,使学生从实验设计者的角度换位思考,纵观及写出实验设计总思路,考虑得到精准实验结果所需考量的每一个细节、注意点,鼓励学生改进实验方案使结果更佳或领会多种实现同一实验目标的实验方法。为帮助刚入学的一年级学生更好地领悟相关内容,还提供了引导问题帮助学生思考,培养学生严谨的科研思维、理论与实践相结合的实验技能、批判性精神及创新思维能力等综合素质。

3. 教材中的实验内容涉及分析化学、物理化学及无机化合物制备等,在知识点上与主教材对应,且有一定延伸和拓展。

4. 优化各实验文字表述和思考题,论述严谨、语言流畅简洁、层次分明、术语规范、图表直观。

5. 更新了实验相关及附录的数据。

6. 结合国外同类教材的编写模式,引进新的教学理念和内容,进一步提升教材质量。

在编写本书的过程中,编者在叙述科学性、准确性、合理性方面做了很大努力,但难免有缺点和错误,诚恳地希望读者对书中不妥和错误之处批评指正。

李雪华　陈志琼

2024 年 5 月

目录

第一篇 基础化学实验基本知识

第一章 | 实验室规则及安全知识

一、基础化学实验的目的

基础化学实验是基础化学课程的重要组成部分。基础化学实验的目的不仅仅是验证理论知识和一些实验现象，理解和掌握实验课程内容，更重要的是学会将理论与实践相结合，并将理论应用于实践中，培养学生严谨的科学态度和综合实验技能。

学生通过实验课的严格训练，掌握规范的化学实验操作、正确记录和处理实验数据、分析实验现象、表述实验结果，学会总结实验规律，给出实验结论。通过自己动手设计和完成实验，培养独立思考和独立解决问题的能力，同时培养严谨的科学态度，从而逐步掌握科学研究方法及实验技能的应用。

二、化学实验室一般规则

1. 首次进化学实验室前，应仔细阅读实验室规则及安全知识。

2. 实验前应认真预习实验教程，阅读有关教材及参考书，明确实验目的与要求，了解实验基本原理和方法，熟悉实验步骤，做好预习报告。

3. 仔细阅读仪器使用指南，按照说明进行操作。不得进行未经许可的实验和操作。

4. 学生进实验室应穿白大褂，禁止穿拖鞋。实验过程应严肃认真，正确操作、认真仔细观察，并及时记录实验现象与数据。根据原始记录，写出实验报告，按时交给教师。

5. 不允许单独一人在实验室工作。实验中的任何事故无论大小均须及时向教师报告。

6. 公用仪器与试剂只能在原处使用，不得随意挪动。

7. 从试剂瓶中取出的试剂，不得再倒回原瓶中。取试剂前应两次阅读标签，以保证药品名称和浓度正确。

8. 勿将试剂瓶盖接口处接触其他表面。为避免试剂瓶盖污染试剂，建议一次只打开一瓶试剂。如果试剂瓶盖只有硬币大小，倒试剂时，用手夹住瓶盖，就不会因弄混瓶盖造成污染。

9. 禁止将食物带进实验室，勿在实验室饮食。

10. 实验中应注意安全，易燃药品应远离火源。保持实验室和桌面干净整洁，不要将杂物随地乱扔，用过的试纸、火柴等放在烧杯中，待实验结束后倒入废物缸。腐蚀性和有毒化品必须按规定回收，切勿将固体废物、腐蚀性液体和有毒试剂倒入水槽。

11. 实验结束前，不得擅自离开实验室。实验完毕，立即清洗仪器，整理药品、仪器及实验台，做好实验室、天平室与仪器室的清洁。关好门、窗及水、电、气源后，方可离开实验室。

三、化学实验室的安全知识

1. 水、电、火防护　首次进实验室,必须了解楼层的所有逃生通道;每次进实验室,首先打开实验室窗户,并保证通风状态良好;确认实验室水、电、气的安装情况,灭火器材存放位置及使用方法,以便应急使用。

2. 危险物质、有毒气体防护　谨慎处理易燃、易爆、有毒及有腐蚀性和剧毒物质。使用危险物质、有毒有害气体或挥发性有毒物质时,应在通风条件良好的地方如通风橱中操作并远离火源。

3. 化学操作防护　在加热试管中的液体时,先将试管外壁擦干,勿将试管对准自己或他人。不要直接加热试管底部,应倾斜试管缓缓加热液体上端到试管底部之间的部位。

4. 化学试剂防护　打开盐酸、硝酸、氨水或过氧化氢等试剂瓶塞时小心气体冲出。嗅闻气味时,不要将鼻直接接近瓶口,而应用手扇闻。使用浓酸、浓碱和洗液时,应避免接触皮肤或溅在衣服上,特别要注意保护眼睛(佩戴防护眼镜)。

5. 个人安全防护　使用热的或腐蚀性液体时,应戴防护眼镜并穿防护外套以保护皮肤和衣物。穿皮鞋会比穿帆布鞋或凉鞋更安全。

6. 化学药品处理　保持台面清洁,及时清除溅落的酸碱。若化学药品溅到眼睛或皮肤上,立即用大量清水冲洗患处,冲洗后,若是皮肤,还应抹上肥皂,并用水清洗。

7. 电气设备使用　要确保电压-电流功率匹配,切勿用湿手接触电源插头;确保水、电处于分离状态。

8. 实验室备用急救包　学生实验室要备有急救包,常见的急救用品包括:医用纱布块、医用弹性绷带、创可贴、医用透气胶带、碘伏消毒液、医用敷贴、医用酒精棉片、清洁湿巾、烫伤药物、急救手册等,以备急救时使用。

四、化学实验操作过程中可能发生的事故与处理

1. 割伤　在伤口上涂抹碘酒后,敷贴创可贴。

2. 烫伤　在伤口上涂抹烫伤药膏或用浓$KMnO_4$溶液擦至灼伤处皮肤变为棕色,再涂抹凡士林或烫伤药膏。

3. 酸碱腐蚀　立即用大量水冲洗。酸灼伤时,用水冲洗后,再用饱和碳酸氢钠、稀氨溶液或肥皂水处理;若为浓硫酸烫伤,须先用脱脂棉揩净,再用水冲洗。若酸溅入眼睛,首先用水冲洗,然后用1%~3%碳酸氢钠溶液处理,再用水冲洗。碱灼伤时,用水冲洗后,再用2%~5%醋酸或3%硼酸溶液处理。若碱溅入眼睛,应用水冲洗,然后用3%硼酸溶液处理,再用水冲洗。经上述处理后,立即送医院治疗。

4. 有毒气体吸入　如果吸入溴、氯或氯化氢等有毒气体,立即离开有毒气体环境,并到室外呼吸新鲜空气,可吸入少量酒精与乙醚混合的蒸气以解毒。如果吸入硫化氢或一氧化碳气体,则立即到室外呼吸新鲜空气。

5. 毒物摄入　可内服一杯稀硫酸铜溶液,用手指触摸喉咙,促使呕吐,然后立即送医院。

6. 触电事故　电器与水隔绝,实验桌面保持干燥、整洁。使用电器设备时,不要用湿手接触电器和插销。遇到触电,不能直接用手拉受害者离开现场,而是立即切断电源;遇到电器着火,应立即切断电源,防止触电。

五、化学实验室的防火、防电与灭火常识

(一) 引起化学实验室火灾的主要原因

（1）易燃物质离火源太近。实验室安全要求：不能使用明火加热。

（2）电线老化、插头接触不良或电器故障等。

（3）化学反应不当导燃，如化学品物性不明、操作不当等。

（4）下列物质彼此混合或接触后易着火，甚至酿成火灾：

活性炭与硝酸铵；

沾染了强氧化剂（如氯酸钾）的衣物；

抹布与浓硫酸；

可燃性物质（木材或纤维等）与浓硝酸；

有机物与液氧；

铝与有机氯化物；

磷化氢、硅烷、烷基金属及白磷等与空气接触。

(二) 灭火方法

化学实验室一旦着火或发生火灾，切勿惊慌，应冷静果断地按表1-1所示方法采取扑灭措施并及时报警。

表1-1　可燃物的灭火方法

燃烧物	灭火方法	说明
纸张、纺织品或木材	沙、水、灭火器	需降温和隔绝空气
油、苯等有机溶剂	CO_2、干粉灭火器、石棉布、干沙等	适用于贵重仪器上的灭火，油、气等燃烧切勿用泡沫灭火器灭火
醇、醚等	水	需冲淡、降温和隔绝空气
电线、电表及仪器	CCl_4、CO_2等灭火器	灭火材料不能导电，切勿用水和泡沫灭火器灭火
可燃性气体	关闭气源，灭火器	尽一切可能切断可燃气源
活泼金属（如钾、钠等）及磷化物与水接触	干砂土、干粉灭火器	绝不能使用水或泡沫、CO_2灭火器
身上的衣物	就地滚动，压灭火焰或脱掉衣服、用专用防火布覆盖着火处	切勿跑动，否则将加剧燃烧

(三) 防触电

首先切断电源，尽快用绝缘物如干燥的木棍或竹竿等，使触电者脱离电源。必要时进行人工呼吸，并立即送医院抢救。

（陈志琼）

第二章 | 基础化学实验常用仪器

一、实验室常用仪器介绍

实验室常用仪器主要以玻璃仪器为主,按其用途可分为容器类仪器、量器类仪器和其他类仪器。

(一)容器类

常温或加热条件下物质的反应容器、贮存容器,包括试管、烧杯、烧瓶、漏斗等,如图 2-1 所示。使用时根据用途和用量选择不同种类和不同规格的容器。

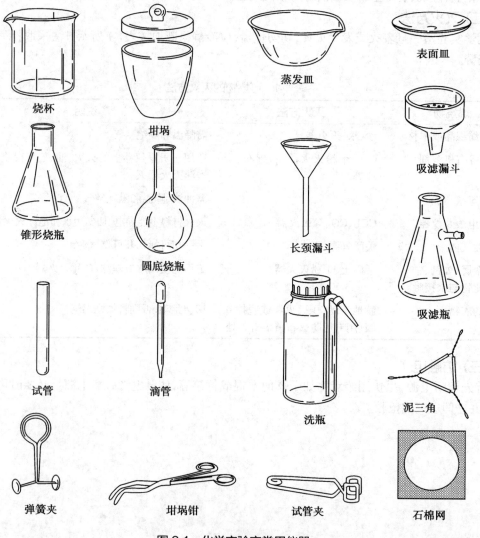

图 2-1　化学实验室常用仪器

(二) 量器类

用于度量或移取一定溶液体积的玻璃仪器,主要有量筒、滴定管、容量瓶、移液管和移液枪等,根据精度不同,分为精量仪器及粗量仪器。量器不可以作为实验容器,例如不可用于溶解、稀释操作,不可量取热溶液,不可加热及长期存放溶液。量器上常注明两种符号:一种为"E",表示"量入"容器;另一种为"A",表示"量出"容器。量器的管颈处刻有一条标线,是所移取的准确体积的标志。

其他类仪器包括玻璃仪器和非玻璃仪器。

二、玻璃仪器的洗涤和干燥

(一) 普通玻璃仪器的洗涤

洗涤玻璃仪器,先用自来水荡洗,根据仪器形状使用相应毛刷蘸取洗涤剂等,沿器壁内外均匀刷洗,然后用自来水冲洗至无泡沫,最后用少量蒸馏水润洗三次。

若仪器沾有污垢,首先用热水或热碱液浸泡,然后用毛刷沾上洗涤剂刷洗,再用自来水冲洗至无泡沫,最后用蒸馏水润洗三次。

若仪器口小、管细、体长,使用毛刷受限时,可用烧杯或烧瓶加热铬酸洗液(铬酸洗液的配制:取 10 g 工业用 $K_2Cr_2O_7$,置于烧杯中。先用少量水溶解,在不断搅拌下缓慢加入 200 mL 工业用浓硫酸,待溶解并冷却后,即可保存于试剂瓶中待用),将洗液转移到仪器中浸泡一段时间,再用自来水连续冲洗,最后用蒸馏水润洗三次。

对于碱式滴定管的洗涤,要注意铬酸洗液不能直接接触橡胶管。洗涤前取下橡胶管。

洗涤玻璃仪器洁净的标准是,水沿器壁自然流下后均匀湿润,不挂水珠。

(二) 普通玻璃仪器的干燥

1. 自然晾干 敞开仪器开口并朝向下方,让水分自然流出,挥发。

需要尽快使用的玻璃仪器可用烤干、吹干、烘干、有机溶剂挥干等方法干燥。

2. 烤干 尽可能倾尽已洁净仪器内壁水分,然后用小火均匀烤干仪器。此方法适合于数量少、体积小的玻璃仪器,如:试管的干燥。

3. 吹干 尽可能倾尽已洁净仪器内壁水分,然后用电吹风或专用的气流烘干机吹干仪器。如:烧杯的干燥。

4. 烘干 尽可能倾尽已洁净仪器内壁水分,然后将仪器放入烘箱中烘干。此方法特别适合数量较多,口径较小的仪器。

5. 有机溶剂挥干 尽可能倾尽已洁净仪器内壁水分,然后用丙酮或酒精等易挥发的有机溶剂润湿仪器内壁,倒出并回收用过的有机溶剂,最后晾干或吹干仪器。

由于度量仪器具有标定的刻度,一般不用毛刷刷洗,可用铬酸洗液浸泡一段时间,再用自来水冲洗,最后用蒸馏水润洗数次。玻璃仪器热胀冷缩,受热后不易恢复体积,因此,容量分析仪器应在标注温度范围内干燥。

三、常用仪器使用方法

(一) 基本度量仪器的使用

1. 滴定管 滴定管主要用于精确放、取一定体积的溶液。滴定管按其构造可分为酸式、碱式或酸碱两用滴定管。酸式滴定管下端有玻璃旋塞,如图2-2(a),通过自由转动旋塞以控制溶液流速,用以盛装或量取酸性

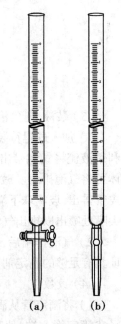

图 2-2 滴定管
(a) 酸式(酸碱两用)滴定管;(b) 碱式滴定管。

及氧化性溶液;碱式滴定管下端连接一软橡胶管,内装有一玻璃珠,通过挤捏玻璃珠可控制溶液的流速,如图2-2(b),用以盛装碱性溶液;酸碱两用滴定管的构造与酸式滴定管相同,但其旋塞材质是聚四氟乙烯,具有耐酸、碱的作用,因此可盛装酸性及碱性两种溶液。

常用的滴定管容积有 25 mL 和 50 mL,最小刻度为 0.1 mL,读数可读到 0.01 mL。此外,还有 10 mL、5 mL、2 mL 和 1 mL 的半微量或微量滴定管,最小刻度为 0.05 mL、0.01 mL 或 0.005 mL。

（1）检漏及装配

1）使用酸式滴定管前,应检查旋塞转动是否灵活或漏液,否则取下旋塞,洗净后用吸水纸吸干或吹干旋塞和旋塞槽。如图 2-3(a),在旋塞的两端涂一层很薄的凡士林,如图 2-3(b)所示的 A、B 处,旋塞中部塞孔两旁只涂极薄一层的凡士林以防堵塞塞孔。将旋塞插入塞槽内并向同一方向旋转旋塞,使旋塞与塞槽接触处呈透明状且转动灵活,若油脂分布不均匀或堵塞小孔,需重新清洗、涂布,最后装水检查是否漏液。

2）碱式滴定管应选择大小合适的玻璃珠和橡胶管,检查滴定管是否漏液,是否能灵活控制液滴流出,如不符合要求,需重新选球径合适的玻璃珠装配。

（2）润洗:使用滴定管前,用待装溶液润洗 2~3 次以除去滴定管内残留水分(保证溶液浓度不变)。向滴定管注入润洗溶液约 10 mL,两手平端滴定管,慢慢转动,使溶液流遍全管。打开酸式滴定管的旋塞或挤压碱式滴定管的玻璃珠,使润洗液从滴定管下端流出,润洗液完全倒掉。

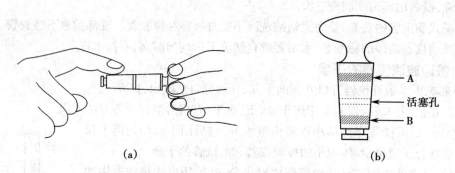

（a）　　　　　　　　（b）

图 2-3　酸式滴定管旋塞及涂凡士林方法
（a）旋塞涂抹凡士林;（b）旋塞各部位。

（3）装液、赶气泡

1）加入过量待装液至酸式滴定管零刻度标线上方,快速旋转旋塞放液,使液体完全充满管尖,利用液流将气泡带出;或将酸式滴定管倾斜至与水平成 15°~30°,缓慢开启旋塞,浸流入管尖的液体可将气泡排出。碱式滴定管需将玻璃珠上端及下端的气泡赶尽,玻璃珠上端气泡可通过挤捏橡皮管排出,玻璃珠下端的气泡则需将橡皮管向上弯曲,挤捏橡皮管玻璃珠,如图 2-4 所示,使溶液从尖嘴处喷出以排出气泡。

2）气泡排出后,调整液面至零刻度或稍低于零刻度以保证具有足够的滴定剂用于滴定分析。

（4）读数

1）将滴定管从滴定管夹上取下,用大拇指与食指或中指轻拿滴定管上端,使其自然垂直,待溶液稳定 1~2 min 后(使附着在内壁上的溶液完全流下后再读数),使视线与凹液面水平,分别读出初始读数或滴定终点时读数。读数时,管壁不应

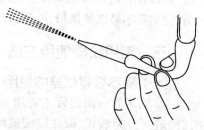

图 2-4　碱式滴定管排出气泡的方法

挂液滴,管尖不应有气泡或悬滴液,读数精确至 0.01 mL。

2)无色溶液或浅色溶液的凹液面清晰可见,应以凹液面下缘实线的最低点为准,如图 2-5(a);有色溶液凹液面的清晰程度较差,如 $KMnO_4$、I_2 溶液等,读数时应以液面两侧最高点为准。

3)采用"蓝带"滴定管读数更准确,其背景设有一条蓝色带状标记,如图 2-5(b)所示。对于无色溶液,凹形液面的上下边缘在滴定管蓝带上相交于某一点,读数时应以该交点为准。若为有色溶液,以液面两侧的最高点为准。采用读数卡可协助读数,如图 2-5(c)。读数卡可用涂有黑长方形的白纸制成,滴定管后面衬一张读数卡,使黑色部分在凹液面下约 1 mm 处,此时即可看到凹液面的反射层成为黑色,读数时以此凹液面下缘最低点为准。

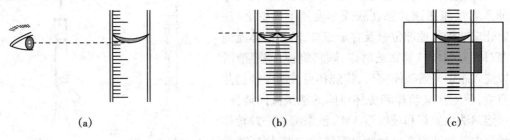

(a)　　　　　　　　　　(b)　　　　　　　　　　(c)

图 2-5　滴定管读数

(a)滴定管读数的方法;(b)蓝条滴定管的读数方法;(c)黑色背景滴定管的读数方法。

(5)滴定

1)滴定管垂直固定在滴定管夹上,确定管尖是否挂液滴,若有,需用容器外壁碰掉液滴。滴定管尖距锥形瓶口 1 cm 左右,样品溶液盛于锥形瓶中,锥形瓶置于一白色衬底之上。滴定时若使用酸式滴定管则采用反握法,用左手开启并控制旋塞,旋塞柄指向右方,用拇指、食指、中指轻轻向内扣住旋塞,手心空握,对旋塞施加指向手心的内扣力,以防旋塞松动或被顶出而漏液。右手握持锥形瓶,需上提锥形瓶,使滴定管下端伸入锥形瓶内约 1~2 cm,边滴边向同一方向作圆周旋转摇动,如图 2-6 所示(不能前后振动,否则会溅出溶液)。滴定速度一般为 $10\ mL \cdot min^{-1}$,即每秒 3~4 滴。滴定接近终点前,一滴一滴地加入,用少量蒸馏水冲洗黏附于锥形瓶内壁的液滴;当色晕消失缓慢,此时即将到达滴定终点,可半滴半滴地加入(即微开旋塞,液滴悬在管尖,用锥形瓶内壁将液滴碰下,再用蒸馏水冲下锥形瓶内壁的液滴),直至到达滴定终点。终点读数时需注意管尖是否挂液滴,数据记录时需减去半滴液滴体积量。

2)酸碱两用滴定管的滴定操作方法与酸式滴定管相似。

3)使用碱式滴定管滴定时,左手拇指和食指挤压玻璃珠稍上缘的胶管,使管内形成一条缝隙,溶液可从玻璃管的尖嘴中流出。根据所挤压的缝隙大小可控制溶液的流速。若手放在玻璃球的下部,松手后,空气会从玻璃管尖端进入而出现气泡。

2. 容量瓶　容量瓶是一种细梨形的平底玻璃瓶,用于配制标准溶液或试样溶液,带有玻璃磨口塞或塑料塞,颈上有一标线,一般表示指定温度下(标记于瓶上)溶液充满至标线时的容积,如图2-7(a)所示。通常有25 mL、100 mL、250 mL、500 mL 和1 000 mL 等各种规格。容量瓶不能用作贮液瓶,配制或稀释后的溶液应转移到贮液瓶中,并洗净容量瓶。

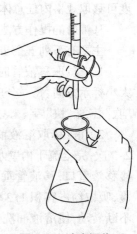

图 2-6　滴定操作

（1）检漏：使用容量瓶前，应检查是否漏液，可注入自来水至容积的 2/3 以上，盖好瓶塞并用右手食指顶住瓶塞，另一只手托住瓶底，将其倒立，观察瓶塞周围是否漏液。若不漏液，将瓶直立后将瓶塞转动 180°，再次倒立并检查，确定容量瓶不漏液后，方可使用。

（2）转移溶液和定容：

1）容量瓶只盛放已溶解的溶液。用固体物质配制成标准溶液时，应将准确称量的固体置于小烧杯中，用总体积 10%~20% 的溶剂溶解后，将溶液定量转移入容量瓶中。若溶质难溶，可加热助溶，但必须待溶液完全冷却至室温再转移，否则将造成体积误差。

2）将溶液转入容量瓶的方法见图 2-7（b），玻璃棒下端伸入容量瓶瓶颈并靠在瓶颈刻度线下内壁上（注意不要让玻璃棒其他部位触及容量瓶口，防止液体流到容量瓶外壁），烧杯口紧靠玻璃棒，倾斜烧杯，使溶液沿玻璃棒流入瓶中。溶液倾完后，将烧杯沿玻璃棒轻提并慢慢直立，使附在玻璃棒和烧杯口间的液滴流回烧杯。用少量溶剂洗涤烧杯和玻璃棒 3 次，洗涤溶液一并转移入容量瓶中。加溶剂至容量瓶总容量的一半，旋摇容量瓶，使瓶内溶液大体混匀。继续加溶剂至标线附近，改用滴管小心滴加溶剂，视线与溶液凹液面及刻度标线水平相切。盖紧瓶塞，反复倒转和摇动容量瓶，使瓶内溶液混合均匀。

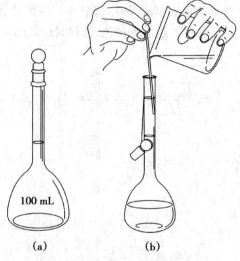

图 2-7　容量瓶及其使用
（a）容量瓶；（b）容量瓶使用。

3）若发现静置容量瓶后液面低于刻度线，这是由于容量瓶内极少量溶液在瓶颈处润湿所致，并不影响所配制溶液的浓度，故不要在瓶内添加溶剂，否则，所配制的溶液浓度将降低。若加溶剂超过标线，需重新配制。

3. 移液管及移液器

（1）移液管：移液管是指在给定温度下（以 TD 标明，通常为 25 ℃），用于准确移取一定体积溶液的量器，精度为 0.01 mL，常用的移液管有 5 mL、10 mL、25 mL 和 50 mL 等规格。习惯上中间为球形的称为大肚移液管，简称移液管，如图 2-8（a）所示，具有分刻度可移取规格内任意体积溶液的称为吸量管，如图 2-8（b）所示。

移液管的操作方法

主要有下列五个步骤：读、淋、吸、拿、放。

1）读：取移液管时，要明确容量的规格、类型、吸量管刻度的大小标示方向、每一分度标示的容量大小，及确认管口上是否刻有"吹"字或"快"字。

2）淋：移取溶液前，彻底洗净移液管，并用少量蒸馏水润洗 2~3 次，完全流干内壁水分。挤出洗耳球内空气，再把球的尖端紧接移液管口，移液管垂直插入液面 1.5 cm 以下，缓慢松开洗耳球囊，吸取约占容积 1/3 体积量的溶液，双手平端移液管中后部，并不断转动，使溶液润洗全管内壁，随后使溶液从移液管管尖流出。重复吸取待移取的溶液润洗管内壁 2~3 次，以确保所移取溶液浓

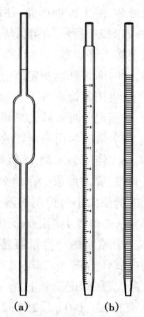

图 2-8　移液管
（a）移液管；（b）吸量管。

度不变。

3）吸与拿：移取溶液时，一般用右手拇指和中指拿住管颈标线上方，将管尖适当插入溶液面1.5~2 cm中（勿接触底部），左手拿洗耳球先把球内空气挤出，再把球的尖端紧接移液管口，缓缓松开左手吸取溶液，随溶液在移液管内上升管尖下移，保持插入液面1.5~2 cm中，当溶液在管内上升至标线以上时，迅速用食指代替洗耳球按住管口，将移液管离开液面，如图2-9（a）所示。

4）放：保持移液管垂直状态，管尖靠在倾斜的器皿液面以上的内壁上，略微放松食指，轻轻转动移液管，使过量液体流出管尖，直到溶液凹液面下缘与标线相平时立即用食指压紧管口；取出移液管，转移入承接溶液的器皿中。在放液过程中，移液管保持垂直，承接器皿稍倾斜而使移液管最大化地接触器皿内壁，使流速均匀形成均匀的内膜，松开食指，让管内全部溶液自然平稳地沿器皿壁流下。流完液体后等待10~15 s或管尖靠壁轻轻旋转几圈取出移液管，如图2-9（b）所示。若管壁上刻有"吹"或"快"字，用洗耳球将管内及管尖残留的溶液全部吹至承接器皿中；否则不可用力使其流出，因校准移液管时已考虑了管尖所保留溶液的体积。

（2）移液器：移液器又称移液枪，是用于定量转移液体的量器，化学实验室常用的是单道微量可调手动移液器，包括0.1 μL~10 mL体积的不同规格。移液器的结构如图2-10所示，推动活塞排出空气，而后松开活塞利用大气压吸入液体；再次推动活塞排出液体，通过控制推动力度以调控被移液体的流速。

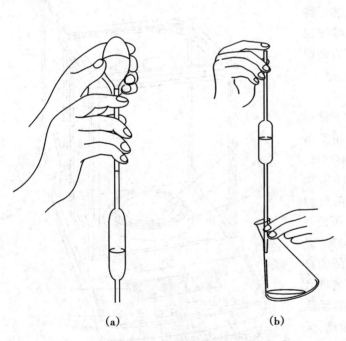

图2-9 移液管的使用
（a）移液管的吸液；（b）移液管的放液。

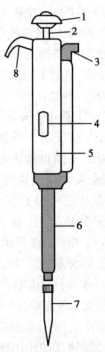

图2-10 移液器的结构
1. 控制按钮；2. 推动杆；3. 枪头卸除按钮；4. 体积显示窗口；5. 套筒；6. 吸液杆；7. 枪头（吸头）；8. 握盖。

移液器的使用方法

1）安装枪头：利用旋转安装法安装枪头（也称吸头），轻轻用力下压，并左右微微转动将移液器垂直插入枪头，使其紧密结合。

2）设定容量：取移液枪时，要明确其容量规格，根据需要设定其体积。将移液器从大体积调为小体积时，逆时针旋转旋钮即可；从小体积调为大体积时，可先顺时针旋转旋钮至刻度超出设定容量值的1/4圈，再回调至设定值，这样可排除机械间隙，保证设定的容量值准确。不要将按钮旋转超出量程，否则会卡住内部机械装置而损坏移液器。

3）吸液操作：一般利用前进移液法吸液。首先连接适当的枪头，用大拇指按下控制钮至第一档，将移液器枪头垂直插入液面下1~6 mm；其中0.1~10 μL容量的移液器枪头插入液面下1~2 mm，2~200 μL容量的移液器枪头插入液面下2~3 mm，1~5 mL容量的移液器枪头插入液面下3~6 mm。缓慢松开控制钮，等待1~3 s，将移液器移出容器前，用试剂瓶口内壁将枪头外壁液体碰掉，确保枪头外壁无液体。当吸取有机溶剂或高挥发液体时，挥发性气体会在套筒室内形成负压，从而产生漏液情况，需要用待吸液预洗4~6次，让套筒室内气体达到饱和从而消除负压。

4）放液操作：将移液枪头垂直插入承液器，缓慢将控制按钮压至第一档并等待约1~3 s，继续按压至第二档，可重复几次，以确保枪头内无剩余液体。

5）移液器使用完毕后，按压弹射键以弹除枪头；把移液器量程调至最大值，使弹簧处于松弛状态以保护弹簧，将移液器垂直放置在移液器架上。当移液器枪头里有液体时，切勿将移液器水平放置或倒置，以免液体倒流腐蚀活塞弹簧。

此外，当转移高黏液体、生物活性液体、易起泡液体或极微量的液体时，一般利用反向移液法，其原理是直接按下按钮至第二档，先吸入多于设定量值的液体，慢慢松开按钮至原位，然后将按钮按至第一档排出设定量值的液体，继续保持按钮于第一档（不再按至第二档），取下有残留液体的枪头，弃之。

（二）电子分析天平

电子分析天平为单盘称量仪器，用于称量物体质量。不同规格的电子分析天平，精度不同，绝对精度分度值达到0.1 mg（即0.000 1 g）的称为万分之一分析天平，是目前实验室常用的电子分析天平，电子分析天平的荷载为100~200 g，如图2-11所示。万分之一分析天平采用电磁平衡传感器，特点是称量准确可靠、显示快速清晰并且具有自动检测系统、简便的自动校准装置以及超载保护等装置。天平的秤盘置于电磁铁上，当样品放在秤盘上，由于样品质量和重力加速度的作用使得秤盘向下运动，天平检测到这个运动并通过电磁铁产生与此重力相抗衡的作用力，这个力与物品的质量成比例。

称量方法

1. 直接称量法　直接称量法用于称量在空气中性质稳定、不吸潮的样品如金属、矿石等。称量时应注意：①不能称量热的物品；②为防止药品腐蚀托盘，所称量的物品不能直接放在托

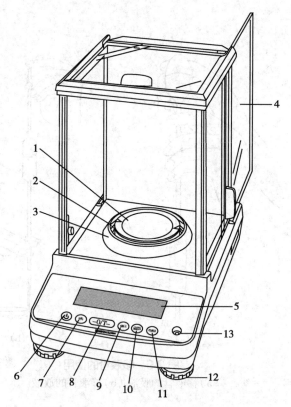

图2-11　电子分析天平

1.托盘；2.托盘支撑；3.托盘圈；4.防风罩；5.显示器部；6.启动键；7."CAL"灵敏度校正键；8."0/T"测定（零点/扣皮重）键；9.单位切换键；10.功能切换键；11.数据输出菜单键；12.水平调节支脚；13.水准器。

盘上,依情况置于称量纸上(称量纸四角沿对角线外延1/4处对折2次成小纸盒,纸盒大小依托盘大小或称量物品的多少而定)、表面皿上或容器中再称量。

(1)调节天平水平:查看水准器中的气泡是否居中,否则调节垫脚使气泡居中天平达水平。顺时针旋转水平调节垫脚时,垫脚伸长,天平上升,相反操作使天平下降。用小毛刷清扫干净托盘周围。

(2)预热:接通电源,至少预热半小时。

(3)调节灵敏度:按“CAL”灵敏度校正键,使用内置砝码的灵敏度校正自动开始,显示[END],返回。

(4)调零或去皮:调节为质量测定方式(以“g”等质量单位显示的状态)。打开防风罩的玻璃门,将容器放在托盘上,再次关闭玻璃门。显示稳定后,按“0/T”键,显示为零。

(5)测定质量:打开玻璃门,将称量器皿或折好的称量纸盒置于称台上,关闭天平门,待显示值稳定后按“去皮”(TARE)键,天平显示“0.0”。将试剂瓶盖取下倒置于桌面,左手拿着试剂瓶,并使瓶口横向对着称量纸盒或称量器皿中心上方约5~10 cm处(防止取试剂时洒落到桌面),小心用专用药勺取出试剂,轻轻抖入称量纸盒中,直至数字显示为所需要的质量,此时关闭玻璃门,显示稳定后,读取显示数值。(注:在读取天平示数时,请确认玻璃门已完全关闭。)

(6)包药:若用称量纸盛样品,样品需按药房包药的方式将药品包好,在称量纸外封写上样品的名称、质量、称量的时间及称量者的姓名。

(7)关闭天平:使用天平后,使用小毛刷进行清洁,调零后,按住启动键不动,直到显示“OFF”,关闭天平,拔掉电源。

2. 差减称量法　差减称量法用于称取吸潮或挥发性的试样。称量步骤是先称量容器(通常是称量瓶)和试样物质的总质量,取出部分样品后再称量剩余质量,两者之差即为取出样品的质量。

大多数固体样品都有一定程度的吸潮现象,因此称量前需将被称物品,预先烘干1~2 h,并盛于称量瓶中,如图2-12(a)所示;烘干后放入干燥器内,如图2-12(b)所示。不能用手直接拿取洁净的称量瓶,应使用干燥的纸条套在称量瓶上夹取,或戴上洁净的细纱手套拿取。取下称量瓶斜放在承接容器的中上方,打开瓶盖,用瓶盖轻轻敲击瓶口,使样品落入承接容器中,如图2-13所示。当倾出的样品接近所需要的质量时,慢慢将瓶竖起,轻敲瓶口,使附在瓶口的试样落在瓶内,盖好瓶盖。勿将样品洒落在承接容器外。

(三) pH计

pH计(或称酸度计)是用来测量溶液酸碱度的仪器,它通过电位测定分析法,即测量浸入溶液中的指示电极和参比电极的电位差来确定溶液的pH。

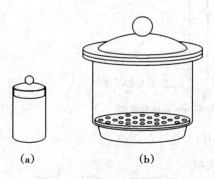

(a)　　　　　(b)

图2-12　称量瓶与干燥器
(a)称量瓶;(b)干燥器。

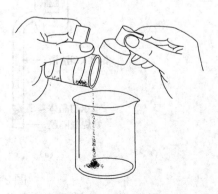

图2-13　敲取试样

1. 原理 pH 计由参比电极与指示电极,或复合电极和精密电位计组成。

(1)参比电极:参比电极有恒定的电极电位,不受溶液的影响,当有微弱电流通过时,电极电位改变微弱。常用的参比电极有饱和甘汞电极和银-氯化银电极。

饱和甘汞电极

饱和甘汞电极(SCE)见图 2-14(a)。在内管中,铂丝浸入糊状氯化亚汞(甘汞)和汞的混合物中。外管是盛有饱和氯化钾溶液的盐桥,可直接浸入待测溶液中。

甘汞电极的半电池表达式是

$$Pt(s)|Hg(1)|Hg_2Cl_2(s)|KCl(饱和)||$$

在电极反应中,氯化亚汞和汞可逆地发生氧化还原反应

$$Hg_2Cl_2(s)+2e^- \rightleftharpoons 2Hg(1)+2Cl^-(aq)$$

由于液态 Hg 和固态 Hg_2Cl_2 活度一致,电极电位的 Nernst 方程是

$$\varphi_{Hg_2Cl_2/Hg}=\varphi_{Hg_2Cl_2/Hg}^{\ominus}-\frac{0.059\,16V}{2}\lg c(Cl^-)^2 \tag{2-1}$$

式(2-1)中 Cl^- 的浓度是固定的(饱和 KCl 的浓度约 4.2 mol·L^{-1}),因此,电极电位是常数,在 25 ℃时为 0.241 5 V。

银-氯化银电极

银-氯化银电极见图 2-14(b),敷有氯化银的银丝浸入经氯化银饱和的氯化钾溶液中。半电池表示为

$$Ag(s)|AgCl(s)|KCl(c)||$$

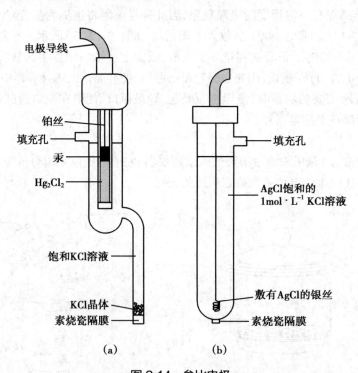

图 2-14 参比电极

(a)饱和甘汞电极;(b)银-氯化银电极示意图。

其半电池反应是

$$AgCl(s) + e^- \rightleftharpoons Ag(s) + Cl^-(aq)$$

根据 Nernst 方程式,电极电位仅与 Cl$^-$浓度相关

$$\varphi_{AgCl/Ag} = \varphi_{AgCl/Ag}^{\ominus} - \frac{0.059\,16\,V}{1}\lg c(Cl^-) \tag{2-2}$$

如同甘汞电极,氯化钾溶液是饱和的。通常该电极体积很小,可在较高温度下使用。

（2）指示电极:指示电极的电极电位对溶液中待测物质有响应。如玻璃 pH 电极是对溶液中氢离子浓度有响应的一种膜电极,当特制的玻璃膜两边氢离子浓度不等时,电极会产生一定电位。

玻璃 pH 电极中玻璃膜结构如图 2-15 所示,膜内为银-氯化银电极,浸在经氯化银饱和的 pH 7 缓冲溶液中。极薄的离子敏感玻璃膜的主要成分是 SiO$_2$(约 70%),其余 30% 由 CaO、BaO、Li$_2$O 和 Na$_2$O 混合而成。玻璃膜焊接于不敏感的玻璃管下端,测量时应浸入溶液中。当外部溶液含有氢离子时,电极组成表示为

$$Ag(s)|AgCl|Cl^-(内),H_3O^+(内)|玻璃膜|H^+(外)$$

25 ℃时其电极电位是

$$\varphi_{glass} = K_{glass} + 0.059\,16\lg a(H_3O^+) = K_{glass} - 0.059\,16pH \tag{2-3}$$

式（2-3）中 K_{glass} 是未知的玻璃电极常数,包括由 Cl$^-$浓度决定的内参比电极的电位、由膜内 H$_3$O$^+$浓度决定的膜电位和玻璃膜两边的不对称电位。

25 ℃时,用饱和甘汞电极、玻璃 pH 电极和待测溶液组成原电池,电池的电动势为

$$E = \varphi_{SCE} - \varphi_{glass} = 0.241\,5 - (K_{glass} - 0.059\,16pH) \tag{2-4}$$

因此,玻璃电极常数 K_{glass} 必须用已知 pH 的标准缓冲溶液校准。

$$pH = \frac{E + K_{glass} - 0.241\,5}{0.059\,16} \tag{2-5}$$

（3）复合电极:现在多数 pH 电极将玻璃电极和银-氯化银外参比电极组装在一个管中形成复合电极（图 2-16）。复合电极中 pH 敏感玻璃电极位于中间,外围被充满了参比电解液的参比电极

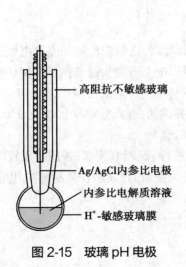

图 2-15　玻璃 pH 电极　　　　　图 2-16　复合电极

所包围。复合电极因其结构紧凑而优于分离的双电极系统。更便捷的电极是在复合电极中加入温度探头,便于进行温度补偿,也被称为三合一电极。

2. FE28 型 pH 计的使用　FE28 型 pH 计(图2-17)是一种高输入阻抗的伏特计,读数为pH单位和毫伏(mV)单位,特点是操作直观、节省空间,使用灵活。pH 测定范围为0~14,分辨率是0.01 pH,测量精度为 ± 0.01 pH;mV 测量范围为–2 000~2 000 mV,分辨率是1 mV,测量精度为± 1 mV。

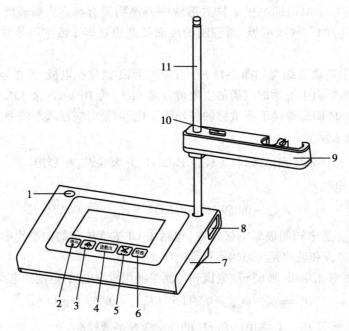

图 2-17　FE28 型 pH 计示意图

1. 电极支架的左侧安装位置;2. 开关按钮;3. 存储/回显;4. 读取/终点方式;5. 模式/设置;6. 校准;7. 外壳;8. 支架杆存储空间;9. 支架臂;10. 紧固按钮;11. 电极支架杆。

(1)安装及开机:安装电极支架,pH 计的电源线与 100~240 V 电源连接,连接电极。短按开关键打开仪器,预热仪器半小时。

(2)校准

1)仪器自动识别温度电极,则显示出 ATC 和样品温度,若仪器未检测到温度电极,则将自动切换到手动温度模式。长按"模式/设置"键,温度值闪烁,按上下箭头键选择温度值(默认设置为25 ℃),按下"读数$\sqrt{A}$"键确认 MTC 温度补偿设置;当前标准缓冲溶液组闪烁,使用上下箭头键选择标准缓冲溶液组并确认;选择校准方式(Lin. 或 Seg.)并确认;选择分辨率(0.1 或 0.01)并确认;选择温度单位(℃或℉)并确认,按下开关键,返回测量界面。

2)根据需要,进行 1 点校准或多点校准(采用 1 点校准,仅调节偏移;采用 2 点校准,斜率和偏移均得到更新;采用 3 点或以上校准,斜率或零点均得以更新,并显示在显示屏的相应位置),标准缓冲溶液的 pH 与温度有关(表 2-1)。

表 2-1 不同温度下标准缓冲溶液的 pH

温度 /℃	邻苯二甲酸氢钾 / 0.05 mol·L⁻¹	KH₂PO₄ + Na₂HPO₄/ (0.025 mol·L⁻¹ + 0.025 mol·L⁻¹)	硼砂 / 0.01 mol·L⁻¹
0	4.00	6.98	9.46
10	4.00	6.92	9.33
15	4.00	6.90	9.27
20	4.01	6.88	9.22
25	4.01	6.86	9.18
30	4.02	6.85	9.14
35	4.03	6.84	9.10
40	4.04	6.84	9.07
50	4.06	6.83	9.01
60	4.10	6.84	8.96

3）清洗并擦净 pH 电极头，将电极插入标准缓冲溶液液面以下 3~5 cm，短按"校准"键，开始校准仪器。通过长按"读数$\sqrt{A}$"键进行自动和手动两种终点方式的切换。显示屏上显示出样品的 pH，小数点开始闪烁，若选择了自动终点模式，当信号稳定后，显示器将自动锁定读数，出现"$\sqrt{A}$"，且小数点停止闪烁。若选择了手动终点模式，当信号稳定后，按下"读数"键记录缓冲液在当前温度下的 pH。

4）若进行 1 点校准，短按"读数"键完成 1 点校准。

5）若进行 2 点校准，用蒸馏水冲洗且擦干电极，将电极放入下一校准缓冲液中，短按"校准"键，根据不同终点方式完成校准。

6）若进行 3 点校准，在 2 点校准基础上，重复步骤 5）的操作。

7）以此类推，可对设备进行 4 或 5 点校准。（注：Seg 线段校准仅对 3 点或更多点校准有意义），按下"退出"键，返回测量界面。

（3）测量 pH

1）短按"模式设置"键，将测量模式调为 pH 测量模式。

2）清洗并擦净 pH 电极头，将其浸入待测样液液面以下 3~5 cm，短按"读数$\sqrt{A}$"键，开始测量。当信号稳定（自动终点方式，出现"$\sqrt{A}$"）或按下"读数$\sqrt{A}$"键（手动终点方式，出现"$\sqrt{M}$"）时仪器停止测量。记录溶液在当前温度下的 pH。

3）将电极移上支架臂，移去被测溶液，用蒸馏水洗净擦干后放入原来的电极浸泡液中。长按"退出"键关闭仪器。

（4）测量 mV：短按"模式设置"键，将测量模式调为 mV 测量模式。测量方法与步骤"（3）"测量 pH 中 2）和 3）操作相同。

(四) 722 型分光光度计

1. 工作原理　分光光度计的基本原理是，在光的照射下，被测物质受到激发，产生对光的吸收效应。物质对光的吸收具有选择性，各种不同的物质都具有其各自的吸收光谱。所以当某单色光通过有色溶液时（图2-18）一部分光被吸收，其余则透过或反射。有色溶液对光的吸收程度与物质

的浓度、液层厚度及入射光的强度有一定的比例关系，即符合Lambert-Beer定律

$$T = \frac{I}{I_0} \tag{2-6}$$

$$A = \lg\frac{1}{T} = \lg\frac{I_0}{I} \tag{2-7}$$

$$A = abc \tag{2-8}$$

式（2-6）中 T 为透光率，I 为透射光强度，I_0 为入射光强度，式（2-7）中 A 为吸光度，式（2-8）中 a 为吸光系数，b 为液层厚度，c 为溶液的浓度。由上式可知，当入射光、吸光系数和溶液的厚度不变时，吸光度随溶液的浓度而变化。

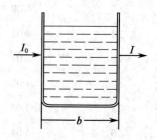

图 2-18 光吸收示意图

2. 光学系统 722型分光光度计是利用近紫外光和可见光（360~800 nm）进行光度分析的仪器。光度分析的主要优点是具有良好的稳定性，重现性，功能完善和方法简便。其光学系统如图2-19所示。由光源灯（钨灯或卤钨灯）发出的连续辐射光线射到聚光透镜上，会聚后再经过反光镜转角90°，反射至入射狭缝与准直镜。入射光线经过准直镜反射后，以一束平行光射向光栅（C-T 单色光器）后进行散射，并依原路稍偏转一个角度反射回来，经过准直镜会聚在出射狭缝上。光经过出射狭缝后，通过聚光透镜进行聚焦，然后通过比色皿，由光门射到光电倍增管上，产生的光电流输入显示器，可光电直读数据。

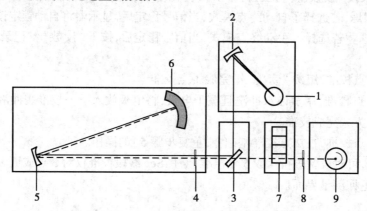

图 2-19 722 型分光光度计的光学系统
1. 光源；2. 聚光镜；3. 反光镜；4. 狭缝；5. 准直镜；6. 光栅；7. 比色皿；
8. 光闸门；9. 光电倍增管。

3. 结构 图2-20是722型分光光度计的主要部件示意图。光源灯发射的复合光经单色光器（光栅）分解为单色光，经由色散元件和狭缝选择单一波长的光。单色光通过样品池吸收后，透过光由检测器（光电倍增管）接收及微电流放大器将信号放大，最后由读数装置显示。

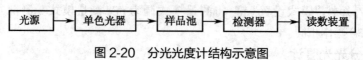

图 2-20 分光光度计结构示意图

4. 比色皿 比色皿，又称样品池或吸收池，它有两个平行的透光面（图2-21）。常用1 cm 的比色皿，厚度更大的比色皿能装盛更多样品而增加吸光度。玻璃比色皿因对紫外光有很强吸收而只用于可见光测定，石英比色皿既可用于紫外光也可用于可见光测定。每台仪器都备有一组成套的

比色皿,它们有相同的光学性质。

取用比色皿的方法很重要,任何一点厚度变化、弯曲变形、斑点、擦毛、刮痕和裂纹都会影响测量结果。因此操作时必须遵守以下几点:

（1）不要拿握透光面。

（2）测量前须用待装溶液少量多次洗涤。盛装溶液不低于比色皿的二分之一。

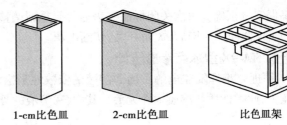

1-cm比色皿 2-cm比色皿 比色皿架

图 2-21 比色皿和比色皿架

（3）用镜头纸擦拭比色皿外壁的水分或污渍,禁用抹布和毛巾擦拭。观察比色皿,外壁不应有纤维、内部不能有气泡。否则,可用硝酸浸泡,但不能超过 3 小时。

（4）将比色皿置于比色皿架中时,注意不要划伤透光面。比色皿应直立,透光面正对比色皿架的窗口。

（5）同时使用两只或两只以上比色皿时,固定一只装空白溶液。

5. 722 型分光光度计的使用方法 722 型分光光度计的仪器外形如图2-22 所示。

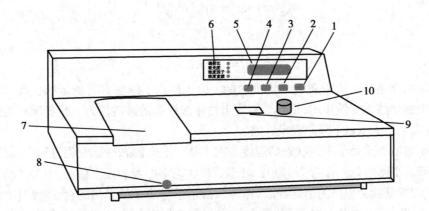

图 2-22 722 型分光光度计

1. 100% 键;2. 0% 键;3. 功能键;4. 模式键;5. 显示窗 4 位 LED 数字;6. 四种标尺（"透射比""吸光度""浓度因子""浓度直读"）;7. 样品室;8. 试样槽架拉杆;9. 波长指示窗;10. 波长调节钮。

（1）预热:接通仪器电源,预热半小时。

（2）调整波长:使用波长调节钮调整仪器当前测试波长,具体波长由指示窗显示,读取波长时目光垂直观察。

（3）置入空白样和待测试样:仪器标准配置中,样品槽架有四个位置,最靠近测试者（最外侧）为"0"位置,往里数依次为"1""2""3"位置,一般在"0"位置放入空白样。

（4）调零:打开试样盖或用不透光材料在样品室中遮断光路,按"0%"键。

（5）调整 100%T:通过推拉试样槽架拉杆让空白样置入样品室光路中,盖下试样盖（自动打开光门）,按"100%"键（一次有误差可加按一次）。

（6）测定样品吸光度:按模式键调为"吸光度"模式,通过拉试样槽架拉杆让不同样品进入光路,从"显示窗"中分别读出各个样品吸光度数值。当拉杆到位时有定位感,到位时请前后轻轻推动以确保定位正确。每次关闭样品室盖后都要重新调整 100%T,再对样品进行测试。

(7) 仪器使用完毕后,关闭开关,切断电源。

(五) FM-9X 型冰点渗透压计

1. 原理 难挥发非电解质稀薄溶液的依数性是指溶液蒸气压下降、沸点升高、凝固点降低和渗透压力,此类性质与溶质本性无关。其中,稀溶液的凝固点降低 ΔT_f 用关系式表示为

$$\Delta T_f = i K_f b_B \qquad (2\text{-}9)$$

式(2-9)中 K_f 为溶剂的凝固点降低常数,水的 K_f 是 1.857 K·kg·mol^{-1},b_B 为溶质的质量摩尔浓度,单位 mol·kg^{-1}。校正因子 i 是溶质分子解离出的粒子个数。非电解质溶质的校正因子 i 为 1;在近似处理的情况下,AB 型强电解质(如 KCl、CaSO$_4$、NaHCO$_3$ 等)及 AB$_2$ 或 A$_2$B 型强电解质如(MgCl$_2$、Na$_2$SO$_4$ 等)的校正因子 i 分别为 2 和 3。

根据 van't Hoff 定律,稀溶液的渗透压力 Π 为

$$\Pi = i c_B RT \qquad (2\text{-}10)$$

式(2-10)中 c_B 为溶质的物质的量浓度,单位 mol·L^{-1},R 为气体常数,T 为绝对温度。

常温下稀的水溶液的质量摩尔浓度和物质的量浓度的数值近乎相等

$$b_B (\text{mol·kg}^{-1}) \approx c_B (\text{mol·L}^{-1}) \qquad (2\text{-}11)$$

因此有

$$\Pi \approx i b_B RT \qquad (2\text{-}12)$$

生物体液的渗透压力有着重要的生理功能。由于冰点下降法具有测量精度高、操作简便、样品量少和对生物样品无变性作用,适合于测定生物体液样品的渗透压力。目前国外生产的渗透压力测定仪器,大多是按冰点下降原理设计的。

冰点是冰与液态水处于平衡状态的温度。在水从液态向固态冷却变化过程中,温度虽达到甚至低于冰点而未结冰的现象称为"过冷"。处于过冷状态下的液态极不稳定,一经扰动便可立刻引起结晶,分子的能量就会以热的形式释放,称为"结晶热"。由于结晶热的存在,使过冷溶液在结冰形成的瞬间温度回升。如图 2-23 所示,图中 A 点为溶液开始冷却,B 点为过冷温度,C 点为溶液开始结冰温度,CD 段为冰点温度稳定时间,DE 段为固态下继续冷却。CD 段出现时的温度,就是冰点。FM-9X 型冰点渗透压计采用高灵敏度的半导体热敏电阻测量溶液的冰点,通过电量转化得到渗透压测定结果。

2. FM-9X 型冰点渗透压力计的使用方法

图 2-24 所示为某仪器厂生产的 FM-9X 型冰点渗透压力计的外观。仪器有一套半导体制冷装置,以不冻液作为冷媒,冷却样品。为使液体在过冷后结晶,仪器还有一套过冷引晶装置,一套高精度的测温系统。通过测量溶液的冰点温度下降值来测定渗透压,选择 300 mmol·L^{-1} 和 800 mmol·L^{-1} 两种不同浓度标准的 NaCl 溶液对仪器进行标定。

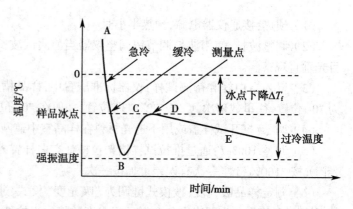

图 2-23 冷却曲线

（1）仪器使用的准备与调整

1）在冷却槽内加入约 60 mL 的不冻液，直到仪器右侧溢流杯中有不冻液排出为止。

2）接通电源，仪器进入等待状态，仪器面板显示冷却槽温度（- - - - 表示温度过高），仪器经约半小时的预热，自动平衡在温度控制点。

（2）标定

1）标定要求：取一只干净且干燥的试管，用玻璃注射器从标准溶液瓶内抽取 0.5 mL 的 300（或 800）mmol·L^{-1} 标准溶液注入试管，对仪器进行正常的标定（早冻或不冻的结果不能作为正常标定）。注射器和试管不得污染标准溶液。

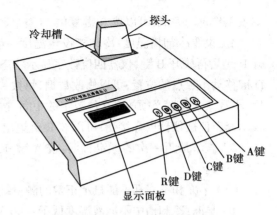

图 2-24　FM-9X 型冰点渗透压力计

2）标定方法：将装有 0.5 mL 标准溶液的试管垂直套向用软纸擦净的测量探头后置入冷却槽，按 C 键进入标定程序，仪器显示"300"。标定值须与所放入仪器的标准溶液相一致，如果有错，仪器将不能进入正常测试。用 D 键可以根据所用标准溶液进行 300 和 800 变换。在确定标定液和所选标定值相同后，按 B 键执行标定功能。标定过程中显示标准溶液温度的变化，当标准溶液温度达到–6 ℃时仪器自动强振，显示标定液的冰点温度，稍后显示"300E"（或"800E"），表示标定结束。按 D 键将标定值存入仪器内存，仪器显示"300P"（或"800P"）。标定结束应及时将测量探头从冷却槽内取出，如长时间将探头置于冷却槽内，会使仪器测量传感器和标准溶液之间被冻结得过硬而容易损坏测量传感器。

标定中按 A 键可以退出标定，回到等待状态，显示冷却槽温度，按 B 键可以查看标定进行时间（单位：s），按 D 键显示冷却槽温度。

（3）样品的测量

1）在试管内加入 0.5 mL 的被测样品溶液，将试管口套在测量探头上后置入冷却槽，按 D 键进入测量程序，测量过程中仪器显示样品温度的变化，当样品温度达到–6 ℃时仪器自动强振，强振后仪器显示的样品温度迅速从–6 ℃回升到样品的冰点温度，在报出测量结果后，及时将测量探头从冷却槽内取出。

2）手动强振用于易产生早冻的样品，在测量过程中可进行人工干预，在刚发生早冻时，通过手动强振的方法测得样品的渗透压近似值。正常测量不需手动强振。

（4）按键辅助功能

1）读出数据：在等待状态按 B 键，显示仪器最后测量的 12 个数据。按下按键，显示测量时间；放开按键，显示测量值。

2）设置时间：按 R 键+D 键，然后先放开 R 键后再放开 D 键，确定使用本功能。在此功能下，仪器四位数字显示状态为"月、日"，小数点所在的位置是可以进行修改的数据位置，用 D 键移位，按 B 键加"1"；A 键减"1"；完成设置月、日设置后，把小数点移至最后一位，按 C 键存入内存；然后仪器四位数字显示状态为"时、分"，用同样方法调整，按 D 键把小数点移至最后一位，按 C 键存入内存。

3）热敏电阻温度和电压线性校正：本功能是在仪器出现内存数据丢失的情况下才使用。在测量试管内放入 0.5 mL 不冻液，将试管口套在测量探头上，置入冷却槽内，按 R 键+C 键，先放开 R 键后放开 C 键，仪器四位数字显示初始状态为"- - 0 0"。手推测量探头进入冷却槽到低位，仪器前二位数据显示的是冷却槽温度，后二位数据显示的是动态时间。当仪器最终显示"- - - -"时，表示本项工作自动完成,可以按 R 键复位。(整个调整过程需要较长时间,一般在一个小时左右。)

4)设置冷却槽温度:冷却槽设定温度一般为–9.0 ℃。按 B 键+R 键,确定使用本功能。先放开 R 键后再放开 B 键,仪器四位数字显示状态为"L‑X X","‑X X"是仪器原冷却槽设置温度,用 D 键移动小数点的位置,可以修改数据,每按一次 B 键可以增加 1,按 A 键减小 1,冷却槽温度设定后,小数点的位置必须放在 2 位数字的中间,按 C 键确认修改完成,在 L 位置下出现又一个小数点,表示修改值被仪器内存接受,可以按 R 键退出。

5)查看最近一次的标定日期:按 A 键+R 键,先放开 R 键后再放开 A 键,可以查看仪器目前标定日期。

(5)早冻和不冻都不能显示正常的测量结果

1)早冻:冷却槽中不冻液温度低于 –9.0 ℃,或被测样品的渗透压力太低;

试管不清洁或被测溶液中有颗粒状杂质(如样品中有结晶);

仪器在有振动的环境下测试样品也容易引起早冻。

通常测量一个样品时间在 300 s 以内,如果测量时间大于 300 s,就应及时观察是否发生了早冻,以便及时中止。如能及时发现早冻,就可中止本次操作,如未能及时发现早冻,仪器将仍按其样品温度的下降而强振,强振后仪器显示"‑ ‑ ‑ ‑",说明本次操作失败。如果早冻未能及时观察发现,试管内的样品和热敏电阻将被冻结,这时不可急于拉下试管,应待其自然融化后取下试管,不然将会损坏热敏电阻。

2)不冻:冷却槽中不冻液温度偏高,或被测样品的渗透压力太高;

强振幅度太小,振动棒在振动过程中打不到试管壁;

被测样品如有气泡也会产生不冻。

若发生不冻,需稀释被测样品;或调整扳动振动棒,使振动中打到试管壁上。

(六)离心机

1. 原理 离心机是通过高速旋转,对不同相(l‑s、l‑l)混合物进行快速分离的专用设备,见图 2‑25(a)。如把装有固液混合物的试管放进离心机的试管套,通过离心机的运转使固体物质沉积于试管底部,可分离液体而保留固体,也可用毛细管抽提液体而遗弃固体。

在旋转离心机前,必须将一支平衡试管装在分离试管相对的位置,以避免离心机的过度振动,否则将会损坏离心机。平衡试管必须与离心试管同样大小,而且装有与待分离混合物同样体积的水。

离心分离法广泛用于医院、食品、工业、科研等单位进行化验、生化试验、分离悬浮液等工作中。

以 LDZ5‑2 低速离心机为例,采用集成电路控制,控制面板见图 2‑25(b)。具有慢启动功能,定时及转速均采用数字显示,方便、直观。该机特设超速报警及自制动系统,当旋转速度超过允许最高转速时,自动发出报警信号并停止运转。该系统对主控制电路系统故障和由于误操作引起的超速运转均具保护功能。

2. 操作方法

(1)将离心机置于平稳台面上。

(2)试料配平:该机装备了自动平衡系统,试料配平较为简单,用目力观察每只试管放置溶液数量近似,然后对称放置到离心隔架内。最大不平衡量不得超过 20 g,各旋转体按表 2‑2 所示对应转速运转,不得超过 5 000 r·min^{-1}(超过后机器将报警),离心少量试液时,可在对称试管内加水平衡。

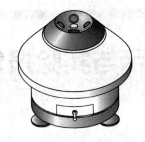 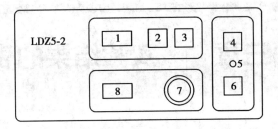

（a）离心机 （b）LDZ5-2低速离心机控制部分示意图

图 2-25 离心机和 LDZ5-2 低速离心机控制部分示意图

1. 定时显示（min）；2. 定时调谐按键；3. 定时手动 / 自动按键；4. 启动按键；
5. 超速保护；6. 电源开关；7. 转速调节旋钮；8. 转速显示（×100 r·min^{-1}）。

表 2-2 LDZ5-2 离心机的转速、离心力和容量

转速/r·min^{-1}	相对离心力/g	单支试管容量/mL	试管/支	总容量/mL	不平衡量 <g
5 000	4 360	50	4	200	20
5 000	4 360	10	12	120	20
3 500	2 100	10	32	320	20

（3）检查

1）调速旋钮 7（SPEED）应在 0 位；

2）欲使用的旋转体应紧固，并确认安装正确；

3）接好电源，插牢插头，接地使用；

4）锁好盖锁。

（4）操作程序

1）接通电源，将电源开关 6（POWER）接到"ON"位置，转速表显示"00"。如需定时，将定时手动自动按键 3（MAN-AUTO），选择"AUTO"，则定时器显示出一个任意随机数并闪动，按下"定时调谐"按键 2（SET），设定时间。

2）按"启动"键 4（START），顺时针转动调整旋钮 7（SPEED），离心机开始做逆时针旋转，观察转速表，调至所需转速。

3）在设定的时间内，显示表做时间减法计时，时间至"00"时，离心机停机运转，START 键上指示灯灭。

4）如需在此转速重复使用，可重新设置所需时间，按"启动"键 4（START）后，离心机可自动在预置的转速和时间内运行。

5）如不需使用定时，或离心时间超过 59 min，此时可将定时手动/自动按键设在"MAN"位，定时表显示的随机数仍做减法，但不定时。如需停止离心可将电源开关键 6（POWER）搬至"OFF"位置。

6）重复使用时，先开启电源开关键 6（POWER）再按启动键 4（START），离心机可自动加速到所设置的转速（仍不定时）。

7）离心完毕，将转速调节旋钮 7（SPEED）旋回"0"位，将电源开关搬到"OFF"。按动开锁按钮，即可开盖取出样品。运转中严禁开盖，或企图在旋转惯性未完时用手制动。

（周春艳 李雪华）

第三章 | 实验结果的表示与实验报告

一、实验误差与有效数字

(一)实验误差

实验误差是普遍存在的,即使严格地进行平行实验,也并不能保证每次都能得到完全相同的结果。每次测量都有实验误差,实验误差源于以下原因。

1. **系统误差** 系统误差是由某些确定的原因造成的,有确定的值,它主要来源于方法误差、仪器误差、试剂误差和操作误差等。系统误差使得测量值总是偏高或偏低,因此可以通过校准测量仪器、改进实验方法、更换试剂或者通过对照实验来消除。

2. **偶然误差** 偶然误差是由某些难以预料的偶然因素引起的,如测定时环境温度、湿度和气压的微小波动,仪器性能的微小变化,以及分析人员对试样处理的微小差异等。即使没有系统误差,偶然误差也会使得测定结果时而比真实值高,时而又偏低。偶然误差虽然不可避免,但它对准确测定的影响可以通过多次重复的平行实验,取测定平均值的方法加以消除。

由于粗心大意或不按操作规程操作等引起的误差属于过失误差,例如错误读数或不正确操作等过失误差必须坚决避免。

(二)准确度和精密度

1. **准确度** 准确度是指测定值(x_i)与真实值(T)符合的程度,准确度的高低用误差来衡量。误差越小,测定结果的准确度越高。

误差又称绝对误差(E),可表示为

$$E = x_i - T \qquad (3\text{-}1)$$

准确度也常用相对误差(E_r)表示,即

$$E_r = \frac{E}{T} \times 100\% \qquad (3\text{-}2)$$

由于相对误差反映出了误差在真实值中所占的比例,这对于衡量测定结果的准确度更为合理。因此,通常用相对误差来表示测定结果的准确度。

2. **精密度** 精密度指平行测定值之间相互接近的程度,其大小用偏差来度量。偏差越小,测定结果的精密度越高。

某次测定值(x_i)与多次测定值的算术平均值($\bar{x}$)之差称为绝对偏差(d),即

$$d = x_i - \bar{x} \qquad (3\text{-}3)$$

每次测定的绝对偏差的绝对值($|d_i|$)之和的平均值称为绝对平均偏差($\bar{d}$),设测定次数为n,则有

$$\bar{d} = \frac{|d_1| + |d_2| + |d_3| + \cdots + |d_n|}{n} \qquad (3\text{-}4)$$

精密度的另一种衡量方法是相对平均偏差($\bar{d_r}$),可表示为

$$\bar{d_r} = \frac{\bar{d}}{\bar{x}} \times 100\% \qquad (3\text{-}5)$$

在讨论实验误差时,标准偏差(s)和相对标准偏差(RSD)也时常用到。

标准偏差的数学表达式为

$$s = \sqrt{\frac{d_1^2 + d_2^2 + d_3^2 + \cdots + d_n^2}{n-1}} \tag{3-6}$$

标准偏差突出了单次测量中较大偏差对测定结果的影响,是表示精密度较理想的指标。

相对标准偏差可表示为

$$\text{RSD} = \frac{s}{x} \times 100\% \tag{3-7}$$

在实际工作中多用相对标准偏差表示分析结果的精密度。

(三)有效数字

有效数字用来表现测量值的精确程度,或者基于测量值的计算结果的精确程度。它由一些确定数字加末位不确定数字构成。例如用最小准确刻度为 1 mL 的量筒测量液体的体积,读到 34 mL,再估读一位体积,如 0.2 mL,于是液体的体积是 34.2 mL。这个测量值有 3 位有效数字,误差是 ± 0.1 mL。

1. 有效数字的位数   确定有效数字的位数有以下规则:

(1)数字 "0":"0" 作为定位时不是有效数字。如 34.2 mL 和 0.034 2 mL 都只有 3 位有效数字。

数的右边有小数点,结尾的 "0" 都是有效数字。如 9.00 cm、9.10 cm、90.0 cm,都有 3 位有效数字。

没有小数点的数,其结尾的 "0" 可能是也可能不是有效数字,不能确定。用科学记数法可以排除这种不确定性。

(2)科学记数法:科学记数法用 $A \times 10^n$ 的形式表示数,其中 A 是小数点前只有一位并且是非零数字的数,n 是整数。在科学记数法中,测量值 900 cm 精确到两位有效数字是 9.0×10^2 cm,精确到三位有效数字是 9.00×10^2 cm。

(3)常用对数中的有效数字:常用对数其小数点前的数字对应于有理数幂的指数,因而其小数点后的数值才是有效数字。例如 pH 2.88 只有两位有效数字,它是氢离子浓度的负对数,此时氢离子的浓度为 1.3×10^{-3} mol·L^{-1}。

2. 准确数   迄今为止讨论的只是带有不确定性的数,然而也会遇到准确数。如数某一物品的数量或定义某一单位时,给出的是确定数。例如9 只试剂瓶,那就是准确的9,而不是8.9 或9.1。同样,1 英寸准确定义为2.54 cm,这里2.54 不能说成三位有效数字,事实上它有无穷多位有效数字,只不过不可能全部写出来,因此有效数字的规则对准确数不适用。在计算中其结果的有效数字位数只取决于不确定数。例如一只试剂瓶的质量是20.1 g,9 只试剂瓶总质量的计算是

$$20.1 \text{ g} \times 9 = 180.9 \text{ g}$$

一些常数或来自于文献数据手册的数据,属于非测定值,其有效数字位数不予考虑或视为无限多位。

3. 数的修约

(1)在实际测量中,常常是多种测量仪器联用,并进行多次测量,当要对多个测量数据进行处理时,需要根据误差的传递规律,对测量数据多余的数字进行取舍,即修约。

(2)修约通常按 "四舍六入五留双" 规则进行处理。即:当约去数为 4 时舍弃,为 6 时则进位,如用三位有效数字修约 1.214 3 和 1.216 2 的结果分别是 1.21 和 1.22;当约去数为 5 而后面无其他数字时,若保留数是偶数(包括 0)则舍去,是奇数则进位,使修约后的最后一位数字为偶数。例如用三位有效数字修约 1.215 的结果是 1.22。

4. 有效数字的运算规则   测量值进行数据处理时,常用下面两条规则来确定计算结果的有效数字:

(1)有效数字的加减计算法:进行有效数字加减计算时,其结果以小数点后最少的位数为准。

因此 34.2＋0.21 的和是 34.4。又如，184.2 g＋2.324 g，计算结果为 184.2＋2.324＝186.524，但因为加数 184.2 g 有最少的小数位数（1 位），而 2.324 g 有 3 位小数，因此结果应该写成 186.5 g。

（2）有效数字的乘除计算法：进行有效数字乘除计算时，其结果以有效数字位数最少的那个数为准。因此 34.2 × 0.21 的积是 7.2，两位有效数字。

做两步或两步以上的计算时，保留中间结果的非有效数字，这样能使计算中因修约而存在的小的误差不致在最后结果中出现。如果使用计算器，简单地输入数字并进行计算，最后修约。

二、实验数据的处理

为了表示实验结果和分析其中的规律，需要将实验中获得的大量实验数据进行归纳和处理，常用的方法有列表法、作图法和数学方程法。

（一）列表法

实验中常见的数据处理方法是列表法。将实验数据按自变量 x 和因变量 y 一一对应排列起来制成三线表格，以清楚地表示两者之间的关系。

每个表均应有表头，表由三线组成，不是特别需要，不能有竖线，表中需注明所示变量的名称与单位，表中数据不能再出现单位，并注意所示数据的有效数字位数。在数据处理过程中，通常选择较简单的变量（如温度、时间、浓度等）作为自变量。

（二）作图法

虽然列表法有时能给出有意义的结论，但实验数据用作图来处理，常常可以更直观地显现数据之间的关联，表现数据变化的规律。根据作图还可求得斜率、截距、外推值等。下列为作图的要求：

1. 选择合理的坐标比例，充分利用坐标纸。两根坐标轴可以有不同比例，数据的零值也可不必在原点上。坐标纸的主要分格应以 1 或 2 或 2.5 或 5 为间隔量或者为 10 的幂的倍数单位，不用 3、7 或其他非倍数值为间隔量，以免造成实验数据点在图上难以定位。

2. 坐标轴标明所用物理量单位。习惯上以自变量为横坐标，因变量为纵坐标。

3. 在坐标上定位实验数据，用点标出。同一实验数据组的点用同一图形符号"○""△""×"或"□"圈住，图形的面积近似等于测量误差的范围，每个点用"工"的长度大小表示出此值的测定标准差。

4. 如果实验数据点看似是落在一条直线上，就用一直线表示，注意不在直线上的数据点要均匀地分布在直线两侧，这样能最佳地拟合实验数据。不能随手勾画直线，也不能用线段连接数据点而画成折线。如果数据点看似在一条光滑的曲线上，就用一条曲线表示，并使曲线尽可能地穿过各实验数据点。或用"Excel"软件拟合。

5. 给出图标题　在作图法中，直线图是处理大量数据的极为有效的方法，也容易得出可信的重要结论。尽管实验变量之间存在许多不同的关系，但线性关系最具吸引力，这不仅因为直线比曲线容易绘制，还因为直线方程的计算也更简单。

（三）计算机软件作图及数学方程法

计算机软件作图及数学方程法即是建立自变量和因变量之间的图形或数学方程，从而阐释各数据之间的关系。数学方程的建立可以利用多种方法，目前，利用计算机技术，使制表和制图更加方便，一些数据处理软件（如 Excel 等）的应用，可简化工作过程，提高效率。

如何利用 Excel 获得线性回归方程：

1. 将数据录入到 Excel 表中（2 列）。

2. 选中所有实验数据，然后在菜单中点击"插入"→"散点图"，即显示点状图。

3. 右击图中任意一数据点,在出现的选项中选择"添加趋势线",则在图中显示直线。

4. 在上面的"趋势线选项中",选择"显示公式",即可在图中显示线性回归方程,根据线性回归方程可以获得直线的斜率和截距。

三、实验报告

实验报告体现了学生对所学化学知识的理解和掌握程度。包括实验预习报告和数据记录与结果分析。

学生进实验室之前必须做好预习,包括仔细阅读实验教程,查阅参考文献,模拟设计者的身份,充分理解并能简述实验设计思路、原理、步骤、实验条件及注意事项,完成预习实验报告。

实验中应按照实验规程操作,认真观察实验现象,记录实验数据。通过参与实验、使用化学试剂和仪器,学生学习如何收集实验数据、观察实验现象,并对这些数据和现象给予解释;在准备和完成实验报告的过程中,学会设计、完成科学实验,报告研究结果。

实验结束后必须上交实验报告,包括数据和现象记录、数据处理和结论。

实验预习报告部分包括实验名称、学生姓名和学号、实验日期;实验目的要求、原理、仪器和试剂、模拟设计实验——参照对应实验的实验步骤,以流程图方式给出该实验的设计思路,在流程图中注明相应的注意事项及缘由。最后对实验数据或者现象进行记录,对结果进行分析讨论,给出实验结论,完成思考题。书写实验报告,要求科学严谨、简洁明了、字迹工整、尊重事实、结论正确。根据实验的目的,本教程的实验从培养学生综合实验技能角度和无机化学、分析化学及物理化学等学科理论与实践相结合的角度,从不同教学层次,综合为以下三段式的化学实验训练内容:基本操作规范化及技能训练实验、以模拟设计者身份培养科学研究思维的综合性实验(容量分析实验、仪器分析、化学原理实验、无机化合物制备实验)、综合实验技能提升的开放设计性实验。下面是无机化合物制备和定量分析两种典型实验的报告格式。

无机化合物制备实验
实验 X　硫酸亚铁铵的制备

姓名＿＿＿＿＿＿＿＿＿＿＿＿　　学号＿＿＿＿＿＿＿＿＿＿＿＿　　日期＿＿＿＿＿＿＿＿＿＿＿＿

一、实验预习报告

(一) 实验目的

……

(二) 实验原理

……

(三) 实验仪器材料与试剂

……

(四) 模拟设计实验——参照本实验步骤,以流程图方式给出本实验的设计思路,在流程图中注明相应的注意事项及缘由。

……

二、数据记录与结果分析

……(此处提前做好实验数据记录的三线表格及数据处理项)

实验日期:＿＿＿＿＿＿＿　　室温:＿＿＿＿＿ ℃　　相对湿度:＿＿＿＿＿＿＿

1. 硫酸亚铁铵的制备

在台秤上称取铁屑重 $m(\text{Fe})_1 =$＿＿＿＿＿ g;

铁屑残渣重 $m(\text{Fe})_2 =$＿＿＿＿＿ g;

硫酸亚铁铵 $m[(\text{NH}_4)_2\text{SO}_4 \cdot \text{FeSO}_4 \cdot 6\text{H}_2\text{O}] =$＿＿＿＿＿ g;

硫酸亚铁铵产率（%）= $\dfrac{产品质量（g）}{理论产量（g）}$ × 100% = _____ 。

2. 产品纯度检验

Fe^{3+}标准溶液	一级	二级	三级
硫酸亚铁铵产品级别			

三、思考题

定量分析实验
实验 X 盐酸溶液浓度的标定

姓名_____ 学号_____ 日期_____

一、实验预习报告

（一）实验目的
……

（二）实验原理
……

（三）实验仪器材料与试剂
……

（四）模拟设计实验——参照本实验步骤，以流程图方式给出本实验的设计思路，在流程图中注明相应的注意事项及缘由。
……

二、数据记录与结果分析
……

实验日期：_____ 室温：_____ ℃ 相对湿度：_____

1. 一级标准物 Na_2CO_3 的称量

称量瓶 + Na_2CO_3 质量（m_1）_____ g

称量瓶 + 剩余 Na_2CO_3 质量（m_2）_____ g

每次滴定的 Na_2CO_3 质量_____ g

2. 溶液配制
……

3. 数据记录及结果分析

样品	1	2	3
指示剂			
终点溶液颜色变化			
$V(Na_2CO_3)$/mL			
$V_初(HCl)$/mL			
$V_终(HCl)$/mL			
$\Delta V(HCl)$/mL			
$c(HCl)$/mol·L^{-1}			
$\bar{c}(HCl)$/mol·L^{-1}			
相对平均偏差 $\bar{d_r}$/%			

4. NaOH 标准溶液浓度的计算
……

三、思考题
……

（陈志琼）

第二篇　基础化学实验课题

第四章 ｜ 基本操作训练实验

实验一　常用容量分析仪器操作练习

【实验目的】

1. 学习常量分析玻璃仪器的规范化操作和注意事项。
2. 掌握溶液配制、转移和滴定分析操作。
3. 熟悉酸碱滴定分析的原理。

【预习作业】

1. 指出玻璃仪器中的容器与量器的区别及使用要求。
2. 简要写出本实验中常用定量分析玻璃仪器:容量瓶、移液管、吸量管、滴定管、锥形瓶规范化操作的注意要点。
3. 查阅酸碱滴定分析相关文献,简要说明酸碱滴定分析的原理、种类及选择指示剂的原则。
4. 结合实验内容,请用流程图列出本实验的操作步骤,并在流程图中标出实验的注意事项。

【仪器材料与试剂】

仪器　烧杯(50 mL,250 mL),量筒(50 mL),锥形瓶(250 mL × 3),容量瓶(100 mL),玻璃棒,洗耳球,移液管(20 mL × 2),吸量管(10 mL),酸式滴定管(25 mL),碱式滴定管(25 mL)或聚四氟乙烯酸碱两用滴定管(25 mL),滴定管架,万分之一电子分析天平。

材料与试剂　无水 Na_2CO_3(A.R.),0.1 mol·L^{-1}(精确至 ± 0.000 1 mol·L^{-1})HCl 溶液,0.1 mol·L^{-1}(精确至 ± 0.000 1 mol·L^{-1})NaOH 溶液,1.000 mol·L^{-1} NaCl 溶液,酚酞,甲基橙。

【实验步骤】

(一)容量仪器的洗涤和干燥练习

参照第二章"基础化学实验常用仪器",练习锥形瓶、容量瓶、移液管、滴定管等仪器的洗涤和干燥。

(二)移液管和吸量管操作练习

1. **移液管**　用一支 20 mL 的移液管,练习从 250 mL 的烧杯中吸入自来水和调节凹液面与刻度线相切,然后将 20.00 mL 水转移至 250 mL 锥形瓶中。重复操作数次直至熟练。

2. 吸量管 用一支 10 mL 吸量管吸取 10.00 mL 水,转移至 250 mL 锥形瓶中。练习润洗、吸液及放液,要求每次放出 2.00 mL 水,直至放完所有液体。重复上述操作数次直至熟练。

(三)容量瓶操作练习

1. 检漏、转移溶液和定容 参照第二章"基础化学实验常用仪器"中容量瓶的操作方法,练习容量瓶的检漏、转移溶液和定容。

2. 溶液配制

(1)配制 0.200 0 mol·L^{-1} NaCl 溶液:取一支 20 mL 移液管,准确移取 20.00 mL 1.000 mol·L^{-1} 的 NaCl 溶液至 100 mL 容量瓶中,加水至刻度线,盖紧瓶塞、充分摇匀。重复上述操作数次直至熟练。

(2)配制 0.1 mol·L^{-1}(精确至 0.000 1 mol·L^{-1})Na$_2$CO$_3$ 标准溶液:在电子分析天平上准确称取无水碳酸钠 1.0~1.1 g(精确至 0.000 1 g),置于洁净的 50 mL 烧杯中,加入蒸馏水 30 mL,用玻璃棒小心搅拌使之溶解。然后用玻璃棒引流将溶液转移入 100 mL 容量瓶中,再用少量蒸馏水淋洗烧杯数次,淋洗液一并转移入容量瓶中。加蒸馏水至刻度标线,盖紧瓶塞、充分摇匀。

(四)锥形瓶操作练习

用移液管准确移取 20.00 mL 自来水于 250 mL 锥形瓶中,右手握持锥形瓶颈,向同一方向作圆周旋转摇动练习。要求溶液在锥形瓶内旋转,不能让溶液飞溅造成损失。重复上述操作数次直至熟练。

(五)滴定操作练习

1. 滴定管 参照第二章"基础化学实验常用仪器"中滴定管操作方法,进行滴定管检漏及装配、润洗、装液、排气泡、滴定和读数等操作练习。

2. 酸碱滴定

(1)以酚酞为指示剂,用 0.1 mol·L^{-1}(精确至 ± 0.000 1 mol·L^{-1})NaOH 溶液作滴定剂,滴定 0.1 mol·L^{-1}(精确至 ± 0.000 1 mol·L^{-1})HCl 溶液。

取洁净碱式或酸碱两用滴定管一支,用自来水检查是否漏液。若不漏液,则依次用蒸馏水和 NaOH 标准溶液润洗 2~3 次,润洗液从管尖弃去。将 NaOH 标准溶液注入滴定管,排除尖端的气泡,调整液面,记录滴定管初始读数。

取 20 mL 洁净移液管一支,用 0.1 mol·L^{-1} HCl 标准溶液润洗 2~3 次。准确移取 HCl 标准溶液 20.00 mL 于 250 mL 锥形瓶中,滴加 2 滴酚酞指示剂,用 NaOH 标准溶液滴定至溶液呈现微红色,且 30 s 内不消失,即为滴定终点。读取并记录消耗的 NaOH 溶液的体积(准确至 ± 0.01 mL)于表 4-1-1 中。重复滴定 3 次。

计算 NaOH 溶液与 HCl 溶液的体积比及体积比的平均值,算出相对平均偏差。

(2)以甲基橙为指示剂,按同样方法,用 0.1 mol·L^{-1} HCl(精确至 ± 0.000 1 mol·L^{-1})溶液滴定 0.1 mol·L^{-1}(精确至 ± 0.000 1 mol·L^{-1})NaOH 溶液至溶液由黄色变为橙色或微红色,颜色保持 30 s 不变即为滴定终点。记录相应数据于表 4-1-2 中,计算 HCl 溶液和 NaOH 溶液的体积比及体积比的平均值,算出相对平均偏差。

【数据记录与结果分析】

日期：_____ 温度：_____℃ 相对湿度：_____

表 4-1-1 NaOH 标准溶液滴定 HCl 标准溶液（$n=3$）

实验序号	1	2	3
指示剂	酚酞	酚酞	酚酞
滴定终点颜色变化			
$V_{初}(NaOH)/mL$			
$V_{终}(NaOH)/mL$			
$V_{消耗}(NaOH)/mL$			
$\overline{V}_{消耗}(NaOH)/mL$			
$c(NaOH)/mol \cdot L^{-1}$			
$V(HCl)/mL$			
$c(HCl)/mol \cdot L^{-1}$			
$\dfrac{V(HCl)}{V_{消耗}(NaOH)}$			
$\dfrac{V(HCl)}{\overline{V}_{消耗}(NaOH)}$			
相对平均偏差 $\overline{d}_r/\%$			

表 4-1-2 HCl 标准溶液滴定 NaOH 标准溶液（$n=3$）

实验序号	1	2	3
指示剂	甲基橙	甲基橙	甲基橙
滴定终点颜色变化			
$V_{初}(HCl)/mL$			
$V_{终}(HCl)/mL$			
$V_{消耗}(HCl)/mL$			
$\overline{V}_{消耗}(HCl)/mL$			
$c(HCl)/mol \cdot L^{-1}$			
$V(NaOH)/mL$			
$c(NaOH)/mol \cdot L^{-1}$			
$\dfrac{V_{消耗}(HCl)}{V(NaOH)}$			
$\dfrac{\overline{V}_{消耗}(HCl)}{V(NaOH)}$			
相对平均偏差 $\overline{d}_r/\%$			

【思考题】

1. 滴定管和移液管在使用前用蒸馏水洗涤后，为什么还要用少量滴定剂或待转移液体润洗？
2. 为何每次滴定从零刻度或略低于零刻度开始？
3. 滴定时，为何以甲基橙为指示剂和以酚酞作指示剂所得的 HCl 和 NaOH 的体积比不同？

（李献锐）

实验二　电子分析天平称量练习

【实验目的】

1. 掌握电子分析天平的基本操作及常用的称量方法。
2. 熟悉称量瓶与干燥器的使用。

【预习作业】

1. 称量的方法有哪几种？直接称量法和差减称量法在操作和使用范围上有何不同？
2. 简述电子分析天平的一般操作程序。
3. 使用电子分析天平时应注意什么问题？
4. 结合实验内容，请用流程图列出电子分析天平称量练习的操作步骤，标明具体的称量方法及实验的注意事项。

【实验原理】

电子分析天平的结构、原理和使用方法参见本书第一部分基础化学实验基本知识，第二章中电子分析天平使用的有关内容。

物质的称量有多种方法，常用的有直接称量法和差减称量法。直接称量法适用于称量洁净干燥的器皿（如小烧杯、表面皿等）以及在空气中性质稳定、不吸潮的试样（如金属、矿石等）。称量操作是首先将容器或称量纸置于天平的秤盘上称量，去除容器或称量纸质量（简称去皮），然后将试样放到容器或称量纸上，称出试样的质量。差减称量法的操作是由两次称量之差得到试样质量的称量方法，并且只要求在一定的质量范围内称量。称量步骤是先称量容器（通常是称量瓶）和试样的总质量，取出部分样品后再称量剩余质量，两者之差即为取出样品的质量。

本实验练习电子分析天平的使用、试剂的取用及干燥器使用的规范化操作，利用常用的称量方法准确称取一定质量的试样。

【仪器材料与试剂】

仪器　万分之一电子分析天平，干燥器，称量瓶，小烧杯（50 mL），药匙，小纸条，称量纸。
材料与试剂　碳酸镁（A.R.），硼砂（A.R.）。

【实验步骤】

（一）检查天平

使用前观察水平仪的气泡位置是否居中,若有偏移,需调整水平调节脚,使气泡位于水平仪中心。

（二）开启天平

接通电源,单击"ON"键,天平自检,显示屏很快出现"0.000 0 g"。如果显示不是"0.000 0 g",则要按一下"→O/T←"键。天平长时间断电之后再使用时,至少需预热 30 min。

（三）直接称量法

准确称出小烧杯的质量和 0.20~0.25 g(精确至 0.000 1 g)碳酸镁。

1. 称量容器　将干净的小烧杯轻轻放在秤盘上,其质量即会自动显示,记录称量数据。

2. 扣除皮重　轻按"→O/T←"键(清零/去皮),显示的数字消失,然后出现"0.000 0 g"字样,容器质量即被扣除。

3. 称量样品　将碳酸镁试剂瓶口置于小烧杯上方,用药匙取出试剂分别借助轻抖,或轻弹,或轻敲等方式小心缓慢地放入小烧杯中,直至符合称量的要求。停止加样,关闭天平门,记录称量数据于表 4-2-1 中。若用称量纸称量的试样,按药房包药方式包好,在称量纸外标注上相应样品信息及日期。

4. 重复实验　按上述方法再重复称量 2 份试样。

（四）差减称量法

准确称出 1.0~1.4 g(精确至 0.000 1 g)硼砂。

1. 平移打开干燥器盖子,用小纸条将盛有硼砂的称量瓶从干燥器中夹住取出,盖好干燥器,将称量瓶置于秤盘上,关好天平门。显示稳定后,按"O/T"键,去皮重并显示"0.000 0 g"字样。

2. 从天平上取出称量瓶,倾斜称量瓶,用瓶盖小心敲击称量瓶口边沿,使一定量的样品抖落入烧杯中,再将称量瓶置于秤盘上称量。此时显示的读数是负值,负号后的数据即为倾出样品的质量。若所示质量达到要求范围,即可记录称量数据于表 4-2-1 中。

3. 按上述方法再重复称量 2 份试样。

4. 若用称量纸称取试样,称好的试样要求按药房包药的方式包好,并写上试剂的名称、质量、称量的时间及称量者的姓名等信息。

（五）称量完毕的操作

称量完毕,取下被称物,轻按"OFF"键,让天平处于待命状态。

使用完毕,用毛刷清扫天平,关好天平门,拔下电源插头,盖上防尘罩,在"使用登记本"上登记。

【注意事项】

1. 称量时,一切操作都要细心。读数时要注意关闭好天平门,以免气流影响使读数不准确。

2. 天平的载重不能超过其限度,称量物体的温度必须与室温相同。

3. 不能在天平秤盘上直接称取试样,应放在洁净的器皿中称量。有腐蚀性或吸湿性的样品都必须置于密闭容器内称量。

4. 称量时,要用镊子或纸条夹取称量物品,也可套上医用手套进行操作,切勿用手直接拿取。

31

【数据记录及结果分析】

日期：_____ 温度：_____℃ 相对湿度：_____

表 4-2-1 电子分析天平称量练习记录

称量方法	试样	质量/g		
		1	2	3
直接称量法	小烧杯			
	样品			
差减称量法	样品			

【思考题】

1. 用差减称量法称量时,如何从称量瓶中倾倒出试样?
2. 影响电子分析天平读数稳定性的因素有哪些?

(赵全芹)

实验三 缓冲溶液的配制、性质和溶液 pH 测量

【实验目的】

1. 学习缓冲溶液及常用等渗磷酸盐缓冲溶液的配制方法。
2. 加深对缓冲溶液性质的理解。
3. 巩固吸量管的规范操作。
4. 掌握移液器的使用方法。
5. 掌握使用 pH 试纸和酸度计测量溶液 pH 的方法。

【预习作业】

1. 缓冲溶液的性质有哪些? 缓冲溶液的 pH 由哪些因素决定?
2. 如何衡量缓冲溶液的缓冲能力大小? 缓冲溶液的缓冲能力与什么因素有关?
3. 如何检测缓冲溶液的 pH 是否发生改变? 是否均需要用 pH 计?
4. 根据本实验的检测手段,说明本实验属于定量分析还是定性分析或半定量分析?
5. 请用流程图阐释本实验是如何设计实验步骤,以验证缓冲溶液所具有的性质及缓冲容量的影响因素,并在流程图中标出每个实验步骤的注意事项。

【实验原理】

缓冲溶液具有抵抗外加的少量强酸或强碱、或适当稀释而保持溶液 pH 基本不变的作用。

缓冲溶液由足够浓度的弱酸(HB,亦称抗碱成分)及其共轭碱(B$^-$,亦称抗酸成分),或弱碱及其共轭酸组成的溶液。在溶液中存在酸碱质子平衡：

$$HB + H_2O \rightleftharpoons H_3O^+ + B^-$$

缓冲溶液的 pH 可用下式计算

$$pH = pK_a + \lg\frac{[B^-]}{[HB]}$$

其中:K_a 为共轭酸的酸解离常数。$\dfrac{[B^-]}{[HB]}$ 称为缓冲溶液的缓冲比。

向缓冲溶液中加入少量强酸(或者少量强碱),会被缓冲溶液中大量的抗酸成分(或者抗碱成分)中和,因此缓冲溶液的缓冲比 $\dfrac{[B^-]}{[HB]}$ 基本保持不变,即缓冲溶液的 pH 保持基本不变。缓冲溶液缓冲能力的大小可用缓冲容量 β 表示。缓冲容量的大小与缓冲溶液总浓度、缓冲比有关。

$$\beta = \frac{dn_{a(b)}}{V\,|dpH|}$$

当缓冲比一定时,缓冲溶液总浓度 $\{[HB]+[B^-]\}$ 越大,缓冲容量 β 越大;当总浓度一定时,缓冲比 $\dfrac{[B^-]}{[HB]}$ 越趋向于 1,缓冲容量 β 越大;当缓冲比 $\dfrac{[B^-]}{[HB]}=1$ 时,缓冲容量 β 达该总浓度 $\{[HB]+[B^-]\}$ 下的极大值。

缓冲溶液主要应用于需要保持稳定的 pH 环境,如:生物体的各组织器官发生的生化反应就需要保持稳定 pH。磷酸盐缓冲生理盐水(phosphate-buffered saline,PBS)是医学上体外细胞培养常用的缓冲液,其渗透压和细胞内液相似,pH 和细胞外液相似,并有较强的缓冲能力。

本实验将学习配制一般的缓冲溶液和 PBS 溶液,并将缓冲溶液和普通溶液进行比对的抗酸、抗碱及适当稀释的实验,验证缓冲溶液的缓冲性质。

【仪器材料与试剂】

仪器　烧杯(50 mL × 6 200 mL × 2 500 mL × 1),试管(5 mL × 12),比色管(10.00 mL × 3),容量瓶(50.00 mL × 1),吸量管或者可调移液器(5.00 mL × 6,1.00 mL × 3)及吸头若干,比色管架,试管架,滴管,玻璃棒,洗瓶,洗耳球,pH 计。

材料与试剂　HAc 溶液(1.000 0 mol·L^{-1},0.500 0 mol·L^{-1},0.100 0 mol·L^{-1}),NaAc 溶液(1.000 0 mol·L^{-1},0.100 0 mol·L^{-1}),1.000 0 mol·L^{-1} NaOH 溶液,1.000 0 mol·L^{-1} HCl 溶液,0.150 0 mol·L^{-1} NaCl 溶液,0.150 0 mol·L^{-1} KCl 溶液,0.150 0 mol·L^{-1} KH$_2$PO$_4$ 溶液,0.100 0 mol·L^{-1} Na$_2$HPO$_4$ 溶液,标准缓冲液(pH = 4.00、6.86、9.18),广泛 pH 试纸,学生自带的试样溶液两份(体积≥50 mL)。

【实验步骤】

(一) 缓冲溶液的配制

1. PBS 缓冲溶液的配制　按照表 4-3-1 中各试剂的用量,使用吸量管或移液器分别移取相应的溶液到 50.00 mL 容量瓶中,配制 pH 为 7.40 的 PBS 缓冲溶液,备用。

2. HAc-NaAc 缓冲溶液的配制　按照表 4-3-2 中试剂的用量,用吸量管或移液器分别移取相应的溶液到 3 支 10.00 mL 比色管中,分别配制 A~C 缓冲溶液,备用。

(二) 缓冲溶液的性质及缓冲容量的影响因素测定

以 0.500 0 mol·L^{-1} HAc 溶液作为对照用的普通溶液,按照表 4-3-3 中试剂的用量,使用 pH 试纸分别检测加入 HCl 溶液、NaOH 溶液或者纯水前后,普通溶液以及缓冲溶液 A、B 和 C 的 pH(加入前为 pH$_1$,加入后为 pH$_2$),记录在表 4-3-3 中,并计算 pH 变化值的绝对值 |ΔpH|。

$$|\Delta pH| = |pH_2 - pH_1|$$

通过比较分析表 4-3-3 的 |ΔpH|,进行以下讨论并总结结论:

1. 与普通溶液比较,缓冲溶液具有哪些缓冲作用?

2. 比较缓冲溶液 A 和 B,当总浓度相同时,缓冲比如何影响缓冲溶液的缓冲容量?

3. 比较缓冲溶液 A 和 C,当缓冲比相同时,总浓度如何影响缓冲溶液的缓冲容量?

4. 影响缓冲能力(缓冲容量)大小的因素主要有哪些?

(三) 准确测量 PBS 缓冲溶液及自带试样溶液的 pH

1. pH 计的校正 按第二章"基础化学实验常用仪器"中 pH 计的使用方法对 pH 计进行校正。

2. 准确测量PBS溶液及自带试样溶液pH 将步骤一中配制好的 PBS 溶液倒入 50 mL 烧杯中,分别使用 pH 计和广泛 pH 试纸测量 pH,并以 $1.000\ 0\ mol\cdot L^{-1}$ HCl 溶液或者 $1.000\ 0\ mol\cdot L^{-1}$ NaOH 溶液调节 PBS 溶液的 pH 至 7.40。

以相同的方法测量自带试样溶液的 pH。将测得的 pH 分别记录在表 4-3-4 中,比较两种方法所测得的各溶液样品 pH 的精确度。

【数据记录及结果处理】

日期:＿＿＿＿＿＿＿＿＿   温度:＿＿＿＿＿＿＿＿℃   相对湿度:＿＿＿＿＿＿＿＿

表 4-3-1 pH = 7.40 的 PBS 缓冲溶液的配制

试剂	KCl	KH₂PO₄	Na₂HPO₄	NaCl
浓度 /(mol·L⁻¹)	0.150 0	0.150 0	0.100 0	0.150 0
用量 /mL	0.86	0.56	4.90	加至 50.00 mL

表 4-3-2 缓冲溶液配制

试管编号	A	B	C
$1.000\ 0\ mol\cdot L^{-1}$ NaAc /mL	2.50	4.00	/
$1.000\ 0\ mol\cdot L^{-1}$ HAc /mL	2.50	1.00	/
$0.100\ 0\ mol\cdot L^{-1}$ NaAc /mL	/	/	2.50
$0.100\ 0\ mol\cdot L^{-1}$ HAc /mL	/	/	2.50

$V_{总}$ /mL

c(NaAc)/mol·L⁻¹

c(HAc)/mol·L⁻¹

缓冲比 = c(NaAc)/c(HAc)

$c_{总} = c$(NaAc)+ c(HAc)/mol·L⁻¹

表 4-3-3 普通溶液及缓冲溶液的抗酸、抗碱和抗稀释测试

测试项目	抗酸测试				抗碱测试				抗稀释测试			
试剂	HAc	A	B	C	HAc	A	B	C	HAc	A	B	C
试剂用量 /mL	1.00	1.00	1.00	1.00	1.00	1.00	1.00	1.00	1.00	1.00	1.00	1.00
pH₁												

测试项目	抗酸测试				抗碱测试				抗稀释测试			
试剂	HAc	A	B	C	HAc	A	B	C	HAc	A	B	C
$1.000\,0\ mol\cdot L^{-1}$ HCl/滴	3	3	3	3								
$1.000\,0\ mol\cdot L^{-1}$ NaOH/滴					3	3	3	3				
H_2O/mL									4.00	4.00	4.00	4.00
pH_2												
$\Delta pH=\lvert pH_2-pH_1\rvert$												

注:表 4-3-3 中用于对照的 HAc 的浓度为 $0.500\,0\ mol\cdot L^{-1}$。

表 4-3-4 PBS 缓冲溶液的配制及自带试样溶液 pH 的测量

试样	PBS 缓冲溶液	自带试样溶液 1	自带试样溶液 2
试纸测 pH			
pH 计测 pH			

【思考题】

1. 请比较和讨论 pH 试纸与 pH 计测量溶液 pH 的准确度。

2. 为何每测量完一种溶液,复合电极需用蒸馏水洗净并吸干后才能测量另一种溶液?

3. 如果只有 HAc 和 NaOH,HCl 和 $NH_3\cdot H_2O$,KH_2PO_4 和 NaOH,能够进行上述实验吗? 你将怎样设计实验?

(赖泽锋)

实验四 溶胶的制备与性质

【实验目的】

1. 掌握溶胶的制备方法。

2. 熟悉溶胶的光学及电学性质。

3. 了解溶胶的净化、聚沉及高分子化合物对溶胶的保护作用。

【预习作业】

模拟设计实验:以流程图方式给出本实验的设计思路,并在流程图的实验步骤中注明相应的注意事项及缘由。

引导问题:

1. 如何按照分散相粒子的大小对分散系进行分类? 它们是否都能透过滤纸和半透膜?

2. 胶体分散系是如何分类的? 溶胶的基本特征有哪些?

3. 分别写出 $Fe(OH)_3$、Sb_2S_3 胶团结构式,并判断电泳时胶粒的运动方向?

4. 为什么溶胶是热力学不稳定系统但又能够相对稳定存在?

5. 试说明加热和加入电解质对溶胶聚沉的影响?

【实验原理】

(一) 溶胶的制备

胶体是物质的一种分散体系,当物质以 1~100 nm 大小的粒子分散于另一种介质中时,就成为胶体分散系。胶体分散系主要包括溶胶、高分子溶液和缔合胶体三类。溶胶的制备通常采用化学反应或物理凝聚方法。

1. 化学反应制备法 利用 $FeCl_3$ 的水解反应制备 $Fe(OH)_3$ 溶胶:将 $FeCl_3$ 溶液逐滴加入沸腾的蒸馏水中并不断搅拌,加完后根据情况可适当延长煮沸时间,得到暗红色的 $Fe(OH)_3$ 溶胶:

$$FeCl_3 + 3H_2O \underset{}{\overset{煮沸}{\rightleftharpoons}} Fe(OH)_3 + 3HCl$$

$$Fe(OH)_3(部分) + HCl \rightleftharpoons FeOCl + 2H_2O$$

$$FeOCl \rightleftharpoons FeO^+ + Cl^-$$

在本制备方式下,$Fe(OH)_3$ 胶核优先吸附与其具有相似组成的 FeO^+ 离子,而形成正溶胶。

利用酒石酸锑钾与 H_2S 的复分解反应制备 Sb_2S_3 溶胶:该溶胶的制备是通过溶解在水中的 H_2S 与酒石酸锑钾的反应而得:

$$2(SbO)K(C_4H_4O_6) + 3H_2S \rightleftharpoons Sb_2S_3 + 2KHC_4H_4O_6 + 2H_2O$$

$$H_2S(过量) + H_2O \rightleftharpoons H_3O^+ + HS^-$$

Sb_2S_3 胶核吸附 HS^-,因而形成负溶胶。

2. 物理凝聚制备法 改换溶剂法制备硫溶胶:根据物质在不同溶剂中溶解度不同的性质,向水中滴入硫的乙醇饱和溶液,由于硫难溶于水,过饱和的硫原子相互聚集,从而形成硫溶胶。

(二) 溶胶的光学及电学性质

溶胶具有较强的光散射现象,当一束光线照射溶胶时,在其垂直方向可看到明显的光路,此现象称为丁铎尔现象。丁铎尔现象是溶胶区别于真溶液的一个基本特征,常用于鉴定试样体系是否为胶体。

溶胶的另一个重要性质是其胶粒表面带有电荷。胶粒带电的原因:①胶核对与其具有相似组成离子的选择性吸附;②胶核表面分子的解离。胶粒的带电性可通过将溶胶置于含有两个电极的 U 形管,即电泳装置来测定。在外加电场作用下,溶胶粒子定向迁移,产生电泳现象。带负电荷的胶粒向正极迁移,带正电荷胶粒向负极迁移。如氢氧化铁胶粒将向负极移动,由此可见其带正电荷;而大部分金属硫化物(如三硫化二锑)胶粒将向正极移动,表明其带负电荷。溶胶胶粒的带电性是其稳定存在的原因之一。

(三) 溶胶的净化

制备的溶胶中,共存的电解质离子会影响溶胶的稳定性。因此,除去杂质离子可使溶胶在较长时间内保持稳定。根据胶粒不能透过半透膜而电解质离子、小分子和水等易通过半透膜的特性,分离和纯化胶体的方式称为渗析法,这种膜称为渗析膜。

(四) 溶胶的聚沉

溶胶的稳定因素有胶粒带电、胶粒表面水合膜的保护作用和布朗运动,其中最主要的稳定因素是胶粒带电。电解质对溶胶的聚沉作用主要通过改变胶粒吸附层结构实现。随着电解质的增加,反离子较多地进入吸附层,胶粒表面所带电荷被反离子中和,吸附层随之变薄,胶粒易聚集变大而产生沉降。反离子价数越高,电解质的聚沉能力越强。如氢氧化铁溶胶是正溶胶,可加入含高价阴离子(如 PO_4^{3-})的溶液使其聚沉。Sb_2S_3 溶胶是负溶胶,带正电荷的高价电解质离子是其聚沉的有效离子,因此,在 Sb_2S_3 溶胶中加入 $AlCl_3$ 比加入等量的 $NaCl$ 聚沉效果更好。

除了电解质的聚沉作用以外,两种带相反电荷的溶胶混合,也可以发生聚沉现象;另外,加热也是使溶胶聚沉的常用方法。

(五) 高分子化合物对溶胶的保护作用

若在溶胶中加入足够量的高分子溶液,高分子化合物可在胶粒周围形成高分子保护层,使胶粒不易发生聚沉,从而增加溶胶的稳定性。

【仪器材料与试剂】

仪器　电泳装置,丁铎尔现象装置,电磁加热搅拌器,酒精灯,烧杯(100 mL×5),量筒(10 mL×4,50 mL×3),大试管,表面皿,滴管,三角架,玻璃棒。

试剂　30 $g·L^{-1}$ $FeCl_3$ 溶液,4 $g·L^{-1}$ 酒石酸锑钾溶液,饱和 H_2S 溶液,硫的乙醇饱和溶液,饱和 $NaCl$ 溶液,0.01 $mol·L^{-1}$ $NaCl$ 溶液,0.01 $mol·L^{-1}$ $CaCl_2$ 溶液,0.01 $mol·L^{-1}$ $AlCl_3$ 溶液,0.1 $mol·L^{-1}$ $NH_3·H_2O$ 溶液,0.1 $mol·L^{-1}$ $KSCN$ 溶液,0.05 $mol·L^{-1}$ $AgNO_3$ 溶液,新配制的 30 $g·L^{-1}$ 动物胶,20 $g·L^{-1}$ $CuSO_4$ 溶液,火棉胶,pH 试纸。

【实验步骤】

(一) 胶体的制备

1. 水解法制备 Fe(OH)$_3$ 溶胶　取 30.0 mL 蒸馏水于小烧杯中,加热至沸,边搅拌边逐滴加入 30 $g·L^{-1}$ $FeCl_3$ 溶液 3.0 mL,继续煮沸 2~3 min,可得 Fe(OH)$_3$ 溶胶,观察制备过程中溶液颜色变化,备用。

2. 复分解法制备 Sb_2S_3 溶胶　取 20.0 mL 4 $g·L^{-1}$ 酒石酸锑钾溶液于小烧杯中,电磁搅拌下逐滴加入约 10.0 mL 饱和 H_2S 溶液,即可得橙红色的 Sb_2S_3 溶胶,备用。

3. 转换溶剂法制备硫溶胶　在小烧杯中加入 20.0 mL 蒸馏水,电磁搅拌下逐滴加入硫的乙醇饱和溶液 2.0~3.0 mL,观察硫溶胶的生成,备用。

(二) 溶胶的性质

1. 溶胶的光学性质——丁铎尔现象　将制备的溶胶分别置于丁铎尔现象装置中,用一束聚焦的可见光源照射溶胶,从垂直于光束方向观察溶胶的丁铎尔现象。再观察蒸馏水和硫酸铜溶液是否具有丁铎尔现象。注意:若 Fe(OH)$_3$ 溶胶的丁铎尔现象不明显,可延长制备过程沸腾时间,使 HCl 充分挥发,并用激光笔检测至有光柱即可证明制备溶胶成功。

2. 溶胶的电学性质——电泳　在 U 形管中注入 Sb_2S_3 溶胶。沿 U 形管两侧的管壁慢慢加入蒸馏水,使水与溶胶之间有明显的界面,水层厚约 1~2 cm,然后将金属电极分别插入水层,接通直流电源,调节电压在 30~110 V,观察溶胶界面的移动。由溶胶界面移动的方向,判断胶粒所带电荷的电性。

(三) 溶胶的净化——渗析

1. 渗析袋的制作　将适量火棉胶倒入干燥洁净的小烧杯中,慢慢转动烧杯,使火棉胶均匀布满器壁形成薄层,倾出多余的火棉胶。倒置烧杯,使火棉胶固化成膜,在烧杯中小心地加入少量蒸馏水,然后轻轻将火棉胶膜与烧杯口分离,注水于容器壁与膜之间,膜即可脱离容器壁,慢慢取出,注意不要撕破。在制备渗析袋并从烧杯内剥离时,注意加水不宜太早,因为若火棉胶中乙醚尚未挥发完全,早加水,膜呈白色不能用;但亦不宜太迟,否则膜变干、变硬不易取出。

2. Fe(OH)₃溶胶的净化 将制备的 Fe(OH)₃ 溶胶注入渗析袋,注意不要让溶液污染渗析袋外面,若外部附有溶液,用蒸馏水冲洗干净。袋口用线扎紧,置于盛有蒸馏水的烧杯中(袋口不要浸入水中)。每隔 10 min 换水一次,并取适量袋外溶液,分别用 0.05 mol·L⁻¹ AgNO₃ 溶液和 0.1 mol·L⁻¹ KSCN 溶液检测 Cl⁻ 和 Fe³⁺,解释实验现象。

(四) 溶胶的聚沉

1. 电解质的聚沉作用 于三支干燥试管中加入 2.0 mL Sb₂S₃ 溶胶,分别向其中滴加 0.01 mol·L⁻¹ NaCl、0.01 mol·L⁻¹ CaCl₂ 和 0.01 mol·L⁻¹ AlCl₃ 溶液,边加边摇,至溶液刚呈现浑浊为止。记录各试管所加溶液的滴数,比较三种电解质聚沉能力大小,解释实验现象。

2. 溶胶的相互聚沉 将 2.0 mL Fe(OH)₃ 溶胶与 2.0 mL Sb₂S₃ 溶胶充分混合,观察并解释实验现象。

3. 温度对溶胶稳定性的影响 将盛有 2.0 mL Sb₂S₃ 溶胶的试管加热至沸,观察并解释实验现象。

(五) 高分子化合物对溶胶的保护作用

取两支大试管,一支试管中加入 2.0 mL 蒸馏水,另一支试管中加入 2.0 mL 新配制的 30 g·L⁻¹ 动物胶溶液,然后在两支试管中分别加入 4.0 mL Sb₂S₃ 溶胶,小心振摇,放置约 3 min 后,向两支试管中分别滴加饱和 NaCl 溶液,观察聚沉现象的差别。

将以上的实验现象及解释原因填写于表格 4-4-1 中。

【数据记录及结果处理】

日期:_____ 温度:_____ ℃ 相对湿度:_____

表 4-4-1 溶胶的制备与性质

实验内容		实验现象	解释
溶胶制备	Fe(OH)₃溶胶		
	Sb₂S₃溶胶		
	硫溶胶		
溶胶的光学性质——Tyndall 现象			
溶胶的电学性质——电泳			
Fe(OH)₃溶胶的净化			
溶胶聚沉	电解质的聚沉作用		
	溶胶的相互聚沉		
	温度对溶胶稳定性的影响		
高分子化合物对溶胶的保护作用			

【思考题】

1. 制备 $Fe(OH)_3$ 溶胶时,需将 $FeCl_3$ 溶液滴入沸水中,试解释其原因。
2. 动物胶为何能使溶胶稳定?
3. 试解释溶胶产生丁铎尔现象的原因。

（刘国杰）

第五章 | 滴定分析实验

实验五　酸碱滴定分析法

【实验目的】

1. 掌握酸碱滴定分析的基本原理及实验操作步骤。
2. 掌握滴定规范化操作及滴定终点的判断方法。
3. 学习酸碱标准溶液的配制及酸性物质或碱性物质的含量测定。
4. 熟悉返滴定法。
5. 学习直接滴定法及实际样品的测定方法。

【预习作业】

1. 滴定中测定与标定有何不同？
2. 标准溶液的配制方法有哪几种？标定标准溶液的方法有哪几种？
3. 酸碱滴定中常用盐酸或氢氧化钠作为标准溶液，为什么？
4. 酸碱滴定中指示剂选择依据是什么？
5. 酸碱指示剂的变色范围是根据 $pK(HIn)$ 计算出来的吗？
6. 指示剂用量的多或少对滴定误差有影响吗？

【实验原理】

酸碱滴定法是以酸碱反应为基础的滴定分析方法。利用酸碱滴定法，可以测定酸性物质或碱性物质的含量，也可以测定能与酸或碱反应的其他物质的含量。测定酸性物质时，用已知浓度的标准强碱溶液与其作用，然后根据所消耗的强碱量，求出被测物质的含量。测定碱性物质时，则用已知浓度的标准强酸溶液与之作用，然后根据所消耗掉的强酸的量来求出被测物质的含量。

对具有酸性（或碱性）且难溶于水的物质，可以通过加入过量的碱（或酸）标准溶液与其充分反应后，再用另一种酸（或碱）溶液返滴定过量的标准溶液。

滴定分析法通常分为三个步骤：标准溶液的配制，标准溶液浓度的标定和试样含量的测定。

在酸碱滴定分析中，常用盐酸和氢氧化钠溶液作为标准溶液。但浓盐酸易挥发，氢氧化钠易吸收空气中的水和二氧化碳，都不能用于直接配制标准溶液。只能先配制成近似浓度的溶液，然后用一级标准物质或标准溶液标定其准确浓度。根据滴定所得到的 $V(NaOH)$ 或 $V(HCl)$ 值和一级标准物质的质量或标准溶液的浓度，可算出待标定标准溶液的浓度。

1. 标定 HCl 溶液常用的一级标准物质无水碳酸钠（Na_2CO_3）或硼砂（$Na_2B_4O_7 \cdot 10H_2O$）。其中碳酸钠易制得纯品，价廉，但易吸收空气中的水和二氧化碳，所以使用前必须在 270~300 ℃加热约 1 h，稍冷后置于干燥器中冷至室温备用。硼砂的摩尔质量较大（381.37 g·mol^{-1}），但因含结晶水，须保持在相对湿度为 60% 的恒湿器中。

2. 标定 NaOH 常用的一级标准物质草酸（$H_2C_2O_4 \cdot 2H_2O$）或邻苯二甲酸氢钾（$KHC_8H_4O_4$，KHP）等。最常用的是邻苯二甲酸氢钾，它易得纯品，稳定且易于保存，摩尔质量较大（$204.22\ g \cdot mol^{-1}$）。

一、盐酸标准溶液浓度的标定

【实验目的】

1. 掌握盐酸标准溶液浓度标定的原理和操作步骤。
2. 巩固酸式滴定管的规范化操作及滴定终点的判断方法。
3. 巩固差减称量法的规范化操作。

【预习作业】

模拟设计实验：以流程图方式给出本实验的设计思路，并在流程图实验步骤中注明相应的注意事项及缘由。

引导问题：

1. 为什么不能将盐酸直接配制成标准溶液使用？
2. 在配制盐酸溶液的过程中，为什么要先加入适量蒸馏水再加入盐酸？
3. 标定盐酸溶液可以用无水碳酸钠（Na_2CO_3），也可以用硼砂（$Na_2B_4O_7 \cdot 10H_2O$），若用甲基橙作为指示剂，哪个更好？
4. 用无水碳酸钠（Na_2CO_3）标定盐酸溶液的浓度，应如何判断滴定终点？

【实验原理】

无水 Na_2CO_3（pK_{b1}=3.75，pK_{b2}=7.62）是常见的二元弱碱，可作为基准物质标定 HCl 溶液。反应式如下：

$$Na_2CO_3 + 2HCl \longrightarrow 2NaCl + H_2O + CO_2 \uparrow$$

若采用 $0.100\ 0\ mol \cdot L^{-1}$ HCl 溶液滴定 $0.100\ 0\ mol \cdot L^{-1}$ Na_2CO_3 溶液，化学计量点时 pH = 3.9，滴定突跃为 pH = 5.0~3.5，可选用甲基橙（变色范围 pH 3.1~4.4）作指示剂。滴定接近终点时，应将溶液煮沸，减少 CO_2 对终点的影响。

HCl 溶液的准确浓度可通过式（5-5-1）计算得到

$$c(HCl) = \frac{2 \times m(Na_2CO_3)}{M_r(Na_2CO_3) \times V(HCl)} \qquad (5\text{-}5\text{-}1)$$

式（5-5-1）中 $m(Na_2CO_3)$ 为 Na_2CO_3 质量，$M_r(Na_2CO_3)$ 为 Na_2CO_3 的摩尔质量（$105.99\ g \cdot mol^{-1}$），$V(HCl)$ 为所消耗 HCl 标准溶液的体积。

【仪器材料与试剂】

仪器　万分之一电子分析天平，称量瓶，酸式滴定管或聚四氟乙烯酸碱两用滴定管（25 mL），烧杯（100 mL，1 L），锥形瓶（250 mL×3），量筒（10 mL，50 mL），称量瓶，试剂瓶，滴定管架，洗瓶，玻璃棒，滴管，酒精灯。

材料与试剂 无水碳酸钠（A.R.），浓盐酸（12 mol·L^{-1}），0.05% 甲基橙指示剂。

【实验步骤】

（一）0.1 mol·L^{-1} HCl 溶液的配制

计算配制 500 mL 0.1 mol·L^{-1} HCl 溶液所需浓盐酸的体积。在通风橱，用 10 mL 量筒量取所需浓盐酸，倒入盛有适量蒸馏水的烧杯中，用少量的蒸馏水洗涤量筒 2~3 次，洗涤液并入烧杯中，加蒸馏水至总体积约 500 mL。充分搅拌均匀，倒入试剂瓶，盖好塞子，得到 0.1 mol·L^{-1} HCl 溶液备用。

（二）HCl 溶液的标定

在分析天平上用差减法精确称取无水 Na$_2$CO$_3$ 0.07~0.09 g（准确至 0.000 1 g）于洁净的 250 mL 锥形瓶中，加入 30 mL 蒸馏水溶解，再加入 1~2 滴甲基橙指示剂，混合均匀后溶液呈黄色。用待标定的 HCl 溶液滴定至溶液由黄色刚刚变为橙色时，暂停滴定，将溶液加热至微沸 2~3 min，剧烈摇动锥形瓶以去除 CO$_2$，溶液又由橙色变为黄色。冷却后继续用 HCl 溶液滴定，至溶液由黄色变为橙色，且 30 s 之内不褪色即为终点。记录滴定消耗的 HCl 溶液体积于表 5-5-1 中。

重复上述滴定操作 2~3 次。测定结果的相对平均偏差应小于 0.2%。根据滴定所消耗的 HCl 溶液的体积和实际参加反应的 Na$_2$CO$_3$ 质量，计算出 HCl 溶液的准确浓度。

【数据记录及结果分析】

日期：_____ 温度：_____℃ 相对湿度：_____

1. 配制 0.1 mol·L^{-1} HCl 溶液 500 mL 所需浓盐酸体积：_____mL。

2. 0.1 mol·L^{-1} HCl 溶液的标定

表 5-5-1 0.1 mol·L^{-1} HCl 溶液的标定

实验序号	1	2	3
m_1（称量瓶 + Na$_2$CO$_3$）/g			
m_2（称量瓶 + 剩余 Na$_2$CO$_3$）/g			
m_1-m_2（Na$_2$CO$_3$）/g			
$V_{初}$（HCl）/mL			
$V_{终}$（HCl）/mL			
$V_{消耗}$（HCl）/mL			
c（HCl）/mol·L^{-1}			
$\bar{c}$（HCl）/mol·L^{-1}			
$\bar{d_r}$/%			

【思考题】

1. 本实验为何选用甲基橙作为指示剂？除了甲基橙，还可以选用其他指示剂吗？

2. 在用 HCl 溶液滴定 Na$_2$CO$_3$ 溶液的过程中，溶液第一次变色后为什么要加热去除 CO$_2$，如果不处理，对滴定终点有什么影响？

（别子俊）

二、氢氧化钠标准溶液浓度的标定

【实验目的】

1. 掌握氢氧化钠标准溶液浓度标定的原理和操作方法。
2. 巩固碱式滴定管的规范化操作及酸碱滴定终点的判断方法。
3. 巩固差减称量法的规范化操作。

【预习作业】

模拟设计实验:以流程图方式给出本实验的设计思路,请在流程图中实验步骤注明相应的注意事项及缘由。

引导问题:

1. 为什么不能将氢氧化钠直接配制成标准溶液使用?
2. 在使用氢氧化钠标准溶液前,常常需要重新标定其浓度,为什么?
3. 常使用邻苯二甲酸氢钾($KHC_8H_4O_4$)作为标定氢氧化钠溶液的基准物质,为什么?还可以使用其他基准物质吗?

【实验原理】

邻苯二甲酸氢钾($KHC_8H_4O_4$,KHP,$pK_{a2}=5.41$)常作为基准物质来标定 NaOH 溶液。反应式如下:

若采用 $0.100\,0\ mol\cdot L^{-1}$ NaOH 溶液滴定 $0.100\,0\ mol\cdot L^{-1}$ KHP 溶液,化学计量点时溶液的 pH = 9.1,可选用酚酞(变色范围 pH 8.2~10.0)作指示剂。

NaOH 溶液的准确浓度可通过式(5-5-2)计算得到

$$c(\text{NaOH}) = \frac{m(\text{KHP})}{M_r(\text{KHP}) \times V(\text{NaOH})} \qquad (5\text{-}5\text{-}2)$$

式(5-5-2)中 m(KHP)为邻苯二甲酸氢钾的质量,M_r(KHP)为邻苯二甲酸氢钾的摩尔质量($204.22\ g\cdot mol^{-1}$),V(NaOH)为消耗的 NaOH 溶液的体积。

【仪器材料与试剂】

仪器　万分之一电子分析天平,百分之一电子分析天平,称量瓶,碱式滴定管或聚四氟乙烯酸碱两用滴定管(25 mL),锥形瓶(250 mL × 3),烧杯(100 mL,1 L),量筒(50 mL),称量瓶,试剂瓶,滴定管架,洗瓶,玻璃棒,滴管。

材料与试剂　固体 NaOH,邻苯二甲酸氢钾($KHC_8H_4O_4$,A.R.),0.1% 酚酞指示剂。

【实验步骤】

(一) 0.1 mol·L⁻¹ NaOH 溶液的配制

计算配制 500 mL 0.1 mol·L⁻¹ NaOH 溶液所需的固体 NaOH 的质量。用百分之一电子分析天平快速称出所需的 NaOH，置于洁净的烧杯中，加适量蒸馏水使之溶解，放冷后加蒸馏水至总体积约 500 mL，充分搅拌均匀，倒入试剂瓶，盖好塞子，得到 0.1 mol·L^{-1} NaOH 溶液备用。

（二）NaOH 溶液的标定

在分析天平上用差减法称取邻苯二甲酸氢钾约 0.28~0.32 g（准确至 0.000 1 g），置于洁净的 250 mL 锥形瓶中，加入 50 mL 蒸馏水溶解，再加入酚酞指示剂 2~3 滴，摇匀，滴加待标定的 NaOH 溶液至溶液刚刚由无色变为微红色，且保持 30 s 不褪色即为滴定终点。记录滴定消耗的 NaOH 溶液体积于表 5-5-2 中。

重复滴定操作 2~3 次，测定结果的相对平均偏差应小于 0.2%。根据消耗的 NaOH 溶液的体积和实际参加反应的邻苯二甲酸氢钾质量，计算 NaOH 标准溶液的浓度。

【注意事项】

1. NaOH 具有强腐蚀性，称量过程不要接触到皮肤或衣物等，尽量不要洒在操作台上。如有洒落，应及时处理。

2. 配制好的 NaOH 溶液须存放于塑料试剂瓶或带橡皮塞的玻璃试剂瓶中。

【数据记录及结果分析】

日期：_____　　温度：_____ ℃　相对湿度：_____

1. 配制 0.1 mol·L^{-1} NaOH 溶液 500 mL 所需的固体 NaOH 的质量：_____ g。

2. 0.1 mol·L^{-1} NaOH 溶液的标定（表 5-5-2）。

表 5-5-2　0.1 mol·L^{-1} NaOH 溶液的标定

实验序号	1	2	3
m_1（称量瓶 +KHP）/g			
m_2（称量瓶 + 剩余 KHP）/g			
m_1-m_2（KHP）/g			
$V_初$（NaOH）/mL			
$V_终$（NaOH）/mL			
$V_消耗$（NaOH）/mL			
c（NaOH）/mol·L^{-1}			
$\bar{c}$（NaOH）/mol·L^{-1}			
$\bar{d_r}$/%			

【思考题】

1. 为什么标定 NaOH 溶液时一般采用酚酞指示剂？除了酚酞，还可以选用其他指示剂吗？

2. 滴定接近终点时，如果用蒸馏水淋洗锥形瓶内壁，对滴定结果有何影响？

（别子俊）

三、食醋总酸度的测定

【实验目的】

1. 理解强碱滴定弱酸过程中溶液 pH 的变化及指示剂的选择。
2. 掌握食醋总酸度的测定方法。

【预习作业】

模拟设计实验:以流程图方式给出本实验的设计思路,并在流程图中实验步骤处注明相应的注意事项及缘由。

引导问题:

1. 为何 NaOH 标准溶液要现标定现用?
2. 实验中如何准确移取食醋样品?为何须将食醋样品稀释后再进行测定?
3. 测定食醋总酸度时,为什么所用蒸馏水不能含有二氧化碳?
4. 能用氨水测定食醋中乙酸的含量吗?

【实验原理】

食醋是一种酸性液态调味品,其中酸性物质主要包括乙酸、乳酸、葡萄糖酸、琥珀酸等,通常乙酸含量最多。在贮存过程中,有机酸能与醇结合生成酯,增加食醋的风味,因此食醋中总酸含量是食醋质量的重要指标。《食品安全国家标准　食醋》(GB 2719-2018)中规定食醋的总酸(以乙酸计)指标≥$3.5 \text{ g·}(100 \text{ mL})^{-1}$。

乙酸是一元弱酸($K_a = 1.75 \times 10^{-5}$),可用强碱 NaOH 标准溶液直接滴定,反应式如下:

$$HAc + NaOH =\!=\!= NaAc + H_2O$$

若食醋试液及 NaOH 标准溶液的初始浓度均为 0.1 mol·L^{-1},化学计量点时 pH 约为 8.7,可选用酚酞作为指示剂,滴定终点时溶液由无色变为微红色。

由于滴定时食醋中可能存在的其他酸也与 NaOH 反应,故滴定所得为总酸度,以 $\rho(\text{HAc})$ $[\text{g·}(100 \text{ mL})^{-1}]$ 表示,可根据下式进行计算

$$\rho(\text{HAc}) = \frac{c(\text{NaOH})\Delta V(\text{NaOH})M(\text{HAc})}{V(\text{食醋}) \times 10} \tag{5-5-3}$$

式(5-5-3)中,$c(\text{NaOH})$ 为 NaOH 标准溶液的浓度(mol·L⁻¹),$\Delta V(\text{NaOH})$ 为滴定所消耗的 NaOH 标准溶液体积(mL),$M(\text{HAc})$ 为乙酸的摩尔质量(60.05 g·mol^{-1}),$V(\text{食醋})$ 为每次滴定对应的食醋样品体积(mL)。

【仪器材料与试剂】

仪器　碱式滴定管或酸碱两用滴定管(25 mL),移液管(20 mL,10 mL),容量瓶(100 mL),锥形瓶(250 mL×3),滴定管架,洗瓶,玻璃棒,滴管。

材料与试剂　食醋(白醋),新鲜标定的 NaOH 标准溶液(0.1 mol·L^{-1}),酚酞指示剂(2 g·L^{-1},乙醇溶液)。

【实验步骤】

取 1 支洁净的 20 mL 移液管,用少量待测食醋样品润洗 3 次。准确移取 20.00 mL 待测食醋于 100 mL 容量瓶中,用新煮沸并冷却的蒸馏水稀释至刻度线,盖上塞子,将溶液充分混匀。

另取 1 支洁净的 10 mL 移液管,用稀释后的食醋试液润洗 3 次。准确移取 10.00 mL 稀释后的食醋试液于 250 mL 锥形瓶中,加 2 滴酚酞指示剂。用新鲜标定的 NaOH 标准溶液滴定,至溶液呈浅粉红色且 30 s 内不褪色,即为终点。

平行滴定 3 份,记录滴定消耗的 NaOH 溶液体积于表 5-5-3 中,由消耗的 NaOH 标准溶液的体积计算食醋的总酸度 $[g \cdot (100\ mL)^{-1}]$。

【数据记录及结果处理】

日期:＿＿＿＿＿＿＿　室温:＿＿＿＿＿＿＿℃　相对湿度:＿＿＿＿＿＿＿

表 5-5-3　食醋总酸度的测定

实验序号	1	2	3
$c(NaOH)/mol \cdot L^{-1}$			
$V_初(NaOH)/mL$			
$V_终(NaOH)/mL$			
$\Delta V(NaOH)/mL$			
$\Delta \overline{V}(NaOH)/mL$			
$\overline{\rho}(HAc)/g \cdot (100\ mL)^{-1}$			
$d_r/\%$			
$\overline{d}_r/\%$			

【思考题】

1. 本实验属于哪类滴定?应怎样选择指示剂?
2. 试分析本实验的误差来源,并讨论可能的误差消除方法。

(林　毅)

四、硼砂含量的测定

【实验目的】

1. 理解强酸滴定弱碱性物质过程中溶液 pH 的变化及指示剂的选择。
2. 掌握硼砂含量的测定方法。

【预习作业】

模拟设计实验:以流程图方式给出本实验的设计思路,并在流程图中实验步骤处注明相应的注意事项及缘由。

引导问题：

1. 实验中应称取多少克硼砂样品？为什么？
2. 本实验中为何选用甲基红作为指示剂？

【实验原理】

硼砂（$Na_2B_4O_7 \cdot 10H_2O$）是一种常见的化工原料，也常用于配制缓冲溶液或制备其他硼化合物。硼砂可与水发生质子传递反应，使溶液呈碱性。因此硼砂是一元弱碱（$K_b = 1.74 \times 10^{-5}$），可采用 HCl 标准溶液直接滴定，反应式如下：

$$Na_2B_4O_7 \cdot 10H_2O + 2HCl \Longrightarrow 2NaCl + 4H_3BO_3 + 5H_2O$$

若硼砂试液及 HCl 标准溶液的初始浓度均为 $0.1\ mol \cdot L^{-1}$，化学计量点时 pH 约为 5.1，可选用甲基红作为指示剂，滴定终点时溶液由黄色变为浅红色。

由滴定反应式可知，在计量点时

$$n(HCl) = 2n(Na_2B_4O_7 \cdot 10H_2O) \tag{5-5-4}$$

因此硼砂的质量分数

$$w(Na_2B_4O_7 \cdot 10H_2O) = \frac{c(HCl)\Delta V(HCl)M(Na_2B_4O_7 \cdot 10H_2O)}{m(样品) \times 2\,000} \times 100\% \tag{5-5-5}$$

式（5-5-5）中，$c(HCl)$ 为 HCl 标准溶液的浓度（$mol \cdot L^{-1}$），$\Delta V(HCl)$ 为滴定所消耗的 HCl 标准溶液的体积（mL），$M(Na_2B_4O_7 \cdot 10H_2O)$ 为硼砂的摩尔质量（$381.37\ g \cdot mol^{-1}$），$m(样品)$ 为每次滴定对应的样品质量（g）。

【仪器材料与试剂】

仪器　万分之一电子分析天平，酸式滴定管或酸碱两用滴定管（25 mL），称量瓶，锥形瓶（250 mL × 3），量筒（100 mL），滴定管架，洗瓶，玻璃棒。

材料与试剂　硼砂样品，新鲜标定的 HCl 标准溶液（$0.1\ mol \cdot L^{-1}$），甲基红指示剂（$2\ g \cdot L^{-1}$，乙醇溶液）。

【实验步骤】

采用电子分析天平，用差减法称取 3 份 0.28~0.38 g（精确至 0.000 1 g）硼砂样品于 250 mL 锥形瓶中，分别加入约 50.0 mL 蒸馏水溶解。分别加 2 滴甲基红指示剂，用新鲜标定的 HCl 标准溶液滴定，至溶液呈浅粉红色且 30 s 内不褪色，即为终点。

平行测定 3 份，记录滴定消耗的 HCl 溶液体积于表 5-5-4 中，由消耗的 HCl 标准溶液的体积计算硼砂的质量分数 $w(Na_2B_4O_7 \cdot 10H_2O)$。

【数据记录及结果处理】

日期：_____　　室温：_____℃　相对湿度：_____

表 5-5-4　硼砂含量的测定

实验序号	1	2	3
$m(样品)/g$			
$c(HCl)/mol \cdot L^{-1}$			

续表

实验序号	1	2	3
$V_{初}(\mathrm{HCl})/\mathrm{mL}$			
$V_{终}(\mathrm{HCl})/\mathrm{mL}$			
$\Delta V(\mathrm{HCl})/\mathrm{mL}$			
$w(\mathrm{Na_2B_4O_7 \cdot 10H_2O})/\%$			
$\overline{w}(\mathrm{Na_2B_4O_7 \cdot 10H_2O})/\%$			
$d_r/\%$			
$\overline{d_r}/\%$			

【思考题】

试分析本实验的误差来源,并讨论可能的误差消除方法。

(林 毅)

五、返滴定法测定阿司匹林药片中乙酰水杨酸的含量

【实验目的】

1. 掌握返滴定法的原理与操作。
2. 熟悉利用酸碱滴定法测定阿司匹林药片中乙酰水杨酸含量的方法。

【预习作业】

模拟设计实验:以流程图方式给出本实验的设计思路,并在流程图中实验步骤处注明相应的注意事项及缘由。

引导问题:

1. 实验中为什么不宜采用直接滴定法测定药片中乙酰水杨酸的含量?
2. 在乙酰水杨酸与过量 NaOH 的反应中,水浴加热样品 15 min 后要迅速用流动水冷却,试述该操作的原因。

【实验原理】

阿司匹林是一种解热镇痛药,它的主要成分是乙酰水杨酸。乙酰水杨酸是有机弱酸($K_a = 3.2 \times 10^{-4}$),微溶于水,易溶于乙醇,在强碱性溶液中水解为水杨酸和乙酸盐,反应式为

由于药片中一般都添加了一定量的赋形剂,如硬脂酸镁、淀粉等不溶物,不宜直接滴定,可采用返滴定法进行测定。

将药片研磨成粉状后定量加入过量的 NaOH 标准溶液,加热一段时间使乙酰基水解完全。以酚酞为指示剂,用 HCl 标准溶液返滴定过量的 NaOH,至粉红色刚刚消失即为终点。

该反应中,1 摩尔乙酰水杨酸消耗 2 摩尔 NaOH。根据最初加入的碱的体积 $V(\text{NaOH})$ 和滴定中消耗 HCl 的体积 $\Delta V(\text{HCl})$,即可求得药品中乙酰水杨酸实际消耗的碱量,从而计算出药品中乙酰水杨酸的质量分数

$$w(\text{乙酰水杨酸}) = \frac{[c(\text{NaOH})V(\text{NaOH}) - c(\text{HCl})\Delta V(\text{HCl})]M(\text{乙酰水杨酸})}{m(\text{药粉}) \times 2} \times 100\% \qquad (5\text{-}5\text{-}6)$$

式(5-5-6)中,$M(\text{乙酰水杨酸})$ 为乙酰水杨酸的摩尔质量(180.16 g·mol^{-1})。

【仪器材料与试剂】

仪器 万分之一电子分析天平,酸式滴定管或酸碱两用滴定管(25 mL),恒温水浴锅,研钵,称量瓶,移液管(20 mL),量筒(100 mL),表面皿,锥形瓶(250 mL × 3),滴定管架,洗瓶,玻璃棒。

材料与试剂 阿司匹林药片,新鲜标定的 NaOH 标准溶液(约 0.1 mol·L^{-1}),新鲜标定的 HCl 标准溶液(约 0.1 mol·L^{-1}),酚酞指示剂(2 g·L^{-1},乙醇溶液)。

【实验步骤】

(一)阿司匹林药片中乙酰水杨酸含量的测定

用研钵将阿司匹林药片研磨成粉末,采用电子分析天平分别准确称取 3 份 0.10 ~0.12 g(精确至 0.000 1 g)药粉于 250 mL 锥形瓶中。用移液管准确加入 20.00 mL 0.1 mol·L^{-1} NaOH 标准溶液后,盖上表面皿轻摇几下,置于约 90 ℃水浴中加热 15 min,之后迅速用流动水冷却至室温。

分别加入约 20.0 mL 蒸馏水和 2~3 滴酚酞指示剂,用 0.1 mol·L^{-1} HCl 标准溶液滴定至红色刚好消失,即为终点。平行滴定 3 次,根据所消耗的 HCl 标准溶液体积计算药片中乙酰水杨酸的质量分数。结果记录于表 5-5-5 中。

(二)空白实验

用移液管准确移取 20.00 mL 0.1 mol·L^{-1} NaOH 标准溶液于 250 mL 锥形瓶中,在与测定药粉样品相同的实验条件下进行加热及冷却。

分别加入约 20.0 mL 蒸馏水和 2~3 滴酚酞指示剂,用 0.1 mol·L^{-1} HCl 标准溶液滴定至红色刚好消失,即为终点。平行滴定 3 次,根据所消耗的 HCl 标准溶液体积计算 $V(\text{NaOH})/\Delta V(\text{HCl})$ 的值。结果记录于表 5-5-6 中。

【数据记录及结果处理】

日期:_____ 室温:_____℃ 相对湿度:_____

表 5-5-5 阿司匹林药片中乙酰水杨酸含量的测定

实验序号	1	2	3
$m(\text{药粉})/\text{g}$			
$c(\text{NaOH})/\text{mol·L}^{-1}$			

续表

实验序号	1	2	3
$V(NaOH)/mL$			
$c(HCl)/mol \cdot L^{-1}$			
$V_{初}(HCl)/mL$			
$V_{终}(HCl)/mL$			
$\Delta V(HCl)/mL$			
$w(乙酰水杨酸)/\%$			
$\overline{w}(乙酰水杨酸)/\%$			
$d_r/\%$			
$\overline{d_r}/\%$			

表 5-5-6 空白实验

实验序号	1	2	3
$c(NaOH)/mol \cdot L^{-1}$			
$V(NaOH)/mL$			
$c(HCl)/mol \cdot L^{-1}$			
$V_{初}(HCl)/mL$			
$V_{终}(HCl)/mL$			
$\Delta V(HCl)/mL$			
$\Delta \overline{V}(HCl)/mL$			
$V(NaOH)/\Delta \overline{V}(HCl)$			
$d_r/\%$			
$\overline{d_r}/\%$			

【思考题】

1. 试分析本实验的误差来源,并讨论可能的误差消除方法。
2. 试查阅文献,指出还可以用哪些方法测定阿司匹林药片中乙酰水杨酸的含量。

(林 毅)

实验六 氧化还原滴定法

【实验目的】

1. 掌握高锰酸钾法和碘量法中标准溶液的配制原理及方法。
2. 学会利用氧化还原滴定原理测定物质含量。
3. 学习自身指示剂和显色指示剂指示终点的方法。

【实验原理】

氧化还原滴定法是以氧化还原反应为基础的一类滴定分析方法,其实质是电子的转移或偏移。氧化还原反应机制复杂,通常反应较慢并伴随副反应。为了保证反应定量且迅速进行,滴定过程中要对反应物浓度、反应温度、反应介质、催化剂等条件进行控制,从而符合滴定分析的要求。

根据滴定剂的种类不同,氧化还原滴定法可分为高锰酸钾法、重铬酸钾法、碘量法等。氧化还原滴定中常用的指示剂包括自身指示剂、显色指示剂和氧化还原指示剂等。例如高锰酸钾法中的高锰酸钾就是自身指示剂;碘量法中,淀粉溶液可以与 I_2 反应生成蓝色复合物,属于显色指示剂;重铬酸钾法中的二苯胺磺酸钠原本无色,滴定终点时被过量的重铬酸钾氧化显紫色,属于氧化还原指示剂。

氧化还原滴定法应用广泛,可以直接测定具有氧化性或还原性的物质,如高锰酸钾法测定过氧化氢含量,重铬酸钾法测定铁矿石中全铁含量,碘量法测定维生素 C、铜离子的含量等;还可以间接测定一些本身不具有氧化性或还原性,但能与氧化剂或还原剂发生定量反应的物质,例如高锰酸钾法测定钙离子含量。

本实验主要涉及高锰酸钾法和碘量法的应用。

一、高锰酸钾法测定过氧化氢含量

【实验目的】

1. 掌握高锰酸钾标准溶液的配制原理及方法。
2. 学会高锰酸钾法测定过氧化氢含量的原理及方法。
3. 巩固分析天平、滴定管、移液管的规范操作。

【预习作业】

模拟设计实验:根据氧化还原滴定原理及相应的 $KMnO_4$ 滴定法原理,参照本实验步骤,以流程图方式给出实验的设计思路,并在流程图中标注滴定反应条件、操作条件以及所采取的可行性实验措施及依据。

引导问题:
1. 配制 $KMnO_4$ 标准溶液时,能否用滤纸代替砂芯漏斗? 为什么?
2. 如何准确读取滴定管中有色溶液的体积?
3. 在 $KMnO_4$ 的标定过程中,需要控制哪些反应条件? 为什么?
4. 高锰酸钾法还可用于测定哪些物质?
5. 测定市售双氧水中 H_2O_2 含量的实验为何不能加热?

【实验原理】

高锰酸钾作为强氧化剂,是氧化还原滴定中常用的标准溶液,在强酸性条件下可被还原为 Mn^{2+},其半反应及电极电位如下:

$$MnO_4^- + 8H^+ + 5e \rightleftharpoons Mn^{2+} + 4H_2O \quad \varphi^\ominus = 1.507\ V$$

$KMnO_4$ 不稳定,而且市售 $KMnO_4$ 试剂中常含有 MnO_2 及其他杂质,因此采用间接法配制

$KMnO_4$ 标准溶液。此外，在 MnO_2 和光的催化作用下，$KMnO_4$ 不仅会发生自身分解反应，还能与水中的微量还原性物质作用，所以标定前需过滤除去溶液中的 MnO_2，并将滤液贮存于棕色瓶中，在暗处放置。

常用一级标准物质 $Na_2C_2O_4$ 来标定 $KMnO_4$（$M_r = 158$ g·mol⁻¹）溶液。在酸性条件下：

$$2MnO_4^- + 5C_2O_4^{2-} + 16H^+ \xlongequal{\quad} 2Mn^{2+} + 10CO_2 \uparrow + 8H_2O$$

室温下该反应较慢，加热可提高反应速率。但反应温度不能太高，否则会导致 $Na_2C_2O_4$ 分解。此外，催化剂 Mn^{2+} 的生成也可以使反应加速。因此滴定前先加少量 $KMnO_4$ 溶液于 $Na_2C_2O_4$，微热。化学计量点时，稍过量的 $KMnO_4$ 使溶液呈微红色，指示滴定终点。

根据滴定时消耗 $KMnO_4$ 溶液的体积及 $Na_2C_2O_4$ 的质量，可以计算出 $KMnO_4$ 标准溶液的浓度。

$$c(KMnO_4) = \frac{2 \times m(Na_2C_2O_4) \times 1\,000}{5 \times M(Na_2C_2O_4) \Delta V(KMnO_4)} \text{ mol} \cdot \text{L}^{-1} \qquad (5\text{-}6\text{-}1)$$

式（5-6-1）中，$m(Na_2C_2O_4)$ 为称取的 $Na_2C_2O_4$ 质量（g），$M(Na_2C_2O_4)$ 为 $Na_2C_2O_4$ 的摩尔质量（134 g·mol⁻¹），$\Delta V(KMnO_4)$ 为滴定所消耗 $KMnO_4$ 溶液的体积（mL）。

过氧化氢是医药上常用的消毒剂，市售双氧水含 H_2O_2 约 3%（g·mL⁻¹）或 30%（g·mL⁻¹）。在酸性溶液中，H_2O_2 与 $KMnO_4$ 的反应为：

$$2MnO_4^- + 5H_2O_2 + 6H^+ \xlongequal{\quad} 2Mn^{2+} + 8H_2O + 5O_2 \uparrow$$

该反应与 $KMnO_4$ 的标定类似，开始时速度较慢，随着 Mn^{2+} 的增加逐渐加快。化学计量点附近，稍过量的 $KMnO_4$ 使体系呈微红色，指示滴定终点的到达。不同的是，由于 H_2O_2 遇热易分解，该反应须在室温下进行。根据消耗 $KMnO_4$ 标准溶液以及试样的体积，可计算样品中 H_2O_2 的含量 $\rho(H_2O_2)$

$$\rho(H_2O_2) = \frac{5 \times c(KMnO_4) \Delta V(KMnO_4) M(H_2O_2)}{2 \times V(H_2O_2) \times 1\,000} \text{ g} \cdot \text{mL}^{-1} \qquad (5\text{-}6\text{-}2)$$

式（5-6-2）中，$c(KMnO_4)$ 为 $KMnO_4$ 标准溶液的浓度（mol·L⁻¹），$\Delta V(KMnO_4)$ 为滴定所消耗 $KMnO_4$ 标准溶液的体积（mL），$M(H_2O_2)$ 为过氧化氢的摩尔质量（34.01 g·mol⁻¹），$V(H_2O_2)$ 表示滴定时对应的双氧水稀释液的体积（mL）。

【仪器材料与试剂】

仪器 万分之一电子分析天平，砂芯漏斗，酸式滴定管或聚四氟乙烯酸碱两用滴定管（25 mL），容量瓶（100 mL×2），锥形瓶（250 mL×3），烧杯（250 mL，100 mL），移液管（20 mL×2，1 mL），量筒（10 mL），洗瓶，洗耳球，称量瓶，玻璃棒，滴管，干燥器，滴定管架。

材料与试剂 $Na_2C_2O_4$（A.R.），$KMnO_4$（A.R.），H_2SO_4 溶液（6 mol·L⁻¹），市售双氧水溶液（3%）

【实验步骤】

（一）$KMnO_4$ 溶液的配制与标定

1. 0.004 mol·L⁻¹ $KMnO_4$ 溶液的配制　称取约0.16 g $KMnO_4$ 固体，在250.0 mL 烧杯中用少量蒸馏水溶解后，继续加水稀释至250.0 mL 刻度。将溶液加热并保持微沸1 h，放置2~3 天后用砂芯漏斗过滤，滤液储存于棕色瓶中，在暗处密闭保存，以待标定。

2. $Na_2C_2O_4$ 标准溶液的配制　准确称取105 ℃干燥至恒重的 $Na_2C_2O_4$ 0.13~0.14 g（精确至0.000 1 g），

在小烧杯中加 20.0 mL 蒸馏水溶解,定量转移至 100.00 mL 容量瓶中,定容,摇匀。

3. KMnO₄ 溶液的标定　用移液管准确移取 20.00 mL Na₂C₂O₄ 标准溶液于锥形瓶中,加 6 mol·L⁻¹ H₂SO₄ 5.0 mL,先从滴定管加入 10.00 mL 高锰酸钾溶液,加热至 40 ℃左右(红色消失),继续用 KMnO₄ 溶液滴定至微红色,30 s 不褪色即为滴定终点。结果记录于表 5-6-1 中,平行测定 3 次。

(二) 市售双氧水中 H_2O_2 含量的测定

用移液管移取 1.00 mL 市售双氧水于 100.00 mL 容量瓶中,加蒸馏水定容,摇匀。移取 20.00 mL 稀释液于锥形瓶中,加入 6 mol·L⁻¹ H₂SO₄ 5.0 mL,用 KMnO₄ 标准溶液滴定至微红色,30 s 不褪色即为滴定终点。结果记录于表 5-6-2 中,平行测定 3 次。

【数据记录及结果分析】

日期:＿＿＿＿＿＿＿＿　温度:＿＿＿＿＿＿＿＿℃　相对湿度:＿＿＿＿＿＿＿＿

表 5-6-1　KMnO₄ 溶液的标定

实验序号	1	2	3
$m(\mathrm{Na_2C_2O_4})/\mathrm{g}$			
$V_{初}(\mathrm{KMnO_4})/\mathrm{mL}$			
$V_{终}(\mathrm{KMnO_4})/\mathrm{mL}$			
$\Delta V(\mathrm{KMnO_4})/\mathrm{mL}$			
$c(\mathrm{KMnO_4})/\mathrm{mol \cdot L^{-1}}$			
$\overline{c}(\mathrm{KMnO_4})/\mathrm{mol \cdot L^{-1}}$			
$\overline{d_r}/\%$			

表 5-6-2　市售双氧水中 H_2O_2 含量的测定

实验序号	1	2	3
$V(\mathrm{H_2O_2})/\mathrm{mL}$			
$c(\mathrm{KMnO_4})/\mathrm{mol \cdot L^{-1}}$			
$V_{初}(\mathrm{KMnO_4})/\mathrm{mL}$			
$V_{终}(\mathrm{KMnO_4})/\mathrm{mL}$			
$\Delta V(\mathrm{KMnO_4})/\mathrm{mL}$			
$\rho(\mathrm{H_2O_2})/\mathrm{g \cdot mL^{-1}}$			
$\overline{\rho}(\mathrm{H_2O_2})/\mathrm{g \cdot mL^{-1}}$			
$\overline{d_r}/\%$			

【注意事项】

1. 使用 KMnO₄ 标准溶液滴定还原性物质时,常用 H₂SO₄ 作为酸性介质。滴定体系的适宜酸度是 0.5~1.0 mol·L⁻¹。若酸度过高,易引起 Na₂C₂O₄ 的分解。

2. 通过式(5-6-1)计算 $c(\mathrm{KMnO_4})$ 时,需考虑每次滴定取用的 Na₂C₂O₄ 溶液体积仅占配制的 Na₂C₂O₄ 标准溶液总体积的 20%,因此计算时要再除以 5。

3. 通过式（5-6-2）计算 $\rho(H_2O_2)$ 时,需考虑对市售双氧水的稀释倍数及取用体积,因此计算时要再乘以 5。

【思考题】

1. 用高锰酸钾法测定 H_2O_2 含量时,能否用 HNO_3、HCl 或 HAc 控制酸度? 为什么?
2. 双氧水为何可用作消毒剂? 使用不当有什么危害?
3. 检测过氧化氢含量的方法还有哪些?

（吕雅娟）

二、碘量法测定维生素 C 含量

【实验目的】

1. 掌握直接碘量法测定维生素 C 的原理和方法。
2. 掌握 I_2 标准溶液、$Na_2S_2O_3$ 标准溶液的配制和标定方法。
3. 学会用淀粉指示剂指示终点的方法。

【预习作业】

模拟设计实验:以流程图方式给出本实验的设计思路,并在流程图中实验步骤处注明相应的注意事项及缘由。

引导问题:

1. 溶解 I_2 时,加入过量 KI 的作用是什么?
2. 哪些方法可用于标定 $Na_2S_2O_3$ 标准溶液?
3. 碘量法测定维生素 C 实验为什么要在弱酸性溶液中进行?

【实验原理】

碘量法是以 I_2 做氧化剂或以碘化物作还原剂进行氧化还原滴定的分析方法。其氧化还原半反应式为:

$$I_2 + 2e^- \rightleftharpoons 2I^- \qquad \varphi^\ominus(I_2/I^-) = 0.535\ V$$

标准电极电位比 $\varphi^\ominus(I_2/I^-)$ 低的还原性物质可用 I_2 标准溶液直接滴定,这种方法称为直接碘量法。直接碘量法只能在酸性、中性及弱碱性溶液中进行。

I_2 是容易升华的固体,难溶于水,但易溶于 KI 溶液。因此,I_2 标准溶液的配制通常是将 I_2 溶解于 KI 溶液并保存于棕色磨口瓶中,用一级标准物质 As_2O_3 标定或用已标定的 $Na_2S_2O_3$ 标准溶液标定。

市售 $Na_2S_2O_3 \cdot 5H_2O$ 常含有杂质,在空气中易风化或潮解,因此不能直接配制为标准溶液。为了防止与溶解的 CO_2 发生反应,通常需加入 Na_2CO_3 作稳定剂,使溶液的 pH 保持在 9~10,用新煮沸并放冷的蒸馏水配制后放置 7~10 天,再用 KIO_3 一级标准物质进行标定。

KIO_3 在酸性溶液中与过量的 KI 反应,定量地析出 I_2,用待标定的 $Na_2S_2O_3$ 溶液滴定析出的 I_2,便可求出 $Na_2S_2O_3$ 溶液的准确浓度。其反应式为:

$$KIO_3 + 5KI + 6HCl \rightleftharpoons 3I_2 + 3H_2O + 6KCl$$

$$I_2 + 2Na_2S_2O_3 \Longrightarrow 2NaI + Na_2S_4O_6$$

由以上反应可知，存在如下的定量关系

$$n(Na_2S_2O_3) = 6n(KIO_3) \tag{5-6-3}$$

$Na_2S_2O_3$ 标准溶液的准确浓度可计算为

$$c(Na_2S_2O_3) = \frac{6m(KIO_3)}{M(KIO_3) \times V(Na_2S_2O_3) \times 1\,000}\ (mol \cdot L^{-1}) \tag{5-6-4}$$

上述滴定反应用淀粉溶液作指示剂。淀粉指示剂应在近终点时（溶液呈浅黄色时）加入，滴定至蓝色变为无色即为滴定终点。

维生素 C（$C_6H_8O_6$）又称抗坏血酸，属于水溶性维生素，广泛存在于水果和蔬菜中。它具有还原性，可直接用 I_2 标准溶液滴定。反应式如下：

从上反应式可知，维生素 C 与 I_2 反应摩尔比为 1∶1。

维生素C易被空气氧化，在碱性溶液中氧化更快，所以滴定常在弱酸性（pH 3~4）条件下进行。终点时，过量的 I_2 与淀粉指示剂生成蓝色配合物。维生素 C 的含量可用式（5-6-5）计算

$$V_C\% = \frac{c(I_2)V(I_2) \times M(C_6H_8O_6)}{m(样品)}\ (mg \cdot g^{-1}) \tag{5-6-5}$$

式（5-6-5）中，m(样品)为每次滴定样品的质量。

【仪器材料与试剂】

仪器 万分之一电子分析天平，百分之一电子分析天平，酸式滴定管或两用滴定管（25 mL），移液管（25 mL×2），容量瓶（250 mL，500 mL），棕色试剂瓶（500 mL×2），量筒（10 mL，50 mL，100 mL），锥形瓶（250 mL×3），烧杯（100 mL，250 mL），滴定管架，洗瓶，玻璃棒，洗耳球。

材料与试剂 药用维生素 C 片剂，果蔬样品（西红柿、橙子、草莓等），KIO_3 基准物质（A.R.），I_2（A.R.），$Na_2S_2O_3 \cdot 5H_2O$（A.R.），Na_2CO_3（A.R.），淀粉溶液（2 g·L^{-1}），HAc 水溶液（2 mol·L^{-1}），H_2SO_4 水溶液（1 mol·L^{-1}），KI 溶液（200 g·L^{-1}）。

【实验步骤】

（一）0.1 mol·L^{-1} $Na_2S_2O_3$ 标准溶液的配制及标定

用百分之一电子分析天平称取 $Na_2S_2O_3 \cdot 5H_2O$ 约 12.50 g 于洁净小烧杯中，加入适量新鲜煮沸并放冷的蒸馏水，溶解后，加入 Na_2CO_3 固体约 0.1 g，用新鲜煮沸并转移至 500 mL 容量瓶中，用放冷的蒸馏水定容至 500.00 mL，转移至棕色瓶中，放置 7~10 天后标定。

用电子分析天平准确称取 0.9~1.0 g（精确至 0.000 1 g）KIO_3 基准物质于洁净干燥小烧杯中，加水溶解后，定量转入 250 mL 容量瓶中，定容，充分摇匀。用移液管吸取 10.00 mL KIO_3 标准溶液 3 份，分别置于 250 mL 洁净锥形瓶中，用量筒依次加入 20.0 mL 200 g·L^{-1} KI 溶液，5.0 mL 1 mol·L^{-1} H_2SO_4 溶液，50.0 mL 蒸馏水，立即用待标定的 $Na_2S_2O_3$ 溶液滴定至浅黄色，然后再用量筒加入 5.0 mL 2 g·L^{-1} 淀粉溶液，继续滴入标准溶液至蓝色恰好变为无色即为滴定终点，记录结果

于表 5-6-3 中。平行标定 3 份,计算 $c(Na_2S_2O_3)$ 及相对偏差。

(二) 0.05 mol·L^{-1} I$_2$ 标准溶液的配制及标定

用百分之一电子分析天平称取 6.60 g I$_2$ 和 10.00 g KI,置于研钵中,加少量蒸馏水,在通风橱中研磨。待 I$_2$ 全部溶解后,将溶液转入 500 mL 容量瓶中,定容至 500.00 mL,充分搅拌,再将溶液转入棕色试剂瓶中,放置暗处保存。

用移液管移取 10.00 mL Na$_2$S$_2$O$_3$ 标准溶液于 250 mL 锥形瓶中,依次用量筒加入 50.0 mL 蒸馏水及 5.0 mL 2 g·L^{-1} 淀粉溶液,然后用 I$_2$ 标准溶液滴定至溶液呈浅蓝色,30 s 内不褪色即为终点,记录结果于表 5-6-4 中。平行标定 3 份并计算 $c(I_2)$ 及相对偏差。

(三) 0.005 mol·L^{-1} I$_2$ 标准溶液的配制

用移液管移取 25.00 mL I$_2$ 标准溶液于 250 mL 容量瓶中,定容,充分摇匀,备用。

(四) 片剂中维生素 C 含量的测定

在分析天平上准确称取 0.15 g 维生素 C 药片粉末(精确至 0.000 1 g),置于 250 mL 锥形瓶中,用量筒依次加入 100.0 mL 新煮沸并冷却的蒸馏水、10.0 mL 2 mol·L^{-1} HAc 溶液和 5.0 mL 2 g·L^{-1} 淀粉溶液,立即用 I$_2$ 标准溶液滴定至出现稳定的浅蓝色,且在 30 s 内不褪色即为终点。记录消耗的 I$_2$ 溶液体积于表 5-6-5 中。平行测定三份,计算片剂中维生素 C 的质量分数 ω(维生素 C)。

(五) 果蔬样品中维生素 C 含量的测定

准确称取 25 g 左右果蔬匀浆样品(如草莓,用绞碎机打成糊状)于洁净干燥小烧杯中,将其转入 250 mL 锥形瓶中,用水冲洗小烧杯 1~2 次。用量筒向锥形瓶中加入 10.0 mL 2.0 mol·L^{-1} HAc 溶液和 5.0 mL 2 g·L^{-1} 淀粉溶液,用 0.005 mol·L^{-1} 的 I$_2$ 标准溶液滴定至试液由红色变为蓝紫色即为终点,记录消耗的 I$_2$ 溶液体积于表 5-6-6 中。平行测定 3 份,计算维生素 C 的质量分数 ω(维生素 C)。

【注意事项】

1. 在标定 Na$_2$S$_2$O$_3$ 溶液时,淀粉指示剂一定要在临近终点(即 I$_2$ 的黄色接近褪去)时加入,否则会有较多的 I$_2$ 被淀粉包藏导致终点滞后。

2. 果蔬样品的前处理应根据样品的实际情况进行选择。如橘子、柚子等应除去果皮、膜、丝络和籽,只取果肉部分进行均浆处理,否则存在于待测液中的这些含纤维较多的部分会吸附维生素 C,影响终点的判断。同时终点的颜色变化要考虑到果肉本身所具有的颜色,不能一概而论。

【数据记录及结果分析】

日期:_____ 室温:_____ ℃ 相对湿度:_____

表 5-6-3 Na$_2$S$_2$O$_3$ 溶液的标定

实验序号	1	2	3
$m(KIO_3)/g$			
$c(KIO_3)/(mol·L^{-1})$			
$V_{始}(Na_2S_2O_3)/mL$			
$V_{终}(Na_2S_2O_3)/mL$			
$\Delta V(Na_2S_2O_3)/mL$			

实验序号	1	2	3
$c(\mathrm{Na_2S_2O_3})/(\mathrm{mol \cdot L^{-1}})$			
$\bar{c}(\mathrm{Na_2S_2O_3})/(\mathrm{mol \cdot L^{-1}})$			
$d_r/\%$			
$\overline{d_r}/\%$			

表 5-6-4　I_2 溶液的标定

实验序号	1	2	3
$c(\mathrm{Na_2S_2O_3})/(\mathrm{mol \cdot L^{-1}})$			
$V(\mathrm{Na_2S_2O_3})/\mathrm{mL}$			
$V_{始}(\mathrm{I_2})/\mathrm{mL}$			
$V_{终}(\mathrm{I_2})/\mathrm{mL}$			
$\Delta V(\mathrm{I_2})/\mathrm{mL}$			
$c(\mathrm{I_2})/(\mathrm{mol \cdot L^{-1}})$			
$\bar{c}(\mathrm{I_2})/(\mathrm{mol \cdot L^{-1}})$			
$d_r/\%$			
$\overline{d_r}/\%$			

表 5-6-5　片剂中维生素 C 含量的测定

实验序号	1	2	3
$m(维生素\ C)/\mathrm{g}$			
$c(\mathrm{I_2})/(\mathrm{mol \cdot L^{-1}})$			
$V_{始}(\mathrm{I_2})/\mathrm{mL}$			
$V_{终}(\mathrm{I_2})/\mathrm{mL}$			
$\Delta V(\mathrm{I_2})/\mathrm{mL}$			
$w(\mathrm{V_C})/(\mathrm{mg \cdot g^{-1}})$			
$\bar{w}(\mathrm{V_C})/(\mathrm{mg \cdot g^{-1}})$			
$d_r/\%$			
$\overline{d_r}/\%$			

表 5-6-6　果蔬试样中维生素 C 含量的测定

实验序号	1	2	3
$m(果蔬试样)/\mathrm{g}$			
$c(\mathrm{I_2})/(\mathrm{mol \cdot L^{-1}})$			
$V_{始}(\mathrm{I_2})/\mathrm{mL}$			
$V_{终}(\mathrm{I_2})/\mathrm{mL}$			

续表

实验序号	1	2	3
$\Delta V(I_2)/mL$			
$w(V_C)/\%(mg \cdot g^{-1})$			
$\overline{w}(V_C)/\%(mg \cdot g^{-1})$			
$d_r/\%$			
$\overline{d_r}/\%$			

【思考题】

1. 维生素 C 有哪些药理作用和临床应用？
2. 维生素 C 固体试样溶解时为何要加入新煮沸并冷却的蒸馏水？
3. 碘量法的误差来源主要有哪些？应采取哪些措施减小误差？

（康 凯）

实验七 配位滴定分析

【实验目的】

1. 掌握铬黑 T 及二甲酚橙指示剂的使用方法。
2. 掌握 EDTA 标准溶液的配制和标定方法。
3. 掌握配位滴定法测定样品中金属离子含量的方法。
4. 了解配位滴定的基本过程。

【实验原理】

乙二胺四乙酸（H_4Y）或乙二胺四乙酸二钠盐（Na_2H_2Y）是一种螯合配体,简称 EDTA,其能与绝大多数金属离子形成稳定的配位化合物,在配位滴定中常用作标准溶液,用于测定某些金属离子的含量。

EDTA 在水中溶解度较小,通常用其易溶于水的 EDTA 二钠盐（$Na_2H_2Y \cdot 2H_2O$）配制标准溶液。采用间接法配制 EDTA 标准溶液,先配制近似的浓度,再用一级标准物质标定。为防止 EDTA 与玻璃中的金属离子作用,配制的 EDTA 标准溶液应贮存于聚乙烯塑料瓶。

标定 EDTA 标准溶液的一级标准物质有 Zn、ZnO、$ZnSO_4$、$CaCO_3$、$MgCO_3$ 等。最常用的一级标准物质是 Zn、ZnO 和 $CaCO_3$。为了减小系统误差,标定 EDTA 标准溶液的条件应尽可能与测定条件相同。例如:测定 Bi^{3+}、Zn^{2+}、Pb^{2+}、Al^{3+} 等离子时,宜用 Zn、ZnO 或 $ZnSO_4 \cdot 7H_2O$ 作一级标准物质,在 pH 5~6 的条件下以二甲酚橙作指示剂进行标定。测定 Ca^{2+}、Mg^{2+} 等离子时,若采用 $CaCO_3$ 作一级标准物质,在 pH = 10 的 NH_3-NH_4Cl 缓冲溶液中,用铬黑 T（EBT）作指示剂进行标定,但 Ca^{2+} 与铬黑 T 指示剂显色灵敏度较差,终点变色不敏锐,而 Mg^{2+} 与铬黑 T 显色灵敏,因此,采用 $MgCO_3$ 作一级标准物质。

铬黑 T pH < 6 时呈酒红色,在 pH=7~11 时呈纯蓝色,在 pH > 12 时呈橙黄色。铬黑 T 与 Mg^{2+} 形成的配位个体为酒红色,因此只有在 pH=7~11 范围内终点才有明显的颜色变化。由于酸度对

EDTA 的存在形式及滴定反应后产生的酸会导致反应逆向进行,无法完全反应,通常用 pH = 10 的 NH_3-NH_4Cl 缓冲溶液维持滴定过程溶液的酸度。滴定前,铬黑 T 先与试样中的 Mg^{2+} 形成酒红色的 Mg-HIn,终点时 EDTA 从 Mg-HIn 中夺取 Mg^{2+} 而将铬黑 T 游离出来,溶液呈纯蓝色。

$$Mg^{2+} + HIn \Longrightarrow Mg\text{-}HIn$$
$$\text{纯蓝色} \qquad \text{酒红色}$$
$$H_2Y^{2-} + Mg\text{-}HIn \Longrightarrow MgY^{2-} + HIn$$
$$\text{酒红色} \qquad\qquad \text{纯蓝色}$$

EDTA 标准溶液的浓度按下式计算

$$c(\text{EDTA}) = \frac{m(\text{MgCO}_3) \times \dfrac{20.00}{250.00}}{M_r(\text{MgCO}_3) \times V(\text{EDTA})} \times 1\,000 \ (\text{mol} \cdot \text{L}^{-1}) \qquad (5\text{-}7\text{-}1)$$

滴定要注意的是,此反应速率不是很快,而且终点指示来自于铬黑 T 的原色,终点颜色变为纯蓝后,过量滴定颜色不会加深,因此接近终点时,加入一滴的滴定剂后要充分振荡,要待变色停止后才继续加入另一滴,直至终点出现。

当复杂试样中的金属离子(例如 Al^{3+})与 EDTA 配合反应较缓慢时,可用返滴定法或置换滴定法来测定。

一、水的硬度的测定

【实验目的】

1. 掌握 EDTA 标准溶液的标定方法。
2. 掌握 EDTA 标准溶液测定 Ca^{2+},Mg^{2+} 含量的方法。
3. 了解配位滴定法的原理。

【预习作业】

模拟设计实验:以流程图方式给出本实验的设计思路,请在流程图中实验步骤注明相应的注意事项及缘由。

引导问题:

1. 水的总硬度如何表示? 根据国家饮用水标准生活用水的总硬度多大时不可饮用?
2. 在测定水样硬度时,可用哪些一级标准物质标定 EDTA 标准溶液?
3. 测定水的总硬度使用何种指示剂来指示滴定的终点? 如何控制待测溶液的酸度?

【实验原理】

水的硬度是指水中钙、镁离子沉淀肥皂水化液的能力,包括碳酸盐硬度(即通过加热能以碳酸盐形式沉淀下来的钙、镁离子,又称:暂时硬度)和非碳酸盐硬度(即加热后不能沉淀下来的那部分钙、镁离子,又称:永久硬度)。

水的硬度常用单位为 $mg \cdot L^{-1}$,国家标准《生活饮用水卫生标准》(GB 5749-2022)规定总硬度(以 $CaCO_3$ 计)限度为 450 $mg \cdot L^{-1}$。

测定水的硬度是在 pH=10 的 NH_3-NH_4Cl 缓冲溶液中进行,以铬黑 T 为指示剂,用 EDTA 标准溶液滴定至待测溶液由酒红色变为纯蓝色即为终点。

滴定前:

$$Mg^{2+} + HIn === Mg\text{-}HIn$$

纯蓝色　　　酒红色

滴定中:

$$H_2Y^{2-} + Ca^{2+} === CaY^{2-} + 2H^+$$

$$H_2Y^{2-} + Mg^{2+} === MgY^{2-} + 2H^+$$

滴定终点时:

$$H_2Y^{2-} + Mg\text{-}HIn === MgY^{2-} + HIn + 2H^+$$

酒红色　　　　　纯蓝色

测定水样中的 Ca^{2+}、Mg^{2+} 含量时,若存在 Fe^{3+}、Al^{3+}、Cu^{2+}、Zn^{2+}、Pb^{2+} 等离子时,对指示剂铬黑 T 有封闭作用,出现终点变色延长的不敏锐现象。可通过加入三乙醇胺溶液掩蔽 Fe^{3+}、Al^{3+} 及加入 Na_2S 溶液掩蔽少量的 Cu^{2+}、Zn^{2+}、Pb^{2+} 等重金属离子。

当分别测定水中 Ca^{2+}、Mg^{2+} 含量时,先加 NaOH 溶液调节待测溶液 pH 至 12,使 Mg^{2+} 形成 $Mg(OH)_2$ 沉淀。再加入钙指示剂,与水中 Ca^{2+} 形成酒红色配合物。当用 EDTA 标准溶液进行滴定时,EDTA 首先与游离的 Ca^{2+} 配位,当溶液中游离的 Ca^{2+} 耗尽时,EDTA 夺取与指示剂配位的 Ca^{2+},使指示剂游离出来,溶液由酒红色变成纯蓝色即为终点。Mg^{2+} 含量则由 Ca^{2+}、Mg^{2+} 总量与 Ca^{2+} 测定值之差计算而得。

根据 EDTA 的用量 $V_1(EDTA)$,可按式(5-7-2)计算出水样的总硬度 c(总硬度)。

$$c(总硬度) = \frac{c(EDTA) \times V_1(EDTA) \times M(CaCO_3)}{V(水样)} \times 1\,000 \ (mg \cdot L^{-1}) \tag{5-7-2}$$

根据 EDTA 的用量 $V_2(EDTA)$,可按式(5-7-3)、式(5-7-4)分别计算出 Ca^{2+} 和 Mg^{2+} 的浓度。

$$c(Ca^{2+}) = \frac{c(EDTA) \times V_2(EDTA) \times M(Ca^{2+})}{V(水样)} \times 1\,000 \ (mg \cdot L^{-1}) \tag{5-7-3}$$

$$c(Mg^{2+}) = \frac{c(EDTA) \times \{V_1(EDTA) - V_2(EDTA)\} \times M(Mg^{2+})}{V(水样)} \times 1\,000 \ (mg \cdot L^{-1}) \tag{5-7-4}$$

或

$$c(Mg^{2+}) = c(总硬度) - c(Ca^{2+}) \ (mg \cdot L^{-1}) \tag{5-7-5}$$

为了减少系统误差,本实验中所用的 EDTA 标准溶液用 $MgCO_3$ 一级标准物质来标定。

【仪器材料与试剂】

仪器　托盘天平、万分之一电子分析天平,酸式滴定管或聚四氟乙烯酸碱两用滴定管(25 mL),锥形瓶(250 mL×3),移液管(20 mL,50 mL),容量瓶(250 mL),烧杯(150 mL,250 mL),聚乙烯塑料瓶(1 000 mL),量筒(5 mL,10 mL×2,50 mL,1 000 mL),玻璃棒,滴定管架。

材料与试剂　乙二胺四乙酸二钠盐(A.R.),3 mol·L⁻¹ HCl 溶液,$MgCO_3$ 基准物质,6 mol·L⁻¹ NaOH 溶液,1.5 mol·L⁻¹ 三乙醇胺,pH=10 的 NH_3-NH_4Cl 缓冲溶液,0.25 mol·L⁻¹ Na_2S 溶液,铬黑 T 指示剂,钙指示剂[1-(2-羟基-4-磺基-1-萘基偶氮)-2-羟基-3-萘甲酸],广泛 pH 试纸。

【实验步骤】

(一) 0.01 mol·L⁻¹ EDTA 溶液的配制

用托盘天平称取约 3.8 g Na$_2$H$_2$Y·2H$_2$O（M_r = 372.26）于 250 mL 烧杯中，加适量蒸馏水溶解，搅拌均匀，稀释至 1.0 L，摇匀，贮存于聚乙烯塑料瓶，备用。

(二) EDTA 标准溶液的标定

用万分之一电子分析天平准确称取一级标准物质 MgCO$_3$（M_r = 84.32）（110 ℃干燥 2 h 至恒重）0.15~0.20 g（精确至 0.000 1 g）于 150 mL 烧杯中，加 5 滴去离子水润湿，盖上表面皿，从烧杯口处缓慢滴加 3 mol·L⁻¹ HCl 溶液 3.0 mL，至 MgCO$_3$ 完全溶解后，加热微沸以去除 CO$_2$，冷却后用去离子水冲洗表面皿，冲洗液与烧杯内液合并，将烧杯内溶液转移至 250 mL 容量瓶，用少量去离子水冲洗烧杯 2~3 次，合并转移至容量瓶中，加去离子水稀释至刻度，摇匀。

准确移取 20.00 mL MgCO$_3$ 标准溶液于 250 mL 锥形瓶中，加入 10.0 mL pH = 10 的 NH$_3$-NH$_4$Cl 缓冲溶液及 2~3 滴铬黑 T 溶液，用 EDTA 标准溶液滴定至溶液由酒红色变为纯蓝色，颜色保持 30 s 不褪即为终点。平行测定三次，数据记录于表 5-7-1 中。

(三) 水样的硬度的测定

1. 总硬度的测定　用移液管准确移取水样 50.00 mL 于 250 mL 锥形瓶中，加入 1~2 滴 3 mol·L⁻¹ HCl 溶液使溶液酸化，加热微沸几分钟以去除 CO$_2$，冷却后加入 2.0 mL 三乙醇胺和 5.0 mL pH = 10 的 NH$_3$-NH$_4$Cl 缓冲溶液及 5 滴 Na$_2$S 溶液，再加 2~3 滴铬黑 T 指示剂，用 EDTA 标准溶液滴定至溶液由酒红色变为纯蓝色，颜色保持 30 s 不褪即为终点。平行测定三次，数据记录于表 5-7-2 中。

2. 水样中 Ca^{2+} 及 Mg^{2+} 含量的测定　用移液管准确移取 50.00 mL 水样于 250 mL 锥形瓶中，加入 1~2 滴 3 mol·L⁻¹ HCl 溶液使溶液酸化，加热微沸几分钟以除去 CO$_2$，冷却后加入 2.0 mL 三乙醇胺溶液和 5.0 mL 6 mol·L⁻¹ NaOH 溶液及适量的钙指示剂（通常取 0.1 g），用 EDTA 标准溶液缓慢滴定，并用力摇动，至溶液由酒红色变为纯蓝色，保持 30 s 不褪色即为终点。平行测定三次，数据记录于表 5-7-3 中。

【数据记录及结果分析】

日期：_____　温度：_____℃　相对湿度：_____

表 5-7-1　EDTA 标准溶液的标定

实验序号	1	2	3
m（MgCO$_3$ 质量）/g			
指示剂			
NH$_3$-NH$_4$Cl 缓冲溶液 /mL			
终点颜色变化			
V（MgCO$_3$）/mL			
$V_{初}$（EDTA）/mL			
$V_{终}$（EDTA）/mL			
ΔV（EDTA）/mL			

续表

实验序号	1	2	3
$c(\text{EDTA})/\text{mmol}\cdot\text{L}^{-1}$			
$\bar{c}(\text{EDTA})/\text{mmol}\cdot\text{L}^{-1}$			
相对平均偏差 $\bar{d_r}/\%$			

表 5-7-2　水样总硬度的测定

实验序号		1	2	3
指示剂				
终点前后颜色变化				
$V(\text{水样})/\text{mL}$				
水样处理	$3\ \text{mol}\cdot\text{L}^{-1}\ \text{HCl}/\text{滴}$			
	加热微沸除 CO_2/min			
	三乙醇胺 $/\text{mL}$			
	$pH=10\ \text{NH}_3\text{-NH}_4\text{Cl}$ 缓冲溶液 $/\text{mL}$			
	$\text{Na}_2\text{S}/\text{滴}$			
测定	$V_\text{初}(\text{EDTA})/\text{mL}$			
	$V_\text{终}(\text{EDTA})/\text{mL}$			
	$\Delta V(\text{EDTA})/\text{mL}$			
	$c(\text{总硬度})/\text{mg}\cdot\text{L}^{-1}$			
	$\bar{c}(\text{总硬度})/\text{mg}\cdot\text{L}^{-1}$			
相对平均偏差 $\bar{d_r}/\%$				

表 5-7-3　水样中 Ca^{2+} 含量及 Mg^{2+} 含量的测定

实验序号		1	2	3
指示剂				
终点前后颜色变化				
$V(\text{水样})/\text{mL}$				
水样处理	$3\ \text{mol}\cdot\text{L}^{-1}\ \text{HCl}/\text{滴}$			
	加热微沸除 CO_2			
	三乙醇胺 $/\text{mL}$			
	$6\ \text{mol}\cdot\text{L}^{-1}\ \text{NaOH}$ 缓冲溶液 $/\text{mL}$			
	钙指示剂 $/\text{g}$			

续表

实验序号		1	2	3
测定	$V_初(EDTA)/mL$			
	$V_终(EDTA)/mL$			
	$\Delta V(EDTA)/mL$			
	$c(Ca^{2+})/mg\cdot L^{-1}$			
	$c(Mg^{2+})/mg\cdot L^{-1}$			
	$\bar{c}(Ca^{2+})/mg\cdot L^{-1}$			
	$\bar{c}(Mg^{2+})/mg\cdot L^{-1}$			
相对平均偏差$\bar{d_r}/\%$				

【思考题】

1. 测定水样总硬度时,为什么要加 pH=10 的 NH_3-NH_4Cl 缓冲溶液?

2. 本实验测定钙、镁含量时,试样中存在少量 Fe^{3+}、Al^{3+}、Cu^{2+}、Zn^{2+}、Pb^{2+}等杂质离子,对测定有干扰吗? 用什么方法可消除 Fe^{3+}、Al^{3+}、Cu^{2+}、Zn^{2+}、Pb^{2+}的干扰?

3. 在水样硬度的测定前,为什么要滴加 1~2 滴 3 $mol\cdot L^{-1}$ HCl 溶液以酸化反应体系? 为什么要加入三乙醇胺和 Na_2S 溶液?

(王英骥)

二、明矾中 $KAl(SO_4)_2\cdot12H_2O$ 含量的测定

【实验目的】

1. 了解返滴定的基本过程。
2. 巩固理解 EDTA 标准溶液的标定方法。
3. 掌握使用二甲酚橙指示剂的条件和方法。
4. 学习配位滴定法测定明矾含量的原理和方法。

【预习作业】

模拟设计实验:以流程图方式给出本实验的设计思路,并在流程图中实验步骤处注明相应的注意事项及缘由。

引导问题:
1. 实验中明矾含量的测定方法有哪些?
2. 哪些情况下宜采用返滴定法?
3. 在明矾含量的测定时采用返滴定法,为什么?
4. 二甲酚橙指示剂在配位滴定中的使用条件是什么?

【实验原理】

明矾$[KAl(SO_4)_2\cdot12H_2O]$又名白矾,是明矾石的提炼品。明矾含量的测定一般都是先测定

其组成中 Al^{3+} 的含量，再换算成明矾的含量。Al^{3+} 的含量测定可采用配位滴定法，但 Al^{3+} 与 EDTA 的配位反应不仅速度缓慢，而且对二甲酚橙指示剂还具有封闭作用，当酸度不高时，Al^{3+} 易水解形成多种多核羟基配合物，因此，Al^{3+} 的含量测定不能用直接滴定法而用返滴定法。其测定方法是：在含 Al^{3+} 的试液中，先定量加入过量的 EDTA 标准溶液，煮沸以加速 Al^{3+} 与 EDTA 的反应，冷却后，加入 HAc-NaAc 缓冲溶液调节 pH 至 5~6，以保证 Al^{3+} 与 EDTA 的定量配位反应，然后以二甲酚橙做指示剂（Al^{3+} 已形成 AlY^- 配合物，不再封闭指示剂），用 Zn^{2+} 标准溶液滴定过量的 EDTA，Zn^{2+} 与过量的 EDTA 反应完全后，Zn^{2+} 开始与二甲酚橙结合转化为紫红色配合物 ZnH_3In^{2-}，由于二甲酚橙为黄色，两者的混合色为橙色，所以溶液颜色变为橙色时，即终点到达。由两种标准溶液的浓度和用量，可以求得 Al^{3+} 的含量。反应过程如下：

$$Al^{3+} + H_2Y^{2-}（过量）+ 2H_2O \Longrightarrow AlY^- + 2H_3O^+$$

$$H_2Y^{2-}（剩余）+ Zn^{2+} + 2H_2O \Longrightarrow ZnY^{2-} + 2H_3O^+$$

$$Zn^{2+} + H_3In^{4-} \Longrightarrow ZnH_3In^{2-}$$

$$（黄色）\qquad （紫红色）$$

滴定过程各配合物的稳定顺序：$AlY^- > ZnY^{2-} > ZnH_3In^{2-}$。

【仪器材料与试剂】

仪器　万分之一电子分析天平，酸式滴定管或酸碱两用滴定管（25 mL），锥形瓶（250 mL×3），移液管（25 mL×3），容量瓶（100 mL，250 mL），烧杯（100 mL×2），试剂瓶（250 mL），量筒（10 mL×3，100 mL），玻璃棒，滴定管架，洗瓶，洗耳球。

材料与试剂　$0.05 \ mol \cdot L^{-1}$ EDTA 溶液，HAc-NaAc 缓冲溶液（pH 4.5），$2 \ mol \cdot L^{-1}$ HCl 溶液，$ZnSO_4 \cdot 7H_2O$（A.R. 或 C.P.），0.5% 的二甲酚橙溶液，明矾试样。

【实验步骤】

（一）$0.05 \ mol \cdot L^{-1} \ Zn^{2+}$ 标准溶液的配制

准确称取 3.6~3.8 g（精确至 ±0.000 1 g）一级标准物质 $ZnSO_4 \cdot 7H_2O$（$M_r = 287.56$）于小烧杯中，用移液管加 2.00 mL 的 $2 \ mol \cdot L^{-1}$ HCl 溶液和少量蒸馏水，溶解后定量转移至 250 mL 容量瓶中，稀释至刻度，摇匀。根据下式（5-7-6）计算 Zn^{2+} 标准溶液浓度

$$c(ZnSO_4 \cdot 7H_2O) = \frac{m(ZnSO_4 \cdot 7H_2O)}{M_r(ZnSO_4 \cdot 7H_2O) \times \dfrac{250.00}{1\,000}} \ (mol \cdot L^{-1}) \qquad (5-7-6)$$

（二）$0.05 \ mol \cdot L^{-1}$ EDTA 溶液浓度的测定

用移液管准确移取 25.00 mL EDTA 溶液于 250 mL 锥形瓶中，加入 100.0 mL 蒸馏水，5.00 mL HAc-NaAc 缓冲溶液及 1.00 mL 二甲酚橙指示剂。用 Zn^{2+} 标准溶液滴定至溶液由黄色变为橙色即为终点。平行滴定三次，数据记录于表 5-7-4，按式（5-7-7）计算 EDTA 的准确浓度。

$$c(EDTA) = \frac{c(ZnSO_4) \times V(ZnSO_4)}{V(EDTA)} \ (mol \cdot L^{-1}) \qquad (5-7-7)$$

（三）明矾中 $KAl(SO_4)_2 \cdot 12H_2O$ 含量的测定

准确称取 1.3~1.4 g（精确至 ±0.000 1 g）已研细的明矾 $\{M_r([KAl(SO_4)_2 \cdot 12H_2O] = 474.4\}$ 试样于小烧杯中，加蒸馏水溶解，定量转移至 100 mL 容量瓶中，用蒸馏水稀释至刻度，摇匀。用移液

管准确移取 25.00 mL 明矾待测液于锥形瓶中,另用移液管吸取 25.00 mL 已标定的 EDTA 溶液与之混合均匀,在沸水浴中加热 10 min,冷却至室温,加入 100.0 mL 蒸馏水,5.00 mL HAc-NaAc 缓冲溶液及 1.00 mL 二甲酚橙指示剂,用 Zn^{2+} 标准溶液滴定至溶液由黄色变为橙色即为终点。平行测定三次,数据记录于表 5-7-5,按式(5-7-8)计算明矾的含量

$$\omega[KAl(SO_4)_2 \cdot 12H_2O] =$$

$$\frac{[c(EDTA)V(EDTA) - c(ZnSO_4)V(ZnSO_4)] \times M_r[KAl(SO_4)_2 \cdot 12H_2O] \times 10^{-3}}{m(样品) \times \dfrac{25.00}{100.00}} (g \cdot g^{-1}) \qquad (5\text{-}7\text{-}8)$$

【注意事项】

1. 在 Al^{3+} 的试液中加入过量 EDTA 标准溶液后,一定要煮沸以加速 Al^{3+} 与 EDTA 的反应。

2. Al^{3+} 与 EDTA 的反应液充分冷却后,调节 pH 至 5~6,以保证 Al^{3+} 与 EDTA 的定量配合。

3. Al^{3+} 与 EDTA 的反应完毕后才加入二甲酚橙作指示剂,用 Zn^{2+} 标准溶液滴定过量的 EDTA。

【数据记录及结果分析】

日期:_____　温度:_____℃　相对湿度:_____

表 5-7-4　EDTA 溶液浓度的测定

实验序号	1	2	3
$m_{称量}(ZnSO_4 \cdot 7H_2O)/g$			
$m_{测定}(ZnSO_4 \cdot 7H_2O)/g$			
指示剂			
终点颜色变化			
$V(ZnSO_4 \cdot 7H_2O)/mL$			
$V_{初}(EDTA)/mL$			
$V_{终}(EDTA)/mL$			
$V_{消耗}(EDTA)/mL$			
$c(EDTA)/mol \cdot L^{-1}$			
$\bar{c}(EDTA)/mol \cdot L^{-1}$			
相对平均偏差 $\bar{d_r}/\%$			

表 5-7-5　明矾含量的测定

实验序号		1	2	3
$m_{称量}(明矾)/g$				
$m_{测定}(明矾)/g$				
$V(明矾)/mL$				
样品处理	0.5 mol·L^{-1} EDTA/mL			
	沸水浴加热/min			
	蒸馏水/mL			
	HAc-NaAc/mL			

续表

实验序号	1	2	3
指示剂			
终点颜色变化			
$V_{初}$（$ZnSO_4 \cdot 7H_2O$）/mL			
$V_{终}$（$ZnSO_4 \cdot 7H_2O$）/mL			
$V_{消耗}$（$ZnSO_4 \cdot 7H_2O$）/mL			
ω（明矾）/$g \cdot g^{-1}$			
$\overline{\omega}$（明矾）/$g \cdot g^{-1}$			
相对平均偏差$\overline{d_r}$/%			

【思考题】

1. 用 EDTA 测定 Al^{3+}时，能采用直接滴定法吗，为什么或者为什么不呢？

2. 用 EDTA 测定 Al^{3+}时，能否用铬黑 T 为指示剂？为什么？

3. Al^{3+}对二甲酚橙有封闭作用，为什么在用 EDTA 标准溶液测定铝含量的返滴定法中还能采用二甲酚橙作指示剂？

（梁洪文）

三、葡萄糖酸钙含量的测定

【实验目的】

1. 巩固理解 EDTA 标准溶液的直接配制方法。
2. 巩固掌握使用铬黑 T 指示剂的条件和方法。
3. 学习应用配位滴定法测定葡萄糖酸钙含量的原理和方法。

【预习作业】

模拟设计实验：以流程图方式给出本实验的设计思路，并在流程图中实验步骤处注明相应的注意事项及缘由。

引导问题：

1. 如何用直接配制法获得 EDTA 标准溶液？
2. 葡萄糖酸钙的含量测定原理是什么？
3. 配位滴定法测定葡萄糖酸钙的含量时采用何种指示剂？
4. 铬黑 T 指示剂的使用条件是什么？本实验中为何要加入辅助指示剂？

【实验原理】

临床上常用的葡萄糖酸钙药物有片剂和针剂两种剂型，其含量的测定常用螯合滴定法。方法是：在葡萄糖酸钙的溶液中，用 pH 10 的 NH_3-NH_4Cl 缓冲溶液来控制溶液的酸度，以铬黑 T 作指示剂，用 EDTA 标准溶液直接滴定。但因 Ca^{2+}与铬黑 T 形成的螯合物（$CaIn^-$）不够稳定，单独使用铬黑 T 会使终点过早到达,为此可先加入少量的 Mg^{2+} 做辅助指示剂,以提高终点变色的敏锐性。为使加入的 Mg^{2+} 不影响测定的结果,本实验在加入葡萄糖酸钙样品之前,先将加入的 Mg^{2+} 用 EDTA 溶液滴定至终点,再加入葡萄糖酸钙样品溶液,然后用 EDTA 标准溶液再次滴定至终点,则滴定葡萄糖酸钙消耗的 EDTA 标准溶液的体积为滴定管中两次滴定终点读数之差,并由此可计算出葡萄糖酸钙的含量。葡萄糖酸钙含量测定的实验步骤如下:

1. 先将 Mg^{2+} 溶液和铬黑 T 加入 NH$_3$-NH$_4$Cl 缓冲溶液中,用 EDTA 标准溶液滴定至溶液由酒红色恰好变为纯蓝色,为第一滴定终点。

2. 在所得溶液中加入葡萄糖酸钙样品溶液,用 EDTA 标准溶液滴定至溶液由酒红色恰好变为纯蓝色,为第二滴定终点。

用于滴定葡萄糖酸钙所消耗的 EDTA 标准溶液与第一滴定无关,故滴定葡萄糖酸钙消耗的 EDTA 标准溶液的体积为滴定管中两次滴定终点体积读数之差。

【仪器材料与试剂】

仪器　万分之一电子分析天平,碱式滴定管或酸碱两用滴定管(25 mL),锥形瓶(250 mL×3),移液管(10 mL,20 mL),容量瓶(250 mL×3),烧杯(250 mL×2),量筒(10 mL×2,50 mL),洗瓶,滴定管架,洗耳球。

材料与试剂　Na$_2$H$_2$Y·2H$_2$O(s,A.R.),1%MgSO$_4$ 溶液,pH 10 的 NH$_3$-NH$_4$Cl 缓冲溶液,葡萄糖酸钙(片剂或针剂),0.5% 铬黑 T 溶液。

【实验步骤】

(一) 0.01 mol·L^{-1} EDTA 标准溶液的配制

在分析天平上准确称取 1.0~1.1 g(精确至 ±0.000 1 g)一级标准物质 Na$_2$H$_2$Y·2H$_2$O(M_r=372.26)于 250 mL 烧杯中,用 50.0 mL 蒸馏水溶解,定量转移至 250 mL 容量瓶中,加蒸馏水稀释至刻度,摇匀。

$$c(\text{EDTA})=\frac{m(\text{EDTA})\times 1\,000}{M_r(\text{EDTA})\times 250.00}\,(\text{mol}\cdot\text{L}^{-1}) \tag{5-7-9}$$

(二) 葡萄糖酸钙待测溶液的配制

在分析天平上准确称取葡萄糖酸钙(M_r=448.6)片剂 1.0~1.1 g(精确至 ±0.000 1 g)于 250 mL 烧杯中,加 50.0 mL 蒸馏水并微热使其溶解,冷却后定量转移至 250 mL 容量瓶中,加蒸馏水稀释至刻度,摇匀。

或用移液管吸取 10.00 mL 针剂葡萄糖酸钙溶液于 250 mL 容量瓶中,加蒸馏水稀释至刻度,摇匀。

(三) 葡萄糖酸钙含量的测定

取蒸馏水 10.0 mL 于 250 mL 锥形瓶中,加入 10.0 mL pH 10 的 NH$_3$-NH$_4$Cl 缓冲溶液,1~2 滴 1% MgSO$_4$ 和 2~3 滴铬黑 T,摇匀。用 EDTA 标准溶液滴定至溶液由酒红色恰好变为纯蓝色,记录滴定管中 EDTA 溶液的读数 V_1。用移液管吸取 20.00 mL 葡萄糖酸钙待测液于上述锥形瓶中,继续用 EDTA 标准溶液滴定至溶液由酒红色恰好变为纯蓝色,记录滴定管中 EDTA 溶液的读数 V_2 于表 5-7-6 中。平行测定三次。由式(5-7-10)计算葡萄糖酸钙的质量分数 ω(片剂)和式(5-7-11)计算质量浓度 ρ(针剂)。

1. 片剂

$$\omega(\text{葡萄糖酸钙})=\frac{c(\text{EDTA})\left[V_2(\text{EDTA})-V_1(\text{EDTA})\right]\times M_r(\text{葡萄糖酸钙})}{m(\text{葡萄糖酸钙})\times\dfrac{20.00}{250.00}}\,(\text{mg}\cdot\text{g}^{-1}) \tag{5-7-10}$$

式（5-7-10）中 m（葡萄糖酸钙）为片剂的质量。

2. 针剂

$$\rho(\text{葡萄糖酸钙}) = \frac{c(\text{EDTA})\left[V_2(\text{EDTA}) - V_1(\text{EDTA})\right] \times M_r(\text{葡萄糖酸钙})}{10.00 \times \dfrac{20.00}{250.00}} \quad (\text{g} \cdot \text{L}^{-1}) \quad (5\text{-}7\text{-}11)$$

【注意事项】

1. 在 pH 10 的 NH_3-NH_4Cl 缓冲溶液中使用铬黑 T。

2. 加入少量 $MgSO_4$ 作为辅助指示剂以免因 Ca^{2+} 与铬黑 T 形成的螯合物不够稳定而使滴定终点提前。

3. 实验中有两个滴定终点，Ca^{2+} 消耗的 EDTA 是第一滴定终点至第二滴定终点之体积。

【数据记录及结果分析】

日期：_____ 温度：_____℃ 相对湿度：_____

表 5-7-6 针剂及片剂中葡萄糖酸钙含量的测定

实验序号	1	2	3
$m(\text{Na}_2\text{H}_2\text{Y} \cdot 2\text{H}_2\text{O})/\text{g}$			
$c(\text{Na}_2\text{H}_2\text{Y} \cdot 2\text{H}_2\text{O})/\text{mol} \cdot \text{L}^{-1}$			
第一终点指示剂			
第二终点指示剂			
第一终点颜色变化			
第二终点颜色变化			
$V(\text{葡萄糖酸钙})/\text{mL}$			
$V_{\text{终点}1}(\text{EDTA})/\text{mL}$			
$V_{\text{终点}2}(\text{EDTA})/\text{mL}$			
$\left[V_{\text{终点}2}(\text{EDTA}) - V_{\text{终点}1}(\text{EDTA})\right]/\text{mL}$			
$\omega(\text{葡萄糖酸钙})/\text{mg} \cdot \text{g}^{-1}$			
$\overline{\omega}(\text{葡萄糖酸钙})/\text{mg} \cdot \text{g}^{-1}$			
$\rho(\text{葡萄糖酸钙})/\text{g} \cdot \text{L}^{-1}$			
$\overline{\rho}(\text{葡萄糖酸钙})/\text{g} \cdot \text{L}^{-1}$			
相对平均偏差 $\overline{d_r}/\%$			

【思考题】

1. 在测定葡萄糖酸钙含量时，为什么要加入少量的 Mg^{2+} 试液？它会影响测定的结果吗？

2. 本实验能否在配制 EDTA 标准溶液时加入 Mg^{2+} 作辅助指示剂？

（梁洪文）

第六章 | 分光光度法实验

实验八　可见分光光度法测定水样中铁含量

【目的要求】

1. 熟悉可见分光光度法测定水样中铁含量的原理和方法。
2. 掌握可见分光光度计的使用方法。

【预习作业】

模拟设计实验:参照本实验步骤,以流程图方式给出本实验水样中铁含量测定的设计思路,并在流程图中的实验步骤注明相应的注意事项及缘由。

引导问题:

1. Lambert-Beer 定律的基本内容是什么? 怎样用两种不同的关系式表示?
2. 分光光度法最常用的定量分析方法有哪些? 它们具体的方法是什么?
3. 如何绘制吸收光曲线? 什么是最大吸收波长?
4. 分光光度计的基本部件有哪些? 各起什么作用?
5. 邻二氮菲法、硫氰酸盐法和磺基水杨酸法测定水样中铁含量的基本原理是什么? 试比较三者的异同。

【实验原理】

分光光度法是一种现代仪器分析方法,它的理论基础是物质的吸收光谱和光的吸收定律。根据所用光源波长不同,分光光度法可分为:可见分光光度法(380~760 nm);紫外分光光度法(200~380 nm);红外分光光度法($780 \sim 3 \times 10^5$ nm)。Lambert-Beer 定律是吸收光谱法的基本定律,它描述物质对单色光吸收的程度与吸光物质的浓度和厚度的关系。根据 Lambert-Beer 定律,当吸光物质的种类、溶剂、溶液温度一定时,具有一定波长的单色光通过一定厚度(b)的有色物质溶液时,有色物质对光的吸收程度(用吸光度 A 表示)与有色物质的浓度(c)呈线性关系

$$A = \varepsilon bc \tag{6-8-1}$$

式(6-8-1)中,c 为物质的量浓度,ε 为摩尔吸光系数,单位为 $L \cdot mol^{-1} \cdot cm^{-1}$,它是各种有色物质在一定波长下的特征常数。若以质量浓度($g \cdot L^{-1}$)表示,则 $A = ab\rho_B$,a 称为质量吸光系数,单位为 $L \cdot g^{-1} \cdot cm^{-1}$。

在分光光度法中,当吸光物质、入射光波长、温度和溶剂一定时,ε、a 为常数,此时溶液的吸光度(A)与有色物质的浓度(c)及吸收池厚度(b)成正比。Lambert-Beer 定律成为分光光度法定量

分析的基础,可用于测定吸光物质的含量。

Lambert-Beer 定律只适合于单色光,通常要选择合适的波长。对某一溶液在不同波长下测定其吸光度,以吸光度对波长作图,得到吸收光谱,从吸收光谱中找出最大吸收波长(λ_{max})作为测定波长。

分光光度法仅适合于微量组分的分析,通常以 A 处于 0.2~0.7 为最佳。

分光光度法常用的定量分析方法有标准比较法和标准曲线法。

标准比较法是指在相同实验条件下配制出标准溶液和试样溶液,分别测出标准溶液和未知物的吸光度

$$A_{标} = abc_{标} \qquad\qquad (6\text{-}8\text{-}2)$$

$$A_{未} = abc_{未} \qquad\qquad (6\text{-}8\text{-}3)$$

因同一实验中所使用的吸收池厚度 b 相等,相同的吸光物质与测定条件,因此 a 亦相同,比较式(6-8-2)与式(6-8-3)得

$$\frac{A_{标}}{A_{未}} = \frac{abc_{标}}{abc_{未}} \qquad\qquad (6\text{-}8\text{-}4)$$

$$c_{未} = \frac{A_{未}}{A_{标}} \times c_{标} \qquad\qquad (6\text{-}8\text{-}5)$$

上述方法称为标准对照法(比较法)。为提高测量的准确度,往往同时测定数个标准溶液的吸光度,并以浓度为横坐标,吸光度为纵坐标,绘制标准曲线(或称工作曲线),在同样条件下,测定被测溶液的吸光度,从标准曲线上查出该吸光度所对应的溶液浓度,这种方法称为标准曲线法,该曲线可用直线方程 $y = ax + b$ 表示,该方程也称为回归方程。

一、邻二氮菲法测定 Fe^{2+} 浓度

邻二氮菲(邻菲罗啉)是目前可见分光光度法测定铁含量的较好试剂。加入试剂的作用分别是:盐酸羟胺是还原剂、邻二氮菲是显色剂、NaAc 溶液是缓冲溶液用来控制溶液的pH。在 pH 为 3~9 的溶液中,邻二氮菲与 Fe^{2+} 生成稳定的橘红色配合物 $[Fe(phen)_3]^{2+}$($\lg K_s = 21.3$),$\varepsilon_{508\ nm} = 1.1 \times 10^4\ L \cdot mol^{-1} \cdot cm^{-1}$,其最大吸收峰位于 450~560 nm 波长范围内;当然邻二氮菲也能与 Fe^{3+} 生成淡蓝色 $[Fe(phen)_3]^{3+}$($\lg K_s = 14.1$),不过其稳定性较 $[Fe(phen)_3]^{2+}$ 差,在实际应用中,先加入还原剂盐酸羟胺把 Fe^{3+} 还原成 Fe^{2+},再与显色剂邻二氮菲作用显色,其反应式如下:

$$2Fe^{3+} + 2NH_2OH \cdot HCl + 2H_2O \Longrightarrow 2Fe^{2+} + N_2 \uparrow + 4H_3O^+ + 2Cl^-$$

【仪器材料及试剂】

仪器 分光光度计,万分之一分析天平,容量瓶(50 mL × 7,1 000 mL),吸量管(1 mL,2 mL × 2,

5 mL,10 mL),滴管,可调移液枪(5 mL,10 mL)。

材料与试剂 8 mmol·L^{-1}邻菲罗啉(新鲜配制)溶液,1.5 mol·L^{-1}盐酸羟胺(临用时配制)溶液,1 mol·L^{-1} NaAc 溶液,2.000 mmol·L^{-1}标准 Fe^{2+}溶液。

【实验步骤】

(一)标准溶液和待测溶液的配制

取 50 mL 容量瓶 7 支,按表 6-8-1 所列的量,用吸量管量取各种溶液加入容量瓶中,加蒸馏水稀释至刻度,摇匀,配成空白溶液、一系列不同浓度的标准溶液以及待测溶液(表 6-8-1)。

表 6-8-1 Fe^{2+}标准溶液及待测溶液配制与吸光度测定

实验序号	1(空白)	2	3	4	5	6	7
2.000 mmol·L^{-1}标准 Fe^{2+}溶液/mL	0	0.40	0.80	1.20	1.60	2.00	—
Fe^{2+}水样溶液/mL	—	—	—	—	—	—	10.00
1.5 mol·L^{-1}盐酸羟胺/mL	1.00	1.00	1.00	1.00	1.00	1.00	1.00
8 mmol·L^{-1}邻菲罗啉/mL	2.00	2.00	2.00	2.00	2.00	2.00	2.00
1 mol·L^{-1} NaAc 溶液/mL	5.00	5.00	5.00	5.00	5.00	5.00	5.00
$V_{总}$(稀释)/mL	50.00	50.00	50.00	50.00	50.00	50.00	50.00
$c_{稀释}$(Fe^{2+})/μmol·L^{-1}							

(二)吸收光谱的测定

取表 6-8-1 中的 4 号溶液,按分光光度计的使用方法(参考第二章"基础化学实验常用仪器的使用"),在 450~560 nm 波长范围内,以 1 号空白作为参比溶液,每隔 10 nm 测定一次溶液的吸光度,在最大吸光度的波长附近可每隔 5 nm 再加测其吸光度。记录实验数据于表 6-8-2 中。

(三)吸光度(A)的测定及标准曲线的绘制

选择 λ_{max} 为入射光波长,以 1 号空白作为参比溶液,测出系列标准溶液的吸光度,记录实验数据于表 6-8-3。并以浓度为横坐标,吸光度为纵坐标,绘制标准曲线,该曲线可用回归方程 $y=ax+b$ 表示。

(四)待测水样中 Fe^{2+}浓度的测定

将待测水样按与标准曲线系列溶液相同的条件下测其吸光度,记录实验数据于表 6-8-3 中。

【数据记录与结果分析】

日期:＿＿＿＿＿＿ 温度:＿＿＿＿℃ 相对湿度:＿＿＿＿

(一)绘制吸收光谱并确定 λ_{max}

根据表 6-8-2 记录的数据,以波长为横坐标,吸光度为纵坐标,在坐标纸上绘制吸收光谱,找出 λ_{max}。

表 6-8-2   邻菲罗啉合亚铁的吸收光谱测定

λ/nm	
A	
λ_{max}/nm	

绘制吸收光谱,请附图 1 于实验报告。

(二) 绘制标准曲线

根据表 6-8-3 记录的数据,以标准 Fe^{2+} 的浓度($\mu mol \cdot L^{-1}$)为横坐标,吸光度(A)为纵坐标绘制标准曲线。

表 6-8-3   标准溶液和待测溶液的吸光度测定

容量瓶编号	1(空白)	2	3	4	5	6	7(样品)
$c_{稀释}$(Fe^{2+})/$\mu mol \cdot L^{-1}$	0.00						
吸光度 A	0.00						

(三) 待测溶液中 Fe^{2+} 浓度的确定

根据待测溶液的吸光度,利用标准对照法和标准曲线法分别计算出原水样溶液中未知的 Fe^{2+}($\mu mol \cdot L^{-1}$)。

标准曲线:请附图 2 于实验报告,列出回归方程及相关系数。

1. 标准曲线法

标准曲线上直接读出待测 Fe^{2+} 的含量为_____($\mu mol \cdot L^{-1}$);

原样品中 Fe^{2+} 含量为_____($\mu mol \cdot L^{-1}$)。

2. 标准对照法

所选取 Fe^{2+} 标准溶液的吸光度_____;

样品的吸光度_____;

原样品中 Fe^{2+} 含量_____($\mu mol \cdot L^{-1}$)。

样品溶液的原浓度 c_2(ρ_2)=从标准曲线找出待测溶液的浓度 c_1(ρ_1) × 稀释倍数 k。

【思考题】

1. 为什么要将被测溶液的吸光度控制在 0.2~0.7 的范围内? 如何控制?
2. 由工作曲线查出的待测铁离子的浓度是否为原始待测 Fe^{2+} 溶液的浓度?
3. 以实验结果说明标准对照法与标准曲线法的优缺点。

二、硫氰酸盐法测定 Fe^{3+} 浓度

可见分光光度法仅适合于有色物质含量的测定,而 Fe^{3+} 的稀溶液几乎是无色的,当加入显色剂 KSCN 时,即产生血红色的络合物 $[Fe(SCN)_6]^{3-}$($lgK_s = 6.4$)。

$$Fe^{3+} + 6SCN^- \Longrightarrow [Fe(SCN)_6]^{3-}$$

溶液颜色的深度与 Fe^{3+} 浓度成正比。当溶液中 SCN^- 浓度增大时,平衡右移,溶液颜色也随之加深。因此,在测定时,一定要使 SCN^- 浓度超过与 Fe^{3+} 反应所需的浓度,且每次的浓度恒定。此

外，为防止 Fe^{3+} 的水解，在溶液中应加入一定量的强酸硝酸。Fe^{3+} 离子还能被 SCN^- 离子慢慢还原为 Fe^{2+} 离子，而使红色变浅，所以在溶液中应当含有少量强氧化剂过二硫酸铵，即 $(NH_4)_2S_2O_8$，其与硝酸一起协同防止 Fe^{3+} 离子的还原。

【仪器材料及试剂】

仪器　分光光度计，容量瓶（50 mL × 7，1 000 mL），吸量管（1 mL，5 mL，10 mL），滴管。

材料与试剂　$0.2\ mol\cdot L^{-1}$ KSCN 溶液，$2\ mol\cdot L^{-1}$ HNO_3 溶液，浓 H_2SO_4，$0.100\ 0\ g\cdot L^{-1}$ Fe^{3+} 标准溶液，$25\ g\cdot L^{-1}$ $(NH_4)_2S_2O_8$ 溶液。

【实验步骤】

（一）标准溶液和待测溶液的配制

取 50 mL 容量瓶 7 支，按表 6-8-4 所列的量，用吸量管量取各种溶液加入容量瓶中，加蒸馏水稀释至刻度，摇匀，配成空白溶液、一系列不同浓度的标准溶液以及待测溶液。

表 6-8-4　Fe^{3+} 标准溶液和待测溶液的配制

容量瓶号	1（空白）	2	3	4	5	6	7（待测）
$0.1\ g\cdot L^{-1}$ Fe^{3+} 标准 /mL	0	0.50	1.00	1.50	2.00	2.50	—
水样 /mL	—	—	—	—	—	—	10
$2\ mol\cdot L^{-1}$ HNO_3 /mL	1.00	1.00	1.00	1.00	1.00	1.00	1.0
$0.2\ mol\cdot L^{-1}$ KSCN /mL	5.00	5.00	5.00	5.00	5.00	5.00	5.00
$25\ g\cdot L^{-1}$ $(NH_4)_2S_2O_8$ /滴	1	1	1	1	1	1	1
$V_{总}$（稀释）/mL	50.00	50.00	50.00	50.00	50.00	50.00	50.00
$\rho_{稀释}$（Fe^{3+}）/$mg\cdot L^{-1}$							

（二）吸收光谱的测定

取表 6-8-4 中的 4 号溶液，按分光光度计的使用方法，在 450~520 nm 波长范围内，以 1 号空白作为参比溶液，每隔 10 nm 测定一次溶液的吸光度，在最大吸光度的波长附近可每隔 5 nm 再加测其吸光度。记录实验数据于表 6-8-5 中。

（三）吸光度（A）的测定及标准曲线的绘制

选择 λ_{max} 为入射光波长（文献记载的 λ_{max} = 480 nm），以 1 号空白作为参比溶液，测出系列标准溶液的吸光度，记录实验数据于表 6-8-6。并以浓度为横坐标，吸光度为纵坐标，绘制标准曲线，该曲线可用回归方程 $y = ax + b$ 表示。

（四）待测溶液中 Fe^{3+} 浓度的确定

根据所测得的供试液的吸光度，利用标准对照法和标准曲线法分别计算出水样中 Fe^{3+} 浓度（$mg\cdot L^{-1}$）。

【数据记录与结果分析】

日期：_____　温度：_____℃　相对湿度：_____

（一）绘制吸收光谱并确定 λ_{max}

根据表 6-8-5 所记录的数据，以波长为横坐标，吸光度为纵坐标在坐标纸上绘制吸收光谱，找出 λ_{max}。

表 6-8-5 吸收光谱测定

λ/nm	
吸光度 A	
λ_{max}/nm	

绘制吸收光谱,请附图 1 于实验报告。

(二)绘制标准曲线

根据表 6-8-6 所记录的数据,以标准 Fe^{3+} 的浓度($mg\cdot L^{-1}$)为横坐标,吸光度(A)为纵坐标绘制标准曲线。

表 6-8-6 标准溶液和待测溶液的吸光度数据记录

容量瓶编号	1(空白)	2	3	4	5	6	7(样品)
$\rho_{稀释}$(Fe^{3+})/$mg\cdot L^{-1}$	0.00						
A	0.00						

标准曲线请附图 2 于实验报告,列出回归方程及相关系数。

(三)待测溶液中 Fe^{3+} 浓度的确定

根据所测的待测溶液的吸光度,利用标准对照法和标准曲线法分别计算出原未知溶液 Fe^{3+} 浓度($mg\cdot L^{-1}$)。

1. 标准曲线法(列出回归方程及相关系数)

标准曲线上直接读出待测 Fe^{3+} 的含量为＿＿＿＿＿＿＿＿＿＿＿($mg\cdot L^{-1}$);

原样品中 Fe^{3+} 含量为＿＿＿＿＿＿＿＿＿＿＿($mg\cdot L^{-1}$)。

2. 标准对照法

所选取标准溶液的吸光度＿＿＿＿＿＿＿＿＿＿＿;

样品的吸光度＿＿＿＿＿＿＿＿＿＿＿;

原样品中 Fe^{3+} 含量＿＿＿＿＿＿＿＿＿＿＿($mg\cdot L^{-1}$)。

【思考题】

在 Fe^{3+} 的显色反应时,为什么要加过量的 KSCN 溶液?

三、磺基水杨酸法测定 Fe^{3+} 浓度

磺基水杨酸(H_2Ssal)是 Fe^{3+} 的显色剂。Fe^{3+} 与磺基水杨酸作用能形成多种配合物,在不同的酸度下生成的配合物的组成和颜色也不同。如 pH 1.8~2.5 时生成紫红色[FeSsal]$^+$;pH 4~8 时生成棕褐色[Fe(Ssal)$_2$]$^-$;pH 8.0~11.5 时生成稳定的黄色[Fe(Ssal)$_3$]$^{3-}$,当 pH > 12 时 Fe^{3+} 易水解生成 Fe(OH)$_3$ 沉淀,不能用于比色测定,故磺基水杨酸法应 pH < 12,且需在恒定不变的 pH 条件下进行。本实验采用在醋酸盐缓冲体系条件下进行测定,此时溶液的 pH 约为 5,Fe^{3+} 与其生成稳定的 1:2 橙色的[Fe(Ssal)$_2$]$^-$配合物,其显色反应式如下:

在实验条件下,先在 420~490 nm 波长范围内,绘制吸收光谱,选择 λ_{max} 为测量用单色光,然后在此波长下用标准曲线法或标准对照法测出未知样品的铁含量。

【仪器材料与试剂】

仪器　可见分光光度计,容量瓶(25 mL×7),吸量管(2 mL×2,1 mL),滴管。

材料与试剂　0.100 0 $g \cdot L^{-1}$ 标准 Fe^{3+} 溶液,100 $g \cdot L^{-1}$ 磺基水杨酸溶液,pH 5.0 的 HAc-NaAc 缓冲溶液,待测水样-铁盐溶液,坐标纸(2 张)。

【实验步骤】

(一)标准溶液和待测溶液的配制

取 25 mL 容量瓶 7 支,按表 6-8-7 所列的量,用吸量管量取各种溶液加入容量瓶中,再用 pH 5 的 HAc-NaAc 缓冲溶液稀释至刻度,摇匀,配成空白溶液、一系列不同浓度的标准溶液以及待测溶液。

表 6-8-7　标准溶液和待测溶液的配制

容量瓶编号	1(空白)	2	3	4	5	6	7(待测)
0.100 0 $g \cdot L^{-1}$ 标准 Fe^{3+} 溶液 / mL	0.00	0.40	0.60	0.80	1.00	1.20	—
水样 / mL	—	—	—	—	—	—	1.00
100 $g \cdot L^{-1}$ 磺基水杨酸溶液 / mL	2.00	2.00	2.00	2.00	2.00	2.00	2.00
$V_{总}$(稀释)/ mL	25.00	25.00	25.00	25.00	25.00	25.00	25.00
$\rho_{稀释}(Fe^{3+})$/ mg $\cdot L^{-1}$							

(二)吸收光谱的测定

在系列标准溶液中,取表 6-8-7 中的 4 号溶液,按分光光度计的使用方法,用 1 cm 比色皿,在 420~490 nm 波长范围内,以 1 号空白作为参比溶液,每隔 10 nm 测定一次溶液的吸光度,在最大吸光度的波长附近可每隔 5 nm 再测其吸光度,记录实验数据(表 6-8-8)。

(三)吸光度(A)的测定及标准曲线的绘制

选择 λ_{max} 为入射光波长(文献记载的 λ_{max} = 466 nm),以 1 号空白作为参比溶液,测出系列标准溶液的吸光度,记录实验数据于表 6-8-9。并以浓度为横坐标,吸光度为纵坐标,绘制标准曲线,该曲线可用回归方程 $y = ax + b$ 表示。

(四)待测水溶液中 Fe^{3+} 浓度的确定

根据待测溶液的吸光度,利用标准对照法和标准曲线法分别计算出水样中铁离子浓度(mg $\cdot L^{-1}$)。

【数据记录与结果分析】

日期:＿＿＿＿＿＿＿＿　温度:＿＿＿＿＿＿＿℃　相对湿度:＿＿＿＿＿＿＿＿

(一)绘制吸收光谱并确定 λ_{max}

根据表 6-8-8 所记录的数据,以波长为横坐标,吸光度为纵坐标在坐标纸上绘制吸收光谱,找出 λ_{max}。

表 6-8-8　测定吸收光谱数据记录

波长 λ/nm	
吸光度 A	
$\lambda_{\max}$/nm	

绘制吸收光谱,请附图 1 于实验报告,列出回归方程及相关系数。

(二)绘制标准曲线

根据表 6-8-9 所记录的数据,以各标准溶液的浓度($mg \cdot L^{-1}$)为横坐标,相应的吸光度值为纵坐标,绘制出标准曲线。

表 6-8-9　标准溶液和待测溶液的吸光度数据记录

容量瓶编号	1(空白)	2	3	4	5	6	7(待测)
Fe^{3+}溶液的含量/$mg \cdot L^{-1}$	0.00						
吸光度 A	0.00						

标准曲线请附图 2 于实验报告,列出回归方程及相关系数。

(三)待测溶液中 Fe^{3+} 浓度的确定

根据待测溶液的吸光度,利用比较法和标准曲线法分别计算出原未知溶液 Fe^{3+} 浓度($mg \cdot L^{-1}$)。

1. 标准曲线法(列出回归方程及相关系数)

标准曲线上直接读出待测 Fe^{3+} 的含量为＿＿＿＿＿＿＿＿＿＿＿＿＿＿＿＿＿＿＿＿($mg \cdot L^{-1}$);

原未知样品中 Fe^{3+} 含量＝从标准曲线查得供试液含量 ×25(倍)为＿＿＿＿＿＿($mg \cdot L^{-1}$)。

2. 标准比较法

所选取标准溶液的吸光度＿＿＿＿＿＿＿＿＿＿＿＿＿＿＿＿＿＿＿＿＿＿＿＿＿;

未知样品中 Fe^{3+} 的吸光度＿＿＿＿＿＿＿＿＿＿＿＿＿＿＿＿＿＿＿＿＿＿＿;

原未知样品中 Fe^{3+} 含量＿＿＿＿＿＿＿＿＿＿＿＿＿＿＿＿＿＿＿＿＿($mg \cdot L^{-1}$)。

【思考题】

1. 实验中为什么要用缓冲溶液定容?

2. 本实验测定吸光度的空白溶液是什么?

(王金玲)

实验九　可见分光光度法测定阿司匹林药片中乙酰水杨酸的含量

【实验目的】

1. 掌握可见分光光度法测定阿司匹林药片的方法。

2. 掌握 722/721 型可见分光光度计的操作方法。

【预习作业】

模拟设计实验:以流程图方式给出本实验的设计思路,并在流程图实验步骤中注明相应的注意事项及缘由。

引导问题：

1. 实验中阿司匹林乙醇溶液可否将溶剂更换为水？
2. 实验中试剂的加样顺序可否颠倒，为什么？
3. 影响实验准确度的因素有哪些？

【实验原理】

阿司匹林（$CH_3COOC_6H_4COOH$）又名乙酰水杨酸，是由水杨酸合成的白色晶体化合物，常以片剂的方式用于退烧、消炎和减轻疼痛。

阿司匹林药片中的主要成分为乙酰水杨酸，在碱性条件下，分子中的酯基可与羟胺反应生成羟肟酸，后者在酸性条件下与三氯化铁形成红色的羟肟酸铁，此物质的理论最大吸收波长为 520 nm，且在一定浓度范围内符合 Lambert-Beer 定律，可采用标准曲线法求出药片中阿司匹林的含量。

【仪器材料与试剂】

仪器　722/721 型分光光度计，容量瓶（25 mL×6），吸量管（1 mL×5,5 mL），滴管，烧杯（100 mL）。

材料与试剂　2.00 mol·L^{-1} NaOH，4.00 mol·L^{-1} HCl，10% FeCl$_3$，0.500 g·L^{-1} 乙酰水杨酸乙醇溶液，7% 盐酸羟胺乙醇溶液，阿司匹林样品溶液（阿司匹林肠溶片，配制成 20 片·L^{-1} 乙醇溶液）。

【实验步骤】

（一）乙酰水杨酸标准溶液和样品溶液的配制

根据表 6-9-1，分别取 0.500 g·L^{-1} 乙酰水杨酸乙醇溶液 0.00 mL，0.50 mL，1.00 mL，1.50 mL，2.00 mL 和阿司匹林样品乙醇溶液 1.00 mL 置于 25 mL 容量瓶中，再各加入 7% 盐酸羟胺乙醇溶液 1.00 mL，2.00 mol·L^{-1} NaOH 1.00 mL，放置 3 min 后，加入 4.00 mol·L^{-1} HCl 溶液和 10% FeCl$_3$ 溶液各 1.00 mL，加水至刻度摇匀，放置 10 min 后，备用。

表 6-9-1　乙酰水杨酸标准溶液和样品溶液的配制

实验序号	1(空白)	2	3	4	5	6	7(样品)
0.500 g·L^{-1} 乙酰水杨酸乙醇溶液 /mL	0.00	0.50	1.00	1.50	2.00	2.50	—
阿司匹林样品溶液 /mL	—	—	—	—	—	—	1.00
7% 盐酸羟胺乙醇溶液 /mL	1.00	1.00	1.00	1.00	1.00	1.00	1.00
2.00 mol·L^{-1} NaOH /mL	1.00	1.00	1.00	1.00	1.00	1.00	1.00
4.00 mol·L^{-1} HCl /mL	1.00	1.00	1.00	1.00	1.00	1.00	1.00
10%FeCl$_3$ /mL	1.00	1.00	1.00	1.00	1.00	1.00	1.00
$V_{总}$(稀释)/mL	25.00	25.00	25.00	25.00	25.00	25.00	25.00
$c_{标准}$(稀释)/mg·L^{-1}							

（二）吸光度（A）的测定及标准曲线的绘制

按 722/721 型分光光度计的使用方法（见第二章"基础化学实验常用仪器"）选择波长 $\lambda_{max}=$ 520 nm 和相应的灵敏度档，以空白溶液作为参比溶液，分别测定各标准溶液的吸光度和待测样品溶液的吸光度。记录于表 6-9-2 中，并以浓度为横坐标，吸光度为纵坐标，绘制标准曲线，给出回归方程及相关系数。

【数据记录与结果分析】

日期：_____   温度：_____℃   相对湿度：_____

（一）乙酰水杨酸标准溶液和样品溶液的吸光度（A）

表 6-9-2   乙酰水杨酸标准溶液和样品溶液的吸光度

实验序号	1（空白）	2	3	4	5	6	7（样品）
$c_{标准}$（稀释）/mg·L^{-1}							
吸光度 A							

（二）乙酰水杨酸标准曲线的绘制

以乙酰水杨酸标准溶液浓度为横坐标,吸光度为纵坐标作图,绘制出标准曲线,并列出回归方程及相关系数。

（三）待测药片中阿司匹林含量的确定

从标准曲线找出阿司匹林样品溶液的浓度为 $\rho_1 =$ _____ mg·L^{-1},原阿司匹林样品溶液的浓度为 $\rho_2 = \rho_1 \times 25$（稀释倍数）= _____ mg·L^{-1},换算出药片中阿司匹林的含量 = _____ mg·片$^{-1}$。

【思考题】

1. 整个测定过程酸度控制是否一致,为什么?
2. 水杨酸与三氯化铁形成的紫色可干扰测定,如何消除?
3. 阅读相关资料指出阿司匹林的结构和理化性质。
4. 通过文献查阅,指出还有何方法测定阿司匹林药片中乙酰水杨酸的含量? 了解阿司匹林在临床的主要作用。

（尹计秋）

实验十   可见分光光度法测定磺基水杨酸合铁(Ⅲ)的组成和稳定常数

【实验目的】

1. 巩固对可见分光光度法基本原理的理解。
2. 掌握分光光度计的使用方法。
3. 了解分光光度法测定溶液中配合物的组成和稳定常数的原理和方法。

【预习作业】

模拟设计实验:参照本实验步骤,以流程图方式给出本实验的设计思路,以测定配合物的最大吸收波长、组成及稳定常数。请在流程图的实验步骤中注明相应的注意事项及缘由。

引导问题:

1. 分光光度法测定物质浓度时显色剂是如何选择的?
2. 本实验是如何控制磺基水杨酸合铁配合物组成的?

3. 本实验为什么选择高氯酸控制溶液的酸度？能够用其他酸代替高氯酸吗？

4. 如何选择测定波长？如何选择合适的参比溶液？本实验的参比溶液是什么？

5. 通过文献查阅,总结测定配合物的组成和稳定常数的方法有哪些？本实验选择哪种方法？

6. 用等摩尔系列法测定配合物的组成时,为什么溶液中金属离子与配体的组成与配合物中金属离子与配体的组成一致时,配合物的浓度最大？

【实验原理】

金属离子 M 和配位体 L 形成配位化合物的反应为

$$M + nL \rightleftharpoons ML_n（忽略离子的电荷）$$

$$K_s = \frac{[ML_n]}{[M][L]^n} \tag{6-10-1}$$

式(6-10-1)中的 n 为配合物的配位数,K_s 为配合物的稳定常数。

如果 M 和 L 都是无色的,而 ML_n 有色,根据 Lambert-Beer 定律 $A = \varepsilon bc$,则此溶液的吸光度与配合物浓度成正比。通过测定溶液的吸光度,可求出该配合物的组成和稳定常数,本实验采用等摩尔系列法进行测定。

所谓等摩尔系列法又称为连续变化法、浓度比递变法,是将相同摩尔浓度的金属离子溶液和配体溶液,在保持金属离子与配体溶液总体积不变的前提下,按照不同的体积比(亦即摩尔浓度之比)混合,以配合物最大吸收波长为入射光,测量该系列混合溶液的吸光度。当溶液中配合物的浓度最大时,配位数 n 为

$$n = \frac{c(L)}{c(M)} = \frac{1-f}{f} \tag{6-10-2}$$

式(6-10-2)中 $c(M)$ 和 $c(L)$ 分别为金属离子和配体的浓度;f 为金属离子在总浓度中所占分数。且有

$$c(M) + c(L) = c = 常数 \tag{6-10-3}$$

$$f = \frac{c(M)}{c} \tag{6-10-4}$$

以吸光度 A 对 f 作图(图 6-10-1)。当 $f=0$ 或 $f=1$ 时,没有加入金属离子或没有加入配体,没有配合物生成,即配合物的浓度为零。当溶液中金属离子与配体的摩尔比与配合物组成一致时,配合物浓度才能最大。图中吸光度值最大处的 f 值,即为配合物浓度达最大时的 f 值。例如:1∶1 型配合物,吸光度值最大处的 f 值为 0.5,1∶2 型的 f 值为 0.34 等。

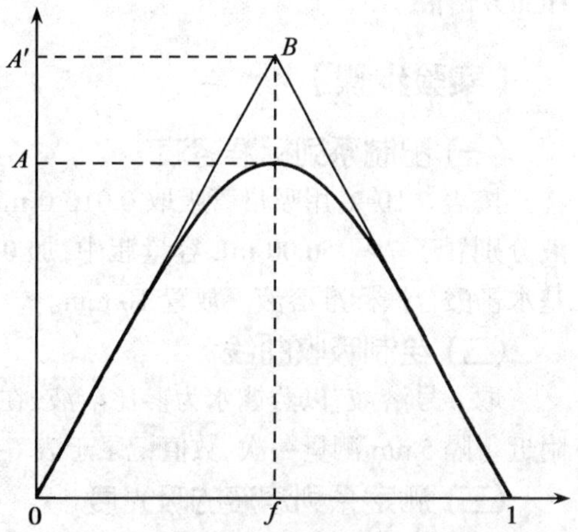

若配合物为 ML,从图 6-10-1 可知,测得的最大吸光度为 A,它略低于延长线交点 B 的吸光度 A',这是因为配合物有一定程度的解离,A' 为配合物完全不解离时的吸光度值,A' 与 A 之间差别愈小,说明配合物愈稳定。由此可计算出配合物的稳定常数

图 6-10-1　吸光度-组成图

$$K_s = \frac{[ML]}{[M][L]} \tag{6-10-5}$$

因配合物溶液的吸光度与配合物的浓度成正比,故

$$\frac{A}{A'} = \frac{[ML]}{c'} \qquad (6\text{-}10\text{-}6)$$

式(6-10-6)中 c' 为配合物未离解时的浓度

$$c' = c(M) = c(L) \qquad (6\text{-}10\text{-}7)$$

而

$$[M] = [L] = c' - c'\frac{A}{A'} = c'\left[1 - \frac{A}{A'}\right] \qquad (6\text{-}10\text{-}8)$$

将式(6-10-6)和式(6-10-8)代入式(6-10-5),整理后得配合物的稳定常数的计算式(6-10-9)

$$K_s = \frac{\dfrac{A}{A'}}{\left[1 - \dfrac{A}{A'}\right]^2 c'} \qquad (6\text{-}10\text{-}9)$$

Fe^{3+} 与磺基水杨酸(H_2Ssal)形成配合物的组成因溶液 pH 不同而不同,在 pH 1.8~2.5 时,生成含一个配体的紫红色配合物;pH = 4~8 时,生成含有两个配体的红色配合物;pH 8~11.5 时,生成含有三个配体的黄色配合物;pH>12 时,有色配合物被破坏而生成 $Fe(OH)_3$ 沉淀。在溶液中,磺基水杨酸无色,Fe^{3+} 在溶液中呈现浅黄色,磺基水杨酸合铁配离子呈紫红色。在配离子的最大吸收波长处,溶液的吸光度与配合物的浓度成正比。因此,通过测定溶液吸光度,可以求出该配合物的组成。本实验是测定 Fe^{3+} 与磺基水杨酸在 pH 2~3 条件下形成配合物的组成和稳定常数,实验中通过加入一定量的 $HClO_4$ 溶液来控制溶液的 pH,其主要优点是 ClO_4^- 不易与金属离子配合,同时其强氧化性还可用于阻止 Fe^{3+} 水解及还原为 Fe^{2+}。

【仪器材料和试剂】

仪器　分光光度计,容量瓶(50 mL×7),吸量管(10 mL×2),滴管 1 支。

材料与试剂　0.010 00 mol·L⁻¹ 磺基水杨酸溶液,0.010 00 mol·L⁻¹ 硫酸铁铵溶液,0.1 mol·L⁻¹ $HClO_4$ 溶液。

【实验步骤】

(一)配制系列标准溶液

按表 6-10-2,用吸量管吸取 0.010 0 mol·L⁻¹ 的磺基水杨酸溶液和 0.010 0 mol·L⁻¹ 硫酸铁铵溶液分别置于 7 只 50.00 mL 容量瓶中,加 0.1 mol·L⁻¹ $HClO_4$ 稀释至刻度,摇匀,即得不同浓度的磺基水杨酸合铁标准溶液。放置 10 min。

(二)绘制吸收曲线

取 4 号溶液,以蒸馏水为参比溶液,在波长 400~700 nm 范围,每隔 10 nm 测一次吸光度,峰值附近每隔 5 nm 测量一次,数值记录于表 6-10-1,绘制吸收曲线,找出最大吸收波长,λ_{max}。

(三)测定系列溶液的吸光度

以该配合物最大吸收波长 λ_{max} 为入射光,测定步骤 1 配制的系列溶液的吸光度,记录结果于表 6-10-2。

【数据记录与结果分析】

日期：_____　温度：_____℃　相对湿度：_____

(一)绘制吸收曲线确定测定波长

表 6-10-1　磺基水杨酸合铁溶液吸收曲线测定

λ/nm	
A	
λ_{max}/nm	

吸收曲线：

$\lambda_{max} =$ _____ nm。

(二)配合物组成

以金属离子物质的量浓度与总物质的量浓度之比为横坐标,吸光度为纵坐标,作 A-f 图,确定溶液 pH 2~3 时配合物组成,并给出分子式。

表 6-10-2　磺基水杨酸合铁溶液配制及吸光度 A 测定

实验序号	1	2	3	4	5	6	7
0.010 0 mol·L^{-1} H_2Ssal 溶液/mL	1.00	2.00	3.00	5.00	7.00	8.00	9.00
0.010 0 mol·L^{-1} $NH_4Fe(SO_4)_2$ 溶液/mL	9.00	8.00	7.00	5.00	3.00	2.00	1.00
0.1 mol·L^{-1} $HClO_4$ 溶液/mL				40			
A							
$f = \dfrac{c(M)}{c}$							

(三)磺基水杨酸合铁的稳定常数

从 A-f 图中,查得最大吸光度 A,延长曲线两边的直线部分,相交于一点,这一点即为配合物未解离时的吸光度 A',求得 c' 并代入式(6-10-9)求出磺基水杨酸合铁的稳定常数。

【思考题】

1. 等摩尔系列法测定配合物的稳定常数有什么条件?
2. 酸度对磺基水杨酸合铁配合物的组成有什么影响?

(秦向阳)

实验十一　紫外分光光度法对维生素 B_{12} 的鉴别与含量测定

【实验目的】

1. 掌握紫外分光光度计的使用方法。
2. 掌握紫外分光光度法定性鉴别维生素 B_{12} 的方法。

【预习作业】

模拟设计实验:参照本实验步骤,以流程图方式给出本实验的设计思路,找出准确测定维生素 B_{12} 含量的实验步骤,并在流程图中的实验步骤注明相应的注意事项及缘由。

引导问题:

1. 写出维生素 B_{12} 的化学结构,其在体内的主要功能有哪些?

2. 简要叙述紫外分光光度法的基本原理。

3. 查阅相关文献,紫外分光光度法测定维生素 B_{12} 的准确度受哪些因素的影响?

4. 查阅《中华人民共和国药典(2025 年版)》,指出维生素 B_{12} 的鉴别、检测方法及紫外分光光度法的要求。

【实验原理】

紫外分光光度法是通过测定在紫外光区(200~400 nm)有特定吸收波长或一定波长范围的被测物质的吸光度,对该物质进行定性和定量分析的方法,且吸收强度与被测物质浓度的关系符合 Lambert-Beer 定律。

维生素 B_{12} 是钴配位化合物(配体为卟啉环,分子式:$C_{63}H_{88}CoN_{14}O_{14}P$,$M_r = 1\ 355.38$),为深红色吸湿性结晶,其注射液标示量为 500 $\mu g \cdot mL^{-1}$、250 $\mu g \cdot mL^{-1}$、100 $\mu g \cdot mL^{-1}$、50 $\mu g \cdot mL^{-1}$ 等。维生素 B_{12} 的注射液在 278 nm、361 nm、550 nm 三个波长处有最大吸收,这三个波长的吸光度的比值,可作为维生素 B_{12} 定性鉴别的依据。其比值范围分别为:

$$A_{361\ nm}/A_{278\ nm} = 1.70 \sim 1.88 \qquad A_{361\ nm}/A_{550\ nm} = 3.15 \sim 3.45$$

其在 361 nm 波长处的吸收强度最大、干扰较少。测定 361 nm 波长处的吸光度,根据维生素 B_{12} 的吸收系数(为 $E_{1\ cm}^{1\%} = 207$),可计算出维生素 B_{12} 的浓度

$$A_{361\ nm} = E_{1\ cm}^{1\%} \cdot b \cdot c \qquad (6\text{-}11\text{-}1)$$

式(6-11-1)中,$E_{1\ cm}^{1\%}$ 指在一定波长时,溶液浓度为 1% [$g \cdot (100\ mL)^{-1}$],液层厚度为 1 cm 时的吸光度数值,A 为溶液的吸光度,b 为液层厚度,c 为溶液浓度。

测定维生素 B_{12} 注射液的含量,浓度单位应表示为 $\mu g \cdot mL^{-1}$。在计算时,需将浓度单位为 1 $g \cdot (100\ mL)^{-1}$ 的吸收系数 $E_{1\ cm}^{1\%}$ 361 nm = 207 换算成浓度单位为 $\mu g \cdot mL^{-1}$ 的吸收系数,即

$$E_{1\ cm}^{1\ \mu g \cdot L^{-1}}\ 361\ nm = \frac{207 \times 100}{10^6} = 207 \times 10^{-4} \qquad (6\text{-}11\text{-}2)$$

【仪器材料与试剂】

仪器　紫外可见分光光度计,容量瓶(10 mL × 3),吸量管(1 mL),烧杯(100 mL),滴管。

材料与试剂　维生素 B_{12} 注射液(500 $\mu g \cdot mL^{-1}$)。

【实验步骤】

(一) 样品溶液的配制

取 3 支维生素 B_{12} 注射液样品,用吸量管各吸取 0.50 mL,分别置于 3 个 10 mL 容量瓶中,加蒸馏水稀释至刻度,摇匀,配成样品溶液。

(二) 维生素 B_{12} 定性鉴别及注射液样品含量测定

用 1 cm 石英比色皿,以蒸馏水作空白,在仪器上找出样品溶液在 278 nm、361 nm 及 550 nm

处的吸收峰,读取吸光度值。每个样品平行测定 3 次,取其平均值。

【注意事项】

1. 样品溶液必须澄清,不得有浑浊。
2. 通常样品溶液的吸光度读数,在 0.2~0.7 之间的误差较小。
3. 在测定不同样品时,应用待测溶液冲洗吸收池 3~4 次,用擦镜纸擦至吸收池的透光面无斑痕(切忌把透光面磨损)。
4. 测定时不要打开仪器的样品池盖。

【数据记录及结果分析】

(一) 维生素 B$_{12}$ 的定性鉴别

计算三个不同波长处的吸光度比值($A_{361\,nm}/A_{278\,nm}$,$A_{361\,nm}/A_{550\,nm}$),并与《中华人民共和国药典(2020 年版)》规定($A_{361\,nm}/A_{278\,nm}=1.70\sim1.88$;$A_{361\,nm}/A_{550\,nm}=3.15\sim3.45$)进行对照(表 6-11-1)。

表 6-11-1　维生素 B$_{12}$ 的吸收光谱测定

λ/nm	361	278	550
A			
$A_{361\,nm}/A_{278\,nm}$:		$A_{361\,nm}/A_{550\,nm}$:	

(二) 维生素 B$_{12}$ 注射液样品含量

根据 361 nm 处测定的吸光度,浓度单位为 µg·mL^{-1} 的吸收系数,及注射液稀释倍数,计算注射液待测样品中维生素 B$_{12}$ 的含量(µg·mL^{-1})。

$$\rho = \frac{A}{E_{1\,cm}^{1\,\mu g \cdot L^{-1}}} = \frac{A}{207 \times 10^{-4}} = A \times 48.31 \ (\mu g \cdot mL^{-1}) \tag{6-11-3}$$

则原维生素 B$_{12}$ 注射液:$\rho_{原} = A \times 48.31 \times 20$(稀释倍数)(µg·mL^{-1})

测定值在所用维生素 B$_{12}$ 注射液浓度标示值(材料和试剂中给定的值)的 90%~110% 之间即可视为合格。

【思考题】

1. 测定前应先在仪器上找出三个最大吸收峰的确切位置,意义何在?
2. 如果取注射液 2 mL 用水稀释 15 倍,在 361 nm 处测得 A 值为 0.698,试计算注射液每毫升含维生素 B$_{12}$ 多少微克?
3. 采用吸光系数法直接测定样品含量有何要求?

(武世奎)

实验十二　荧光分光光度法测定维生素 B$_2$ 的含量

【实验目的】

1. 掌握荧光分光光度法测定物质含量的原理和方法。

2. 了解荧光光度计的基本构造。

3. 学会 930 型荧光光度计的使用。

【预习作业】

模拟设计实验:参照本实验步骤,以流程图方式给出本实验的设计思路,并在流程图中注明相应的注意事项及缘由。

引导问题:

1. 在荧光测定过程中,设定的激发光波长为什么比发射光波长短? 能否相等?

2. 物质分子产生荧光的条件是什么?

3. 在对多种维生素混合物的测量中,能否使用吸收光谱法测定维生素 B_2 的含量?

【实验原理】

某些物质受紫外光或可见光照射激发后,能发射出比激发光频率低(波长较长)的光,称为荧光。利用物质的荧光特征进行定性、定量分析的方法称为荧光分析法。

荧光物质不同,其特征激发光波长和荧光波长不同,这是荧光定性分析的基础。

当荧光物质的浓度极低时,荧光强度 F 与溶液质量浓度 ρ 有如下关系

$$F = 2.3\Phi I_0 ab\rho \tag{6-12-1}$$

式(6-12-1)中 Φ 为荧光效率,I_0 为入射光强度,a 为荧光物质的质量吸光系数,b 为样品池厚度。

对于同一荧光物质,当 I_0 及 b 固定时,荧光强度与该荧光物质的质量浓度成正比,这就是荧光定量分析的依据。

$$F = K'\rho \tag{6-12-2}$$

维生素 B_2 又称核黄素,是橙黄色结晶性粉末,其结构式如下:

维生素 B_2 分子式:$C_{17}H_{20}N_4O_6$($M_r = 376.37$)

维生素 B_2 的 $0.1\ mol \cdot L^{-1}$ HAc 溶液在紫外光照射下,发出黄绿色荧光,可直接进行荧光测定。激发波长可选择 360 nm、400 nm 或 420 nm,发射波长为 530 nm。

【仪器材料与试剂】

仪器 930 型-荧光分光光度计,万分之一分析天平,容量瓶(25 mL × 6,50 mL,1 000 mL),吸量管(1 mL,5 mL),小烧杯(100 mL),滴管,玻璃棒。

材料与试剂 $0.1\ mol \cdot L^{-1}$ HAc 溶液,维生素 B_2 结晶(生化试剂),维生素 B_2 片剂(待测)。

【实验步骤】

(一)维生素 B_2 标准溶液的配制

准确称取维生素 B_2 约 10.0 mg 置于小烧杯中,用少量 $0.1\ mol \cdot L^{-1}$ HAc 溶液溶解,转移至

1 000 mL 容量瓶,用 0.1 mol·L⁻¹ HAc 溶液稀释至刻度,摇匀,得到 10.0 μg·mL⁻¹ 维生素 B₂ 的储备标准溶液,低温、避光保存。

取 6 支 25 mL 容量瓶,分别加入 0.00 mL、0.50 mL、1.00 mL、1.50 mL、2.00 mL、2.50 mL 维生素 B₂ 的备用标准溶液,用 0.1 mol·L⁻¹ HAc 溶液稀释至刻度,摇匀,得系列维生素 B₂ 标准溶液。

(二)维生素 B₂ 标准曲线的绘制

按照荧光光度计的使用方法,接通电源,预热 10 min。选择 360 nm 或 400 nm 为激发波长,530 nm 为发射波长。用 0.1 mol·L⁻¹ HAc 溶液作参比溶液对仪器进行校正,将读数调至零;用浓度最大的标准溶液,调节荧光读数为满刻度。固定条件不变,按由稀至浓的顺序,测定系列标准溶液的荧光强度。根据所记录数据,以溶液浓度为横坐标,荧光强度为纵坐标,绘制标准曲线。

(三)试样测定

取待测维生素 B₂ 片剂一片,准确称量(精确至 0.000 1 g)后置于研钵研成粉末,用少量 0.1 mol·L⁻¹ HAc 溶液溶解,转移并稀释定容至 1 000 mL,贮存于棕色试剂瓶中。

取待测溶液 2.50 mL,置于 50 mL 容量瓶中,用 0.1 mol·L⁻¹ HAc 溶液稀释至刻度,摇匀。在与测定标准溶液相同条件下,测定待测样品的荧光强度。从标准曲线上查出对应的质量浓度 $\rho_{测}$,得到待测溶液维生素 B₂ 的质量浓度 $\rho_{样品}$。由测得溶液浓度,计算片剂中维生素 B₂ 的含量。

【数据记录及结果分析】

(一)维生素 B₂ 标准曲线的绘制

日期:＿＿＿＿＿＿＿＿　温度:＿＿＿＿＿＿＿＿℃　相对湿度:＿＿＿＿＿＿＿＿

表 6-12-1　维生素 B₂ 测定标准曲线的绘制和试样测定

实验序号	0	1	2	3	4	5	试样
m(维生素 B₂)/mg			10.0				—
$\rho_{贮备}$(维生素 B₂)/μg·mL⁻¹			10.0				—
$V_{标}$(维生素 B₂)/mL	0	0.50	1.00	1.50	2.00	2.50	—
$V_{总}$(0.1 mol·L⁻¹ HAc 稀释后)/mL			25.00				50.00
$\rho_{标}$(维生素 B₂)/μg·mL⁻¹	0	0.20	0.40	0.60	0.80	1.00	—
F							
m(待测片剂)/mg				—			

绘制标准曲线:根据表 6-12-1 记录的数据,以标准维生素 B₂ 的质量浓度(μg·mL⁻¹)为横坐标,荧光强度(F)为纵坐标绘制标准曲线。

标准曲线的回归方程为＿＿＿＿＿＿＿＿＿＿＿＿,相关系数为＿＿＿＿＿＿;

标准曲线上直接读出维生素 B₂ 的质量浓度 $\rho_{测}$ 为＿＿＿＿＿＿＿(μg·mL⁻¹)。

(二)试样维生素 B₂ 片剂浓度

$$\omega(\text{维生素B}_2)\% = \frac{\rho_{测}(\mu g \cdot mL^{-1}) \times 20(\text{稀释倍数}) \times 1\ 000\ mL \times 10^{-3}}{m\ (\text{待测片剂})} \quad (mg \cdot mg^{-1}) \quad (6\text{-}12\text{-}3)$$

【思考题】

1. 什么是激发光谱? 什么是发射光谱?
2. 为何用 $0.1 \ mol \cdot L^{-1}$ HAc 溶液来配制维生素 B_2 溶液?
3. 若选择 420 nm、440 nm 作为激发波长时,对测定结果有无影响?

(周昊霏)

第七章 | 化学原理实验

实验十三　稀溶液的依数性及其应用

【实验目的】

1. 掌握凝固点降低法测定溶质相对分子质量的原理和方法。
2. 学会使用冰点渗透压计并能准确测定溶液的渗透浓度及渗透压。
3. 学会用显微镜并了解动物血红细胞在不同渗透浓度溶液中的形态。
4. 学会用 0.10 ℃分度温度计。

【预习作业】

模拟设计实验:以流程图方式给出本实验测定溶质相对分子质量的设计思路,请在流程图实验步骤中注明相应的注意事项及原因。

引导问题:

1. 常用测定物质相对分子质量的方法有哪些? 实验中常用哪些方法? 为什么?
2. 浓度 $c_{os} \approx b_B$ 在什么条件下成立?
3. 为何溶剂和稀溶液的冷却曲线不同? 理想状态下冷却曲线的特征有哪些?
4. 凝固点降低实验中为什么要在冰水浴中加入较多粗盐?
5. 在渗透压测定实验中溶液为什么会出现过冷现象? 实验中应如何解决?
6. 实验时,尽管配制的葡萄糖溶液中葡萄糖溶解较慢,但也不能用玻璃棒搅拌以加快溶解,为什么?

【实验原理】

溶解难挥发的溶质形成稀溶液时,溶液的物理性质,如凝固点、渗透压等与纯溶剂不同,其性质的改变与溶质的量成正比,而与溶质的本性无关,这些性质统称为稀溶液的依数性。利用稀溶液的依数性,能准确地测定溶质的相对分子质量。

溶液的凝固点(T_f)低于溶剂的凝固点(T_f^0)。对于非电解质稀溶液,若其凝固点降低值为 ΔT_f,则有如下关系式

$$\Delta T_f^0 = T_f^0 - T_f = K_f b(B) \tag{7-13-1}$$

K_f 为溶剂的摩尔凝固点降低常数(K·kg·mol^{-1}),可从化学手册中查出其值。

根据下式

$$b(B) = \frac{m(B)\big/M(B)}{m(A)} \times 1\,000 \tag{7-13-2}$$

87

式（7-13-2）中，$b(B)$ 为溶液的质量摩尔浓度（$mol \cdot kg^{-1}$）；$m(B)$ 为溶质的质量（g）；$M(B)$ 为溶质的分子质量（$g \cdot mol^{-1}$）；$m(A)$ 为溶剂质量（g）。故得

$$M(B) = \frac{K_f m(B)}{m_A \Delta T_f} \times 1\,000 \tag{7-13-3}$$

通过实验测定的其他数值代入式（7-13-3），即可求出溶质的相对分子质量 $M(B)$（$g \cdot mol^{-1}$）。并计算测定的相对误差 E_r。

$$E_r(\%) = \frac{实验值 - 理论值}{理论值} \times 100\% \tag{7-13-4}$$

在溶液逐渐冷却时，通常用冷却曲线记录过程温度的变化，如图 7-13-1 所示。溶液中析出冰时释放了凝固热，溶液温度会迅速回升，并使溶液温度保持在短时间内的相对恒定，之后继续降低。溶剂（a）与稀溶液（b）的冷却曲线不同，稀溶液逐渐析出冰以后，使溶液的浓度逐渐增加，导致稀溶液的温度不像溶剂那样，没有恒定阶段，可将回升后的最高温度看作是稀溶液的凝固点 T_f。

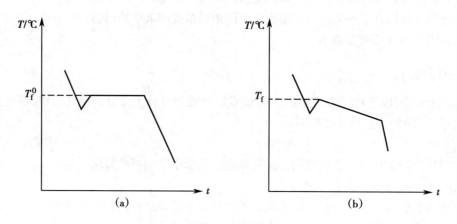

图 7-13-1　冷却曲线
（a）纯溶剂的冷却曲线；（b）稀溶液的冷却曲线。

冰点渗透压计是一种利用溶液凝固点降低的性质来测定溶液渗透压和渗透浓度的装置。非电解质稀溶液的凝固点降低与渗透浓度之间有下列关系

$$c_{os} \approx b(B) = \frac{\Delta T_f}{K_f} \tag{7-13-5}$$

式（7-13-5）中，c_{os} 为溶液的渗透浓度（$mol \cdot L^{-1}$）；以水为溶剂的稀溶液密度约等于 $1\ g \cdot cm^{-3}$，故

$$M(B) = \frac{m(B)}{m(A)c_{os}} \times 1\,000 \tag{7-13-6}$$

将一定质量的非电解质溶解在一定质量的溶剂中，通过冰点渗透压计测量出该溶液的渗透浓度，根据式（7-13-6）就可计算出该溶质的相对分子量 $M(B)$。

对稀溶液，其渗透压与渗透浓度及温度的关系如下

$$\Pi = c_{os} RT \tag{7-13-7}$$

Π 为溶液的渗透压（kPa）；R 为理想气体常数（$8.314\ J \cdot mol^{-1} \cdot K^{-1}$）；$T$ 为溶液的绝对温度（K）。

一定温度下，渗透浓度与渗透压成正比。因此，可以直接通过渗透浓度的大小来比较两溶液

渗透压的高低。渗透浓度大的溶液称为高渗溶液,渗透浓度小的称为低渗溶液。若用半透膜将两种渗透浓度不同的溶液分隔开,将发生渗透现象,溶剂从低渗溶液经过半透膜进入高渗溶液。

渗透浓度的测定在临床医学和其他领域都有广泛应用。临床上是以正常人血浆的渗透浓度($280\sim320$ mmol·L^{-1})为标准,规定在此渗透浓度(或渗透压)定溶液范围内的为等渗溶液。若溶液的渗透浓度低于 280 mmol·L^{-1} 称为低渗溶液,高于 320 mmol·L^{-1} 称为高渗溶液。红细胞在等渗溶液中形态正常;在高渗或低渗溶液中,形态都会发生变化。

一、凝固点降低法测定葡萄糖的摩尔质量

【仪器材料与试剂】

仪器　万分之一分析天平,温度计(0.10 ℃),放大镜,干燥大试管(40 mm × 150 mm),套管,烧杯(500 mL),移液管(50 mL),洗耳球,搅拌器,量筒(100 mL)。

材料与试剂　葡萄糖(A.R.,固体),粗盐或食盐,冰块,蒸馏水。

【实验步骤】

(一) 葡萄糖的称取

在万分之一分析天平上准确称取 4.2~5.1 g(精确至 0.000 1 g)葡萄糖于洁净干燥的大试管中。

(二) 测定稀葡萄糖溶液的平均凝固点

用移液管准确吸取 50.00 mL 蒸馏水,放入盛有葡萄糖的大试管中,摇动试管使葡萄糖全部溶解(不能用玻璃棒搅拌!)。大烧杯中加入少量自来水、足量的冰块和粗盐,混匀(使冰水浴温度在-5 ℃以下);如图 7-13-2 所示,将大试管插入套管内,放在大烧杯中。

用搅拌器搅动大试管内的葡萄糖溶液使其慢慢冷却,同时借助放大镜密切注意观察温度计的读数,适时补充适量冰块和粗盐,并移除多余的融化冰水,当稀葡萄糖溶液的温度足够低时,直至成为过冷溶液后,溶液中的溶剂逐渐凝结析出冰。此时,停止搅拌,仔细观察温度的变化,并多次记录回升后的温度,找出相对恒定的最高值(精确至 0.01 ℃),并取平均值。

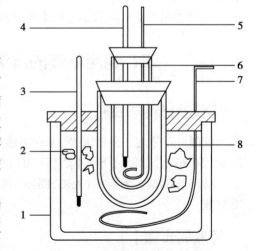

图 7-13-2　凝固点测定装置图
1. 烧杯;2. 冰块;3,4. 温度计;5,7. 搅拌器;6. 大试管;8. 外套管。

取出大试管,流水冲洗试管下部外表,直至试管内的冰全部融化,将含有原溶液的大试管再插入套管内,重复测定凝固点的操作,平行测定三次。任意两个测定值之差不得超过 0.05 ℃,均值即为葡萄糖溶液的凝固点 T_f。

(三) 测定溶剂的凝固点

将同一大试管洗净,用配制溶液的蒸馏水洗涤 3 次后,取此蒸馏水约 50 mL,放入大试管中,按上述方法测定蒸馏水的凝固点 T_f^0,并取平均值。

【数据记录与结果分析】

将水的摩尔凝固点降低常数 K_f(1.86 K·kg·mol^{-1})及各测定值代入式(7-13-3),计算所测定的

葡萄糖分子量。按式(7-13-4)计算测定的相对误差。将数据和结果记录在表 7-13-1 中。

日期:＿＿＿＿＿＿＿＿＿＿ 温度:＿＿＿＿＿＿＿＿＿＿ ℃ 相对湿度:＿＿＿＿＿＿＿＿＿＿

表 7-13-1 凝固点降低法测定葡萄糖的分子量

实验序号	1	2	3
$m(\text{A})/\text{g}$			
$m(\text{B})/\text{g}$			
$T_f/℃$			
$T_f^0/℃$			
$\Delta T_f/℃$			
$M(\text{B})/\text{g}\cdot\text{mol}^{-1}$			
$E_r/\%$			

【注意事项】

实验中使用大量冰块且温度较低,在搅拌的过程中注意保护玻璃套管、试管和温度计,以免碎裂。

【思考题】

1. 血清、尿液等生物样品的凝固点是否能用本实验方法测定? 为什么? 凝固点降低法适合测定哪类物质的相对分子量?

2. 能否用沸点升高法测定葡萄糖的相对分子质量?

二、利用溶液的渗透浓度测定葡萄糖的摩尔质量

【仪器材料与试剂】

仪器 万分之一分析天平,冰点渗透压计,渗透压测定专用试管(2 mL),吸量管(1 mL),移液管(50 mL),洗耳球,干燥小烧杯(100 mL),容量瓶(100 mL)。

材料与试剂 葡萄糖(A.R.,固体),渗透浓度 c_{os} 为 0.300 mol·kg^{-1} 和 0.800 mol·kg^{-1} NaCl 标准溶液。

【实验步骤】

(一)葡萄糖溶液的制备

在万分之一分析天平上准确称量 9.1~9.5 g(精确至 0.000 1 g)葡萄糖于 100 mL 洁净干燥的小烧杯中,用移液管准确吸取 50.00 mL 蒸馏水,放入盛有葡萄糖的小烧杯中,使葡萄糖全部溶解(不用玻璃棒搅拌!)。

(二)冰点渗透压计的校正

实验前,仔细阅读冰点渗透压计的使用说明。按照冰点渗透压计的使用方法开启冰点渗透压计,使仪器中的冷却池降到适当的冷却温度(−10 ～ −8 ℃)。

用吸量管取 0.50 mL 渗透浓度为 0.300 mol·kg^{-1} 的 NaCl 标准溶液于干燥的渗透压测定专用的 2 mL 小试管中，在冰点渗透压计上测定其渗透浓度，反复调整测量值稳定在 0.300 mol·kg^{-1} 处；再用吸量管取 0.50 mL 渗透浓度为 0.800 mol·kg^{-1} 的 NaCl 标准溶液于另一个干燥的专用小试管中，在冰点渗透压计上测定其渗透浓度，反复调整其值稳定在 0.800 mol·kg^{-1} 处。

（三）测定葡萄糖溶液的渗透浓度（渗透压）

用吸量管取 0.50 mL 已配制好的葡萄糖溶液于干燥的专用小试管中，在冰点渗透压计上测定其渗透浓度，重复测定三次。取平均值作为该葡萄糖溶液的渗透浓度。

【数据记录与结果分析】

按式（7-13-6）计算葡萄糖的相对分子质量，并按式（7-13-4）计算测定的相对误差。将数据和结果记录在表 7-13-2 中。

日期：_____　　温度：_____℃　相对湿度：_____

表 7-13-2　利用溶液的渗透浓度测定葡萄糖的分子量

实验序号	1	2	3
$m(A)/g$			
$m(B)/g$			
$c_{os}/mol·L^{-1}$			
$M(B)/g·mol^{-1}$			
$E_r/\%$			

【思考题】

1. 室温下用冰点渗透压计测定出溶液渗透浓度后，如何确定溶液渗透压？
2. 用冰点渗透压计测定溶液的渗透浓度时，应注意哪些问题？

（傅　迎）

三、冰点渗透压计的应用

【仪器材料与试剂】

仪器　普通显微镜，载玻片 ×5，冰点渗透压计，渗透压测定专用小试管（2 mL），试管（20 mL），吸量管（1.00 mL），洗耳球，干燥小烧杯（100 mL），量筒，胶头滴管 ×5，玻璃棒。

材料与试剂　NaCl 标准溶液（c_{os}=0.30 mol·L^{-1} 和 0.80 mol·L^{-1}），NaCl 高渗溶液（c_{os}=0.35 mol·L^{-1}），NaCl 低渗溶液（c_{os}=0.050 mol·L^{-1}），生理盐水，葡萄糖溶液（54 g·L^{-1}），聚乙烯醇滴眼液，动物血液，抗凝剂。

【实验步骤】

（一）冰点渗透压计的校正
方法同第一篇第二章中"三、常用仪器使用方法"。

（二）溶液渗透压的测定

用吸量管移取 0.50 mL 高渗溶液（0.35 mol·L⁻¹ NaCl）于干燥的渗透压测定专用小试管中，在冰点渗透压计上测定渗透浓度，重复测定三次，取平均值作为该溶液的渗透浓度。分别用 0.50 mL 低渗溶液（0.050 mol·L⁻¹ NaCl）、等渗溶液（生理盐水、54 g·L⁻¹ 葡萄糖溶液）、聚乙烯醇滴眼液代替 0.50 mL 高渗溶液重复上述实验，记录各种溶液的渗透浓度于表 7-13-3 中。

（三）红细胞悬液的制备

取新鲜的动物（小白鼠或大白兔）血液 1.00 mL，加入 20.0 mL 含抗凝剂（0.050 mol·L⁻¹ 枸橼酸钠或 EDTA 二钠盐溶液 10 滴）的等渗溶液，轻轻搅拌均匀后备用。

（四）观察红细胞的形态

取五支试管，分别加入 1.00 mL 0.35 mol·L⁻¹ NaCl 溶液、0.050 mol·L⁻¹ NaCl 溶液、生理盐水、54 g·L⁻¹ 葡萄糖溶液和聚乙烯醇滴眼液，每支试管中加入 0.10 mL 红细胞悬液，轻轻摇匀，15~20 分钟后，在普通显微镜上观察红细胞的形态。

实验前，仔细阅读普通显微镜的使用方法并调试好显微镜。从五支试管中分别取一滴溶液放在不同的载玻片上，刮去多余的溶液，分别将载玻片放在显微镜上，观察并记录红细胞的形态于表 7-13-4 中。

【数据记录与结果分析】

日期：_____ 温度：_____ ℃ 相对湿度：_____

表 7-13-3 溶液渗透浓度的测定

实验序号	1	2	3
0.35 mol·L⁻¹ NaCl			
0.050 mol·L⁻¹ NaCl			
生理盐水			
54 g·L⁻¹ 葡萄糖			
聚乙烯醇滴眼液			

表 7-13-4 红细胞在不同渗透浓度溶液中的形态

溶液	0.35 mol·L⁻¹ NaCl	0.050 mol·L⁻¹ NaCl	生理盐水	54 g·L⁻¹ 葡萄糖	聚乙烯醇滴眼液
红细胞形态					

【思考题】

1. 红细胞在低渗、等渗和高渗溶液中各呈什么形态？如何解释这些现象？
2. 为什么在淡水中游泳眼睛会感到胀痛，而在海水中游泳感觉会好得多？

（白天语）

实验十四　置换法测定镁的相对原子量

【实验目的】

1. 掌握电子分析天平的使用。
2. 掌握气体体积的测量方法。
3. 掌握镁的相对原子量测定原理与方法。

【预习作业】

模拟设计实验：以流程图方式，写出本实验测定镁原子量的设计步骤，并注明各步骤的注意事项及原因。

引导问题：

1. 置换法测定镁的原子量的原理是什么？
2. 检查漏气与否的操作原理是什么？
3. 开始测定体积前量气管内的气泡没有赶尽，对实验结果有何影响？
4. 如果镁条表面上的氧化膜未擦除干净，对实验结果有何影响？
5. 反应后如没有完全冷却就记录滴定管液面位置，对实验结果有何影响？
6. 读取读数时，为什么要使量气管和漏斗中的液面保持在同一水平面上？

【实验原理】

镁是活泼金属，与稀硫酸发生置换反应产生氢气。反应式如下：

$$H_2SO_4 + Mg \xrightarrow{\quad\quad} H_2 \uparrow + MgSO_4$$

准确称取一定质量的金属镁，与过量的稀硫酸反应，在一定温度（t）和压力（p）下测出被置换出来的氢气的体积 $V(H_2)$，根据化学计量关系和理想气体状态方程 $pV = nRT$，可计算出 $n(Mg)$

$$n(Mg) = n(H_2) = \frac{p(H_2) \times V(H_2)}{R \times T} \tag{7-14-1}$$

式（7-14-1）中，$p(H_2)$ 为氢气的分压（kPa），$V(H_2)$ 为收集到的反应气体的体积（L），R 为气体常数（8.314 J·mol^{-1}·K^{-1}），T 为绝对温度（273.15 $+ t$ ℃）（K）。

由于量气管（滴定管）内收集的氢气是被水蒸气所饱和的，根据分压定律，若量气管内气压等于大气压时，其压力 p 是氢气分压 $p(H_2)$ 与饱和水蒸气压 $p(H_2O)$ 的总和，即

$$p_{大气压} = p(H_2) + p_{饱和}(H_2O) \tag{7-14-2}$$

$$p(H_2) = p_{大气压} - p_{饱和}(H_2O) \tag{7-14-3}$$

镁的相对原子量 $A_r(Mg)$ 可以通过下式计算

$$A_r(Mg) = \frac{m(Mg)}{n(Mg)} = \frac{m(Mg) \times R \times T}{\left[p_{大气压} - p_{饱和}(H_2O)\right] \times V(H_2)} \tag{7-14-4}$$

式（7-14-4）中，$m(Mg)$ 为镁条的质量，$n(Mg)$ 为镁条的物质的量。

【仪器材料与试剂】

仪器 万分之一电子分析天平,温度计,气压计,铁架台,量气管(50 mL 碱式滴定管),大试管(20 mL),长颈漏斗(×2)或长滴管,量筒(10 mL)。

材料与试剂 镁条(约 25~35 mg),具塞导管,橡皮管,细砂纸,2 mol·L^{-1} H$_2$SO$_4$ 溶液,甘油,橡皮塞。

【实验步骤】

(一)称量

用万分之一电子分析天平准确称取三份已用砂纸或 2 mol·L^{-1} 稀硫酸去除表面氧化膜的干净镁条,每份重在 0.03 g 左右(±0.000 1 g),并用铅笔分别标上 1、2 和 3 数字,分别包好。

(二)安装仪器

按图 7-14-1 装配好仪器,向量气管(50 mL 碱式滴定管)内注水至略低于刻度"0"的位置。上下移动漏斗,以赶尽附着在胶管和量气管内壁的气泡。

(三)检查装置的气密性

将连接量气管和大试管的塞子塞紧,把漏斗缓慢下移一段距离,并固定在一定位置上。量气管中的液面稍有下降,待液面稳定后读数,3 min 后再次读数,若两数据相同,说明装置不漏气;否则说明装置漏气,必须检查并塞紧各接口处。重复气密性试验,直至系统不漏气为止。

(四)装硫酸、贴镁条

取下大试管,用量筒量取 5.0 mL 2 mol·L^{-1} H$_2$SO$_4$ 溶液经长颈漏斗小心注入试管底部(切勿使酸沾在试管壁上)。稍稍倾斜试管,用少量甘油或水将镁条湿润一下,贴在试管壁内上部,确保镁条不与硫酸接触。调整量气管液面,使之尽量接近 0 刻度,并装好试管,塞紧橡皮塞。重复气密性试验,确保装置不漏气。

(五)记录初始液面位置

把漏斗移至量气管右侧,使两者的液面保持在同一水平面上,记下量气管中初读数 $V_{初}$。

(六)化学反应

适当倾斜铁架台,让镁条与稀硫酸接触(尽量不让硫酸冲出试管进入量气管),反应产生的氢气进入量气管中。为避免管内压力过大,在管内液面下降时,漏斗也相应地向下移动,使两者的液面大体上保持在同一水平面上。

(七)记录终读数

反应完全后,用自来水淋洗试管外壁,待整个系统冷却至室温,使漏斗与量气管的液面处于同一水平面上,记下液面读数。稍等 1~2 min,再次读数,如两次读数相等,表明反应体系温度已与室温一致,否则继续冷却后读数,直至连续两次读数相等为止,记录终读数 $V_{终}$。取下大试管,倒出溶液,将试管冲洗干净。

(八)记录室温和反应进行时所对应的大气压

平行测定 3 次。将数据记录于表 7-14-1 中,根据测量数据计算结果,并根据镁的理论原子量计算镁原子量测定的相对误差。

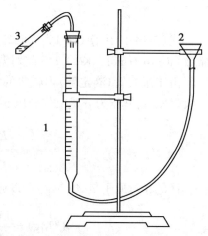

图 7-14-1 测定镁原子量装置示意图
1. 量气管;2. 漏斗;3. 大试管。

【数据记录与结果分析】

日期：＿＿＿＿＿＿＿＿ 温度：＿＿＿＿＿℃ 相对湿度：＿＿＿＿＿＿＿＿

表 7-14-1 置换法测定镁的原子量

实验序号	1	2	3
$m(\mathrm{Mg})/\mathrm{g}$			
$V(\mathrm{H_2SO_4})/\mathrm{mL}$			
$V_{初}/\mathrm{mL}$			
$V_{终}/\mathrm{mL}$			
$V(\mathrm{H_2})/\mathrm{mL}$			
T/K			
$p_{大气压}/\mathrm{kPa}$			
$p_{饱和}(\mathrm{H_2O})/\mathrm{kPa}$			
$p(\mathrm{H_2})/\mathrm{kPa}$			
$A_{\mathrm{r}}(\mathrm{Mg})$			
$\overline{A_{\mathrm{r}}}(\mathrm{Mg})$			
$A_{\mathrm{r}理论}(\mathrm{Mg})$			
相对平均误差 $E_{\mathrm{r}}/\%$			

（1 atm = 760.15 mmHg = 101.325 kPa，水的饱和蒸气压可从附录中查到）

$$E_{\mathrm{r}} = \frac{A_{\mathrm{r}}(\mathrm{Mg})_{测定值} - A_{\mathrm{r}}(\mathrm{Mg})_{理论}}{A_{\mathrm{r}}(\mathrm{Mg})_{理论}} \times 100\% \qquad (7\text{-}14\text{-}5)$$

【思考题】

1. 分析可能导致本实验产生测定误差的原因。
2. 反应时试管中的硫酸冲入量气管对实验测定结果会有影响吗？

（宋　慧）

实验十五　化学反应速率与活化能的测定

【实验目的】

1. 掌握浓度、温度、催化剂对化学反应速率的影响。
2. 通过测定 $(\mathrm{NH_4})_2\mathrm{S_2O_8}$ 氧化 KI 的化学反应速率，计算反应级数、速率常数及活化能。
3. 掌握作图法处理实验数据的方法。

【预习作业】

模拟设计实验：参照本实验步骤，以流程图方式给出本实验的设计思路，并在流程图中注明相应实验步骤的注意事项及原因。

引导问题:

1. 影响化学反应速率的因素主要有哪些?如何影响?
2. 本实验以 $(NH_4)_2S_2O_8 + 3KI = (NH_4)_2SO_4 + K_2SO_4 + KI_3$ 为研究对象,怎样测定其反应速率?
3. 如何测定化学反应中各个反应物的反应级数?
4. 升高温度可以加快化学反应速率,为什么?
5. 如何测定化学反应的活化能?
6. 催化剂可以改变化学反应速率,为什么?

【实验原理】

在水溶液中,$(NH_4)_2S_2O_8$ 与 KI 的氧化还原反应如下

$$(NH_4)_2S_2O_8 + 3KI = (NH_4)_2SO_4 + K_2SO_4 + KI_3$$

或

$$S_2O_8^{2-} + 3I^- = 2SO_4^{2-} + I_3^- \tag{7-15-1}$$

其反应速率为

$$v = kc(S_2O_8^{2-})^m c(I^-)^n \tag{7-15-2}$$

式(7-15-2)中,v 是反应速率;k 是速率常数;m 是 $S_2O_8^{2-}$ 的反应级数;n 是 I^- 的反应级数;m 与 n 之和为反应总级数。

为了测定反应速率,必须知道在一段时间内 $S_2O_8^{2-}$ 浓度的变化。其反应的平均速率可以表示为

$$\bar{v} = -\frac{\Delta c(S_2O_8^{2-})}{\Delta t} \tag{7-15-3}$$

可以用平均速率近似地代替起始时的瞬时速率

$$v = -\frac{\Delta c(S_2O_8^{2-})}{\Delta t} \approx kc(S_2O_8^{2-})^m c(I^-)^n \tag{7-15-4}$$

为了测定出在 Δt 时间内 $S_2O_8^{2-}$ 浓度的变化,在 $(NH_4)_2S_2O_8$ 与 KI 溶液混合前,先在溶液中加入确定量的 $Na_2S_2O_3$ 和淀粉溶液,反应生成的 I_3^- 能很快与 $Na_2S_2O_3$ 反应,生成无色的 $S_4O_6^{2-}$ 和 I^-:

$$2S_2O_3^{2-} + I_3^- = S_4O_6^{2-} + 3I^- \tag{7-15-5}$$

主反应生成的 I_3^- 能与淀粉作用,使溶液变为蓝色。但反应体系中加入的少量 $Na_2S_2O_3$ 能更快速地与 I_3^- 反应,所以实验开始时看不到蓝色,当 $Na_2S_2O_3$ 耗尽时,溶液变蓝。

由反应式(7-15-1)和式(7-15-5)的关系可知,$S_2O_8^{2-}$ 减少的量为 $S_2O_3^{2-}$ 减少量的一半,所以

$$\Delta c(S_2O_8^{2-}) = \frac{\Delta c(S_2O_3^{2-})}{2} \tag{7-15-6}$$

由于少量的 $Na_2S_2O_3$ 在 Δt 内完全耗尽,所以 $\Delta c(S_2O_8^{2-})$ 就是 $Na_2S_2O_3$ 的起始浓度。记录从反应开始到溶液出现蓝色所用的时间 Δt,由式(7-15-4)求得反应速率

$$v = -\frac{\Delta c(S_2O_3^{2-})}{2\Delta t} = \frac{c(S_2O_3^{2-})}{2\Delta t} \tag{7-15-7}$$

即

$$v = -\frac{\Delta c(S_2O_8^{2-})}{\Delta t} = \frac{c(S_2O_3^{2-})}{2\Delta t} = kc(S_2O_8^{2-})^m c(I^-)^n \tag{7-15-8}$$

对式(7-15-8)两边取对数,可得

$$\lg v = \lg k + m\lg c(S_2O_8^{2-}) + n\lg c(I^-) \tag{7-15-9}$$

固定 I^- 的浓度不变,测定不同 $S_2O_8^{2-}$ 浓度条件下的反应速率,以 $\lg v$ 对 $\lg c(S_2O_8^{2-})$ 作图,得一条直线,斜率为 $S_2O_8^{2-}$ 的反应级数 m;同理,当固定 $S_2O_8^{2-}$ 的浓度不变,改变 I^- 的浓度,以 $\lg v$ 对 $\lg c(I^-)$ 作图,得一条直线,其斜率为 I^- 的反应级数 n;根据 m、n 可计算出反应级数$(m+n)$,并由速率方程求出一定温度下反应的速率常数 k。

根据 Arrhenius 方程式,速率常数 k 与反应温度 T 有如下关系

$$\lg k = -\frac{E_a}{2.303RT} + \lg A \tag{7-15-10}$$

式(7-15-10)中,A 为指前因子,R 为气体常数($8.314\ \text{J·mol}^{-1}\text{·K}^{-1}$),$T$ 为绝对温度,E_a 为反应的活化能(J·mol^{-1} 或 kJ·mol^{-1})。

测得不同温度下的速率常数 k 值,以 $\lg k$ 对 $\dfrac{1}{T}$ 作图,可以得一条直线,由直线的斜率$\left(-\dfrac{E_a}{2.303R}\right)$ 可求出反应的活化能 E_a。

【仪器材料与试剂】

仪器　锥形瓶($100\ \text{mL} \times 8$),试管($10\ \text{mL} \times 1$),量筒($10\ \text{mL} \times 6$),温度计,秒表,恒温水浴锅(或槽),搅拌器。

材料与试剂　$0.2\ \text{mol·L}^{-1}\ (NH_4)_2S_2O_8$ 溶液,$0.2\ \text{mol·L}^{-1}\ KI$ 溶液,$0.01\ \text{mol·L}^{-1}\ Na_2S_2O_3$ 溶液,$0.2\ \text{mol·L}^{-1}\ KNO_3$ 溶液,$0.02\ \text{mol·L}^{-1}\ Cu(NO_3)_2$ 溶液,$0.2\ \text{mol·L}^{-1}\ (NH_4)_2SO_4$ 溶液,0.2% 淀粉溶液。

【实验步骤】

(一)浓度对化学反应速率的影响

在室温条件下,按表 7-15-1 中实验组 1~5 的用量,用 10 mL 量筒分别取相应体积的 KI、KNO_3、$(NH_4)_2SO_4$、$Na_2S_2O_3$、淀粉溶液置于 100 mL 干燥锥形瓶中,混合均匀,用量筒取相应体积的 $(NH_4)_2S_2O_8$ 溶液,快速将 $(NH_4)_2S_2O_8$ 溶液加到锥形瓶里,同时启动秒表计时,并不断摇动锥形瓶,当溶液开始出现蓝色时,立即停止计时,记录溶液变蓝所需的时间及反应温度。

为了保证溶液离子强度和总体积维持不变,KI 和 $(NH_4)_2S_2O_8$ 的不足量用 KNO_3 和 $(NH_4)_2SO_4$ 补充。

表 7-15-1　浓度、温度对化学反应速率的影响

	实验序号	1	2	3	4	5	6	7	8
试剂用量/mL	$0.01\ \text{mol·L}^{-1}\ Na_2S_2O_3$	4.0	4.0	4.0	4.0	4.0	4.0	4.0	4.0
	0.2% 淀粉溶液	2.0	2.0	2.0	2.0	2.0	2.0	2.0	2.0
	$0.2\ \text{mol·L}^{-1}\ KI$	10.0	10.0	10.0	5.0	2.5	10.0	10.0	10.0
	$0.2\ \text{mol·L}^{-1}\ KNO_3$	—	—	—	5.00	7.50	—	—	—
	$0.2\ \text{mol·L}^{-1}\ (NH_4)_2SO_4$	7.5	5.0	—	—	—	5.0	5.0	5.0
	$0.2\ \text{mol·L}^{-1}\ (NH_4)_2S_2O_8$	2.5	5.0	10.0	10.0	10.0	5.0	5.0	5.0
$c\{(NH_4)_2S_2O_8\}/\text{mol·L}^{-1}$									
$c(KI)/\text{mol·L}^{-1}$									
$c(Na_2S_2O_3)/\text{mol·L}^{-1}$									
反应温度/K									
$\Delta t/\text{s}$									
$v/\text{mol·L}^{-1}\text{·s}^{-1}$									

根据表 7-15-1 中 1~3 组的结果进行相互比较，分析 $S_2O_8^{2-}$ 浓度的改变对反应速率的影响。根据 3~5 组的结果进行相互比较，分析 I^- 浓度的改变对反应速率的影响。

（二）温度对化学反应速率的影响

按表 7-15-1 中实验组 6 的用量，用量筒分别取相应体积的 KI、$(NH_4)_2SO_4$、$Na_2S_2O_3$、淀粉溶液置于 100 mL 锥形瓶中，用量筒取 5.0 mL 0.2 $mol\cdot L^{-1}$ $(NH_4)_2S_2O_8$ 溶液于干燥大试管中，将含溶液的锥形瓶和大试管分别置于恒温水浴(高出室温 10 ℃)中加热约 5 分钟，将大试管中的 $(NH_4)_2S_2O_8$ 溶液快速加到锥形瓶中，同时启动秒表，并不断摇动锥形瓶，待溶液刚呈现蓝色，停止计时，记录所需的时间和温度，填入表 7-15-1 实验组 6 中。

按照同样方法在 0 ℃ 的冰水混合物中(或高于室温约 20 ℃)条件下，重复上述实验，记录反应时间和温度，填入表 7-15-1 实验组 7 中。

根据表 7-15-1 中 2 组、6 组和 7 组的结果进行相互比较，分析温度的改变对化学反应速率的影响。

（三）催化剂对化学反应速率的影响

Cu^{2+} 对本反应有催化功能，加入微量 Cu^{2+} 可以使反应速率大大加快。按表 7-15-1 中实验组 8 的试剂用量在室温下实验，加 $(NH_4)_2S_2O_8$ 溶液前，先加 2 滴 0.02 $mol\cdot L^{-1}$ $Cu(NO_3)_2$ 溶液于锥形瓶中，记录反应时间。根据 2 组与 8 组的结果进行比较，分析催化剂 $Cu(NO_3)_2$ 对化学反应速率的影响。

【数据记录与结果分析】

日期：_____　温度：_____℃　相对湿度：_____

（一）反应级数和速率常数的计算

由表 7-15-1 的实验数据计算出反应的平均速率。根据组 1~3 的数据，以 $\lg v$ 对 $\lg c(S_2O_8^{2-})$ 的曲线，求出相对于 $S_2O_8^{2-}$ 的反应级数 m；同理，根据组 3~5 的数据，以 $\lg v$ 对 $\lg c(I^-)$ 的曲线，得出 I^- 的反应级数 n。最后根据以上的数据处理结果求出速率常数 k，将结果记录于表 7-15-2 中。

表 7-15-2　反应级数和速率常数

实验序号	1	2	3	4	5
$\lg v$					
$\lg c(S_2O_8^{2-})$					
$\lg c(I^-)$					
m					
n					
k					
$\bar{k}$					

（二）活化能的计算

根据表 7-15-1 中实验组 2、6 和 7 的数据，计算不同温度下对应的 k 值，以 $\lg k$ 对 $\dfrac{1}{T}$ 作图，由直线的斜率求出反应的活化能 E_a，将结果记录于表 7-15-3 中。

表 7-15-3　反应活化能

实验序号	2	6	7
k			
$\lg k$			
$\dfrac{1}{T}$/K^{-1}			
E_a/$kJ \cdot mol^{-1}$			

根据以上实验结果,请分别讨论浓度、温度和催化剂对反应速率的影响。

【注意事项】

$(NH_4)_2S_2O_8$ 溶液需要新配制,若长时间放置易分解。

【思考题】

1. 在表 7-15-1 实验组 1~5 中分别添加 $(NH_4)_2SO_4$ 及 KNO_3 溶液,其作用是什么?

2. 实验中加入一定量的 $Na_2S_2O_3$ 和淀粉溶液,它们的作用各是什么? $Na_2S_2O_3$ 用量过多或过少对实验结果有什么影响?

3. 溶液变蓝后,体系中的反应是否停止了?

(李振泉)

实验十六　最大气泡压力法测定乙醇溶液的表面张力

【实验目的】

1. 掌握最大气泡压力法测定溶液表面张力的原理和方法。

2. 通过测定系列浓度乙醇溶液的表面张力,深入理解溶液浓度与表面张力、表面吸附量的关系。

3. 学会使用表面张力计算表面活性物质的饱和吸附量及其分子横截面积的方法。

【预习作业】

模拟设计实验:以流程图方式,写出最大气泡压力法测定表面张力的设计步骤,并注明各步骤的注意事项及原因。

引导问题:

1. 什么是表面张力? 影响液体表面张力的主要因素有哪些?

2. 最大气泡压力法测定表面张力实验中,系统漏气将对实验有何影响? 应如何检查系统是否漏气?

3. 毛细管管口为何要刚好与液面相切?

4. 为何表面张力的测定要按溶液浓度从稀到浓的顺序?

5. 实验是否需要在恒温条件下进行,为什么?

【实验原理】

由于液体表层分子受力不均衡,液体表面都有趋于收缩的基本特性。沿着液体表面作用于单位长度线段上的收缩张力称为表面张力,其方向为沿着表面切线并指向表面缩小的方向。

影响液体表面张力的因素包括温度、压力及溶液的组成及浓度等。例如,在一定温度和压力下,水的表面张力随加入溶质的种类和浓度的不同而发生变化。能够降低溶剂表面张力的物质称为表面活性物质。当溶液中表面活性物质浓度增加时,溶液的表面张力随之减小,此时溶液界面的浓度大于溶液内部的浓度,溶液界面浓度与溶液内部浓度的差值,称为表面吸附量。溶质的表面吸附量与溶液的表面张力、组成之间的关系符合吉布斯(Gibbs)等温吸附方程

$$\Gamma = -\frac{c}{RT} \times \frac{\mathrm{d}\sigma}{\mathrm{d}c} \tag{7-16-1}$$

式(7-16-1)中,Γ 为表面吸附量(mol·m^{-2}),σ 为溶液的表面张力(N·m^{-1}),T 为热力学温度(K),c 为溶质的浓度(mol·L^{-1}),R 为气体常数(8.314 J·mol^{-1}·K^{-1}),$\frac{\mathrm{d}\sigma}{\mathrm{d}c}$ 为等温条件下表面张力随浓度的变化率。等温条件下 σ 与 c 关系曲线如图 7-16-1 所示。在 $\sigma\sim c$ 曲线上的任意浓度对应点 K 作切线,切线斜率即为表面张力随浓度的变化率 $\frac{\mathrm{d}\sigma}{\mathrm{d}c}$,由式(7-16-1)即可计算出溶质的表面吸附量。若进一步以浓度 c 为横坐标,以表面吸附量 Γ 为纵坐标,可以得到 $\Gamma = f(c)$ 关系曲线(图 7-16-2)。

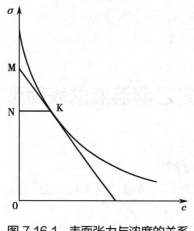

图 7-16-1　表面张力与浓度的关系

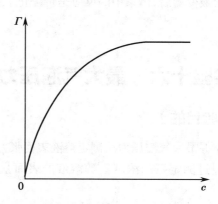

图 7-16-2　表面吸附量与浓度的关系

表面活性物质分子结构中同时含有亲水和疏水基团。若将表面活性物质分子溶于水,其亲水基团倾向于进入水相中,而疏水基团力图离开水相指向空气一侧。因此,表面活性物质易于吸附在水溶液的表面从而降低了水的表面张力(或表面能)。如图 7-16-3(a)所示,在浓度较小时,表面活性物质分子零散地排列在水溶液的表面。随着溶质浓度的进一步增加,表面活性物质分子逐渐占据的表面积随之增大。当浓度增加至一定程度时,表面活性物质分子占据了所有的表面,如图 7-16-3(b),表面活性物质分子在液面上形成单分子吸附层,此时单位面积表面吸附的溶质分子数称为饱和吸附量或最大吸附量,用符号 Γ_∞ 表示。若进一步增加溶质的浓度,表面上的分子数不再增加,而是进入溶液中并聚集形成胶束,如图 7-16-3(c)所示。

表面吸附量 Γ、饱和吸附量 Γ_∞ 与浓度 c 的关系符合朗格缪尔(Langmuir)提出的等温方程式

$$\Gamma = \Gamma_\infty \times \frac{Kc}{1+Kc} (\mathrm{mol \cdot m^{-2}}) \tag{7-16-2}$$

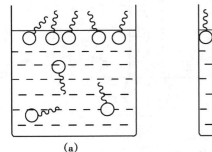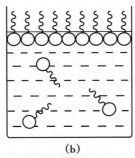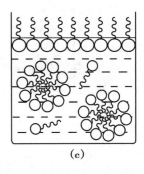

图 7-16-3　不同浓度情况下表面活性物质分子在溶液中的排布状态

（a）$c < \Gamma_\infty$；（b）$c = \Gamma_\infty$；（c）$c > \Gamma_\infty$。

式（7-16-2）中 K 为一常数。将其稍作变换，得

$$\frac{c}{\Gamma} = \frac{c}{\Gamma_\infty} + \frac{1}{K\Gamma_\infty} \qquad (7\text{-}16\text{-}3)$$

若以浓度 c 为横坐标，以浓度与表面吸附量的比值 $\frac{c}{\Gamma}$ 为纵坐标作图，可得一条直线，直线斜率的倒数即为饱和吸附量 Γ_∞。

当溶液表面吸附的溶质分子数量达到饱和状态时，在液面上形成单分子吸附层，因此，可以用饱和吸附量 Γ_∞ 求出单个溶质分子的横截面积 S

$$S = \frac{1}{\Gamma_\infty N_A} (\mathrm{m}^2) \qquad (7\text{-}16\text{-}4)$$

式（7-16-4）中 N_A 为阿伏伽德罗（Avogadro）常数（6.02×10^{23}）。

由于分子通常很小，故一般使用 nm^2 单位，则式（7-16-4）校正为

$$S = \frac{10^{18}}{\Gamma_\infty N_A} (\mathrm{nm}^2) \qquad (7\text{-}16\text{-}5)$$

本实验采用最大气泡法测定不同浓度乙醇水溶液的表面张力，通过数据处理求出表面吸附量 Γ、饱和吸附量 Γ_∞ 及乙醇分子的横截面积 S。

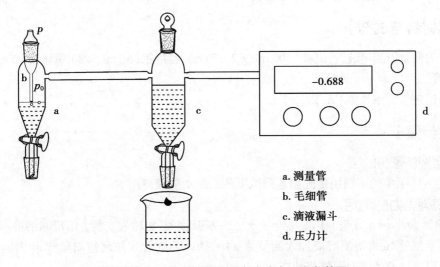

a. 测量管
b. 毛细管
c. 滴液漏斗
d. 压力计

图 7-16-4　最大气泡法测定溶液表面张力装置

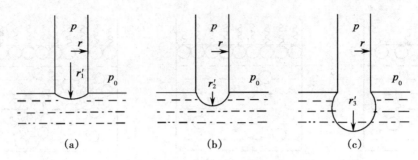

图 7-16-5　气泡产生过程中曲率半径的变化
（a）$r_1' > r$；（b）$r_2' = r$；（c）$r_3' > r$。

最大气泡法测量表面张力的装置如图 7-16-4 所示。实验时，使毛细管 b 管口与测量管 a 中待测溶液的液面刚好相切，打开滴液漏斗 c 下方的活塞放水增大体系的体积从而使压力 p_0 减小，连接大气的毛细管尖气体被大气压压至管口的液面，导致气泡在管口处生成。当气泡在毛细管口逐渐长大时，其曲率半径先变小后增大，如图 7-16-5 所示。当气泡的曲率半径刚好等于毛细管的半径时，其曲率半径最小。此时气泡内外的压力差达到最大值，此压力差的数值可由压力计 d 读出。随后，气泡从毛细管口逸出，测量管中气压得到补偿，压力差数值恢复至较小值。在气泡逸出过程中，最大压力差 Δp 及气泡的最小曲率半径 r_2'（等于毛细管的半径 r）与溶液的表面张力 σ 之间的关系满足杨-拉普拉斯（Young-Laplace）公式

$$\Delta p = p - p_0 = \frac{2\sigma}{r} \tag{7-16-6}$$

由于毛细管的半径难以测定，因此通常使用一种已知表面张力的液体作为标准溶液。用同一根毛细管分别测定标准溶液和待测溶液产生气泡时的最大压力差，代入式（7-16-6），并将所得到的两个方程式相除，最后可由式（7-16-7）计算得到待测溶液的表面张力

$$\frac{\sigma}{\sigma'} = \frac{\Delta p}{\Delta p'} \tag{7-16-7}$$

式（7-16-7）中，σ 和 σ' 分别为标准溶液和待测溶液的表面张力（N·m^{-1}），Δp 和 $\Delta p'$ 分别为标准溶液和待测溶液产生气泡时的最大压力差（kPa）。

【仪器材料与试剂】

仪器　表面张力测定装置，烧杯（500 mL×2），50 mL 容量瓶（50 mL×8），吸量管（5 mL、10 mL、20 mL），滴管。

材料与试剂　无水乙醇（A. R.），纯水。

【实验步骤】

（一）溶液的配制
根据表 7-16-1 中的试剂用量配制系列浓度的乙醇水溶液待用。

（二）表面张力的测定
1. 在滴液漏斗 c（带支管）中加入约三分之二体积的水（勿超过支管），用待测溶液润洗 3~4 次测量管 a 及毛细管 b，将待测溶液加入测量管 a 中，插入毛细管 b 并调整测量管 a 中溶液量，使毛细管管口与待测溶液的液面刚好相切。

2. 接通压力计 d 电源,打开滴液漏斗 c 上方塞子,在系统与大气连通的情况下采零,随后将滴液漏斗 c 上方塞子盖上形成密闭系统。打开滴液漏斗 c 下方旋塞使漏斗中的水滴出,则系统压力逐渐低于外界大气压。关闭旋塞并维持 1~2 分钟,如压力计示数数值稳定,说明系统不漏气。

3. 再次打开滴液漏斗 c 下方旋塞使水缓慢滴下,将观察到毛细管口有气泡逸出,调节旋塞使毛细管口逸出气泡的速度控制在 8~10 秒一个。记录压力差最大值,连续记录 3 次,将数据填入表 7-16-1 中。注意 3 次最大压力差的数值相差不能超过 0.05 kPa。

4. 将所有溶液按照从稀到浓的顺序进行表面张力的测定。每次更换测定的溶液时,都要将测量管中的溶液全部放出,并用待测溶液润洗测量管 a 及毛细管 b。

【注意事项】

1. 测量时尽量使温度不要有明显变化。
2. 润洗测量管时,应避免溶液冲入支管中影响气路连通,造成压力计读数不准确。
3. 所有数据测定必须使用同一根毛细管。

【数据记录及结果处理】

日期:_____　温度:_____℃　相对湿度:_____

表 7-16-1　乙醇溶液表面张力的测定

编号	1	2	3	4	5	6	7	8
$V_{乙醇}$/mL	0.00	0.50	1.00	2.00	4.00	8.00	12.00	16.00
$V_{总}$/mL	50.00	50.00	50.000	50.00	50.00	50.00	50.00	50.00
Δp_1/kPa								
Δp_2/kPa								
Δp_3/kPa								
$\Delta \bar{p}$/kPa								
$c_{乙醇}$/mol·m^{-3}								
σ/N·m^{-1}								
$b = c \times \dfrac{d\sigma}{dc}$	—							
Γ/mol·m^{-2}	—							
c/Γ	—							
Γ_∞/mol·m^{-2}	—							
S/nm^2	—							

(一) 作 σ~c 关系曲线

以浓度 c 为横坐标,乙醇溶液表面张力 σ 为纵坐标,作 σ~c 关系曲线,根据曲线说明 σ 随 c 的变化规律。

(二) 计算不同浓度下的表面吸附量 Γ

在曲线 σ~c 上,对应任意浓度对应曲线上点 K 作曲线的切线及 x 轴的平行线,分别交 y 轴于 M、

N 两点, 见图 7-16-1。从坐标纸上读出 M、N 两点之间的距离 b($b = c \times \dfrac{d\sigma}{dc}$), 代入式 (7-16-1) 计算不同浓度下的表面吸附量 Γ。

(三) 作 $\Gamma \sim c$ 关系曲线

以浓度 c 为横坐标, 以表面吸附量 Γ 为纵坐标, 作 $\Gamma \sim c$ 关系曲线, 根据曲线说明 Γ 与 c 的关系。

(四) 作 $\dfrac{c}{\Gamma} \sim c$ 关系曲线

以浓度 c 为横坐标, 以 $\dfrac{c}{\Gamma}$ 为纵坐标, 作 $\dfrac{c}{\Gamma} \sim c$ 关系曲线, 计算乙醇的饱和吸附量 Γ_∞ 及单分子所占的横截面积 S。

【思考题】

1. 测定液体表面张力的方法有哪些? 各有何优缺点?
2. 什么是表面活性物质? 评价表面活性物质性能的指标都有哪些?
3. 表面活性物质在医药学及生活中都有哪些应用?

(廖传安)

第八章　化合物制备实验

实验十七　氯化钠的纯化

【实验目的】

1. 掌握溶解、过滤、蒸发、浓缩、结晶、干燥等基本操作。
2. 掌握提纯食盐的原理、方法以及检验其纯度的方法。
3. 了解沉淀溶解平衡在无机物纯化中的应用。

【预习作业】

模拟设计实验:参照本实验的原理及步骤,以流程图方式写出本实验纯化氯化钠的实验步骤和设计思路,并在流程图中注明各步骤的注意事项及依据。

引导性问题:

1. 氯化钠在临床上有哪些应用?
2. 固体物质的提纯方法有哪些?
3. 何谓重结晶? 氯化钠是否可以用重结晶法来提纯?
4. 固液分离的常用方法有哪些? 应如何选择? 减压过滤时应该注意哪些细节?
5. 为什么本实验除杂时先除去 SO_4^{2-},再除 Ca^{2+}、Mg^{2+}、Fe^{3+}? 是否可以改变沉淀剂加入顺序?
6. 蒸发浓缩时为什么不能蒸干?

【实验原理】

粗食盐中有 Ca^{2+}、Mg^{2+}、Fe^{3+}、K^+ 和 SO_4^{2-} 等可溶性杂质和泥沙等不溶性杂质,在制成试剂级 NaCl 之前,必须除去这些杂质且避免引入新的杂质。不溶性杂质可通过溶解后过滤的方法除去。而可溶性杂质则可选择适当的试剂(如 $BaCl_2$、Na_2CO_3、NaOH 等)使其生成难溶化合物,再过滤除去。

首先,在粗食盐溶液中加入过量的 $BaCl_2$ 溶液,以除去 SO_4^{2-},

$$Ba^{2+} + SO_4^{2-} =\!=\!=\!= BaSO_4\downarrow$$

过滤除去 $BaSO_4$ 沉淀。然后在滤液中加入 NaOH 和 Na_2CO_3 溶液,以除去 Ca^{2+}、Mg^{2+}、Fe^{3+} 和过量的 Ba^{2+}。

$$Mg^{2+} + 2OH^- =\!=\!=\!= Mg(OH)_2\downarrow$$

$$2Mg^{2+} + 2OH^- + CO_3^{2-} =\!=\!=\!= Mg_2(OH)_2CO_3\downarrow$$

$$Ca^{2+} + CO_3^{2-} =\!=\!=\!= CaCO_3\downarrow$$

$$Fe^{3+} + 3OH^- =\!=\!=\!= Fe(OH)_3\downarrow$$

$$Ba^{2+} + CO_3^{2-} =\!=\!=\!= BaCO_3\downarrow$$

过滤除去沉淀,用稀 HCl 溶液调节溶液的 pH 至 2~3,除去溶液中过量的 NaOH 和 Na_2CO_3。

$$H_3O^+ + OH^- \rightleftharpoons 2H_2O$$

$$2H_3O^+ + CO_3^{2-} \rightleftharpoons 3H_2O + CO_2\uparrow$$

易溶的 K^+ 不能用上述方法除去,但可在蒸发和结晶过程中留在滤液中,趁热减压过滤除去。残留的 HCl 在干燥过程中可被除去。

【仪器材料与试剂】

仪器　台秤,玻璃漏斗,漏斗架,布氏漏斗,抽滤瓶,电热套,蒸发皿,量筒(10 mL,50 mL),试管(10 mL × 6),玻璃棒,烧杯(50 mL × 2,100 mL),药匙,滴管。

材料与试剂　粗食盐,6 mol·L^{-1} HCl 溶液,6 mol·L^{-1} HAc 溶液,6 mol·L^{-1} NaOH 溶液,1 mol·L^{-1} $BaCl_2$ 溶液,1 mol·L^{-1} Na_2CO_3 溶液,$(NH_4)_2C_2O_4$ 饱和溶液,镁试剂,滤纸,广泛 pH 试纸,95% 乙醇溶液。

【实验步骤】

(一) 粗食盐的提纯

1. **称量和溶解**　称取 5.0 g 粗食盐于 100 mL 烧杯中,加入 25.0 mL 蒸馏水,搅拌并加热使其溶解,溶解后如有泥沙等不溶性杂质,可常压过滤除去。

2. **除去 SO_4^{2-}**　当溶液微沸时,边搅拌边逐滴加入 2.0 mL 1 mol·L^{-1} $BaCl_2$ 溶液(注意:$BaCl_2$ 溶液有毒,废液应回收),继续加热 5 min,静置,取少量上清液于小试管中,滴加 2 滴 6 mol·L^{-1} HCl 溶液,再滴加 1 mol·L^{-1} $BaCl_2$ 溶液 2~3 滴。如果混浊,需向原液继续滴加 $BaCl_2$ 溶液,直至 SO_4^{2-} 沉淀完全。继续加热 5 min,静置冷却后常压过滤,收集滤液于洁净小烧杯中。

3. **除去 Ca^{2+}、Mg^{2+}、Fe^{3+} 和过量的 Ba^{2+} 离子**　继续加热滤液至微沸,边搅拌边向其中加入 1.0 mL 6 mol·L^{-1} NaOH 和 2.0 mL 饱和 Na_2CO_3 溶液除去 Ca^{2+}、Mg^{2+}、Fe^{3+} 和过量的 Ba^{2+} 离子,继续加热 5 min,静置冷却后,取少量上层清液于试管中,滴加几滴 Na_2CO_3 溶液,检查有无沉淀生成。若无沉淀生成,常压过滤,收集滤液于蒸发皿中。

4. **除去剩余的 OH^- 和 CO_3^{2-} 离子**　向滤液中逐滴加入 6 mol·L^{-1} HCl 溶液,至滤液 pH 2~3(用广泛 pH 试纸测定)为止。

5. **蒸发干燥**　小火加热蒸发上述滤液,浓缩至稀糊状(注意:不可将溶液蒸干!)。趁热减压过滤,尽量将结晶抽干,将晶体转移至洁净蒸发皿中。小火加热炒干,冷却至室温,称重,计算产率。

(二) 产品纯度的检验

取粗盐和本实验所得精制食盐各 1.0 g,分别置于 50 mL 烧杯中,用 5.0 mL 蒸馏水溶解(若粗盐溶液浑浊则须过滤)。将粗盐和精盐澄清溶液分别盛于 3 对小试管中(每支试管取澄清溶液 1.0 mL),组成对照组以检验它们的纯度。

1. **SO_4^{2-} 的检验**　在第一对照组溶液中分别加入 2 滴 6 mol·L^{-1} HCl 溶液,使溶液呈酸性。再加入 2~3 滴 1 mol·L^{-1} $BaCl_2$ 溶液。如有白色沉淀,即证明有 SO_4^{2-} 存在。记录结果于表 8-17-1。

2. **Ca^{2+} 的检验**　在第二对照组溶液中分别加入 2 滴 6 mol·L^{-1} HAc 溶液,使溶液呈酸性。再加入 3~5 滴饱和 $(NH_4)_2C_2O_4$ 溶液,如有白色沉淀,即证明有 Ca^{2+} 存在。记录结果于表 8-17-1。

3. **Mg^{2+} 的检验**　在第三对照组溶液中分别加入 3~5 滴 6 mol·L^{-1} NaOH 溶液,使溶液呈碱性。

再加入 1 滴镁试剂,如有天蓝色沉淀,即证明有 Mg^{2+} 存在。记录结果于表 8-17-1。

【注意事项】

1. 加入沉淀剂煮沸过程中,如果溶剂蒸发过多,应适当补充溶剂,避免氯化钠结晶析出。
2. 加入沉淀剂后,应煮沸并静置后再过滤。

【数据记录与结果分析】

日期:＿＿＿＿＿＿　温度:＿＿＿＿＿＿＿℃　相对湿度:＿＿＿＿＿＿＿

(一) 粗食盐的提纯

粗食盐 $m(NaCl)=$＿＿＿＿ g,精制食盐 $m(NaCl)=$＿＿＿＿ g。

$$产率(\%)=\frac{精制食盐的质量}{粗食盐的质量}\times100\%=\underline{\qquad\qquad}。$$

(二) 产品纯度的检验

表 8-17-1　产品纯度检验结果

项目	实验方法	粗食盐溶液	精制食盐溶液
SO_4^{2-} 的检验	加入 $BaCl_2$ 溶液	现象: 结论:	现象: 结论:
Ca^{2+} 的检验	加入饱和 $(NH_4)_2C_2O_4$ 溶液	现象: 结论:	现象: 结论:
Mg^{2+} 的检验	加入"镁试剂"	现象: 结论:	现象: 结论:

【思考题】

1. 本实验中,能否用其他酸来除去多余的 CO_3^{2-}?
2. 在检验 SO_4^{2-} 时,为什么要加入盐酸溶液?

(乔秀文)

实验十八　硫酸亚铁铵的制备

【实验目的】

1. 了解复盐制备的基本原理。
2. 练习水浴加热、常压过滤、减压过滤、蒸发、浓缩、结晶和干燥等基本操作。
3. 学习用目视比色法检验产品质量。

【预习作业】

模拟设计实验:根据本实验的原理,以流程图方式写出本实验的实验步骤及设计思路,并在制备流程图中标出反应条件、实验操作条件及依据。

引导问题:

1. 无机化合物制备的基本原则是什么?

2. 铁屑的油污如何处理?

3. 反应过程中溶液被蒸发如何处理?

4. 蒸发浓缩到什么程度,为什么?

5. 目视比色法的原理是什么?$(NH_4)_2SO_4 \cdot FeSO_4 \cdot 6H_2O$ 的等级应如何确定?

【实验原理】

硫酸亚铁铵$[(NH_4)_2SO_4 \cdot FeSO_4 \cdot 6H_2O]$又称莫尔盐,是浅蓝色透明晶体,比一般的亚铁盐稳定。它在空气中不易被氧化,溶于水但不溶于乙醇。在定量分析中,常用硫酸亚铁铵来配制亚铁离子的标准溶液。

硫酸亚铁铵在水中的溶解度比组成它的组分 $FeSO_4$ 或$(NH_4)_2SO_4$ 的溶解度都要小,因此只需要将浓度较高的 $FeSO_4$ 溶液与$(NH_4)_2SO_4$ 溶液混合即得硫酸亚铁铵晶体。

本实验先将铁屑溶于稀 H_2SO_4,制得 $FeSO_4$ 溶液,再加入$(NH_4)_2SO_4$ 固体并使其全部溶解,经浓缩、冷却即得溶解度小的硫酸亚铁铵晶体。

$$Fe + H_2SO_4 \Longrightarrow FeSO_4 + H_2 \uparrow$$

$$FeSO_4 + (NH_4)_2SO_4 + 6H_2O \Longrightarrow (NH_4)_2SO_4 \cdot FeSO_4 \cdot 6H_2O$$

由于 Fe^{2+} 容易被氧化成 Fe^{3+},因此在实验过程中要加入强酸 H_2SO_4,防止 Fe^{2+} 氧化成 Fe^{3+}。

产品中的杂质 Fe^{3+} 含量可用比色法来鉴定。因 Fe^{3+} 能与过量的 SCN^- 生成血红色的$[Fe(SCN)_6]^{3-}$。在产品溶液中加入 SCN^- 后,若溶液呈较深的红色,则表明产品中含 Fe^{3+} 较多,反之表明产品中含 Fe^{3+} 较少。将它所呈现的红色与$[Fe(SCN)_6]^{3-}$标准溶液颜色进行比较,找出与之深浅程度一致的标准溶液,则该标准溶液所示 Fe^{3+} 含量为产品的杂质 Fe^{3+} 含量,依此便可确定产品的等级。检测标准为 1 g 一、二、三级硫酸亚铁铵的含 Fe^{3+} 限量分别为 0.05 mg、0.10 mg 及 0.20 mg。

【仪器材料与试剂】

仪器 台秤,分析天平,锥形瓶(250 mL),烧杯(50 mL),水浴锅(内径 16 cm),量筒(20 mL×2,25 mL),容量瓶(250 mL),吸量管(1.0 mL×2,2.0 mL),目视比色管(25.0 mL×4),减压过滤装置,蒸发皿,滤纸。

材料与试剂 铁屑,$(NH_4)_2SO_4$ 固体,10% Na_2CO_3 溶液,3.0 mol·L^{-1} H_2SO_4 溶液,3.0 mol·L^{-1} HCl 溶液,25% 乙醇溶液,25% KSCN 溶液,Fe^{3+}标准溶液,一级试剂(含 Fe^{3+} 0.05 mg),二级试剂(含 Fe^{3+} 0.10 mg),三级试剂(含 Fe^{3+} 0.20 mg)。

【实验步骤】

(一)铁屑的净化

称取 4.0 g 铁屑于锥形瓶中,加入 20.0 mL 10% Na_2CO_3 溶液,水浴加热约 10 min,倾去碱液,并用去离子水洗净铁屑。

(二)硫酸亚铁的制备

向盛有铁屑的锥形瓶中加入 25.0 mL 3.0 mol·L^{-1} H_2SO_4 溶液,水浴加热约 30 min(在通风橱中进行)。在加热过程中,应经常摇动锥形瓶以加速反应,并适当添加少量水分。待反应至无气泡产生后,趁热减压过滤。将滤液转移到小烧杯中,分别用 1.0 mL 3.0 mol·L^{-1} H$_2$SO$_4$ 和新鲜去离子水洗涤锥形瓶和铁屑残渣(Fe^{2+}在强酸性介质中较稳定,加入硫酸是为了防止滤液中的 Fe^{2+}转化为 Fe^{3+})。再次减压过滤,合并滤液于蒸发皿中。

收集铁屑残渣,用滤纸吸干后称重,计算参与反应的铁屑质量和需要的硫酸铵质量。

(三)硫酸亚铁铵的制备

按上述计算值称量硫酸铵并加入硫酸亚铁溶液中。水浴加热,充分搅拌使其完全溶解。继续蒸发浓缩至溶液表面出现晶膜,停止加热,静置,冷却至室温,即得硫酸亚铁铵晶体。减压过滤,用少量乙醇洗涤晶体两次,取出晶体置于两张滤纸之间,轻压以吸干母液。晾干,称重,计算理论产量与产率。

(四)产品检验

不同级别 Fe^{3+}标准溶液的配制:

1. Fe^{3+}标准溶液配制　准确称取0.431 7 g NH$_4$Fe(SO$_4$)$_2$·12H$_2$O 溶解,并定容至250.00 mL 得 8.95 × 10^{-3} mol·L^{-1} Fe^{3+}标准溶液。

2. 一级试剂(含Fe^{3+} 0.05 mg)配制　取Fe^{3+}标准溶液0.25 mL 于25.00 mL 目视比色管中,加 2.00 mL 2.0 mol·L^{-1} HCl 溶液和1.00 mL 1.0 mol·L^{-1} KSCN 溶液,加蒸馏水定容至25.00 mL。

3. 二级试剂(含Fe^{3+} 0.10 mg)配制　取Fe^{3+}标准溶液0.5 mL 于25.00 mL 目视比色管中,加 2.00 mL 2.0 mol·L^{-1} HCl 和1.00 mL 1.0 mol·L^{-1} KSCN 溶液,加蒸馏水定容至25.00 mL。

4. 三级试剂(含Fe^{3+} 0.20 mg)配制　取Fe^{3+}标准溶液1.00 mL 于25.00 mL 目视比色管中,加 2.00 mL 2.0 mol·L^{-1} HCl 和1.00 mL 1.0 mol·L^{-1} KSCN 溶液,加蒸馏水定容至25.00 mL。

称取约 1.0 g 上述硫酸亚铁铵样品于 25.00 mL 目视比色管中,用 15.0 mL 新鲜去离子水溶解,加 2.00 mL 3.0 mol·L^{-1} HCl 和 1.00 mL 25% KSCN 溶液,加蒸馏水稀释至 25.00 mL,摇匀。与标准溶液进行目视比色,确定产品的等级。

【注意事项】

1. 铁屑在使用之前必须净化。

2. 铁屑与 H$_2$SO$_4$ 溶液的反应须在通风橱中进行。

3. 反应完成后,别用 1.0 mL 3.0 mol·L^{-1} H$_2$SO$_4$ 和不含氧的蒸馏水洗涤锥形瓶和铁屑残渣,以防止滤液中的 Fe^{2+}转化为 Fe^{3+}。

【数据记录及结果分析】

日期:＿＿＿＿＿＿＿＿　室温:＿＿＿＿＿＿＿＿℃　相对湿度:＿＿＿＿＿＿＿＿

(一)硫酸亚铁铵的制备

铁屑的质量 $m_{始}$(Fe)=＿＿＿＿＿＿＿＿＿＿＿＿＿＿＿＿ g;

铁屑残渣重 $m_{终}$(Fe)=＿＿＿＿＿＿＿＿＿＿＿＿＿＿＿＿ g;

参加反应的铁屑质量=＿＿＿＿＿＿＿＿＿＿＿＿＿＿＿＿ g;

硫酸亚铁铵产量 m[(NH$_4$)$_2$SO$_4$·FeSO$_4$·6H$_2$O]=＿＿＿＿＿＿ g;

硫酸亚铁铵产率(%)=$\dfrac{m[(NH_4)_2SO_4·FeSO_4·6H_2O] \times M(Fe)}{[m_{始}(Fe)-m_{终}(Fe)] \times M[(NH_4)_2SO_4·FeSO_4·6H_2O]} \times 100\% = $＿＿＿＿＿＿。

（二）产品纯度检验

Fe³⁺标准溶液	一级（Fe³⁺ 0.05 mg）	二级（Fe³⁺ 0.10 mg）	三级（Fe³⁺ 0.20 mg）
$(NH_4)_2SO_4 \cdot FeSO_4 \cdot 6H_2O$ 产品级别			

【思考题】

1. 什么是复盐？与形成它的简单盐相比复盐有什么特点？
2. 在蒸发及浓缩过程中，若发现溶液变为黄色，可能是什么原因？应如何处理？
3. 如何计算硫酸亚铁铵的产率？应根据铁的用量还是硫酸铵的用量？

（于 昆）

实验十九 转化法制备硝酸钾

【实验目的】

1. 了解复分解反应制备盐类及利用温度对物质溶解度的影响进行分离的方法。
2. 掌握重结晶法的基本原理和操作方法，进一步巩固溶解、加热、结晶、过滤等操作。

【预习作业】

模拟设计实验：参照本实验的原理及步骤，以流程图方式写出本实验通过转化法制备硝酸钾的实验步骤和设计思路，并在流程图中注明各步骤的注意事项及依据。

引导性问题：

1. 无机化合物常用的制备方法有哪些？
2. KNO_3 的制备方法有哪些？请指出各方法的优缺点。
3. 什么是重结晶法？操作时注意事项主要有哪些？
4. 本实验中如何确定各原料的加入量？硝酸钾的理论产量是多少？

【实验原理】

工业上，通常采用转化法制备硝酸钾晶体，其反应为：

$$NaNO_3 + KCl \Longrightarrow NaCl + KNO_3$$

硝酸钾等四种盐类在不同温度下的溶解度见表 8-19-1。由于反应式是可逆的，利用温度对物质溶解度的不同影响，可促使反应向生成产物的方向移动，并将产物进行分离，从而提高硝酸钾晶体的产率和纯度。

表 8-19-1 不同温度下硝酸钾等四种盐类的溶解度 [单位：$g \cdot (100\ g)^{-1} H_2O$]

温度 / ℃	0	10	20	30	40	60	80	100
KNO_3	13.3	20.9	31.6	45.8	63.9	110.0	169.0	246.0
KCl	27.6	31.0	34.0	37.0	40.0	45.5	51.1	56.7

续表

温度/℃	0	10	20	30	40	60	80	100
NaNO₃	73.0	80.0	88.0	96.0	104.0	124.0	148.0	180.0
NaCl	35.7	35.8	36.0	36.3	36.6	37.3	38.4	39.8

从表 8-19-1 中数据可看出,氯化钠的溶解度随温度变化不大,氯化钾、硝酸钠和硝酸钾在较高温下具有很大的溶解度,而硝酸钾在低温下溶解度明显减少。根据上述物质溶解度随温度变化的差异大小,可将硝酸钠和氯化钾的混合液进行加热浓缩,使氯化钠达到饱和并析出大量晶体。在 120 ℃左右,由于硝酸钾的溶解度较大,高温时处于不饱和状态,趁热过滤可除去大部分氯化钠,再将滤液自然冷却至室温。此时,硝酸钾溶解度随温度下降而急剧下降,在室温时以晶体形式大量析出,从而得到硝酸钾粗产品。再经重结晶,即可得到硝酸钾纯品。

【仪器材料与试剂】

仪器　硬质试管(300 mL),小试管(10 mL×2),量筒(50 mL),烧杯(500 mL,100 mL),温度计(200 ℃),铁架台,台秤,玻璃棒,砂芯漏斗,吸滤瓶,循环水真空泵,电陶炉,蒸发皿,表面皿。

材料与试剂　硝酸钠(化学纯,C.P.),氯化钾(化学纯,C.P.),AgNO₃ 溶液(0.1 mol·L⁻¹),HNO₃ 溶液(5 mol·L⁻¹),二甲基硅油。

【实验步骤】

(一)硝酸钾的制备

称取 22.0 g 硝酸钠和 15.0 g 氯化钾于 300 mL 硬质试管中,加入 35.0 mL 去离子水。将试管置于油浴中加热(试管用铁夹垂直地固定在铁架台上;用 500 mL 烧杯盛约 300 mL 的二甲基硅油作为油浴,插入温度计,烧杯放在电陶炉上进行加热),油浴烧杯外与试管内液相水平处画一标记线,油浴温度控制在 140~160 ℃,搅拌使固体完全溶解,继续加热搅拌,使溶液蒸发浓缩至原体积的 2/3。这时试管内有大量晶体析出,趁热减压过滤,并迅速将滤液倒出。滤液盛于小烧杯中,自然冷却至室温,此时析出的晶体为硝酸钾粗产品,减压过滤,晶体称重,计算理论产量和粗产率,记录结果于表 8-19-2。

(二)硝酸钾的纯化

预留少量(约 0.03 g)粗产品供纯度检验外,剩余的粗产品通过重结晶进行纯化。将粗产品转移入蒸发皿中,按粗产品∶水 =2∶1(质量比)的比例,加入一定量的去离子水,小火加热,并搅拌,待晶体全部溶解后,停止加热。将溶液自然冷却至室温,待充分析出晶体后减压过滤。所得晶体置于表面皿上,放入 120 ℃烘箱中烘干,冷却,称重,计算产率,记录结果于表 8-19-2。

(三)产品纯度检验

分别取 0.03 g 粗产品和重结晶得到的产品放入两支小试管中,各加入 3.0 mL 去离子水配成溶液。在溶液中分别滴加 1 滴 5 mol·L⁻¹ HNO₃ 溶液和 2 滴 0.1 mol·L⁻¹ AgNO₃ 溶液,观察现象,进行对比,记录结果于表 8-19-2。

【注意事项】

1. 加热反应物时,由于采用油浴及其温度超过 100 ℃,硬质试管外不能挂水,否则易引起爆沸。

2. 热过滤后,滤液不能骤冷,以防晶体过细。

3. 重结晶时,若溶液沸腾,晶体还未全部溶解,可再加入少量蒸馏水继续搅拌至溶解。

【数据记录及结果分析】

日期:＿＿＿＿＿＿＿＿　　温度:＿＿＿＿＿＿＿＿℃　相对湿度:＿＿＿＿＿＿＿＿

表 8-19-2　实验数据及结果处理

物质	质量/g	产率/%	纯度检验现象
$NaNO_3$		—	—
KCl		—	—
KNO_3(理论值)		—	—
KNO_3 粗产品			
KNO_3 纯品			

【思考题】

1. 硝酸钾的制备过程中,为何第二次减压过滤后得到的晶体是粗产品?

2. 根据溶解度数据,计算本实验应分别有多少 NaCl 和 KNO_3 晶体析出(不考虑其他盐存在时对溶解度的影响)?

3. 实验中为何要趁热过滤除去 NaCl 晶体? 为何要小火加热?

4. 将粗产品重结晶时,粗产品和水的比例如何确定?

5. KNO_3 晶体中混有 KCl 和 $NaNO_3$ 晶体时,应如何提纯?

(黄　静)

第九章 | 综合及研究性实验

实验二十　醋酸解离平衡常数的测定与食醋中 HAc 含量的测定

【实验目的】

1. 掌握测定解离平衡常数及解离度的方法。
2. 掌握 pH 计的使用方法。
3. 掌握酸碱滴定法测定食醋中 HAc 的含量的方法。

【预习作业】

模拟设计实验：参照本实验的原理及步骤，以流程图方式写出本实验如何测定 HAc 的解离平衡常数与食醋中 HAc 的含量，并在流程图中标出测定步骤中的注意事项及依据。

引导问题：

1. 弱酸的解离平衡常数的意义是什么？
2. 可以用哪些方法测定弱酸的解离平衡常数？
3. 配制不同浓度的 HAc 溶液时所用容量瓶是否需要干燥？测定不同浓度的 HAc 溶液 pH 时所用小烧杯是否需要干燥？
4. 测定不同浓度的 HAc 溶液 pH 时为何溶液要按由稀到浓的顺序测定？

【实验原理】

醋酸是一元弱酸，$K_a = 1.76 \times 10^{-5}$，在水溶液中存在如下解离平衡：

$$HAc + H_2O \rightleftharpoons H_3O^+ + Ac^-$$

一定温度下，解离达到平衡时

$$K_a = \frac{[H_3O^+][Ac^-]}{[H_2O][HAc]} \approx \frac{[H_3O^+]^2}{c} \qquad (9\text{-}20\text{-}1)$$

$$\alpha = \frac{[H_3O^+]}{c} \qquad (9\text{-}20\text{-}2)$$

式（9-20-1）、式（9-20-2）中 $[H_3O^+]$、$[Ac^-]$、$[HAc]$ 为平衡体系中各物质平衡浓度，K_a、α 分别为 HAc 的解离平衡常数和解离度，c 为 HAc 溶液的原始浓度，可用 NaOH 标准溶液滴定测得。测定 HAc 溶液的 pH 可知 $[H_3O^+]$，从而计算 HAc 溶液的解离度和解离平衡常数。

食醋是一种酸性液态调味品。食醋中酸性物质通常包括乙酸、乳酸、葡萄糖酸、琥珀酸等，其中以乙酸含量最多，因此食醋中总酸含量是食醋质量的重要指标。《食品安全国家标准　食醋》

（GB 2719—2018）中规定食醋的总酸（以乙酸计）指标≥3.5 g·(100 mL)$^{-1}$。醋酸在食醋中的含量一般约为3.5~5.0 g·(100 mL)$^{-1}$，可以用 NaOH 标准溶液直接滴定。由于滴定突跃范围在碱性区域，故常用酚酞作为指示剂。

【仪器材料与试剂】

仪器　pH 计，碱式滴定管（25 mL）或聚四氟乙烯酸碱两用滴定管（25 mL），锥形瓶（250 mL×3），容量瓶（50 mL×4,100 mL），移液管（10 mL,25 mL），吸量管（5 mL），小烧杯（100 mL×4），温度计，滴定管架。

材料与试剂　0.1 mol·L^{-1} NaOH 标准溶液（精确到 0.000 1），0.1 mol·L^{-1} HAc 溶液，市售食醋，酚酞指示剂，pH = 6.86 和 pH = 4.00 的标准缓冲溶液。

【实验步骤】

（一）HAc 解离度和解离平衡常数的测定

1. HAc 溶液浓度的测定　用移液管吸取 25.00 mL 0.1 mol·L^{-1} HAc 置于锥形瓶中。加入 2 滴酚酞指示剂，用已知准确浓度的 NaOH 标准溶液滴定至溶液呈微红色且 30 s 内不褪色，即为滴定终点。采用相同方法平行测定三次，所消耗 NaOH 标准溶液的体积记于表 9-20-1 中，计算 HAc 溶液的准确浓度。

2. 配制不同浓度的HAc 溶液　取 4 个 50 mL 的容量瓶，分别加入 2.50 mL、5.00 mL、25.00 mL、50.00 mL 已知准确浓度的 HAc 溶液，配制系列不同浓度的 HAc 溶液，并计算稀释后的 HAc 溶液的浓度。

3. 测定HAc 溶液的pH　将40 mL 上述四种不同浓度的HAc 溶液分别转移至四只干燥小烧杯中，按溶液由稀到浓的顺序分别在pH 计上测定它们的pH。（pH 计的用法详见第二章"基础化学实验常用仪器"）。

根据实验测得的数据和 HAc 溶液的不同浓度，按式（9-20-2）和式（9-20-1）分别计算出 HAc 的解离度和解离平衡常数，将结果记录于表 9-20-2 中。

（二）食醋中 HAc 含量的测定

1. 食醋待测溶液的配制　用移液管吸取市售食醋 10.00 mL，置于 100 mL 容量瓶中，用蒸馏水稀释至刻度线，摇匀。

2. 食醋中HAc 含量的测定　用移液管吸取 25.00 mL 食醋待测溶液，置于锥形瓶中。加入 2 滴酚酞指示剂，用已知准确浓度的 NaOH 标准溶液进行滴定，滴定至溶液呈微红色并在 30 s 内不褪色，即为滴定终点。采用相同方法平行测定三次，数据记于表 9-20-3 中，按式（9-20-3）计算食醋中 HAc 含量

$$\rho(\text{HAc}) = \frac{c(\text{NaOH}) \times V(\text{NaOH}) \times M(\text{HAc})}{25.00 \times \dfrac{10.00}{100.00} \times 1\,000} \times 100\,[\text{g}\cdot(100\text{ mL})^{-1}] \tag{9-20-3}$$

$$M(\text{HAc}) = 60.05 \text{ g}\cdot\text{mol}^{-1}$$

【数据记录及结果处理】

日期：_____ 温度：_____℃ 相对湿度：_____

表 9-20-1 HAc 溶液浓度的测定

实验序号	1	2	3
指示剂			
终点颜色变化			
$V(\text{HAc})/\text{mL}$			
$V_{初}(\text{NaOH})/\text{mL}$			
$V_{终}(\text{NaOH})/\text{mL}$			
$\Delta V(\text{NaOH})/\text{mL}$			
$c(\text{NaOH})/\text{mol·L}^{-1}$			
$c(\text{HAc})/\text{mol·L}^{-1}$			
$\overline{c}(\text{HAc})/\text{mol·L}^{-1}$			
相对平均偏差 $\overline{d_r}/\%$			

表 9-20-2 HAc 溶液解离度和解离平衡常数的测定

实验序号	1	2	3	4
$c_{原始}(\text{HAc})/\text{mol·L}^{-1}$				
$V_{原始}(\text{HAc})/\text{mL}$	2.50	5.00	25.00	50.00
$V_{总}(\text{HAc 稀释后})/\text{mL}$	50.00	50.00	50.00	50.00
$c_{稀释}(\text{HAc})/\text{mol·L}^{-1}$				
pH				
$[\text{H}_3\text{O}^+]/\text{mol·L}^{-1}$				
α				
K_a				
$\overline{K_a}$				
相对平均偏差 $\overline{d_r}/\%$				

表 9-20-3 市售食醋中 HAc 含量的测定

实验序号	1	2	3
指示剂			
终点颜色变化			
$V_{原始}(\text{HAc})/\text{mL}$			
$V_{总}(\text{稀释后 HAc})/\text{mL}$			
$V_{待测液}(\text{稀释后 HAc})/\text{mL}$			
$V_{初}(\text{NaOH})/\text{mL}$			
$V_{终}(\text{NaOH})/\text{mL}$			
$\Delta V(\text{NaOH})/\text{mL}$			
$c(\text{NaOH})/\text{mol·L}^{-1}$			
$\rho(\text{HAc})/\text{g·mL}^{-1}$			
$\overline{\rho}(\text{HAc})\%/\text{g·mL}^{-1}$			
相对平均偏差 $\overline{d_r}/\%$			

【思考题】

1. 解离度和解离平衡常数在反映电解质性质时有何区别与联系？相同温度下,不同浓度的 HAc 溶液的解离度是否相同？其解离平衡常数是否相同？

2. 如果改变测定温度,则 HAc 溶液的解离度和解离平衡常数有无变化？

3. 在 NaOH 溶液滴定 HAc 溶液的实验中能否选用甲基红作为指示剂？若选用其作为指示剂,滴定结果是偏高还是偏低？

(李 蓉)

实验二十一 茶叶中钙、镁及铁含量的测定

【实验目的】

1. 掌握配位滴定法测定茶叶中钙、镁含量的原理和方法。
2. 掌握可见分光光度法测定茶叶中铁含量的原理和方法。
3. 学习茶叶的灰化处理方法。

【预习作业】

模拟设计实验:参照本实验的原理及步骤,以流程图方式分别写出配位滴定法测定茶叶中钙、镁含量以及可见分光光度法测定茶叶中铁含量的实验步骤和设计思路,并在流程图中注明各步骤的注意事项及依据。

引导性问题:

1. 请给出 EDTA 的结构和主要理化性质。
2. 溶液的 pH 对配合物的稳定性有何影响？
3. 如何消除样品中干扰金属离子对测定结果的影响？
4. 如何分别测量样品中钙、镁的含量？
5. 为什么采用邻二氮菲法测定样品中的 Fe^{2+} 含量？

【实验原理】

组成茶叶中的化学元素主要是 C、H、O 和 N,而且含有人体必需的 Ca、Mg、Fe 等多种微量元素。将茶叶在空气中置于敞口的蒸发皿或坩埚中加热,经氧化分解而烧成灰烬,再用酸溶解,可对处理后样品中的钙、镁及铁等多种元素含量进行分析。

选用配位滴定法可测得钙和镁总量。在 pH=10 的条件下,以铬黑 T 为指示剂,用 EDTA 标准溶液进行滴定。样品中的 Fe^{3+}、Al^{3+} 会干扰 Ca^{2+}、Mg^{2+} 的测定,滴定前需要加入三乙醇胺进行掩蔽。

茶叶中铁含量较低,可用分光光度法测定。首先用盐酸羟胺将 Fe^{3+} 还原成 Fe^{2+}:

$$2Fe^{3+} + 2NH_2OH \cdot HCl == 2Fe^{2+} + 4H^+ + N_2\uparrow + 2Cl^- + 2H_2O$$

邻二氮菲与 Fe^{2+} 生成稳定的橙红色的配合物如下:

在 20 ℃时,配合物的 lg$K_稳$ = 21.3,摩尔吸收系数 $\varepsilon_{508\,nm}$ = 1.10 × 10^4 L·mol^{-1}·cm^{-1}。需要注意的是,若溶液的 pH < 2,该显色反应速度较慢;若溶液的 pH > 9,则生成 Fe^{2+} 的氢氧化物沉淀。

【仪器材料与试剂】

仪器　可见分光光度计,万分之一分析天平,容量瓶(50 mL × 8,250 mL × 2),吸量管(25 mL,10 mL),量筒(10 mL,25 mL),碱式滴定管或酸碱两用型滴定管(25 mL 或 50 mL),锥形瓶(250 mL × 5),小烧杯(100 mL),蒸发皿或坩埚,玻璃漏斗,定量滤纸,玻璃棒等,滴定管架。

材料与试剂　6 mol·L^{-1} NH$_3$·H$_2$O 溶液,6 mol·L^{-1} HCl 溶液,0.010 0 mol·L^{-1} EDTA 标准溶液,0.010 g·L^{-1} Fe^{2+}标准溶液,25% 三乙醇胺溶液,NH$_3$-NH$_4$Cl 缓冲液(pH = 10),HAc-NaAc 缓冲液(pH = 4.6),0.1% 邻二氮菲溶液,1% 盐酸羟胺溶液,1% 铬黑 T,市售茶叶,去离子水等。

【实验步骤】

(一) 茶叶灰化及试液的制备

首先把干燥的茶叶研磨粉碎,然后准确称量茶叶细末 6~8 g(精确至 0.000 1 g),置于蒸发皿中,加热使之完全灰化,冷却后加入 10.0 mL 6 mol·L^{-1} HCl 溶液。

将溶液转移至小烧杯中,用约 20.0 mL 去离子水分三次洗涤蒸发皿,洗涤液全部并入小烧杯,然后用 6 mol·L^{-1} NH$_3$·H$_2$O 溶液调节 pH 为 6~7,使其产生沉淀。在沸水浴中加热 30 min,过滤,用去离子水洗涤烧杯和滤纸。滤液全部转移至 250 mL 容量瓶中,用去离子水稀释至刻度线,摇匀,贴上标签,标明为 Ca^{2+}、Mg^{2+}待测试液 1#。

用 10.0 mL 6 mol·L^{-1} HCl 溶液重新溶解滤纸上的沉淀,然后用去离子水洗涤滤纸 2 次,滤液全部转移至 250 mL 容量瓶中,用去离子水稀释至刻度线,摇匀,贴上标签,标明为 Fe^{2+}待测试液 2#。

(二) 茶叶中钙镁总含量的测定

从 1# 容量瓶中准确吸取 25.00 mL 试液置于 250 mL 锥形瓶中,加入 5.0 mL 三乙醇胺,再加 15.0 mL NH$_3$-NH$_4$Cl 缓冲溶液,摇匀。加入 2 滴铬黑 T 指示剂,用 0.010 0 mol·L^{-1} EDTA 标准溶液进行滴定,数据记于表 9-21-1 中。采用相同方法平行测定三次,利用 EDTA 溶液的体积,计算 c(Ca^{2+} 和 Mg^{2+}),以 CaO 的质量分数表示茶叶中钙镁总量。

(三) 茶叶中铁含量的测定

1. 邻二氮菲亚铁标准曲线的绘制　分别准确移取 0 mL、1.00 mL、2.00 mL、3.00 mL、4.00 mL、5.00 mL、6.00 mL Fe^{2+}标准溶液,置于 7 只依次编号的 50 mL 容量瓶中,然后分别加入 5.0 mL 盐酸羟胺溶液,5.0 mL 的 HAc-NaAc 缓冲溶液,5.00 mL 邻二氮菲溶液,用去离子水定容至刻度线,摇匀,放置 10 min。设定可见分光光度计的测定波长为 508 nm,以空白溶液作为对照,分别测定 Fe^{2+} 标准溶液的吸光度,数据记于表 9-21-2 中。以被测溶液中铁含量为横坐标,相应的吸光度为纵坐标,绘制邻二氮菲亚铁的标准曲线并拟合线性回归方程。

2. 茶叶中铁含量的测定　从 2# 容量瓶中准确移取 2.50 mL 待测试液,置于 50 mL 容量瓶中,后续操作同 3.1。采用相同方法平行测定三次,数据记于表 9-21-3 中。然后利用线性回归方程求得 $\rho_{稀释}(Fe^{2+})$,以 Fe_2O_3 质量分数 $\omega(Fe_2O_3)$ 表示茶叶中的铁含量。

【数据记录及结果分析】

日期:＿＿＿＿＿＿＿　温度:＿＿＿＿＿＿＿℃　相对湿度:＿＿＿＿＿＿＿

茶叶粉末样品的质量:＿＿＿＿＿＿＿ g

(一) 茶叶中总 Ca、Mg 质量分数的测定

表 9-21-1　茶叶中总 Ca、Mg 质量分数 ω 的测定

实验序号	1	2	3
待测试液 1#/mL	25.00	25.00	25.00
三乙醇胺/mL	5.0	5.0	5.0
NH_3-NH_4Cl 缓冲溶液/mL	15.0	15.0	15.0
指示剂			
$V_{初}(EDTA)/mL$			
终点颜色变化			
$V_{终}(EDTA)/mL$			
$\Delta V_{消耗}(EDTA)/mL$			
$c(Ca^{2+}和Mg^{2+})/mol\cdot L^{-1}$			
$\bar{c}(Ca^{2+}和Mg^{2+})/mol\cdot L^{-1}$			
茶叶中总 Ca、Mg 质量分数 $\omega(CaO)/g\cdot g^{-1}$			
平均质量分数 $\bar{\omega}(CaO)/g\cdot g^{-1}$			
相对平均偏差 $\bar{d}_r$			

以 CaO 的质量分数表示茶叶中的钙镁总量

$$\omega(CaO)=\frac{c(EDTA)\times\Delta V_{消耗}(EDTA)\times M_r(CaO)}{m(样品)\times\dfrac{25.0}{250.00}\times 1\,000}\times100\%\,(g\cdot g^{-1}) \qquad (9\text{-}21\text{-}1)$$

$$M_r(CaO)=56.077\,4$$

(二) 茶叶中 Fe 质量分数的测定

表 9-21-2 标准曲线的测定

实验序号	1	2	3	4	5	6	7
Fe^{2+}标准溶液/mL	0	1.00	2.00	3.00	4.00	5.00	6.00
盐酸羟胺/mL	5.0	5.0	5.0	5.0	5.0	5.0	5.0
HAc-NaAc 缓冲溶液/mL	5.0	5.0	5.0	5.0	5.0	5.0	5.0
邻二氮菲/mL	5.00	5.00	5.00	5.00	5.00	5.00	5.00
$V_{总}$(稀释)/mL	50.00	50.00	50.00	50.00	50.00	50.00	50.00
$\rho_{稀释}(Fe^{2+})/g \cdot L^{-1}$							
吸光度 A							
线性回归方程							
R^2							

绘制标准曲线及拟合线性回归方程。

表 9-21-3 茶叶中 Fe 质量分数 ω 的测定

实验序号	1	2	3
待测试液 2#/mL	2.50	2.50	2.50
盐酸羟胺/mL	5.0	5.0	5.0
HAc-NaAc 缓冲溶液/mL	5.0	5.0	5.0
邻二氮菲/mL	5.00	5.00	5.00
$V_{总}$(稀释)/mL	50.00	50.00	50.00
吸光度 A			
$\rho(Fe^{2+})/g \cdot L^{-1}$			
$\overline{\rho}(Fe^{2+})/g \cdot L^{-1}$			
茶叶中铁的质量分数 $\omega(Fe_2O_3)/g \cdot g^{-1}$			
平均质量分数 $\overline{\omega}(Fe_2O_3)/g \cdot g^{-1}$			
相对平均偏差 $\overline{d_r}$			

以 Fe_2O_3 的质量分数表示茶叶中的铁含量

$$\omega(Fe_2O_3) = \frac{\rho(Fe^{2+}) \times 50.00}{m(样品) \times \dfrac{2.50}{250.00} \times 1\,000} \times \frac{M_r(Fe_2O_3)}{2 \times M_r(Fe)} \times 100\% (g \cdot g^{-1}) \tag{9-21-2}$$

$$M_r(Fe_2O_3) = 159.688, \quad M_r(Fe) = 55.845$$

【思考题】

1. 简述分光光度法测定铁的原理,用该法测得的铁含量是否为茶叶中亚铁含量? 为什么?
2. 为什么 pH 为 6~7 时,能将 Fe^{3+} 与 Ca^{2+}、Mg^{2+} 完全分离?
3. 测定 Ca^{2+}、Mg^{2+} 时,为什么加入三乙醇胺溶液? 测定 Fe^{2+} 时,为什么加入盐酸羟胺溶液?

(苟宝迪)

第十章 | 开放设计性实验

实验二十二 开放设计性实验

【实验项目】

1. NH_3 解离常数 K_b 测定。
2. 小苏打样品中 $NaHCO_3$ 含量测定。
3. 明矾样品中 Al^{3+} 含量测定。
4. 铜盐样品中 Cu^{2+} 含量测定。
5. 蛋壳中 Ca^{2+} 含量测定。

【实验目的】

1. 查阅资料,自主设计实验方案,培养综合实验技能。
2. 掌握定量测定某些物质含量的分析方法。
3. 掌握化学实验规范化基本操作。
4. 掌握实验数据处理方法。

【仪器材料与试剂】

仪器 万分之一分析天平,台秤,可见分光光度计,pH 计,电炉,水浴加热锅,滴定台,酒精灯,三脚架,石棉网,吸量管(1 mL,2 mL,5 mL,10 mL,20 mL),移液管(10 mL×2,25 mL×2),量筒(5 mL,10 mL,25 mL),酸式滴定管(25 mL),碱式滴定管(25 mL)或两用滴定管(25 mL),比色管(25 mL×6),烧杯(50 mL×6,100 mL,250 mL),锥形瓶(250 mL×3),容量瓶(50 mL×3,100 mL×3,250 mL),玻璃棒,胶头滴管,称量瓶,漏斗,滤纸等。

材料与试剂

1. 待测物质 $NH_3 \cdot H_2O$(1.0 mol·L^{-1})溶液,明矾样品,小苏打样品,铜盐样品,蛋壳样品。
2. 一级标准物质 无水 Na_2CO_3(A.R.),$KHC_8H_4O_4$(A.R.),$CuSO_4 \cdot 5H_2O$(A.R.),$MgSO_4 \cdot 7H_2O$(A.R.),$ZnSO_4 \cdot 7H_2O$(A.R.)。
3. 其他试剂 6 mol·L^{-1} H_2SO_4 溶液,6 mol·L^{-1} HCl 溶液,0.1 mol·L^{-1} HCl 溶液,6 mol·L^{-1} HNO_3 溶液,蒸馏水,pH=10 的 NH_3-NH_4Cl 缓冲溶液,0.1 mol·L^{-1} NaOH 溶液,1.0 mol·L^{-1} HAc-NaAc 缓冲溶液,6.0 mol·L^{-1} $NH_3 \cdot H_2O$ 溶液,0.01 mol·L^{-1} EDTA 溶液,0.05 mol·L^{-1} EDTA 溶液,95% 乙醇,三乙醇胺等。
4. 指示剂 酚酞,甲基橙,铬黑T(s),二甲酚橙,钙红指示剂(s),广泛pH 试纸等。

【具体要求】

(一) 实验方案设计

1. 组队　学生以4~5的人数为限,自行组成团队(考核前1~2周)。

2. 设计并提交项目方案　每个团队提交五个项目方案。

团队成立后,成员一起通过查阅文献资料,结合【仪器材料与试剂】中提及的仪器、材料、试剂、表 10-22-1 中检测试样用量范围等信息,设计每个项目的实验方案,列出仪器设备、试剂用量、试剂浓度等内容。

要求每个项目提交 1 个方案。方案内容包括:实验目的、实验原理、仪器、试剂、实验步骤、数据记录表格、参考文献。

(二) 实验方案操作考核与结果

1. 项目方案审阅　教师对每个团队的五个项目方案进行评判和纠错,并评分。

2. 考核项目确定　教师从五个项目中指定其中一个项目作为团队考核的内容。

3. 操作考核　教师根据团队人数,将每个考核项目分成4~5个具有连续性和相对独立性的操作内容。团队所有成员在规定时间内,依次按项目方案步骤独立完成教师指定的操作内容,教师记录学生操作过程中的具体表现,并给予评分。

4. 完成项目报告　操作考核结束后,团队要在指定的时间内进行数据处理,完成项目报告。

5. 汇报与答辩　每个团队由一名成员代表汇报项目完成情况(包括实验现象、实验数据、实验结果、结论、讨论、参考文献等)。汇报完毕后,团队所有成员对教师或其他团队提出的问题进行答辩。教师根据该团队汇报和答辩的完整性、流畅性和准确性等进行评分。

6. 提交项目报告　根据答辩意见修改并提交项目报告。

表 10-22-1　实验项目

序号	实验项目	检测试样用量范围
1	NH_3 解离常数 K_b 的测定	10.00 mL
2	小苏打样品中 $NaHCO_3$ 含量测定	1.000 0 ~1.200 0 g
3	明矾中样品中 Al^{3+} 含量测定	1.300 0 ~1.400 0 g
4	铜盐样品中 Cu^{2+} 含量测定	0.700 0 ~0.800 0 g
5	蛋壳中 Ca^{2+} 含量测定	0.150 0 ~0.200 0 g

方案可参考表 10-22-1 中检测样品的用量范围,计算出一级标准物质及其他试剂所需的量,并根据仪器精度及分析的误差要求,尽可能提高检测结果准确度。

(三) 成绩构成

成绩由项目方案、操作、项目报告、汇报与答辩四部分构成,详见表 10-22-2。

表 10-22-2　实验考核评分表

考核时间:_____年____月___日　星期____　节次____

课程		教　师	
年级		专　业	
项目编号		实验室	

续表

考核编号	1	2	3	4	5
姓名					
班组					
学号					
操作内容					
操作时长					
不规范操作等事项					
实验操作/50分					
项目方案/25分					
实验报告(数据处理、结果与结论)/20分					
答辩/5分					
合计得分					

【提示】

1. 在一定吸收波长范围内,$[Cu(NH_3)_4]^{2+}$浓度与吸光度的关系参见表 10-22-3。

表 10-22-3　$[Cu(NH_3)_4]^{2+}$浓度与吸光度的关系

$[Cu(NH_3)_4]^{2+}$浓度 c/mol·L^{-1}	0.002~0.01
吸光度 A	0.1~0.5

2. 制备$[Cu(NH_3)_4]^{2+}$溶液时,Cu^{2+}浓度与NH_3溶液浓度的参考比:

$$1:200~1:40$$

3. 0.15~0.20 g 蛋壳的溶解与消化大概需要 3.0~4.0 mL 的 6 mol·L^{-1} HNO$_3$,可加热助溶。

4. 一级标准物质的称量范围一般为计算量的 ±10%。

5. 如使用 25.00 mL 规格的滴定管,标准溶液消耗量控制在 20.00 mL 左右,置于锥形瓶内待测溶液也控制在 5.00 mL 的倍数。

6. 设计实验方案时,把固体物质样品配成 100.00 mL 溶液,每次取 20.00 mL 样品溶液进行测定。

【思考题】

1. 用 pH 计测定不同浓度的 NH_3 溶液 pH 时,为何要以由稀到浓的顺序进行?

2. 在用滴定法进行小苏打中 $NaHCO_3$ 含量测定时,为何接近终点时需剧烈振摇溶液?

3. 明矾中样品中 Al^{3+} 含量测定为何不宜采用直接滴定法?

4. 使用可见分光光度计测试时,是否一定要测定样品最大吸收波长?在测定最大吸收波长过程中,能否根据互补光原理缩小测定范围?

5. 如何测定蛋壳中 Mg^{2+} 含量?

(李福森)

Part I   Experiment Essentials in Basic Chemistry

Chapter 1	Laboratory Rules and Safety Information

1. The Purpose of Experiments in Basic Chemistry

The experiment is an important part of Basic Chemistry. Beyond to help students confirm chemical theories and chemical phenomena so as to understand and grasp the contents of Basic Chemistry, the more important purpose of it is to help them study the scientific experimental methods, learn to combine theory with practice, and apply theory to practice, so as to cultivate rigorous scientific attitude and comprehensive experimental skills.

By following strict experimental discipline, students should master standard chemical experimental techniques, learn to record and process experimental data, express their results accurately, and analyze experimental phenomena or problems correctly in order to draw valid conclusions ; learn to summarize the experimental rules, and give the experimental conclusions. By the exercises of experiment design and completion, cultivate the original capacity to think and solve problems independently. Meanwhile, foster the scientific rigor, master the research methods and apply the experimental skills.

2. General Rules in the Laboratory

(1) Before entering the chemistry laboratory for the first time, you must read the laboratory guidelines and safety rules carefully.

(2) Before the experiment, preview the Experiment Instruction Book and read the relevant textbooks and references to understand the purposes, principles, methods and procedures of the experiments. Get ready with the preliminary report for the experiment.

(3) Read the instrumental operating manual carefully. Follow instructions carefully and do not perform unauthorized experiments and operations.

(4) Wear a white lab coat in the laboratory and are not allowed to wear slippers. Be serious and correct operation in your experiments. Observe the experiment phenomena and record experiment data carefully. Complete experiment reports based on the source recordings in time.

(5) Never work alone in the laboratory. Report all accidents, no matter how minor, to the instructor in a timely manner.

(6) Common instruments and sharing reagents are only allowed to be used at their original places but not allowed to move anywhere.

(7) Never return chemicals to their original container. Always read the label twice before using a chemical reagent. Be sure the concentration, as well as the name of the reagent is correct.

(8) Don't touch the inside of the reagent bottle stoppers with other surfaces. Switching reagent bottle stoppers will invariably contaminate the reagent. To avoid this contamination, it is recommended to open only one bottle of reagent at a time. If the stopper is the penny head type, hold it between the fingers of the hand you are pouring with. If you do this, you can be certain you are not mixing up stoppers or contaminating the reagent when pouring the reagent.

(9) Do not bring food into the laboratory. Don't drink or eat in the laboratory.

(10) Ensure safety during experiments. All flammable chemicals should be kept away from any source of ignition. Keep the lab and the table top clean and tidy. Do not dispose of insoluble items on the floor. Used test paper, matches, etc. should be placed in a beaker and be deposed of in designated containers after the experiment finished. Corrosive and toxic chemicals must be recycled in accordance with regulations. Never depose of solid waste, caustic liquids and toxic reagents into sinks.

(11) Do not leave the lab before the ending of the experiment without authorization. Only be allowed to leave after the experiment finished, the work site and the instruments have been cleaned, the reagents have been tidied up, the power and water source been turned off, windows and doors been closed.

3. Safety Information

(1) Protection against water, electricity, and fire: When entering the laboratory for the first time, you must understand all the escape routes. Every time you enter the laboratory, first open the laboratory window and ensure good ventilation. Confirm the installation of water, electricity and gas in the laboratory, the storage location of the fire extinguishing equipment and the method of use for emergency use.

(2) Hazardous substance and toxic gases protection: Be cautious of flammable, explosive, toxic, corrosive and other hazardous substances. When using or dealing with these hazardous substance, poisonous and harmful gases or volatile toxic substances, perform at a well-ventilated place such as a fume hood and far away from any flame.

(3) Chemical operation protection: When heating liquids in test tubes, dry the outside wall at first, never point the tube toward yourself or anyone else. Never heat the test tube directly at the bottom but tilt the tube and heat it gently between the bottom of the tube and the top of the liquid.

(4) Chemical reagents protection: When opening reagent bottles of hydrochloric acid, nitric acid, ammonia or hydrogen peroxide, be careful that the reagent dashes out. Do not smell directly near the bottle but use your hand to slightly waft the scent over toward your nose. When using concentrated acid, concentrated base, or cleaning solution, avoid the chemical spilling on skin or cloth. Especially protect eyes from chemical injure (wearing protective glasses).

(5) Personal safety protection: Wear protective glasses and a lab apron to protect your eyes, skin and clothing whenever you are working with hot or corrosive liquids. Leather shoes are preferred to canvas or open-toed shoes.

(6) Chemicals treatment: Keep the table tops clean. Wipe up acid and base spills promptly. If you

spill a chemical on your eyes or skin, flush the area immediately with plenty of water, then wash the area with soap and water if the treated place is skin.

(7) Use of electrical equipment: When using electrical equipment, be sure of the voltage-current-power matching. Never touch the electric connector with a wet hand and make sure that the water and the electricity are separated.

(8) Laboratory spare first aid kit: The first-aid kit is required for the student's laboratory. Common first-aid kits for emergency use include: medical gauze block, medical elastic bandage, band-aid, medical breathable tape, iodophor disinfectant, medical applicator, medical alcohol cotton film, clean wipes, burns, first aid manuals, etc.

4. The Treatment of Accidents in Chemistry Experiments

(1) Cut: Coat the injured area with adhesive bandages after applying iodine.

(2) Scald: Daub the wound with scald medicament, or wet the wound with a concentrated $KMnO_4$ solution till the skin turns brown, then apply vaseline or scalding ointment.

(3) Acid or base corrosion: Rinse with a great deal of water at once. For acid burn, after rinsing, treat with saturated sodium bicarbonate solution, or diluted ammonia, or soapy water. In case of chemical burn caused by concentrated sulfuric acid, it is necessary to wipe with cotton wool before rinsing with water. If the eye is spattered in by acid, wash with water and then treat with sodium bicarbonate solution 1%-3%, followed by rinse with water. For alkali burn, after rinsing, treat with acetic acid 2%-5% or boric acid 3% solutions. If the eye is splashed by an alkali solution, wash with water and then treat with 3% boric acid solutions, followed by rinsing with water. After the above treatments, send to the hospital for further therapy.

(4) Toxic gas inhalation: If inhaling toxic gases such as bromine, chlorine or hydrogen chloride, leave the toxic atmosphere immediately and breathe fresh air outside. A small amount of alcohol mixed with ether can be inhaled to detoxify. If inhaling hydrogen sulfide or carbon monoxide gas, take a breath of fresh air outside immediately.

(5) Poison intake: Drink a cup of diluted cupric sulfate solution, touch the throat with a finger to bring anabole, and then go to the hospital.

(6) Electric shock accident: Keep electric appliance isolated from the water and the lab bench dry and tidy. When using electrical equipment, do not touch the electric appliance and the plug with wet hands. In the event of electric shock, never attempt to remove the victim from the scene with your hand directly, but cut off the power supply immediately. If the electric appliance is on fire, turn off the power immediately to prevent electric shock and then extinguish the fire.

5. Common Sense on Fire Prevention, Anti-electricity and Fire-Extinguishment in the Chemical Laboratory

5.1　Some main causes of fire in the lab

1) Flammable materials near the fire. Laboratory safety requirements: Do not use open flame heating.

2) Wire aging, connector badness and electric equipment trouble.

3) Improper chemical reaction, such as unclear chemical properties and improper operation.

4) Mixing the following together may cause fire:

Activated carbon and ammonium nitrate;

Clothing contaminated by strong oxidants such as potassium chlorate;

Rag and concentrated sulfuric acid;

Flammable materials, such as wood and fiber, and concentrated nitric acid;

Organic and liquid oxygen;

Aluminum and organic chlorides;

Hydrogen phosphide, silane, metal alkyl or white phosphorus contacting air.

5.2 Fire-extinguishing methods

Once a fire burns in the lab, do not panic, but extinguish the fire by following the methods in Table 1-1 and call the fire brigade in time.

Table 1-1 Extinguishing Methods for Inflammable

Inflammable	Extinguishing method	Note
Paper, textile or wood	Sand, water, fire extinguishers	Need cooling and isolated from the air
Organic solvents such as oil, benzene etc.	CO_2 or dry-powder fire extinguisher, asbestos cloth, dry sand, etc.	Applicable for valuable instruments. Do not use a foam fire extinguisher to extinguish oil, gas, etc.
Alcohol, ether etc.	Water	Need to dilute, cool and be apart from air
Wire, electric meters or instruments	CCl_4, CO_2 extinguishers	Extinguish material unable to conduct electricity. Do not use water and foam extinguisher
Flammable gas	Close the gas, fire extinguisher	Do everything possible to cut off the gas source
Active metals such as potassium and sodium, or phosphide contacting water	Dry sand, dry-powder fire extinguisher	Do not use water, foam or CO_2 extinguishers
Clothing	Roll on the ground to put out the fire or put off clothing, cover the clothing with fireproofing material	Do not run, otherwise it aggravates burning

5.3 Protection against electric shock

Cut off the power supply first, use insulators such as dry wooden sticks or bamboo poles as soon as possible to make the electric shocker out of the power supply. Treat with artificial breathing when necessary and sent to the hospital for rescue immediately.

(CHEN Zhi Qiong)

Chapter 2 | Ordinary Instruments in Basic Chemistry Experiments

1. Introduction of Ordinary Instruments in the Chemical Laboratory

In the laboratory, common instruments include various types of glassware, such as containers and volumetric equipment, categorized by their specific uses.

1.1 Containers

A container is any receptacle used to hold substances during storage or heating at room temperature or elevated temperatures. Common examples include test tubes, beakers, flasks, and funnels, as shown in Figure 2-1. Choose containers of appropriate types and specifications based on their intended use and

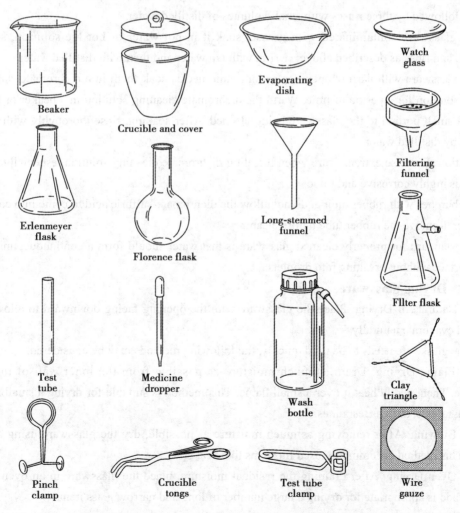

Figure 2-1   Common laboratory equipment in chemistry

the quantity of material involved.

1.2 Volumetric Glassware

Volumetric glassware refers to glass containers designed to measure liquid volumes accurately and to transfer solutions. Common types include graduated cylinders, burettes, volumetric flasks, pipettes, and volumetric pipettes. These items vary in their degree of accuracy. Volumetric glassware should not be used as general-purpose containers—for example, for dissolving, diluting, heating, holding hot solutions, or long-term storage. Each item is marked to indicate its calibration type: "TC" (to contain) means the item holds the specified volume when filled to the calibration line, while "TD" (to deliver) means it delivers the specified volume when dispensed to the calibration line. Other instruments include glassware and non-glassware.

2. Cleaning and Drying Glassware

2.1 Cleaning glassware

Glassware should first be soaked and / or scrubbed with tap water. Then, use a brush with detergent to clean both the inside and outside surfaces. Rinse thoroughly with plenty of tap water until no foam remains, followed by three rinses with small volumes of distilled water.

For glassware contaminated with grease, soak it in hot water or hot lye solution, scrub with detergent, and rinse as described above — first with tap water and then with distilled water.

For glassware with narrow openings or long, thin necks, soak them in a dichromate–sulfuric acid cleaning solution for a period of time. Warm the dichromate cleaning solution in a beaker or flask, then transfer a small portion to the glassware being cleaned. After soaking, rinse thoroughly with tap water, followed by distilled water.

Caution: Exercise extreme care when handling dichromate cleaning solution, especially when it is hot, as it is highly corrosive and toxic.

For burettes with rubber tubing, do not allow the dichromate-sulfuric acid to come into contact with the rubber. Remove the rubber tube before cleaning.

The standard for properly cleaned glassware is that water should form a continuous, uniform film on the surface without breaking into droplets.

2.2 Drying glassware

(1) Natural Air Drying: Place the glassware with the opening facing downward to allow water to drain and evaporate naturally.

If the glassware needs to be used quickly, the following methods may be considered.

(2) Flame Drying: Drain as much moisture as possible from the inner wall of the cleaned glassware. Then, gently heat it over a small flame. This method is suitable for drying a small number of small glass items, such as test tubes.

(3) Blowing: After removing as much moisture as possible, dry the glassware using an electric blower. This method is commonly used for items like beakers.

(4) Oven Drying: After draining the residual moisture, place the glassware in an oven at 105 ℃. This method is appropriate for drying a large number of long and narrow glass items.

(5) Drying with Organic Solvents: Drain as much residual moisture as possible, then rinse the

glassware with a volatile solvent such as acetone or ethanol. Recover the solvent if necessary. Finally, air-dry or use a blower to complete the drying.

Additional Notes on Cleaning Volumetric Glassware

Since volumetric glassware has calibrated markings, it is generally not cleaned with a brush. Instead, it can be soaked in chromic acid cleaning solution for a period of time, then rinsed with tap water, followed by multiple rinses with distilled water.

Glassware expands and contracts with temperature changes. Because an object that expands upon heating may not return exactly to its original volume upon cooling, volumetric glassware should be heated or dried only within the specified calibration temperature range.

Since volumetric glassware has a calibrated scale, it is generally not cleaned with a brush. Instead, it can be soaked in chromic acid cleaning solution for a period of time, then rinsed with tap water, followed by several rinses with distilled water.

Glassware expands and contracts with temperature changes, and an item that expands when heated may not return to its exact original volume when cooled. Therefore, volumetric glassware should only be heated or dried within the temperature range indicated by its calibration mark.

3. Operation of Instrument

3.1   Operation of basic volumetric glassware

(1) Burettes: A burette is a graduated glass tube with a stopcock at one end, used for accurately delivering known volumes of liquids, especially during titrations. There are different types of burettes—acid burettes, base burettes, and polytetrafluoroethylene (PTFE) burettes—each with a slightly different structure.

An acid burette consists of a long, uniformly narrow glass tube marked with volume graduations and fitted with a ground-glass stopcock. It is designed for handling acidic or oxidative reagents, as shown in Figure 2-2(a).

A base burette is fitted with a rubber tube that contains a glass ball and a short delivery tip. It is used for delivering alkaline solutions, as shown in Figure 2-2(b).

A PTFE burette has a structure similar to that of the acid burette but features a stopcock made of polytetrafluoroethylene (PTFE). This gives it resistance to both acids and bases, allowing it to function like an acid burette while offering greater chemical durability.

A conventional burette is typically graduated in 0.1 mL increments and comes in volumes of 25 mL or 50 mL. The reading precision can be estimated to 0.01 mL. In contrast, semimicro and micro burettes come in smaller volumes—10 mL, 5 mL, 2 mL, or 1 mL—with finer graduations down to 0.05 mL, 0.01 mL, or even 0.005 mL, allowing for more precise titrations in small-scale experiments.

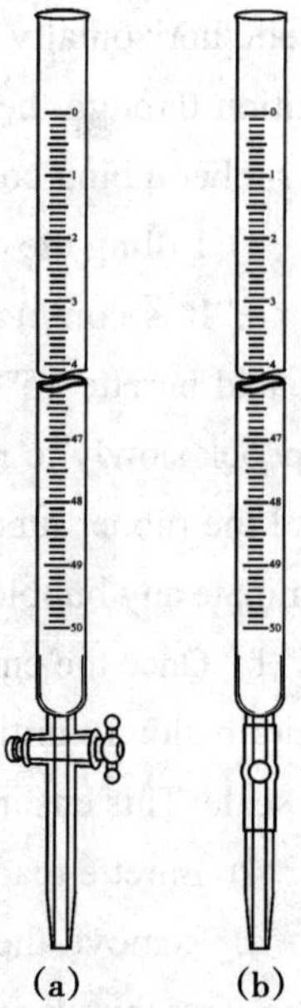

(a)   (b)

Figure 2-2   Burettes
(a) Acid (PTFE) burette;
(b) Base burette.

1) Checking Liquid-Tightness and Assembly

a. Acid Burette: Before using an acid burette, check to ensure it is intact and functioning properly. Dry the stopcock with a soft tissue, then apply a small amount of vaseline (or stopcock grease). Spread a thin, even layer around the stopcock, Figure 2-3(a). avoiding excess grease near the hole and ensuring none enters the bore, Figure 2-3(b). Insert the stopcock and rotate it to distribute the grease evenly. The stopcock should have a uniform, transparent layer of grease and must not leak.

b. Base Burette: Base burettes do not require greasing. However, the glass bead should fit tightly within the rubber tubing to ensure a good seal and prevent leakage.

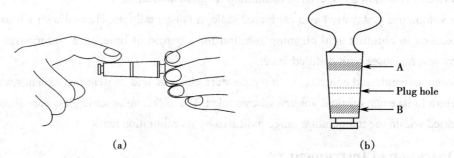

(a)   (b)

Figure 2-3   Stopcock of Acid Burette and Greasing Method

(a) Grease the stopcock; (b) Parts of the stopcock.

2) Rinsing: Before filling the burette with the titration solution, rinse it 2–3 times with about 10 mL of the same solution to remove any residual water and ensure the correct concentration. Hold the burette horizontally and rotate it to coat the entire inner surface with the rinsing solution. Expel the rinse solution through the stopcock—either by opening the stopcock in an acid burette or by gently pinching the rubber tubing containing the glass bead in a base burette.

3) Filling the operation solution and removing air bubbles

a. It is common practice to slightly overfill a burette, then either fully open the stopcock or tilt the acid burette 15°–30° from the horizontal plane and open the stopcock slowly to remove air bubbles. For a base burette, gently bend the rubber tube and pinch the glass bead to eject liquid and eliminate any bubbles (Figure 2-4).

b. Once the entire burette is free of bubbles, allow the liquid to drain slowly until the meniscus aligns with the zero mark on the scale. This ensures there is enough titrant for the titration.

4) Burette reading

a. Remove the burette from the clamp and hold it upright

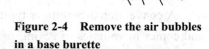

Figure 2-4   Remove the air bubbles in a base burette

using your thumb and index or middle finger. Wait 1–2 minutes after the liquid stabilizes before taking a reading, ensuring that any liquid adhering to the inner wall has fully settled or drained.

b. To accurately measure the volume delivered or added, read the scale at eye level, aligned with the bottom of the meniscus. Record both the initial and final volumes, and calculate the difference to determine the total volume of solution delivered. When reading, make sure no droplets are clinging to the inner wall of the burette or hanging from the tip. The reading should be precise to the nearest 0.01 mL.

c. For colorless or light-colored solutions, the meniscus is usually clear, and the bottom of the meniscus is taken as the reading point, as shown in Figure 2-5(a). For dark or colored solutions (e.g., $KMnO_4$, I_2), the meniscus is less distinct, so the reading should be taken at the top of the meniscus. The reading shown in Figure 2-5(a) is 23.55 mL.

d. When using a burette with a colorless solution, it may be difficult to see the bottom of the meniscus. The blue strip technique can aid in accurate readings, as shown in Figure 2-5(b). Align your eyes at the point where the two curved meniscus lines intersect. For colored solutions, align your eye with the top of the meniscus. The reading in Figure 2-5(b) is 25.00 mL.

e. The most accurate readings are obtained using a meniscus illuminator, as shown in Figure 2-5(c). This device features a white and a black field. Position the black field about 1 mm below the meniscus; this causes the meniscus to appear black. The bottom of the darkened meniscus is used as the reading level. The reading in Figure 2-5(c) is 32.45 mL.

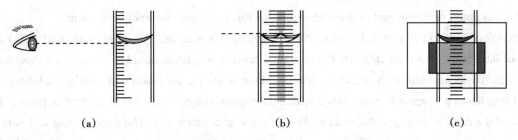

(a)   (b)   (c)

Figure 2-5   Read the burette

(a) The way of reading volume for burette. (b) The way of reading volume for blue Strip burette. (c) The way of reading volume by black background for burette.

5) Titration

a. The burette should be clamped vertically on the stand. Any droplet remaining on the burette tip should be removed by gently touching it to the outer wall of the receiving container. The titration is performed using the sample solution placed in an Erlenmeyer flask, which should rest on a sheet of white paper to provide contrast. The burette tip should be positioned approximately 1 cm above the neck of the flask.

For acid burettes, the reverse grip method is used during titration. The stopcock is operated with the left hand, while the burette is held with the right hand, applying gentle inward pressure on the stopcock using the thumb, index, and middle fingers to prevent leakage. The conical flask (Erlenmeyer flask) is swirled with the right hand, and the burette tip should be inserted 1–2 cm into the neck of the flask by gently lifting the flask.

During titration, the flask should be rotated in a consistent circular direction, as shown in Figure 2-6. Do not shake the flask back and forth, as this may cause spillage.

The recommended delivery rate is approximately 10 mL per minute, or 3–4 drops per second. As the titration approaches the end point, reduce the rate to a stepwise drop-by-drop pace. Rinse any droplets adhering to the inner wall of the flask with a small amount of distilled water. When the color halo fades slowly, it indicates that the end point is near.

At this stage, you may add half a drop of titrant by slightly opening the stopcock to suspend a drop at the tip, then gently touch the droplet to the inner wall of the flask to release it. Afterward, rinse the flask wall with distilled water to ensure the droplet mixes completely.

Finally, if any droplet remains hanging from the burette tip, do not include its volume in the final reading.

b. The titration operation using PTFE burettes is similar to that of acid burettes.

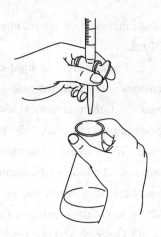

Figure 2-6　Titration operation

c. For base burettes, pinch the rubber tubing just above the glass ball—using your thumb and index finger—to create a small gap, allowing the solution to flow out of the burette tip. The flow rate can be adjusted by changing the size of the gap.

Do not pinch the lower part of the rubber tube, as this may cause air bubbles to form.

(2) Volumetric Flasks: A volumetric flask (also called a measuring flask or graduated flask) is a piece of laboratory glassware calibrated to contain a precise volume of liquid at a specific temperature. Volumetric flasks are commonly used for accurate dilutions and the preparation of standard solutions.

These flasks are typically pear-shaped with a flat bottom and are made of either glass or plastic. The mouth of the flask is usually fitted with a plastic snap cap or screw cap. The neck is long and narrow, with an etched graduation ring. This ring indicates the exact volume the flask contains when filled to that mark at the calibration temperature, as shown in Figure 2-7(a).

Volumetric flasks come in various sizes, typically ranging from 25 mL, 100 mL, and 250 mL to 500 mL and 1 000 mL.

Volumetric flasks should not be used for long-term storage. Once a solution is prepared and mixed in the flask, it should be transferred to a suitable storage container. The volumetric flask should then be rinsed and cleaned promptly.

1) Checking of liquid-tightness: Fill the flask with water to about two-thirds of its volume. Hold the stopper firmly in place with your index finger and grip the body of the flask with your other hand. Invert the flask and swirl or shake it vigorously. If there is no leakage, return the flask to an upright position, rotate the stopper 180°, then invert the flask again to confirm that it is liquid-tight.

2) Transfer and constant volume of solution

a. Volumetric flasks are used only for containing prepared solutions, not for dissolving solids directly. A weighed sample should first be dissolved in a beaker using about 10%–20% of the final solvent volume. The solution is then transferred into a volumetric flask of appropriate size and diluted to the calibration mark with solvent. If the solute is difficult to dissolve, gentle heating may be used during dissolution. However, the solution must be cooled to room temperature before transferring, to avoid volume errors due to thermal expansion.

b. The correct method for transferring a solution into a volumetric flask is shown in Figure 2-7(b).

The lower end of a glass rod should extend into the neck of the flask and rest just below the calibration mark. To prevent the liquid from flowing onto the outer wall, no other part of the glass rod should touch the flask. Position the beaker near the upper part of the glass rod and tilt it slightly so that the solution flows smoothly along the rod into the flask. As the solution transfers, gently raise the beaker while keeping contact with the glass rod, then slowly return it to an upright position to allow any remaining droplets to run back into the beaker.

Rinse the beaker and glass rod three times with small amounts of solvent, and pour the rinsing liquid into the flask (until about half full). Swirl the solution to mix thoroughly. Finally, use a dropper to carefully add solvent until the bottom of the meniscus aligns with the center of the calibration mark, ensuring your eye is at the same level as the mark. The final solution should be thoroughly mixed by swirling or by inverting the flask several times.

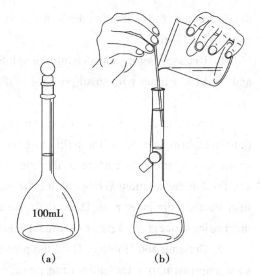

Figure 2-7　Volumetric Flask and Its Use
(a) Volumetric flask; (b) Operation.

c. If the meniscus is slightly below the calibration mark due to residual solution clinging to the inner wall of the flask neck, do not add more solvent—this does not significantly affect the final concentration. However, if the meniscus is above the calibration mark, the solution must be discarded and prepared again, as the concentration will be incorrect.

(3) Volumetric pipette and Pipettor

1) Volumetric pipette: Volumetric pipettes, also known as bulb pipettes or transfer pipettes, are designed to deliver a single, precise volume of liquid. They have a large bulb and a long, narrow stem with a single graduation mark. This mark indicates the exact volume the pipette is calibrated to deliver at a specific temperature (typically 25 ℃, marked as "TD"—to deliver). Common volumes include 5 mL, 10 mL, 25 mL, and 50 mL. These pipettes allow extremely accurate volume measurements, with typical accuracy reaching ± 0.01 mL.

Volumetric pipettes are widely used in analytical chemistry for preparing standard solutions from stock solutions and for precise titrations, as shown in Figure 2-8(a).

Measuring pipettes, in contrast, have a straight, uniform bore with multiple graduation marks, allowing delivery of variable volumes. They are shown in Figure 2-8(b).

There are five steps on operation of volumetric pipettes: "reading", "rinsing", "drawing", "holding" and "draining".

a. Reading before Operation, it is necessary to confirm the type, range,

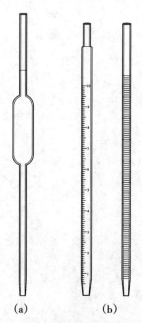

Figure 2-8　Pipettes
(a) Transfer pipettes;
(b) Measuring pipettes.

the direction of the calibration mark, the scale between graduated lines , and the word "吹" or "快" on the nozzle as well.

b. Rinsing: Before transferring the solution, the volumetric pipette should be thoroughly cleaned and rinsed 2–3 times with small portions of distilled water, allowing the water to drain completely each time.

Then, rinse the pipette with the solution to be measured: squeeze the air out of the rubber bulb (aurilave), bring the tip of the bulb close to the top of the pipette, and immerse the pipette vertically about 1.5 cm below the surface of the liquid. Slowly release the pressure on the bulb to draw up about one-third of the solution. While holding the pipette horizontally, rotate it to ensure that the rinse solution fully contacts the inner wall. Drain the rinse solution through either the tip or the top opening. Repeat this rinsing process 2–3 times to maintain solution concentration consistency.

c. Drawing and Holding: Hold the pipette vertically with your thumb and middle finger, keeping your grip just above the calibration mark. Immerse the pipette 1.5–2 cm below the surface of the solution, taking care not to touch the bottom of the container, Figure 2-9(a).

Using your other hand, place the rubber bulb over the top of the pipette and gently draw the liquid in until it slightly exceeds the calibration mark. Remove the bulb quickly and immediately place your index finger over the top opening to stop the flow.

d. Draining: Allow the liquid to slowly drain until the bottom of the meniscus aligns exactly with the calibration mark. This can be done by slightly loosening the pressure of your index finger and gently rotating the pipette between your thumb and middle finger.

Once adjusted, touch the tip of the pipette to the side of a waste container to remove any droplets clinging to the outside. Then, with the pipette held vertically, release your finger to allow the solution to

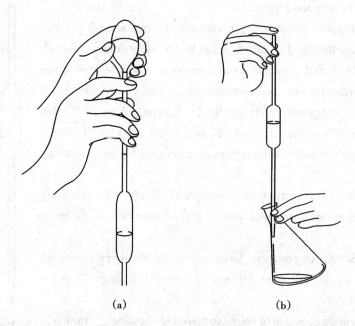

(a)   (b)

Figure 2-9   Operation of pipettes
(a) Drawing; (b) Draining operating pipettes.

drain into the receiving vessel. The pipette tip should be in contact with the inside wall of the vessel to enable smooth, splash-free delivery.

Most volumetric pipettes are calibrated "to deliver" (TD), meaning a small amount of liquid remains in the tip. After draining, wait 10–15 seconds—capillary action will allow part of this liquid to flow out, Figure 2-9(b).

Do not blow out or shake the remaining liquid unless the pipette is marked with the Chinese character "吹" (blow-out) or "快" (fast delivery), indicating that it is designed to be emptied completely. Otherwise, the residual liquid is already accounted for in the calibration.

The operation of measuring pipettes is the same as the transfer pipettes.

2) Pipettor: A pipettor, also known as a micropipette, is used to transfer precise volumes of liquid. The most common type is the single-channel pipettor (Figure 2-10). Pipettors are available in a wide range of volume capacities, typically from 0.1 μL to 10 mL.

Micropipettes operate by creating a partial vacuum above the liquid-holding chamber. By selectively releasing this vacuum, the device draws up and dispenses the desired volume of liquid.

Operation of pipettors

a. Installing the Pipette Tip: To install the pipette tip (also known simply as the "tip"), press the pipettor vertically into the tip using a gentle twisting motion to ensure a secure fit.

b. Setting the Volume: Before use, confirm the pipettor's volume range and set the desired volume. Turn the adjustment knob counterclockwise to increase the volume and clockwise to decrease it. When decrease the volume, first rotate the knob about 1/4 turn below the desired volume, then adjust back to the target setting. This helps eliminate mechanical backlash and improves accuracy.

Do not rotate the knob beyond its upper or lower limits, as this may damage the internal mechanism.

c. Aspirating Liquid: Attach a suitable pipette tip. Press the control button to the first stop using your thumb, then immerse the tip vertically into the liquid to the proper depth:

1–2 mm for 0.1–10 μL tips.

2–3 mm for 2–200 μL tips.

3–6 mm for 1–5 mL tips.

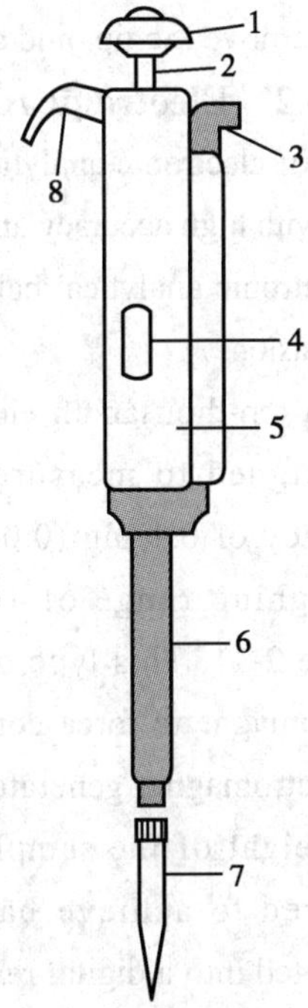

Figure 2-10   Structure of pipettor
1.Push button; 2. Push button rod; 3. Tip Ejector; 4. Display cover; 5. Handle; 6. Tip Ejector collar; 7. Pipettor tip; 8. Grip cover.

Release the button slowly to draw up the liquid. Wait 1–3 seconds to stabilize, then gently touch the pipette tip against the inner wall of the container to remove any clinging droplets.

When working with organic solvents or volatile liquids, vapor pressure may build up in the pipette's internal chamber, causing leakage. To avoid this, pre-rinse the tip 4–6 times to saturate the air space and eliminate negative pressure.

d. Dispensing Liquid: Hold the pipette tip vertically in the target container. Slowly press the control button to the first stop and wait 1–3 seconds. Then press to the second stop to expel any remaining liquid. This ensures complete delivery.

e. Ejecting the Tip & After-Use Handling: Press the "tip ejector" button to discard the used tip. Before storing the pipettor, set it to its maximum volume to relieve spring tension. Store it vertically on a pipette stand.

Never store the pipettor horizontally or upside down if liquid remains in the tip, as this may cause liquid to flow back and corrode the piston spring.

Note:

When transferring high-viscosity liquids, bioactive samples, foamy liquids, or trace volumes, press the button directly to the second stop to aspirate slightly more than the required volume. Slowly release the button, then dispense by pressing only to the first stop to deliver the set volume. Hold at the first stop, remove the tip, and discard it — do not press to the second stop again, to avoid overdrawing.

3.2   Electronic Analytical Balance

An electronic analytical balance is a single-pan analytical instrument capable of measuring weight or mass with high accuracy and precision. Different types of electronic analytical balances offer different levels of precision.

A ten-thousandth electronic analytical balance is designed to measure small masses with an accuracy of 0.1 mg (0.000 1 g), typically within a weighing range of 100–200 g, as shown in Figure 2-11. This type of balance operates using electromagnetic force compensation (EFC), where an electromagnet generates a force that counteracts the weight of the sample. The amount of force required to achieve balance is measured and converted into a digital reading.

Electronic analytical balances with EFC technology are known for their high accuracy and reliability, fast and clear display, automatic self-check functions, simple automatic calibration systems, and overload protection.

The weighing methods

(1) Direct Weighing: Direct weighing is suitable for samples that are stable in air and non-hygroscopic, such as metals or ores. When performing direct weighing:

a. Do not weigh hot samples.

b. Samples should not be placed directly on the balance pan to avoid corrosion. Instead, place

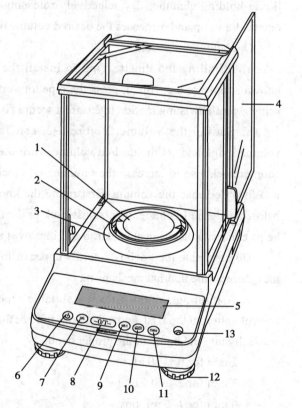

Figure 2-11   Electronic analytical balance
1. Tray; 2. Tray support; 3. Tray circle; 4. Draft shield; 5. Display portion; 6. Start switch; 7. "CAL" sensitivity calibration key; 8. "0/T" Determination (zero/buckle weight) key; 9. Unit switch; 10. Function switch; 11. Data output menu key; 12. Leveling pad; 13. Leveling equipment.

them on a piece of folded weighing paper (fold the four corners twice to form a tray, sized according to the balance pan or sample mass), or in a suitable weighing container.

Step-by-Step Procedure:

Level the Balance

Adjust the leveling feet until the bubble in the spirit level is centered. Turn the leveling feet clockwise to raise the balance, and counterclockwise to lower it. Clean the weighing pan using a soft brush.

Warm Up the Balance

Power on the balance and allow it to warm up for at least 30 minutes before use.

Calibrate Sensitivity

Press the "CAL" button to initiate automatic internal calibration using the built-in standard weight. Wait for the display to show [END] before proceeding.

Tare the Container

Set the weighing mode to display mass in grams ("g"). Open the draft shield doors and place the weighing container or folded paper tray on the pan. Close the doors. Once the display stabilizes, press the "0/T" or "TARE" button to zero the balance.

Weigh the Sample

Open the draft shield, carefully remove the lid of the sample container and place it face-up on the bench. Hold the container with your left hand, positioning its opening 5–10 cm above the center of the pan to prevent spills. Use a medicine spoon to gently transfer the sample into the weighing container or paper tray. Close the draft shield doors and read the weight after the display stabilizes.

Package the Sample

Wrap the weighed sample using weighing paper in the manner used for pharmaceuticals. Label the package with the sample name, weight, weighing date, and the name of the person who performed the weighing.

Turn Off and Clean

After weighing, clean the balance with a soft brush. Reset the balance to zero, press the power button until "OFF" appears, and unplug the instrument.

(2) Indirect Weighing: Indirect weighing involves first weighing a container—typically a weighing bottle—together with its contents, then transferring a portion of the contents to another vessel, and reweighing the container. The difference between the two weights corresponds to the mass of the transferred material.

This method is especially useful for hygroscopic or volatile substances, as the container can remain sealed during the weighing process.

Many solid substances absorb moisture from the atmosphere, which alters their composition. In such cases, the solid should be placed in a weighing bottle and dried in an oven for 1–2 hours before weighing, Figure 2-12(a). After drying, the bottle should be transferred to a desiccator to cool to room temperature in a moisture-free environmentg, Figure 2-12(b).

To transfer the sample from the weighing bottle to another container:

Wrap a strip of paper around the bottle and its stopper to ensure a secure grip.

Use the stopper to gently tap and guide the sample into the receiving vessel (see Figure 2-13).
Be careful not to spill any material during transfer.

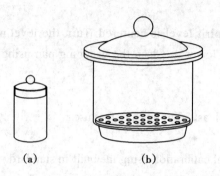

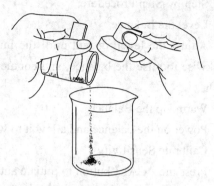

Figure 2-12   Weighing bottle and desicator
(a) Weighing bottle; (b) Desicator.

Figure 2-13   Knock off the samples

3.3   pH Meter

A pH meter, also known as an acidometer, is used to measure the pH of a solution through potentiometry. In this method, the potential difference between an indicator electrode and a reference electrode immersed in the solution is measured.

(1) Principle: A pH meter consists of a reference electrode, an indicator electrode, and a precise potentiometer.

1) Reference Electrodes: A reference electrode must have a stable potential that remains unaffected by the solution in which it is immersed. It should also show minimal changes when a small current flows through it. The most commonly used reference electrodes in routine measurements are the saturated calomel electrode (SCE) and the silver-silver chloride electrode.

Saturated Calomel Electrode (SCE)

A schematic diagram of a commercial saturated calomel electrode (SCE) is shown in Figure 2-14(a). The working part of the electrode consists of a platinum wire immersed in a slurry of solid mercurous chloride (calomel), liquid mercury, and aqueous saturated potassium chloride. This part is contained in the inner tube. The outer tube serves as a potassium chloride salt bridge, allowing the electrode assembly to be placed directly into the solution for measurement.

The calomel electrode half-cell may be represented as

$$Pt(s) \,|Hg(l) \,| \, Hg_2Cl_2(s)|, KCl(sat'd) \, \|$$

Mercurous chloride is reduced and elemental mercury is oxidized in the reversible electrode reaction

$$Hg_2Cl_2(s) + 2e^- \rightleftharpoons 2Hg(l) + 2Cl^-(aq)$$

Since the activities of the liquid Hg and solid Hg_2Cl_2 are both unity, the potential of the electrode is described by the Nernst equation

$$\varphi = \varphi_{Hg_2Cl_2/Hg}^{\ominus} - \frac{0.059\ 16\,V}{2} \lg c(Cl^-)^2 \tag{2-1}$$

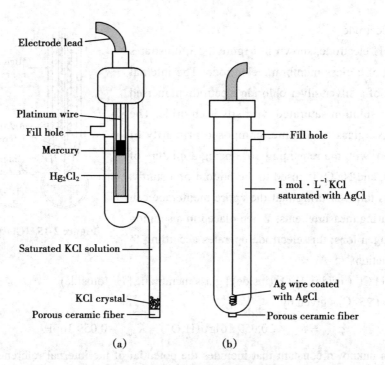

Figure 2-14　Reference electrode
(a) Saturated calomel electrode; (b) Silver-silver chloride electrode.

The concentration of Cl⁻ in equation (2-1) is fixed (saturated KCl is about 4.2 mol·L⁻¹), so the electrode potential remains constant, 0.241 5 V at 25 °C, as long as the salt bridge solution is not permitted to mix with the test solution.

Silver-silver Chloride Electrode

The silver-silver chloride electrode, shown in Figure 2-14 (b), consists of a silver wire coated with silver chloride that is immersed in a potassium chloride solution saturated with silver chloride. The half-cell is represented as

$$Ag(s) \mid AgCl(s)\mid KCl(c) \parallel$$

for which the half-reaction is

$$AgCl(s) + e^- \Longrightarrow Ag(s) + Cl^-(aq)$$

According to the Nernst equation, the potential of the electrode depends only on the concentration of Cl⁻

$$\varphi_{AgCl/Ag} = \varphi_{AgCl/Ag}^{\ominus} - \frac{0.059\ 16\ V}{1} \lg c(Cl^-) \tag{2-2}$$

This electrode, like the calomel electrode, the potassium chloride solution is saturated. Usually the electrode is small and can be used at higher temperatures.

2) Indicator Electrodes：An indicator electrode has a potential that responds to specific species in the test solution. The glass pH electrode is a type of membrane electrode that develops a potential based on the difference in hydrogen ion concentration across a special glass membrane. When the hydrogen ion concentration on both sides of the membrane is unequal, a potential is generated.

Glass pH Electrode

The glass pH electrode, shown in Figure 2-15, illustrates the construction of a glass membrane electrode. The internal element consists of a silver-silver chloride electrode immersed in a pH 7 buffer solution saturated with silver chloride. The thin, ion-selective glass membrane, composed primarily of SiO_2 (about 70%), with the remaining 30% being a mixture of CaO, BaO, Li_2O, and Na_2O, is fused to the bottom of a sturdy, nonreactive glass tube, ensuring that the entire membrane can be submerged during measurements. When placed in a solution containing hydrogen ions, this electrode operates according to the following reaction:

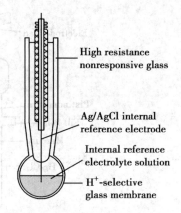

Figure 2-15 Glass pH electrode

Ag(s)| AgCl | Cl^- (inside), H_3O^+ (inside) | glass membrane | H^+ (outside)

whose potential at 25 °C is given by

$$\varphi_{glass} = K_{glass} + 0.059\ 16 \lg a(H_3O^+) = K_{glass} - 0.059\ 16 \text{pH} \tag{2-3}$$

where K_{glass} is an unknown constant that includes the potential of the internal reference electrode with a constant concentration of Cl^-, a potential at the glass membrane due to the concentration of internal H_3O^+, and a term known as the asymmetry potential.

If a cell is constructed at 25 °C with a saturated calomel electrode and a glass pH electrode when determining the pH of a solution, the electromotive force of the cell is given by

$$E = \varphi_{SCE} - \varphi_{glass} = 0.241\ 5 - (K_{glass} - 0.059\ 16 \text{pH}) \tag{2-4}$$

therefore, K_{glass} must be determined by calibration with a standard buffer of known pH

$$\text{pH} = \frac{E + K_{glass} - 0.241\ 5}{0.059\ 16} \tag{2-5}$$

3) Combination electrode: Nowadays, most pH electrodes are available as combination electrodes, physically integrated with an external silver-silver chloride reference electrode, all enclosed in a single tube (Figure 2-16). In these combination electrodes, the glass pH electrode is positioned in the center, surrounded by the reference electrode, which is filled with a reference electrolyte. These combination electrodes offer the advantage of being more compact than a separate two-electrode system. Another convenient option is the composite electrode, which includes a temperature probe, enabling simple temperature compensation. This type is also known as a three-in-one electrode.

(2) Operation of the FE28 pH meter: The FE28 pH meter (Figure 2-17) is a voltmeter with high input impedance, intuitive flexible operation and saving space. The voltage readout is calibrated to read in pH units and millivolts (mV). The pH scale ranges from 0-14 with an

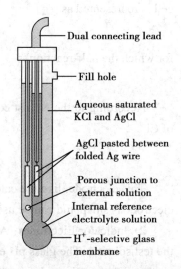

Figure 2-16 Combination electrode

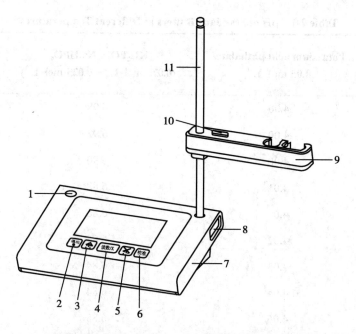

Figure 2-17   A diagram of FE28 pH meter
1. Left installation location side of the electrode bracket rod;
2. On/off switch; 3. Store/Echo; 4. Read/End way; 5. Mode/Setting;
6. Calibration; 7. Shell; 8. Storage space of bracket rod; 9. Bracket
arm; 10. Fasten button; 11. Electrode bracket rod.

accuracy of measurements to ± 0.01 pH and resolution of 0.01 pH; the mV scale ranges -2 000-2 000 mV with an accuracy of ± 1 mV and resolution of 1 mV.

1) Installing: Install the electrode rod, connect the power cable of pH meter to the 100-240 V power supply, and connect the electrode. Press the on/off switch down to warm the instrument up for 0.5 h.

2) Calibration

a. The temperature of ATC and samples can be displayed automatically. Otherwise, the manual temperature mode should be switched from the automatical mode. Press the "模式/设置" button for a long time, the temperature value will flash, then select the temperature value (the default setting is 25 ℃) by pressing the arrow keys, finally set the MTC temperature compensation by pressing "读数 $\sqrt{A}$" key. Select the standard buffer solution by arrow keys, and select the calibration method (Lin. or Seg.), resolution (0.1 or 0.01), temperature unit (℃ or ℉), then return to the measurement interface by pressing the "on/off" switch.

b. 1-point calibration or multi-point calibration is needed (1 point calibration can adjust offset only; slope and offset can be updated by 2-point calibration; the slope or zero can be updated and shown in the corresponding position of the display by 3- point or more calibration). The pH of standard buffer is related to temperature (Table 2-1).

Table 2-1 pH of Standard Buffers at Different Temperatures

Temperature/ °C	Potassium acid phthalate/ 0.05 mol·L⁻¹	KH₂PO₄ + Na₂HPO₄/ (0.025 mol·L⁻¹ + 0.025 mol·L⁻¹)	Sodium tetraborate/ 0.01 mol·L⁻¹
0	4.00	6.98	9.46
10	4.00	6.92	9.33
15	4.00	6.90	9.27
20	4.01	6.88	9.22
25	4.01	6.86	9.18
30	4.02	6.85	9.14
35	4.03	6.84	9.10
40	4.04	6.84	9.07
50	4.06	6.83	9.01
60	4.10	6.84	8.96

c. Clean and wipe the pH electrode tip, place the electrode below the standard buffer solution surface by 3-5 cm, and begin the calibration by pressing the "校准" button. Switch the automatic or manual ending mode by pressing "读数$\sqrt{A}$" key for a long time. When the signal is stable, "$\sqrt{A}$" appeared, the display will lock the reading automatically. If manual ending mode is selected, record the pH value of the buffer by pressing "读数$\sqrt{A}$" till the signal is stable, and "$\sqrt{M}$" appears.

d. For 1-point calibration, complete it by pressing the "读数$\sqrt{A}$" key.

e. For 2-point calibration, rinse the electrode with distilled water and dry it, place the electrode in the next calibration buffer, and complete the calibration by pressing "校准" key.

f. For 3-point calibration, repeat the step e on the basis of 2-point calibration.

g. By analogy, the device can be calibrated by 4-point or 5-point calibration. (Note: Seg line calibration is only meaningful for 3-point or multi-point calibration.) Return to the measurement interface by pressing the "退出" key.

3) Measurement of pH

a. Set pH measurement mode by pressing the "模式设置" key.

b. Clean and wipe the pH electrode tip, immerse the electrode below the solution surface by 3-5 cm, and measure the pH of solution by pressing the "读数$\sqrt{A}$" key. Complete the measurement after the signal is stable (automatic end mode, "$\sqrt{A}$" appears) or by pressing "读数$\sqrt{A}$" (manual end mode, "$\sqrt{M}$" appears). Record pH value of the solution at the current temperature.

c. Place the electrode on the bracket arm and remove the sample solution. Clean the electrode with distilled water and dry it. Power off the pH meter by pressing the "退出" key for a long time.

4) Measurement of mV: Set mV measurement mode by pressing the "模式设置" key. The operation steps are the same as the measurement of pH on b and c steps of the part "3)".

3.4   722-Spectrophotometer

(1) Principle: The absorption of energy by ions and molecules provides the basis for both qualitative and quantitative analysis. It is known that substances absorb certain wavelengths of radiation. When a monochromatic light passes through the colored solution (Figure 2-18), a portion of the light is absorbed and the rest is transmitted and reflected. The degree of absorption of the color of the solution has a certain proportional relationship with the concentration of material, the thickness of the liquid layer, and the intensity of incident light, which is in line with the Lambert-Beer's law

$$T = \frac{I}{I_0} \tag{2-6}$$

$$A = \lg \frac{1}{T} = \lg \frac{I_0}{I} \tag{2-7}$$

$$A = abc \tag{2-8}$$

where I is the intensity of transmitted radiant power, I_0 is the intensity of incident radiant power, T is the transmittance, A is the absorbance, a is the absorptivity, b is the thickness, and c is the concentration. The last equation is named as Lambert-Beer's law. The direct, linear relationship between absorbance and concentration is often used as fundamental test of a system's conformity to Lambert-Beer's law. Deviations from this linear behavior are the result of chemical phenomena such as changes in equilibria and solute-solvent or solute-solute interactions or of instrumental factors such as nonmonochromatic radiant energy, stray radiant energy, and multiple-reflection effects.

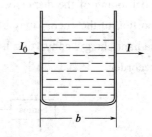

Figure 2-18   Schematic of light absorption

(2) The optical system of 722-spectrophotometer: 722-spectrophotometer is used for photometric analysis at wavelengths ranging from 360 nm to 800 nm, the wavelengths of near ultraviolet and visible lights. The main advantages of spectrometric method are nice stability, reproducibility, functional and a relatively simple methodology. The optical system of 722-spectrophotometer is shown in Figure 2-19.

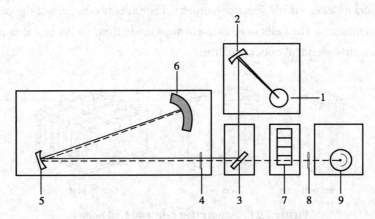

Figure 2-19   The optical system of 722-spectrophotometer

1. Light source; 2. Mirrored lens; 3. Reflecting mirror; 4. Slit; 5. Collimating mirror; 6. Grating; 7. Sample cell; 8. Shutter; 9. Photomultiplier tube.

143

White light from a light source (Tungsten lamp or halogen lamp) is focused by a mirrored lens and reaches a reflecting mirror. The continuous radiation emitted by the light source lamp (halogen lamp) strikes the condenser lens, converges and then passes through the mirror corner 90° and is reflected to the entrance slit and the collimating mirror. After the incident light is reflected by the collimating mirror, a parallel beam of light is emitted toward the grating (C-T monochromator) and is scattered and reflected by a slight deflection at an angle, converging on the exit slit through the collimating mirror. The light goes through the exit slit, through the condenser lens for focusing, through the sample cell, and then gates to pHotomultiplier tube by the shutter, the resulting photocurrent is inputed to the display, the optical data can be read directly.

(3) Structure of 722-Spectrophotometer: The fundamental requirements of a spectrophotometer are illustrated by the simplified schematic presentation (Figure 2-20). Radiation over a broad range of wavelengths emitted from the source is separated into nearly individual components by the monochromator (prism or grating with slit system). A particular wavelength is selected by proper positioning of the dispersive element in the monochromator and is then passed to the sample where a portion of the energy may be absorbed. The photoelectric detector measures the amount of transmitted radiant energy, converting it to an electrical current that is amplified to give a reading on a meter or a recorder.

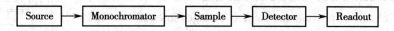

Figure 2-20　Schematic presentation of a spectrophotometer structure

(4) Cells: Sample containers, called cells or cuvettes, are characterized by having two flat, parallel windows through which the radiation passes (Figure 2-21). The rectangular cell of 1-cm path length is certainly the most widely used of various types. Longer-path-length cells get more analyte in the optical beam and thereby increase the measured absorbance. Glass cells are suitable for measurements with visible radiation but cannot be used in the ultraviolet because of their strong absorption. Quartz cells can be used in either ultraviolet or visible spectrophtometry. Instruments often are designed to accommodate a set of cells simultaneously. The cells in a set are always made from the same batch of glass or quartz, and therefore have nearly identical optical qualities.

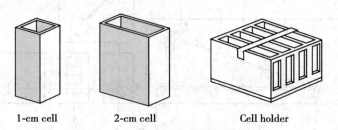

1-cm cell　　　　2-cm cell　　　　Cell holder

Figure 2-21　Absorption cells and Cell holder

The handling of cells is extremely important. Any variation in the cell (such as a change in cell width or the curvature of the glass, stains, smudges, or scratches) will cause varying results. To avoid significant experimental errors, several rules must be followed:

1) Do not handle the optical walls of a cell (through which the light beam will pass).

2) Always rinse the cell with several portions of the solution before taking a measurement. Never fill a cell with solutions less than half-full when measuring.

3) Wipe the moisture or stain on the outer wall of the cell with a clean lens paper. Never wipe cells with towels or handkerchiefs. Inspect to insure that no thread remains on the outside and that small air bubbles are not present on the inside walls. Otherwise, it can be soaked in nitric acid, but not for more than 3 hours.

4) When inserting a cell into a cell-holder, avoid any possible scratching of the cell in the optical path, make the optical walls face toward the windows of the holder. Be sure that the cell is set upright.

5) When using two or more cells simultaneously, use one of them for the blank solution and the others for the various samples to be measured, and insert the cell for blank solution in the nearest cabin of the holder. If absorption spectra are being run on several different samples at the same time, matched cells must be used.

(5) Operation of 722-spectrophotometer: The exterior of a 722 spectrophotometer is shown in Figure 2-22.

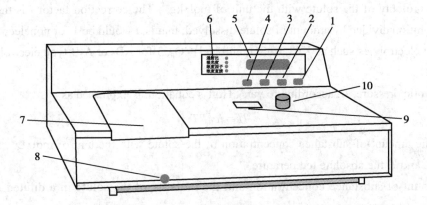

Figure 2-22   722-spectrophotometer
1. 100%T-adjust key; 2. Zero-adjust key; 3. Function key; 4. Mode key 5. Display;
6. Four scales ("transmittance" , "absorbance" , "concentration factor" ,
"concentration direct reading"); 7. Sample chamber; 8. Sample-holder pull;
9. Wavelength scale window; 10. Wavelength selector knob.

1) Warming up: Power on the instrument switch,warm the instrument up for 0.5 h.

2) Adjusting wavelength: Adjust the current test wavelength of the instrument by using the wavelength selector knob. The wavelength value is shown in the wavelength scale window on the left side, near the knob. The wavelength value should be observed vertically.

3) Putting in the samples: There are four positions on the sample rack in the instrument's standard configuration. The sample position closest to the tester in the object tank is called the "0" position, followed by "1" "2" and "3" , generally a blank sample is placed in the "0" position.

4) Zero-adjust: Open the sample chamber cover or block the optical path in the sample chamber with opaque shielding material, then press the "0%" key.

5) 100%T-adjust: Put the blank solution and samples into the sample rack rod in the sample chamber, close the sample cover (the light door will be opened automatically) and press the "100%" key (If there is an error, press again).

6) Absorbance measure: Set "Absorbance" mode by pressing the mode key. Pull different samples into the optical path by pulling the sample-holder pull. Read out the absorbance values of each sample separately from the display. Always readjust 100% T after closing the cover of sample chamber, and then determine the absorbance.

7) Turn off the switch and unplug the power after the instrument is used up.

3.5 FM-9X Osmometer

(1) Principle: Properties of solutions that depend on the amount of solute are colligative properties. These properties include vapor pressure lowering, boiling point elevation, freezing point depression, and osmotic pressure. Among them, the freezing-point depression of the solution, ΔT_f, is expressed as

$$\Delta T_f = iK_f b_B \tag{2-9}$$

where K_f is the freezing-point depression constant of the solvent, which is $1.857\ \mathrm{K \cdot kg \cdot mol^{-1}}$ for water, and b_B is the molality of the solute with the unit of $\mathrm{mol \cdot kg^{-1}}$. The correction factor i is the amount of particles in solution divided by amount of solute dissolved; that is, i would be 1 for nonelectrolyte solute, 2 for AB type electrolytes such as KCl, $CaSO_4$ and $NaHCO_3$, 3 for AB_2 or A_2B type electrolytes such as $MgCl_2$, Na_2SO_4.

The osmotic pressure, Π, according to van't Hoff's equation, is expressed as

$$\Pi = ic_B RT \tag{2-10}$$

where c_B is the amount-of-substance concentration of the solute with the unit of $\mathrm{mol \cdot L^{-1}}$, and R is the gass constant, and T, the absolute temperature.

The amount-of-substance concentration and the molality of the solute in a diluted solution are nearly equal in value at room temperature

$$b_B(\mathrm{mol \cdot kg^{-1}}) \approx c_B(\mathrm{mol \cdot L^{-1}}) \tag{2-11}$$

therefore,

$$\Pi \approx ib_B RT (\mathrm{kPa}) \tag{2-12}$$

The osmotic pressure of body liquid is of important physiologic functions. The freezing-point depression is often used to measure the osmotic pressure in body liquid because it is simple to determine, and the measurement is at lower temperature that biological samples will not be ruined. And also, it reaches higher precision because of its larger value of K_f. Most instruments measuring the osmotic pressure in the world are designed on the principle of the freezing-point depression.

The freezing point is the temperature at which the ice and the liquid solvent are in equilibrium. During the cooling process, the solvent may not solidify when the temperature reaches the freezing point, that is the "undercooling". The liquid solvent is so unstable that it will crystallize at once when some disturbances occur, and its molecules will release the heat called "crystallization heat". The crystallization heat will raise the temperature of the super cooling liquid. Figure 2-23 shows the cooling

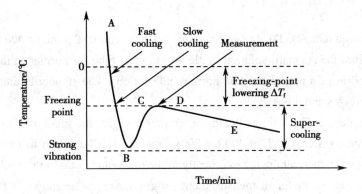

Figure 2-23   The cooling curve

curve, in which A is start of cooling, B represents the undercooling, and C refers to the temperature when solid forms, the CD segment is the freezing point temperature stabilization time, and the DE segment is solid state and continues to cool. From C to D the temperature will last for a period, which is the freezing point of the liquid. FM-9X osmometer is designed to adopt a highly sensitive semiconductor thermistor to measure the freezing point and to transform the measured current into an osmotic pressure display.

(2) Operation for FM-9X osmometer: The osmometer is equipped with a semiconductor refrigeration setting which a nonfreezing solution is used as the cooling media (Figure 2-24). There is a vibrator for causing crystallization, and a highly sensitive measuring system to measure the freezing point and to determine the osmotic pressure of the sample. This osmometer should be calibrated with a 300 mmol·L^{-1} or 800 mmol·L^{-1} standard NaCl solution to match its precision.

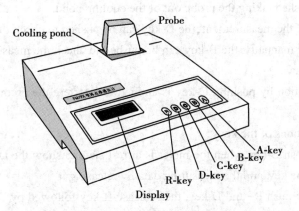

Figure 2-24   FM-9X Freezing-point Osmometer

1) Preparation and adjustment of osmometer

a. Fill in the cooling pond with 60 mL of nonfreezing solution till the liquid flows off from the overflowing tube on the right side of the osmometer.

b. Plug in the meter to warm up for 30 min. The osmometer at rest will reach the reference point automatically and its display will show the temperature of the cooling pond. If the display shows "- - - -", the temperature is much higher.

2) Calibration

a. Calibration requirements: Take a clean and dry test tube, extract 0.5 mL of 300 (or 800) mmol·L^{-1} standard solution from the standard solution bottle into the test tube for normal calibration (The results of early or non-freezing cannot be used as normal calibration). The standard solution should not be contaminated by syringes and tubes.

b. Calibration method: To calibrate the instrument, be sure that the small tube and the glass injector are dry and clean and transfer 0.5mL of 300 (or 800) mmol·L^{-1}NaCl solution from a storage bottle into the tube with the injector, then set the tube vertically to the probe and put it in the cooling pond.

Push C-key to set the meter in measurement program, the meter shows "300" as the osmotic concentration of the standard NaCl solution. If a 800 mmol·L^{-1} NaCl solution is used, push the D-key to switch the display. Then push B-key for calibration. The display shows the temperature change of NaCl solution and when the temperature reaches −6 °C the vibrator will vibrate strongly, then the display will show the freezing point followed by 300E (or 800E) to end the calibration. Push D-key to store the calibration,and the display shows "300P" (or "800P"). After the finish of calibration the probe must be taken out of the cooling pond to avoid damaging the sensor of the probe.

In the process of the measurement, the A-key can be pushed to withdraw. The measuring time (unit: second) can be checked by pushing the B-key and the temperature be checked by pushing the D-key.

3) Measure the sample solution

a. Fill in a dry tube with the sample, clean and dry the probe with soft tissue, and set the tube vertically to the probe and put it in the cooling pond, then push D-key to set the meter in measurement program. The meter shows the temperature change and when the temperature reaches −6 °C the vibrator will vibrate strongly, then the display will show the freezing point followed by the osmotic concentration of the sample. After finished taking the probe out of the cooling pond.

b. In the process of the measurement, the D-key can be pushed to check the temperature, the C-key can be pushed to vibrate manually, the B-key can be pushed to check the measuring time and the A-key can be pushed to withdraw.

Manipulating vibration by pushing C-key is applied to interfere the premature freezing unless the freezing is normal.

4) Additional functions of the keys

a. Sensing data: Push B-key when the meter is at rest state to show the last 12 data, obtaining the time by pushing down the key, and the measuring data by releasing it.

b. Setting the time: push R- and D-key, then release R-key followed by D-key to set the function. The display shows the month and day by four digits. Push D-key to shift the decimal point that indicates the digits being changed, pushing B-key for adding by 1 and A-key for reducing by 1. Then shift decimal point to the right and push C-key to store the date. After that the display shows the hour and minute, operate the keys the same way can set the time.

c. Standardizing the temperature of thermistor and the linearity of voltage: This function is used when the instrument loses the storaged data. Transfer 0.5 mL of nonfreezing solution into the tube and set it vertically to the probe and put them in the cooling pond. Push R-key plus C-key and then release R-key followed by D-key to set the function, the display shows "- - 0 0" (Error! No index). Push the probe to the lower part of the colling pont, the meter shows four digits, in which the first two are for temperature and the last two are the time. Finally a "- - - -" appears on the display indicating the end, then push R-key to finish the reset. It needs about 1 hour to complete the process.

d. Setting the temperature of cooling pond: Generally the temperature of cooling pond is set by −9.0 °C. Push B-key plus R-key, then release R-key followed by B-key, the meter shows four digits as "L - X X" where the "- X X" gives the original temperature. Push D-key to shift the decimal point that indicates the digits being changed when pushing B-key for adding by 1 and A-key for reducing by 1. Then shift decimal point between two "X" s and push C-key to store the date. After that the display shows the decimal point after "L" as the data accepted, push R-key for ending.

e. Examining the date of calibration: Push A-key plus R-key and then release R-key followed by A-key, the meter shows the last date for calibration.

5) Premature freezing and nonfreezing of the sample: Both the premature and the nonfreezing of the sample can not reveal the correct measuring results.

a. Premature freezing: Premature freezing may take place when the temperature of the nonfreezing solution in cooling pond is lower than −9.0 °C, or the osmotic pressure of the sample is too low; or the test tube is not clean or there are some particle impurities such as crystallization in the sample; or there is any vibration to the instrument.

Generally, one measurement can finish within 300 seconds. If the measure time is longer than 300 s, the premature freezing occurs, the measurement should be sopped. Otherwise the meter will show "- - - -" after vibration to inform of the failure. In this case the sample tube and the thermistor are frozen together, and be attention that never pull the tube off unless the iced sample melts.

b. Nonfreezing: Nonfreezing of the sample may take place when the temperature of the nonfreezing solution in cooling pond is higher than −9.0 °C, or the osmotic pressure of the sample is too high; or the vibrator is too weak to beat the wall of the tube; or there are some bubbles in sample.

If nonfreezing occurs, it needs to dilute the sample, or strengthen the vibration.

3.6 Centrifuges

(1) Principle: A centrifuge is a special machine that rotates rapidly to separate solid from a mixture of different phases (l-s, l-l), as shown in Figure 2-25 (a). When a test tube containing a mixture of a liquid and solid is placed in a test tube holder in the centrifuge, the solid can be "packed" into the bottom of the test tube by the rotatory motion of the centrifuge. Then the liquid can be decanted (poured off) into another container leaving the solid behind. Sometimes we use a capillary pipet to withdraw the liquid and leave the solid in the test tube.

Before the centrifuge is turned on, a "balanced tube" must be placed opposite the test tube of interest to prevent excessive vibration, which will destroy the centrifuge otherwise, The balance tube should be the same size as the test tube that contains the mixture to be separated, and it should contain a volume of water equal to the volume in the other test tube.

Centrifugal separation is widely applied in hospitals, food and industrial departments, and research institutes to perform chemical and biochemical examinations, separation of suspension, and so on.

Now many centrifuges are improved for controlling. These improvements will be illustrated by the use of LDZ5-2 centrifuge. It is controlled by a integrated circuit, its control board is shown in Figure 2-25 (b).

It will start up tardily, and it has convenience and direct digital displays of timing and speed. It is also designed to equip the over-speed alarm and the self-brake system. The system can protect the main control circuit and overspeed operation caused by wrong operation.

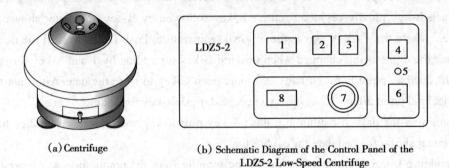

(a) Centrifuge   (b) Schematic Diagram of the Control Panel of the
LDZ5-2 Low-Speed Centrifuge

Figure 2-25 Centrifuge and Schematic Diagram of the Control Panel of the LDZ5-2 Low-Speed Centrifuge
1. Timer (min); 2. Time set; 3. AUTO/MAN timing; 4. Start; 5. Over-speed protection; 6. Power; 7. Speed adjuster; 8. Rotate speed ($\times 100$ r·min^{-1}).

(2) Procedure for LDZ5-2 centrifuge

1) Place the centrifuge on a stable platform.

2) Balance the samples. The centrifuge is equipped with an automatic balancing system, making it easy to balance the samples. The amount of solution in each test tube should be estimated visually, and then the test tubes should be placed symmetrically in the centrifuge. The maximum allowable imbalance should not exceed 20 g, and each rotor must operate at the corresponding speed indicated in Table 2-2, not exceeding 5 000 r·min^{-1} (the centrifuge will alarm if this limit is exceeded). When centrifuging a small amount of test solution, balance with water in the opposite test tube.

Table 2-2 Rotate Speed, Centrifugal Force and Volume of LDZ5-2 Centrifuge

Rotate speed /(r·min^{-1})	Relative centrifugal force /g	Volume of test tube /mL	Test tubes/ number	Overall volume /mL	Imbalance <g
5 000	4 360	50	4	200	20
5 000	4 360	10	12	120	20
3 500	2 100	10	32	320	20

3) Examination

a. Ensure that the speed knob is set to "0".

b. Make sure the test tubes are properly placed and securely tightened.

c. Check that the power is connected, the plug is inserted, and the lid is closed.

d. Verify that the centrifuge is plugged in and properly grounded.

4) Operational program

a. Turn on the power switch (6) to the "ON" position. The indicator light should turn on, and the speed display will show "00". If timing is needed, select "AUTO" by pressing the "Manual / Auto" key (3). The timing display will flash. Then, press the "Set Time" key (2) to set the desired time.

b. Press the "Start" key (4). Turn the adjustment knob (7) clockwise to set the desired speed. The centrifuge will start rotating counterclockwise. Observe the tachometer and adjust to the required speed.

c. During the set time, the display will count down. When the time reaches "00", the centrifuge will stop, and the indicator on the "Start" key will turn off.

d. If necessary, repeat the process at the same speed. You can reset the time if needed. After pressing the "Start" key (4), the centrifuge will run automatically at the preset speed and time.

e. If timing is not needed or the centrifuging time exceeds 59 minutes, switch the AUTO / MAN timing setting to "MAN". The timer will still show a random number, but it will no longer be timed. You must stop the centrifugation manually by turning the power switch (6) to the "OFF" position at the end.

f. When used repeatedly, first turn on the power switch (6) and then press the "Start" key (4). The centrifuge will automatically accelerate to the set speed (untimed).

g. After centrifugation is finished, return the speed adjuster to "0" and turn off the power switch (6). Move the power switch to "OFF". Open the lid and remove the test tubes. Never open the lid while the machine is running or try to stop the machine manually.

(ZHOU Chunyan; LI Xuehua)

Chapter 3 | Expressions of Experiment Results and the Experiment Report

1. Experimental Errors and Significant Figures

1.1 Experimental Error

Experimental error is ubiquitous. Even if the parallel determinations are strictly performed, we usually cannot precisely obtain the same results. Each measurement is subject to experimental error. Experiment error arises from the following causes.

(1) Systematic error: Systematic errors have a definite value, an assignable cause, and are of the same magnitude for replicated measurements operated in the same way. Systematic error results from method error, instrument error, reagent error and operation error. Systematic error causes data to be either higher or lower than the actual value, it can be avoided through calibration of measuring device, improvement of experimental method, changing reagents or by comparing with a known standard.

(2) Random error: Random error results from unpredictable reasons such as the small variation of surrounding temperature, humidity, pressure, performance of measuring device and measurer's treatment. Random error, in the absence of systematic error, makes data higher or lower than the actual value. Random error always occurs, but its effect on the accurate measurement can be eliminated by taking the average value of many parallel repeating measurements.

Occasionally the fault occurs because of negligence or non-compliance with operating procedures, such as taking a wrong reading, or an incorrect operation, etc., which must be avoided.

1.2 Accuracy and Precision

(1) Accuracy: Accuracy refers to the closeness of a single measurement (x_i) to its true value (T). Accuracy is represented by error, the smaller the error, the higher the accuracy.

This definition of error is also named as absolute error (E), which is given by

$$E = x_i - T \tag{3-1}$$

This definition of error is also named as absolute error. Another representation of accuracy often used is relative error (E_r).

$$E_r = \frac{E}{T} \times 100\% \tag{3-2}$$

Since the relative error reflects the proportion of error in the true value, it is more reasonable to measure the accuracy of the measurement. Therefore, the relative error is usually used to indicate the accuracy of the measurement results.

(2) Precision: Precision refers to the degree of closeness between parallel measured values. Precision is represented by deviation, the smaller the deviation, the higher the precision.

The difference between a certain measured value (x_i) and the arithmetic mean ($\overline{x}$) of the multiple measured values is called the absolute deviation (d), that is

$$d = x_i - \overline{x} \tag{3-3}$$

The average value of the sum of the absolute values ($|d_i|$) of the absolute deviations of each measurement is called the absolute mean deviation ($\overline{d}$), and the number of measurements is n, then

$$\overline{d} = \frac{|d_1| + |d_2| + |d_3| + \cdots + |d_n|}{n} \tag{3-4}$$

Another method of evaluating precision is to determine the relative mean deviation ($\overline{d_r}$), which can be calculated as

$$\overline{d_r} = \frac{\overline{d}}{\overline{x}} \times 100\% \tag{3-5}$$

When discussing experimentals , the concept of standard deviation (s) and relative standard deviation (RSD) is in common use.

The standard deviation is defined as

$$s = \sqrt{\frac{d_1^2 + d_2^2 + d_3^2 + \cdots + d_n^2}{n-1}} \tag{3-6}$$

The standard deviation highlights the impact of larger deviations in a single measurement on the measurement, which is an indication of better precision.

The relative standard deviation can be expressed as

$$\text{RSD} = \frac{s}{\overline{x}} \times 100\% \tag{3-7}$$

In practice, the relative standard deviation is used to indicate the precision of the analytical results.

1.3   Significant Figures

To indicate the precision of a measured number or a result of calculations on measured numbers, the concept of significant figures is often used, which are those digits in a measured number or a calculated numbers that include all certain digits plus a final one having some uncertainty. When measuring the volume of a liquid with a cylinder graduated accurately in 1 milliliter, for instance, we have a certain value of 34 mL plus an estimated value, 0.2 mL, thus the volume of the liquid is 34.2 mL. This measured value has 3 significant figures, its error is ± 0.1 mL.

(1) Number of significant figures: To count the number of significant figures in a given measured quantity, you observe the following rules.

1) Digit "zero" : All digits are significant except zeros at the beginning of the number. Thus, 34.2 mL and 0.034 2 mL all contain three significant figures.

Terminal zeros ending at the right of the decimal point are significant. Each of the following has three significant figures: 9.00 cm, 9.10 cm, and 90.0 cm.

Terminal zeros in a number without an explicit decimal point may or may not be significant. More generally, any uncertainty can be removed in such case by expressing the measurement in scientific notation.

2) Scientific notation: Scientific notation is the representation of a number in the form $A \times 10^n$, where A is a number with a single nonzero digit to the left of the decimal point and n is an

integer. In scientific notation, the measurement 900 cm precise to two significant figures is written 9.0×10^2 cm.

3) Significant figures in a common logarithm: A common logarithm has the number of digits at the left of the decimal point corresponding to the power of a rational number, thus whose digits at the right of the decimal point are significant figures. Therefore a pH, the minus logarithm of the concentration of hydrogen ion, 2.88 has two significant figures, and the concentration of hydrogen ion is 1.3×10^{-3} mol·L^{-1}.

(2) Exact numbers: So far, only numbers that involve uncertainties are discussed. However, exact numbers are also encountered. An exact number is a number that arises when counting items or sometimes when defining a unit. For example, when saying there are 9 reagent bottles on a table, that means exactly 9 not 8.9 or 9.1. Also, the inch is defined to be exactly 2.54 centimeters; the 2.54 here should not be interpreted as a measured number with three significant figures. In effect, the 2.54 has an infinite number of significant figures, but of course it would be impossible to write out an infinite number of digits. The conventions of significant figures do not apply to exact numbers. The number of significant figures in a calculation result depends only on the numbers of significant figures in quantities having uncertainties. For example, the calculation of the total mass of 9 bottles, suppose one reagent bottle has a mass of 20.1 grams, is

$$20.1 \text{ g} \times 9 = 180.9 \text{ g.}$$

Some data from constants or bibliographic data books are non-measured values whose significant digits are not considered or treated as infinite.

(3) Rounding off a number

1) In the actual measurement, often a plurality of measuring instruments is used in combination, and multiple measurements are performed. When multiple measurement data is to be processed, it is necessary to make a trade-off to the extra digits of the measurement data according to the law of error transmission, that is, rounding off.

2) The rounding is usually handled according to the rules as follows. That is: when the digit removed is 4, simply drop it and all digits farther to right, and when it is 6, add 1 to the last digit to be retained and drop all digits farther to the right. Thus rounding off 1.214 3 and 1.216 2, for instance, to three significant figures gives to 1.21 and 1.22, respectively. When the digit removed is 5, and the digit after that is zero or null, the last digit retained is added to by 1 to make it even if it is odd or remains unchanged if it is even. Thus rounding off 1.215, for instance, to three significant figures gives 1.22.

(4) Significant figures in calculations: When measuring data for data processing, the following two rules are commonly used to determine the significant figure of calculation results.

1) Addition and subtraction: When adding or subtracting measured quantities, give as many of decimal digits in answer as there are in the measurement with the least number of decimal digits. Therefore, the sum of 34.2 + 0.21 is 34.4. Now consider the addition of 184.2 g and 2.324 g. On a calculator, you find 184.2 + 2.324 = 186.524. But because the quantity of 184.2 g has the least number of decimal places - one, whereas 2.324 g has three - the answer is 186.5 g.

2) Multiplication and division: When multiplying or dividing measured quantities, give as many significant figures in answer as there are in the measurement with the least number of significant

figures. Therefore, the product of 34.2 × 0.21 is 7.2, has two significant figures.

In doing a calculation of two or more steps, it is desirable to retain nonsignificant digits for intermediate answers. This ensures that accumulated small errors from rounding do not appear in the final result. If using a calculator, simply enter numbers one after the other, performing each arithmetic operation and rounding off only the final answer.

2.   Treatments of Experimental Data

To express the experimental results and to find the rules in experiment, it needs to deal with a great lot of experimental data by means of tabling, graphing and mathematic equation.

2.1   Tabling

It is very common for experiments to result in tables full of data. List the experimental data in the order of a dependent variable y corresponding to its independent variable(s) x to form a three-line table so that the relationship between variables is clear.

Each table should have a concise title. The table consists of three lines. If it is not particularly needed, there must be no vertical lines. The name and unit of the variable shown in the table should be noted. The data in the table can no longer be taken with the unit. Pay attention to the number of significant figures for each of the data. Usually, the simpler variables such as temperature, time and concentration are selected as independent variables.

2.2   Graphing

While it is sometimes possible to come to meaningful conclusions from tables, it is often easier to discern relationships between variables visually using appropriate graphs. A graph shows how one variable changes as another is varied. Furthermore, the slop, the intercept and the extrapolated value can be obtained by graphing. The guidelines below should help how to prepare readable graphs.

(1) Select logical scales that utilize as much of the graph paper as possible. For many graphs, the two axes will have different scales, and the zero value will not be at origin. Each major division should represent 1, 2, 2.5 or 5 units or some power of ten. Never use 3, 7 or other non-multiple values that make it difficult to locate points on the graph.

(2) Label the axes and indicate the physical quantity of units used. Conventionally the horizontal axis is chosen for independent variable, and the vertical axis for dependent variable.

(3) Locate the points and put a dot at the proper locations. Circle the dots with one of such figures as "O", "△", "×" or "□", which area is about equal to the range of measuring error, and each point uses the length of the " I " to indicate the standard deviation of the value.

(4) If the points appear to fall on a straight line, use a straight line to represent them, and pay attention to the data points that are not on the line to be evenly distributed on both sides of the line, so as to best fit the experimental data. Do not sketch straight lines and do not connect the dots with straight line segments. If the points seem to fall on a smooth curve draw the best curve possible through the data. Or fit with "excel" software.

(5) Title the graph: Among the graphs, the line graph is an extremely efficient way to present large amounts of data and, at the same time, it permits important conclusions to be drawn easily and with confidence. Although many different relationships exist between experimental variables, linear

relationships are especially attractive, not only because straight lines are easier to be drawn than curves, but also because the equations of straight lines are simpler to be calculated.

2.3 Computer Software Mapping and Mathematical Equation

Computer software mapping and mathematical equation method is to establish the graph or mathematical equation between the independent variable and the dependent variable, so as to explain the relationship between the data. The establishment of mathematical equations can use a variety of methods. Now, the use of computer technology makes both tabling and graphing more convenient, some data processing software (such as Excel, etc.) application can simplify the work process, improve efficiency.

How to use excel to get a linear regression equation:

(1) Enter the data into the excel table (column 2).

(2) Select all the experimental data, then click "Insert" → "Scatter plot" in the menu to display the dot plot.

(3) Right-click on any data point in the graph and select "Add trendline" from the options that appear, and immediately display the line in the graph.

(4) In the "Trend line options" above, select "Show formula" to display the linear regression equation immediately. The slope and intercept of the line can be obtained from the linear regression equation.

3. Experiment Reports

The experiment reports demonstrate for students a personal understanding of the nature of chemistry. Including experiment preview report and data recording and result analysis.

Students should carefully prepare before they come to the laboratory, including carefully reading the textbooks, reviewing the references, simulating the identity of the designer, fully understanding and briefly describing the experimental design ideas, principles, procedures, experimental conditions, and precautions to complete the preparatory work. Finish preview lab report.

In their laboratory period, they should follow the instruction, observe and record earnestly. By participating in experiments with the chemicals and the equipments , students learn to collect data from measurements, to observe changes and to interpret the data and observations. In preparing and performing their experiment reports , students learn the skills of planning, carrying out, and reporting on the results of real investigations.

At the end of the laboratory period, they should hand in the report forms on which they have recorded their data and observations, as well as any calculations and conclusions based on these data and observations.

An experiment preview report includes a title, student's name and ID, date; objectives (purposes), principles, apparatus and reagents, simulation design experiment - according to the experimental steps, the design idea of the experiment is given in the form of flow chart, and the corresponding precautions and reasons are indicated in the flow chart. At last, the experimental data or phenomena are recorded, and the results are analyzed and discussed, and finally answer the questions. The common requirement for an experiment report is being scientific, precise and clear, clean and tidy, factual, and correct.

According to the aim of the experiment, from the perspective of cultivating students' comprehensive experimental skills and the combination of theory and practice of "Inorganic Chemistry", "Analytical Chemistry" and "Physical Chemistry", and the different levels of teaching, the experiments in this textbook are divided into the following three-stage chemistry experiment training content: basic operation standardization and skill training experiment, comprehensive experiment of cultivating scientific thinking by simulation designer (volumetric analysis, instrumental analysis, chemical principle, inorganic compound preparation), and comprehensive experimental skill improvement self-designed experiments. The following are two typical report forms of inorganic compound preparation and quantitative analysis.

Inorganic compound preparation experiment

Experiment X   Preparation of Ammonium Iron(II) Sulfate

Name_____ Student ID_____ Date_____

1. Experiment Preview Report

1.1   Objectives

......

1.2   Principles

......

1.3   Apparatus, Materials and Reagents

......

1.4   Simulated Design Experiment: Present the experimental design as a flowchart, clearly indicating the corresponding precautions and the rationale behind each step.

......

2. Data Recording and Result Analysis

(Three-line form and data processing items for experimental data recording in advance)

Date:_____ Room Temperature:_____°C   Relative Humidity_____

(1) Preparation of Ammomium Iron(II) Sulfate

Weigh iron filings $m(\text{Fe})_1 = $_____ g;

The residue of iron filings $m(\text{Fe})_2 = $_____ g;

$m[(\text{NH}_4)_2\text{SO}_4\cdot\text{FeSO}_4\cdot 6\text{H}_2\text{O}] = $_____ g.

$$\text{Yield of }(\text{NH}_4)_2\text{SO}_4\cdot\text{FeSO}_4\cdot 6\text{H}_2\text{O}(\%) = \frac{\text{Weight of product (g)}}{\text{Theoretical yield (g)}}\times 100\% = \underline{\hspace{2cm}}.$$

(2) Test the purity of the product

Fe^{3+} standard solution	Grade 1	Grade 2	Grade 3
Grade of the product			

3. Questions

Quantitative analysis

Experiment X   Standardization of HCl Concentration

Name_____ Student ID_____ Date_____

1. Experiment Preview Report

1.1   Objectives

......

1.2   Principles
......

1.3   Apparatus, Materials and Reagents
......

1.4   Simulated Design Experiment: Present the experimental design as a flowchart, clearly indicating the corresponding precautions and the rationale behind each step.
......

2. Data Recording and Result Analysis

(Three-line form and data processing items for experimental data recording in advance)

Date:_____   Room Temperature:_____°C   Relative Humidity:_____

(1) Weighing Primary Standard, Na_2CO_3

Weighing bottle + Na_2CO_3 (m_1)   _____ g;

Weighing bottle + Na_2CO_3 retained (m_2)   _____ g;

Mass of Na_2CO_3 ($m_1 - m_2$)   _____ g;

Mass of Na_2CO_3 in each titration   _____ g.

(2) Solution preparation
......

(3) Data record and result analysis

Samples	1	2	3
Acid base indicator			
Color change at the end of titration point			
$V(Na_2CO_3)$ / mL			
$V_{Initial}$ (HCl) / mL			
V_{Final} (HCl) / mL			
ΔV(HCl) / mL			
c(HCl) / mol·L^{-1}			
$c_{Average}$(HCl) / mol·L^{-1}			
Relative mean deviation $\overline{d_r}$ / %			

(4) Calculation of NaOH concentration
......

3. Questions
......

(CHEN Zhiqiong)

Part II   Experiments in Basic Chemistry

Chapter 4	Experiments of Basic Operation Practice

Experiment 1   Operation of Volumetric Analysis Instruments

【 OBJECTIVES 】

(1) To master the standardized operation and the matters needing attention of volumetric glassware.

(2) To master general laboratory techniques including preparation and transferring of solution, operation of acid-base titration analysis and so on.

(3) To learn the principles of acid-base titration analysis.

【 PRE-LAB ASSIGNMENTS 】

(1) Point out the difference between a container and a measuring apparatus, and then explain the operating requirements.

(2) Briefly outline key points for using quantitative analysis glassware including volumetric flask, volumetric pipette, graduated pipette, burette and Erlenmeyer flask.

(3) Review literature on acid-base titration. Briefly describe rules of indicator selection, principle and types of acid-base titration, respectively.

(4) Simulated design experiment: Present the experimental design as a flowchart, clearly indicating the corresponding precautions and the rationale behind each step.

【 Apparatus, Reagents, and Materials 】

Apparatus   Beaker(50 mL, 250 mL), graduated cylinder(50 mL), Erlenmeyer flask(250 mL × 3), volumetric flask(100 mL), pipet bulb, volumetric pipet(20 mL × 2), graduated pipette(10 mL), acid burette(25 mL), base burette(25 mL) or PTFE burette(25 mL), burette stand, 0.1 mg- electronic analytical balance, stirring rod.

Reagents and Materials   0.1 mol·L^{-1} (accurate to ± 0.000 1 mol·L^{-1}) HCl solution, 0.1 mol·L^{-1} (accurate to ± 0.000 1 mol·L^{-1}) NaOH solution, 1.000 mol·L^{-1} NaCl solution, Na$_2$CO$_3$ (A.R.), phenolphthalein, methyl orange

【PROCEDURES】

1. Cleaning and Drying of Volumetric Glassware

Clean and dry Erlenmeyer flask, volumetric flask, volumetric pipette, and burette according to the method indicated in Chapter 2, Part I.

2. Operation of Pipettes

2.1   Volumetric Pipettes

Practice drawing tap water from a 250 mL beaker to a 20 mL pipette and adjusting the meniscus to the calibration mark, then transferring the water to a 250 mL Erlenmeyer flask. Repeat the above practice until you are proficient.

2.2   Graduated Pipettes

Take a 10 mL graduated pipette, practice transferring 10.00 mL of water from a beaker to a 250 mL Erlenmeyer flask. Practice rinsing, drawing and draining with tap water. It is required to deliver liquid of 2.00 mL each time until all the 10.00 mL liquid drains out to the flask. Repeat the practice until you are proficient.

3. Operation of Volumetric Flask

3.1   Checking of Liquid-tightness, Transferring and Fixing volume of the Solution

Refer to the operating procedures for volumetric flasks in Chapter 2, practice leak testing, transferring solutions, and setting the volume.

3.2   Preparing Solution

(1) Preparing $0.200\ 0\ mol \cdot L^{-1}$ NaCl solution: Transfer 20.00 mL of $1.000\ mol \cdot L^{-1}$ NaCl solution from a reagent bottle to a 100 mL volumetric flask with a 20 mL pipette, dilute with water to the 100-mL mark and invert the flask several times to ensure complete mixing. Repeat the practice several times until you are proficient.

(2) Preparing standard solution of Na_2CO_3: 1.0 g-1.1 g (accurate to 0.000 1 g) of pure Na_2CO_3 was weighed out accurately using 0.1 mg-electronic analytical balance and transfer it into a 50 mL beaker. Add 30 mL of distilled water and stir the solution with a stirring rod until the sodium carbonate is dissolved completely. Then the solution was transferred into a 100 mL volumetric flask. Rinse the beaker several times with a small amount of distilled water and transfer it to the volumetric flask, add distilled water to the 100-mL mark and mix well.

4. Operation of Erlenmeyer Flask

Take a 250 mL Erlenmeyer flask, and then transfer 20.00 mL of tap water into it with a 20 mL pipette. Hold the neck of the Erlenmeyer flask with right hand. And swirl it in a consistent circular motion. Ensure the solution rotates within the flask to avoid splashing loss. Repeat the above practice until you are proficient.

5. Operation of Burette and Acid-Base Titration

5.1   Burette

According to the operation techniques of burettes in Chapter 2, check liquid-tightness and assemble the acidic burette and basic burette. Practice rinsing, filling liquid, removing bubbles, titrating and reading the burettes.

5.2　Acid-Base Titration

(1) With phenolphthalein as the indicator, titrate $0.1\ mol\cdot L^{-1}$ (accurate to $\pm\ 0.000\ 1\ mol\cdot L^{-1}$) HCl solution with $0.1\ mol\cdot L^{-1}$ (accurate to $\pm\ 0.000\ 1\ mol\cdot L^{-1}$) NaOH solution.

Take a clean base burette or PTFE burette, check liquid-tightness with tap water. If it doesn't leak, rinse the burette with distilled water and rinse it again with about 5 mL to 6 mL $0.1\ mol\cdot L^{-1}$ NaOH standard solution for 2-3 times. Pour $0.1\ mol\cdot L^{-1}$ NaOH standard solution directly from the reagent bottle into the burette. Remove the air bubbles, adjust the liquid level, and then read the scale as the initial volume, such as $V_{initial}=0.01\ mL$.

Rinse three 250 mL Erlenmeyer flasks with distilled water for 2-3 times. With a 20 mL pipette, accurately transfer 20.00 mL of $0.1\ mol\cdot L^{-1}$ HCl standard solution into one Erlenmeyer flasks. Add 2 drops of phenolphthalein and titrate with $0.1\ mol\cdot L^{-1}$ NaOH standard solution until a faint pink color appears and persists for 30 seconds at least. Record the volume of NaOH solution as V_{final} in Table 4-1-1. Repeat the titration for 3 times.

Calculate the volume ratio of NaOH solution to HCl solution and the relative deviation.

(2) Using methyl orange as the indicator, titrate $0.1\ mol\cdot L^{-1}$ (accurate to $\pm\ 0.000\ 1\ mol\cdot L^{-1}$) NaOH solution with $0.1\ mol\cdot L^{-1}$ (accurate to $\pm\ 0.000\ 1\ mol\cdot L^{-1}$) HCl solution in the same way until the color of the solution becomes orange or a faint pink and the color does not disappear in 30 seconds. Record the corresponding data in Table 4-1-2, calculate the volume ratio of HCl solution to NaOH solution and the relative deviation.

【DATA AND RESULTS】

Date:＿＿＿＿＿＿　Temperature:＿＿＿＿＿℃　Relative Humidity:＿＿＿＿＿

Table 4-1-1　Titration of HCl standard solution with NaOH standard solution($n=3$)

Experiment No.	1	2	3
Indicator	Phenolphthalein	Phenolphthalein	Phenolphthalein
Color of Solution at the End of Titration			
$V_{initial}$(NaOH)/mL			
V_{final}(NaOH)/mL			
$V_{consume}$(NaOH)/mL			
$\overline{V}_{consume}$(NaOH)/mL			
c(NaOH)/mol$\cdot L^{-1}$			
V(HCl)/mL			
c(HCl)/mol$\cdot L^{-1}$			
$\dfrac{V(HCl)}{V_{consume}(NaOH)}$			
$\dfrac{V(HCl)}{\overline{V}_{consume}(NaOH)}$			
$\overline{d}_r$/%			

Table 4-1-2   Titration of NaOH standard solution with HCl standard solution($n = 3$)

Experiment No.	1	2	3
Indicator	Methyl orange	Methyl orange	Methyl orange
Color of Solution at the End of Titration			
$V_{initial}$ (HCl) / mL			
V_{final} (HCl) / mL			
$V_{consume}$(HCl) / mL			
$\overline{V}_{consume}$ (HCl) / mL			
c(HCl) / mol·L^{-1}			
V(NaOH) / mL			
c(NaOH) / mol·L^{-1}			
$\dfrac{V_{consume}(HCl)}{V(NaOH)}$			
$\dfrac{\overline{V}_{consume}(HCl)}{V(NaOH)}$			
$\overline{d}_r$ /%			

【QUESTIONS】

(1) Why do burettes and pipettes need to be moistened with a small amount of solution after being washed with distilled water before use?

(2) Why should the scale of a burette be adjusted to the zero mark or below the zero mark before the titration?

(3) During titration, why is the volume ratio of HCl to NaOH different when methyl orange and phenolphthalein are used as the indicator, respectively?

(LI Xianrui)

Experiment 2   Weighing Practice with an Electronic Analytical Balance

【OBJECTIVES】

(1) To master the basic operations of electronic analytical balance and common weighing methods.

(2) To understand the usage of weighing bottle and desiccator.

【PRE-LAB ASSIGNMENTS】

(1) How many kinds of weighing methods are there? Describe the differences between the direct weighing and the weighing by difference in respect of operation process and scope of application.

(2) Briefly explain the general operation procedures of using an electronic analytical balance.

(3) What precautions should be taken when using an electronic analytical balance?

(4) Simulated Design Experiment: Present the experimental design as a flowchart, clearly indicating the corresponding precautions and the rationale behind each step.

【 PRINCIPLES 】

The structure, principles and usage methods of electronic analytical balances are referred to Chapter 2 of Part I.

A sample can be weighed in many ways, the most commonly used ones are direct weighing and weighing by difference. Direct weighing is suitable for weighing clean and dry vessels (such as small beakers, surface dishes, etc.) and samples that are stable in air and nonhygroscopic (such as metals or ores, etc.). In direct weighing, first placing a receiving vessel or a sheet of weighing paper on the pan and weighed, removing the mass of the container or weighing paper, and then putting the sample on the container or weighing paper to weigh the mass of the sample. The operation of weighing by difference is to obtain the mass of the sample from the difference between two weighing, and only requires weighing within a certain mass range. The weighing procedure involves first measuring the total mass of the container (usually a weighing bottle) along with the sample. After transferring a portion of the sample to another vessel, the container with the remaining sample is reweighed. The difference between the two measurements corresponds to the mass of the transferred sample.

In this experiment, we practice standardized operations including the use of electronic analytical balances, proper reagent handling, and desiccator operation to accurately weigh samples of specific mass using conventional weighing methods.

【 APPARATUS, REAGENTS AND MATERIALS 】

Apparatus   0.1 mg-Electronic analytical balance, desiccator, weighing bottle, beaker (50 mL), spatula, a slip of paper and weighing paper

Reagents and Materials   Magnesium carbonate (A.R.) and borax (A.R.)

【 PROCEDURES 】

1. Checking the Balance

Check the balance carefully. Make sure that the balance is in horizontal state by checking the water level behind the stand of the balance. Otherwise, adjust the base-screws until the bubble moves to the center of the level indicator.

2. Turning on the Balance

Turn on the balance using an "on / off" switch. Once the balance is on and has gone through its initial calibration check, the digital display will show "0.000 0 g". If not, push the tare button or "O / T" button. Pre-heat the balance for at least 30 minutes if it is switched on after being disconnected with power for a long time.

3. Direct Weighing

Place a clean container in the center of the pan and close the sliding glass doors. When the green dot on the left of digital screen disappears (indicating that the weight is stable), the weight (g) of the container will appear in the unit area of the display. Then push the tare button or "O / T" button to deduct the weight of the container. Carefully add 0.20 - 0.25 g (accurate to 0.000 1 g) of magnesium carbonate to the container. Stop adding samples, close the balance door, and record the weighing data in Table 4-2-1. Repeat the weighing twice according to the above method.

4. Weighing by Difference

Take a weighing bottle containing borax with a slip of paper out of a desiccator and place it in the center of the pan. Push the tare button or "O/T" button till the reading of "0.000 0 g" appear.

After that, transfer 1.0 g - 1.4 g (accurate to 0.000 1 g) of borax sample into a clean and dry beaker by hitting the rim of the weighing bottle with its lid right above the beaker. Record the sample mass in Table 4-2-1 when the weighing sample is within the required range. Repeat the weighing for another 2 times for borax sample. If weighing paper is used to measure the sample, the weighed sample should be wrapped in the manner of pharmacy packaging. The package should be labeled with information such as the name of the reagent, the mass, the time of weighing, and the name of the person who performed the weighing.

5. Weighing Completed

After weighing, remove the weighing container from the pan. Push the "on/off" button to turn off the balance. Then clean the balance with a brush. Write down the status of the balance in the register book and sign your name.

【NOTES】

(1) When weighing, you should be careful with all operations. Ensure that the balance door is closed before recording the weight.

(2) Do not exceed the load limit of the balance The temperature of the weighing object must be the same as room temperature.

(3) The sample can not be directly weighed on the balance pan, and should be weighed in a clean vessel. Corrosive or hygroscopic samples must be weighed in a closed container.

(4) When weighing, use tweezers or paper clips to take the weighing items, you can also put on medical gloves for the operation, do not take them directly by hand.

【DATA AND RESULTS】

Date:_____ Temperature:_____℃ Relative Humidity:_____

Table 4-2-1   Weighing practice with an electronic analytical balance

Weighing Method	Sample	Mass/g		
		1	2	3
Direct weighing	Beaker			
	Sample			
Weighing by difference	Sample			

【QUESTIONS】

(1) How should samples be transferred from the weighing bottle when using the weighing-by-

difference method?

(2) What factors affect the reading stability of electronic analytical balances?

(ZHAO Quanqin)

Experiment 3   Preparation, pH Measurement and Properties of Buffer Solutions

【OBJECTIVES】

(1) To prepare buffer solutions and isotonic phosphate-buffered saline (PBS).

(2) To analyse the fundamental properties of buffer solutions.

(3) To refine pipetting techniques using measuring pipettes.

(4) To master the operation of the adjustable air displacement micropipettes.

(5) To measure solution pH using pH indicator papers and a pH meter.

【PRE-LAB ASSIGNMENTS】

(1) What are the key properties of buffer solutions, and what factors determine their pH?

(2) How is buffer capacity measured, and what factors are related to a buffer solution's buffering ability?

(3) How can pH changes in buffer solutions be detected, and is a pH meter always required?

(4) Classify this experiment as quantitative, qualitative, or semi-quantitative based on the analytical methods employed.

(5) Simulated Design Experiment: Present the experimental design as a flowchart, clearly indicating the corresponding precautions and the rationale behind each step.

【PRINCIPLES】

A buffer solution is an aqueous solution consisting of two components: a weak acid (HB, called anti-base component) and its conjugate base (B^-, called anti-acid component), a weak base and its conjugate acid, or an acid salt of polyprotic acid and its secondary salt. There is a proton-transferring equilibrium between the two components.

$$HB + H_2O \rightleftharpoons H_3O^+ + B^-$$

The pH of a buffer solution can be calculated by the Henderson-Hasselbalch equation:

$$pH = pK_a + \lg \frac{[B^-]}{[HB]}$$

wherein, K_a is the acid dissociation constant of the conjugate acid HB and $\frac{[B^-]}{[HB]}$ is called the buffer ratio.

When adding a small amount of a strong acid or a strong base, it will be neutralized by a large amount of an acid-resistant component (or an alkali-resistant component) in the buffer solution, so that the buffer ratio $\frac{[B^-]}{[HB]}$ of the buffer solution remains essentially unchanged, thus the pH of the buffer

165

solution is maintained. The buffer ability can be expressed by buffer capacity, β, whose value depends on the total concentration (c_{total} = [HB] + [B⁻]) and $\dfrac{[B^-]}{[HB]}$ of the solution. The definition of the buffer capacity is expressed below.

$$\beta = \frac{dn_B}{V|dpH|}$$

The buffer capacity increased with the total concentration of the buffer solution. And the closer to 1 the value of the buffer ratio $\dfrac{[B^-]}{[HB]}$, the greater the buffer capacity. Given the total concentration, the buffer capacity reaches maximum when the buffer ratio is equal to 1.

Buffer solutions are primarily used to maintain a stable pH environment, such as in biochemical reactions occurring within the tissues and organs of living organisms. PBS, a common buffer in medical applications for in vitro cell culture, mimics intracellular fluid osmolarity and extracellular fluid pH while exhibiting strong buffering capacity.

This experiment involves preparing standard buffer solutions and phosphate-buffered saline (PBS). The buffering properties will then be validated by comparing the resistance of buffer solutions to acids, bases, and dilution against ordinary solutions.

【 APPARATUS, REAGENTS, AND MATERIALS 】

Apparatus   Beakers (50 mL × 6, 200 mL × 2, 500 mL × 1), test tubes (5 mL × 12), colorimetric tubes (10.00 mL × 3), volumetric flask (50.00 mL × 1), measuring pipettes / adjustable air displacement micropipettes (5.00 mL × 6, 1.00 mL × 3) and a number of tips, colorimetric tube support, test tube rack, dropper, glass rod, washing bottle, rubber suction bulb, pH meter.

Reagents and Materials   HAc solutions (1.000 0, 0.500 0 and 0.100 0 mol·L⁻¹), NaAc solutions (1.000 0 and 0.100 0 mol·L⁻¹), NaOH solution (1.000 0 mol·L⁻¹), HCl solution (1.000 0 mol·L⁻¹), NaCl solution (0.150 0 mol·L⁻¹), KCl solution (0.150 0 mol·L⁻¹), KH_2PO_4 solution (0.150 0 mol·L⁻¹), Na_2HPO_4 solution (0.100 0 mol·L⁻¹), standard buffer solutions (pH = 4.00, 6.86 and 9.18), universal pH indicator papers, two sample solutions (volume ⩾ 50 mL) brought by students themselves.

【 PROCEDURES 】

1. Preparation of Buffer Solutions

1.1   Preparation of PBS Buffer Solution (pH = 7.40)

According to the volumes of the reagents in Table 4-3-1, use measuring pipettes or adjustable air displacement micropipettes to transfer the corresponding solutions into a 50.00 mL volumetric flask, and prepare PBS buffer solution whose pH is equal to 7.40.

1.2   Preparation of HAc-NaAc Buffer Solutions

According to the volumes of the reagents in Table 4-3-2, use measuring pipettes or adjustable air displacement micropipettes to transfer the corresponding solutions into 3 colorimetric tubes (10 mL), in order to prepare buffer solutions A, B and C, respectively.

2. Determination of Buffer Solution Properties and Factors Influencing Buffer Capacity

Prepare a 0.500 0 mol·L⁻¹ HAc solution as the non-buffered control. Following the reagent volumes in Table 4-3-3, measure the pH of the control solution and buffer solutions A, B, and C before (pH_1) and after (pH_2) adding HCl, NaOH, or distilled water using pH indicator papers. Record all the values in Table 4-3-3 and calculate the absolute pH change $|\Delta pH|$.

$$|\Delta pH| = |pH_2 - pH_1|$$

Analyze and compare the $|\Delta pH|$ values from Table 4-3-3 to address the following questions and summarize the conclusions:

(1) What buffering properties do buffer solutions exhibit compared to non-buffered solutions?

(2) For buffer solutions A and B (equal total concentration), how does the buffer ratio affect their buffer capacity?

(3) Point out the differences between the buffer capacity of the buffer solutions with different total concentrations and equivalent buffer ratios.

(4) What are the primary factors affecting buffer capacity?

3. Determination of pH of PBS Solutions and Students' Own Samples

(1) Calibration of pH meter: Calibrate the pH meter according to the instruction in Chapter 2 Ordinary Instruments in Basic Chemistry Experiments.

(2) Determination of pH Values of PBS Solutions and Students' Own Samples: Transfer the prepared PBS solutions and your own sample solutions into three 50 mL beakers, respectively, and detect their pH using pH indicator papers and pH meter sequentially. Enter the data into Table 4-3-4.

Compare the pH values tested by different methods. Are they what you had expected? Make your proposal about waste emissions and protecting environment based on the pH values of your own sample solutions.

【DATA AND RESULTS】

Date::_____   Temperature:_____ ℃   Relative Humidity:_____

Table 4-3-1   Preparation of PBS buffer solution, pH = 7.40

Reagents	KCl	KH_2PO_4	Na_2HPO_4	NaCl
$c/\text{mol}\cdot\text{L}^{-1}$	0.150 0	0.150 0	0.100 0	0.150 0
Volume/mL	0.86	0.56	4.90	Fill to 50.00 mL

Table 4-3-2   Preparation of HAc - Ac⁻ buffer solutions

Solutions No.	A	B	C
1.000 0 mol·L⁻¹ NaAc/mL	2.50	4.00	/
1.000 0 mol·L⁻¹ HAc/mL	2.50	1.00	/
0.100 0 mol·L⁻¹ NaAc/mL	/	/	2.50
0.100 0 mol·L⁻¹ HAc/mL	/	/	2.50
V_{total}/mL			

continued

Solutions No.	A	B	C
$c(NaAc)/mol \cdot L^{-1}$			
$c(HAc)/mol \cdot L^{-1}$			
$c(NaAc)/c(HAc)$			
$c_{total} = c(NaAc) + c(HAc)/mol \cdot L^{-1}$			

Table 4-3-3   Properties of buffer solutions

Testing items	Anti-acid properties				Anti-base properties				Anti-dilution properties			
Reagents	HAc	A	B	C	HAc	A	B	C	HAc	A	B	C
Volume / mL	1.00	1.00	1.00	1.00	1.00	1.00	1.00	1.00	1.00	1.00	1.00	1.00
pH_1												
$1.000\ 0\ mol \cdot L^{-1}\ HCl/drops$	3	3	3	3								
$1.000\ 0\ mol \cdot L^{-1}\ NaOH$					3	3	3	3				
H_2O / mL									4.00	4.00	4.00	4.00
pH_2												
$\Delta pH = |pH_2 - pH_1|$												

Notice: the concentration of HAc solution used as control in Table 4-3-3 is $0.500\ 0\ mol \cdot L^{-1}$

Table 4-3-4   pH Determination of PBS solutions and student's own samples

Sample Name	PBS buffer solution	Sample 1	Sample 2
pH (pH paper)			
pH (pH meter)			

【QUESTIONS】

(1) Compare and discuss the accuracies of pH indicator paper and pH meter.

(2) Why should the combination electrode be washed with distilled water and dried with tissues to determine the pH of a new solution after each measurement?

(3) If there are only HAc and NaOH, HCl and $NH_3 \cdot H_2O$, or KH_2PO_4 and NaOH, can the above experiments be carried out? If they can, how will you design the experiments?

(LAI Zefeng)

Experiment 4   Preparation and Properties of Sols

【OBJECTIVE】

(1) To master the preparation method of sols.

(2) To be familiar with the optical and electrical properties of sols.

(3) To understand the purification and coagulation of sols, and the protection of macromolecular compounds on sols.

【 PRE-LAB ASSIGNMENTS 】

Simulated Design Experiment: Present the experimental design as a flowchart, clearly indicating the corresponding precautions and the rationale behind each step. Preview questions:

(1) How to classify the dispersing system according to the size of dispersed phase? Can they permeate the filter paper or semi-permeable membrane?

(2) How to classify the colloid disperse system? What are the basic properties of a sol?

(3) Write the micelle structure of $Fe(OH)_3$ sol and Sb_2S_3 sol separately, and indicate the direction of movement of the colloidal particles during electrophoresis in an electric field ?

(4) Why are the sols a thermodynamically unstable system and a kinetically stable system?

(5) Explain the reason why heating and electrolytes can cause the coagulation of sols?

【 PRINCIPLES 】

1. Preparation of Sols

A colloidal dispersion is a mixture in which particles ranging from 1 to 100 nm in size are dispersed in another medium. Colloidal dispersions can be classified into three types: sols, macromolecular solutions and association colloids. Generally, sols are prepared by chemical reaction or physical condensation.

1.1   Chemical Reaction Method

Preparation of $Fe(OH)_3$ sol by hydrolysis of $FeCl_3$: A dark red $Fe(OH)_3$ sol can be prepared by dropping $FeCl_3$ solution into boiling water.

$$FeCl_3 + 3H_2O \xrightleftharpoons{boiling} Fe(OH)_3 + 3HCl$$

$$Fe(OH)_3 + HCl \rightleftharpoons FeOCl + 2H_2O$$

$$FeOCl \rightleftharpoons FeO^+ + Cl^-$$

Thus $Fe(OH)_3$ colloidal nuclei would be positively charged by adsorbing FeO^+ which is similar to $Fe(OH)_3$ to form a positive sol.

Preparation of Sb_2S_3 sol: Sb_2S_3 sol is prepared by the reaction of H_2S dissolved in water with potassium antimony tartrate.

$$2(SbO)K(C_4H_4O_6) + 3H_2S \rightleftharpoons Sb_2S_3 + 2KHC_4H_4O_6 + 2H_2O$$

$$H_2S\,(excess) + H_2O \rightleftharpoons H_3O^+ + HS^-$$

The Sb_2S_3 colloidal nuclei would be negatively charged by adsorbing HS^- to form a negative sol.

1.2   Physical Condensation Method

Preparation of sulfur sol: Based on the difference in solubility of sulfur in different solvents, a saturated solution of sulfur in ethanol is added dropwise to water. Because sulfur is insoluble in water, sulfur atoms gather together to form sulfur sol.

2. Optical and Electrical Properties of Sols

When sols are irradiated with a strong beam of light, a conical beam can be seen in the perpendicular direction of the incident light because the colloidal particles reflect and scatter the light. This phenomenon is called the Tyndall effect. The Tyndall effect can be used to distinguish sols from true solutions.

Another important property of sols is that colloidal particles become charged due to dissociation or selective absorption. The electrical property of sols can be determined by an electrophoresis apparatus, which consists of a U-tube and two electrodes. The movement of charged colloidal particles in an electric field is called electrophoresis. When the direct current is applied to the U-tube, each electrode attracts particles of opposite charge. Negative sols accumulate around the positive electrode and positive sols accumulate around the negative electrode. For example, $Fe(OH)_3$ sol moves to the negative electrode because of its positive charge, while Sb_2S_3 sol moves to the positive electrode because of its negative charge. The charging of colloidal particles is one of the key factors contributing to their stability.

3. Purification of Sols

The presence of electrolyte ions can destabilize sols. Therefore, removing electrolyte ions can keep sols stable for a longer time. The method of separating and purifying colloids is called dialysis. This process is based on the characteristic that colloidal particles cannot pass through a semipermeable membrane, while electrolyte ions, small molecules, and water molecules can easily pass through the semipermeable membrane. This membrane is known as the dialysis membrane.

4. Coagulation of Sols

The stability of sols depends on several factors: the electrical property of the sols, the protective effect of the hydrated film surrounding colloidal particles, and Brownian motion. Among these, the electrical property is the most important stabilizing factor.

Coagulation by electrolytes primarily occurs through alterations in the structure of colloidal particles. When electrolytes are added, more counterions migrate from the diffusion layer to the adsorption layer. This process neutralizes the surface charges on colloidal particles and reduces the thickness of the adsorption layer. Consequently, the stability of the sol decreases, ultimately leading to coagulation. The coagulation ability depends on the charge of the counterions - the higher the charge, the stronger the coagulation effect. $Fe(OH)_3$ sol is positively charged, so solutions containing multivalent anions (such as PO_4^{3-}) exhibit stronger coagulation ability. Sb_2S_3 sol is a negative sol, so the most effective coagulating electrolytes are those that have a high positive charge. This explains why $AlCl_3$ is more effective than an equivalent amount of NaCl in coagulating Sb_2S_3 sol.

In addition to coagulation by electrolytes, mixing two types of sols with opposite charges and heating can also lead to the coagulation of sols.

5. Protective Effect of Macromolecules on Sols

When an adequate amount of macromolecular solution is added to a sol, the macromolecules form a protective layer around the colloidal particles. This layer enhances the stability of the sol and prevents coagulation of the colloidal particles.

【 APPARATUS, REAGENTS AND MATERIALS 】

Apparatus   U-shaped tube (electrophoresis apparatus), an instrument for Tyndall effect, a magnetic stirrer, an alcohol lamp, beaker (100 mL × 5), graduated cylinder (10 mL × 4, 50 mL × 3), test tube, a watch glass, medicine dropper, tripod stand and a glass rod.

Reagents   30 $g \cdot L^{-1}$ ferric chloride, 4 $g \cdot L^{-1}$ antimony potassium tartrate, saturated hydrogen sulfide solution, saturated sulfide solution in ethanol, saturated NaCl solution, 0.01 mol·L^{-1} NaCl, 0.01 mol·L^{-1} CaCl$_2$, 0.01 mol·L^{-1} AlCl$_3$, 0.1 mol·L^{-1} NH$_3$·H$_2$O, 0.1 mol·L^{-1} KSCN, 0.05 mol·L^{-1} AgNO$_3$, 30 g·L^{-1} gelatin, 20 g·L^{-1} CuSO$_4$, celloidin, and pH indicator papers.

【 PROCEDURES 】

1. Preparation of Sols

1.1   Preparation of Fe(OH)$_3$ Sol

In a 100-mL beaker containing 30.0 mL of distilled water brought to boiling, 3.0 mL of 30 g·L^{-1} FeCl$_3$ solution is added dropwise under vigorous stirring. The mixture is maintained at boiling for 2–3 minutes to form a stable Fe(OH)$_3$ sol, during which color changes should be observed. The prepared sol is then stored in a labeled container for subsequent use.

1.2   Preparation of Sb$_2$S$_3$ Sol

Transfer 20.0 mL of a 4 g·L^{-1} antimony potassium tartrate solution into a small beaker. Under constant stirring, slowly add approximately 10.0 mL of saturated H$_2$S solution dropwise until an orange-red Sb$_2$S$_3$ sol forms. Store the resulting sol for subsequent use.

1.3   Preparation of Sulfur Sol

Add 20.0 mL of distilled water into a small beaker. Under constant stirring, slowly add 2.0-3.0 mL of an ethanol-saturated sulfur solution dropwise until sulfur sol forms. Store the resulting sol for subsequent use.

2. Properties of Sols

2.1   Tyndall Effect

Place the prepared sols separately in the Tyndall effect apparatus and irradiate them with a strong beam of light. Observe the Tyndall phenomenon from a direction perpendicular to the light path. For comparison, test distilled water and a 20 g·L^{-1} CuSO$_4$ solution under the same conditions to observe their Tyndall effects.

2.2   Electrical Properties of Sols - Electrophoresis

Place the Sb$_2$S$_3$ sol in the electrophoresis apparatus and carefully layer distilled water over both ends of the sol, maintaining a water layer thickness of approximately 1–2 cm. Insert the electrodes into the distilled water, apply a direct current of 30–110 V, and observe the direction of the sol interface movement to determine the electrical charge carried by the colloidal particles.

3. Purification of Sols - Dialysis

3.1   Preparation of Dialysis Bag

Place a suitable amount of celloidins in a clean small beaker and swirl it gently. After allowing it to stand for approximately one minute, invert the beaker. Once the celloidin has solidified into a thin film, carefully peel it away to obtain a dialysis bag.

3.2   Purification of Fe(OH)$_3$ Sol

Transfer the Fe(OH)$_3$ sol into the dialysis bag, ensuring no solution contaminates the outer surface. If contamination occurs, rinse it immediately with distilled water. Securely fasten the opening of the bag and suspend it in a beaker filled with distilled water. Replace the water every 10 minutes, and test for chloride ions (using silver nitrate) and ferric ions (using KCNS). Document the test results at each interval.

4. Coagulation of Sols

4.1 Coagulation by Electrolytes

Prepare three test tubes, each containing 2.0 mL of Sb_2S_3 sol. To the first tube, add 0.01 $mol \cdot L^{-1}$ NaCl dropwise while shaking. Similarly, add 0.01 $mol \cdot L^{-1}$ $CaCl_2$ to the second tube and 0.01 $mol \cdot L^{-1}$ $AlCl_3$ to the third tube, continuing the dropwise addition with shaking until persistent precipitation occurs. Record the number of drops required for each electrolyte to induce coagulation, then compare and interpret the results.

4.2 Intercoagulation of Sols

Mix 2.0 mL of $Fe(OH)_3$ sol with 2.0 mL of Sb_2S_3 sol in a small test tube. Observe the resulting phenomenon and provide an explanation.

4.3 Coagulation by Heating

Heat the test tube containing 2.0 mL of Sb_2S_3 sol to boiling. Observe and explain the resulting phenomenon.

5. Protective Effect of Macromolecules on Sols

Add 2.0 mL of distilled water to one test tube and 2.0 mL of freshly prepared 30 $g \cdot L^{-1}$ gelatin solution to another. To each test tube, add 4.0 mL of Sb_2S_3 sol, gently swirl to mix, and allow to stand for 3 minutes. Subsequently, introduce saturated NaCl solution to both test tubes and observe the comparative differences in their behavior.

Record the above experimental phenomena and explain the neasons in table 4-4-1.

【DATA AND RESULTS】

Date:_____   Temperature:_____℃ Relative Humidity:_____

Table 4-4-1   Preparation and properties of sols

Experimental content		Phenomenon	Explanation
Preparation of sols	$Fe(OH)_3$ sol		
	Sb_2S_3 sol		
	sulfur sol		
Tyndall effect			
Electrophoresis			
Purification of $Fe(OH)_3$ sol			
Coagulation of sols	Coagulation by electrolytes		
	Intercoagulation of sols		
	Coagulation by heating		
Protective effect of macromolecules on sols			

【QUESTIONS】

(1) In the preparation of $Fe(OH)_3$ sol, $FeCl_3$ solution must be added dropwise to boiling water. Explain the scientific rationale behind this procedure.

(2) What is the mechanism by which gelatin stabilizes the sol?

(3) Provide a theoretical explanation for the Tyndall effect observed in colloidal solutions.

(LIU Guojie)

Chapter 5 | Experiments of Titration Analysis

Experiment 5　Acid-Base Titration Analysis

【OBJECTIVES】

(1) To master the principles and procedures of acid-base titration.

(2) To master standardized titration operation and determine the ending point of the titration.

(3) To learn how to prepare standard solutions and how to analyze acidic and basic substances.

(4) To learn the basic operation of back titration.

(5) To learn the direct titration and the analytical method of the real samples.

【PRE-LAB ASSIGNMENTS】

(1) What is the difference between titration and standardization?

(2) How many methods can we use to prepare a standard solution? How many methods can we use to standardize a standard solution?

(3) Why are HCl and NaOH solutions often used as standard solutions in acid-base titration?

(4) What criteria do we use in selecting the indicator for acid-base titration?

(5) Is the color change range of an acid-base indicator calculated from pK_{HIn}?

(6) Does the amount of indicator used has any influence on titration error?

【PRINCIPLES】

Acid-base titration is a titration analysis based on acid-base reaction. It can be used to determine the concentration of acids and bases, and can also be used to determine the concentration of substances that react with an acid or a base. When an acidic sample is analyzed, a strong basic solution with known concentration is used. The concentration of the acidic compound is calculated based on the amount of the base consumed. When a basic sample is analyzed, a strong acidic solution with known concentration is used. The concentration of the basic substance is calculated by the amount of the acid consumed.

The insoluble acidic substance can be neutralized by adding a certain excess of alkali, and the remainder alkali is titrated by another standard acidic solution, which is known as back titration. For the insoluble basic substance the method is also applicable.

The titration analysis usually involves three steps: preparing the standard solutions, standardizing the concentration of the standard solutions, and determining the content of the samples.

In a typical acid-base analysis, hydrochloric acid or sodium hydroxide solution is used as the standard solution. Due to the fact that hydrochloric acid is volatile and sodium hydroxide absorbs moisture and carbon dioxide from the air, their standard solutions cannot be prepared directly. A solution with approximate concentration required is prepared first. Its accurate concentration is then standardized by a primary standard substance or another standard solution with known accurate concentration. The concentration of solution can be calculated according to the value of V(NaOH) or V(HCl) obtained by titration and the mass of primary standard substance or the concentration of standard solution.

The common primary standard substances used to standardize HCl solution include anhydrous sodium carbonate (Na_2CO_3) and borax ($Na_2B_4O_7 \cdot 10H_2O$). Sodium carbonate is readily available in high purity form and is inexpensive. Since it absorbs moisture and CO_2 from the air, however, it must be dried at 270 – 300 °C for about one hour and kept it in a desiccator after cooling down somewhat. Borax has a large molar mass ($381.37\ g \cdot mol^{-1}$) but contains lattice water and must be kept in an environmental chamber kept at approximately 60% relative humidity.

The common primary standard substances used to standardize NaOH solution include oxalic acid ($H_2C_2O_4 \cdot 2H_2O$) and potassium acid phthalate ($KHC_8H_4O_4$, KHP). The most common used primary standard substance is potassium acid phthalate because it has large molar mass ($204.22\ g \cdot mol^{-1}$), high stability, and readily availability in high purity form.

1. The Standardization of the Concentration of HCl Solution

【OBJECTIVES】

(1) To master the principles and procedures of the standardization of the concentration of HCl solution.

(2) To consolidate standardized operation of acidic burette and determine the ending point of the titration.

(3) To consolidate the procedures of the differential weighing method.

【PRE-LAB ASSIGNMENTS】

Simulated Design Experiment: Present the experimental design as a flowchart, clearly indicating the corresponding precautions and the rationales behind each step.

Preview questions:

(1) Why hydrochloric acid cannot be directly prepared into a standard solution for use?

(2) Why is distilled water added to the reagent bottle before hydrochloric acid during the preparation of hydrochloric acid solution?

(3) Which is a better choice to standardize HCl solution when methyl orange is used as the indicator, $Na_2B_4O_7 \cdot 10H_2O$ or Na_2CO_3?

(4) How to determine the titration endpoint during the standardization of the concentration of HCl solution using Na_2CO_3?

【PRINCIPLES】

Anhydrous Na_2CO_3 (pK_{b1} = 3.75, pK_{b2} = 7.62) is often used to titrate HCl solution. The reaction is as follows:

$$Na_2CO_3 + 2HCl \xrightarrow{\hspace{1cm}} 2NaCl + H_2O + CO_2 \uparrow$$

Here we have the titration of $0.100\ 0\ mol \cdot L^{-1}$ Na_2CO_3 by $0.100\ 0\ mol \cdot L^{-1}$ HCl. The stoichiometric point is pH = 3.9. And the interval of inflection point of titration in pH is 5.0 to 3.5. So methyl orange fits reasonably well with its color change interval of pH = 3.1-4.4. When the end point of titration is coming, the solution should be boiled to reduce the effect of CO_2.

The accurate concentration of HCl solution can be calculated according to the following equation

$$c(HCl) = \frac{2 \times m\ (Na_2CO_3)}{M_r(Na_2CO_3)\ V\ (HCl)} \tag{5-5-1}$$

In equation 5-5-1, $m(Na_2CO_3)$ is mass of Na_2CO_3; $M_r(Na_2CO_3)$ is molar mass of Na_2CO_3 ($105.99\ g \cdot mol^{-1}$); $V(HCl)$ is the volume of HCl solution consumed.

【APPARATUS, REAGENTS AND MATERIALS】

Apparatus　0.1 mg-electronic analytic balance, acidic burette or PTFE burette (25 mL), beaker (100 mL, 1 L), conical flask (250 mL × 3), graduated cylinder(10 mL, 50 mL), weighing bottle, reagent bottle, burette stand, washing bottle, glass rod, dropper, alcohol burner

Reagents and Materials　Anhydrous sodium carbonate (A.R) , concentrated hydrochloric acid solution ($12\ mol \cdot L^{-1}$), 0.05% methyl orange indicator solution

【PROCEDURES】

1.1　Preparation of $0.1\ mol \cdot L^{-1}$ HCl Solution

Calculate the volume of concentrated HCl solution needed to prepare 500 mL of $0.1\ mol \cdot L^{-1}$ HCl solution. Then measure it by 10 mL graduated cylinder and pour the acid into the beaker containing a moderate amount of distilled water. Wash out the 10 mL measuring cylinder 2-3 times with a small amount of distilled water and add the washings to the beaker. Replenish the beaker with distilled water to 500 mL and stir evenly. Transfer the solution to the reagent bottle and insert the stopper.

1.2　Standardization the Concentration of HCl Solution

Weigh accurately pure Na_2CO_3 0.07-0.09 g (0.000 1g precisely) with analytic balance using the differential weighing method to a clean 250 mL conical flask. Add 30 mL distilled water to dissolve Na_2CO_3. Add 2 drops of methyl orange indicator and mix the solution sufficiently to homogenization. Then the solution becomes yellow. Release the acid to the conical flask slowly from the burette. Continue the addition until the solution in the conical flask just changes from yellow to orange. Then stop the addition and boil the solution in the conical flask to 2-3 minutes, shake it to remove CO_2. The color of the solution changes from orange to yellow again. After cooling down, continue the titration until the solution became faint yellow and the color does not disappear in at least 30 seconds. This marks the end point of the titration. Record the volume of the standard hydrochloric acid solution used in the titration to Table 5-5-1.

Repeat the titration process 2-3 times until the relative error of the analytical results is below 0.2%. From the weights of sodium carbonate and the volumes of hydrochloric acid employed, the strength of the acid could be calculated for each titration.

【DATA AND RESULTS】

Date:_____   Temperature:_____°C   Relative Humidity:_____

(1) Use_____mL concentrated HCl solution to prepare 500 mL of $0.1\ mol\cdot L^{-1}$ HCl solution

(2) Standardization of the concentration of HCl solution (Table 5-5-1)

Table 5-5-1   Standardization of the concentration of HCl solution

Experiment No.	1	2	3
m_1 (weighing bottle + Na_2CO_3)/g			
m_2 (weighing bottle + remaining Na_2CO_3)/g			
m_1-m_2 (Na_2CO_3)/g			
$V_{Initial}$(HCl)/mL			
V_{Final}(HCl)/mL			
$\Delta V_{Consumed}$(HCl)/mL			
c(HCl)/mol$\cdot L^{-1}$			
$\bar{c}$(HCl)/mol$\cdot L^{-1}$			
$\bar{d_r}$/%			

【QUESTIONS】

(1) Why was methyl orange selected as an indicator? Besides methyl orange, are there any other indicators that can be used?

(2) In the titration of HCl by Na_2CO_3, what is the reason for remove CO_2 by boiling the solution when the color first changes? What will happen if CO_2 haven't been removed?

2. The Standardization of the Concentration of NaOH

【OBJECTIVES】

(1) To master the principles and procedures of the standardization of the concentration of NaOH solution.

(2) To consolidate standardized operation of basic burette and determine the ending point of the titration.

(3) To consolidate the procedures of the differential weighing method.

【PRE-LAB ASSIGNMENTS】

Simulated Design Experiment: Present the experimental design as a flowchart, clearly indicating the corresponding precautions and the rationales behind each step.

Preview questions:

(1) Why NaOH cannot be directly prepared into a standard solution for use?

(2) Why do standard NaOH solutions often need to be recalibrated for concentration before use?

(3) Why is potassium hydrogen phthalate (KHC$_8$H$_4$O$_4$) commonly used as a primary standard substance for titrating sodium hydroxide solutions? Can other primary standard substances be used?

【PRINCIPLES】

Potassium acid phthalate (KHC$_8$H$_4$O$_4$, KHP, pK_{a2} = 5.41) is often used to titrate NaOH solution. The reaction is as follows:

At the stoichiometric point, the pH of the solution is 9.1. Phenolphthalein can be chosen as the indicator as the discoloration range of pH is around 8.2 to 10.0. According to the reaction equation above, at stoichiometric point, we have the following equations to calculate the accurate concentration of NaOH according to mass of KHC$_8$H$_4$O$_4$ titrated and the volume of NaOH solution consumed.

$$c(\text{NaOH}) = \frac{m(\text{KHP})}{M_r(\text{KHP}) \times V(\text{NaOH})} \tag{5-5-2}$$

In equation 5-5-2, m(KHP) is mass of KHC$_8$H$_4$O$_4$; M_r(KFP) is molar mass of KHC$_8$H$_4$O$_4$ (204.22 g·mol^{-1}); V(NaOH) is the volume of NaOH solution consumed.

【APPARATUS, REAGENTS AND MATERIALS】

Apparatus　0.1 mg-electronic analytic balance, 0.01 g-electronic analytical balance, basic burette or PTFE burette (25 mL), conical flask (250 mL × 3), graduated cylinder (50 mL), beaker (100 mL, 1 L), weighing bottle, burette stand, washing bottle, reagent bottle, glass rod, dropper

Reagents and Materials　Solid of sodium hydroxide, potassium hydrogen phthalate (KHC$_8$H$_4$O$_4$, A.R), 0.1% phenolphthalein indicator

【PROCEDURES】

2.1　Preparation of 0.1 mol·L^{-1} NaOH Solution

To calculate the mass of solid sodium hydroxide, you need to prepare 500 mL of 0.1 mol·L^{-1} NaOH solution. Quickly weigh out the solid sodium hydroxide needed with the 0.01 g-electronic analytical balance, and put it into the beaker. Add a moderate amount of distilled water to dissolve it. After it has cooled down to room temperature, replenish the beaker with distilled water to 500 mL and stir evenly. Transfer the solution to the reagent bottle and insert the stopper.

2.2　Standardization the Concentration of NaOH Solution

Weigh out the mass of potassium acid phthalate between 0.28-0.32 g (0.000 1 g precisely) with analytic balance using the differential weighing method to a clean 250 mL conical flask. Add 50 mL of distilled water to dissolve potassium acid phthalate. Add 2 drops of phenolphthalein indicator and mix the solution sufficiently to homogenization. Release the basic solution to the conical flask slowly from the burette. Continue the addition until the solution in the conical flask just changes from colorless to faint pink. The endpoint is reached when the color does not disappear in at least 30 seconds. Record the volume of the standard NaOH solution used in the titration to Table 5-5-2.

Repeat the titration process 2-3 times until the relative error of the determination is below 0.2%. The concentration of the standard NaOH solution could be calculated according to the mass of the potassium acid phthalate and the volumes of sodium hydroxide solution consumed in titration.

【POINTS FOR ATTENTION】

(1) NaOH is strong corrosive. During the process of weighing, do not contact with skin and clothing and avoid dripping it on the bench. If there is any spillage, it should be dealt with immediately.

(2) The prepared NaOH solution should be stored in a plastic reagent bottle or glass reagent bottle with a rubber stopper.

【DATA AND RESULTS】

Date:_____ Temperature:_____°C Relative Humidity:_____

(1) Use _____ g of solid of NaOH to prepare 500 mL of 0.1 mol·L^{-1} NaOH solution.

(2) Standardization of the concentration of NaOH solution. (Table 5-5-2)

Table 5-5-2   Standardization of the concentration of NaOH solution

Experiment No.	1	2	3
m_1 (bottle + KHP)/g			
m_2 (bottle + remaining KHP)/g			
$m_1 - m_2$ (KHP)/g			
V_{Inatial}(NaOH)/mL			
V_{Final}(NaOH)/mL			
$\Delta V_{\text{Consumed}}$(NaOH)/mL			
c(NaOH)/mol·L^{-1}			
$\bar{c}$(NaOH) /mol·L^{-1}			
$\bar{d_r}$/%			

【QUESTIONS】

(1) Why was phenolphthalein selected as an indicator? Besides phenolphthalein, are there any other indicators can be used?

(2) What is the reason for washing the inner surface of conical flask with distilled water when close to the endpoint of titration?

(BIE Zijun)

178

3.　Determination of Total Acidity in Vinegar

【OBJECTIVE】

(1) Understanding the change of pH during the titration of weak acid with strong base and the principles for selecting indicator.

(2) Mastering the method for determining the total acidity of vinegar.

【PRE-LAB ASSIGNMENTS】

Simulated Design Experiment: Present the experimental design as a flowchart, clearly indicating the corresponding precautions and the rationale behind each step.

Preview questions:

(1) Why the NaOH standard solution should be calibrated just before use?

(2) How to accurately transfer the vinegar sample in the experiment? Why should the vinegar sample be diluted before testing?

(3) When measuring the total acidity, the distilled water used must not contain carbon dioxide. Why?

(4) Can ammonia be used to determine the content of acetic acid in vinegar?

【PRINCIPLES】

Vinegar is a kind of liquid acidic condiment containing starch, sugar, and spirit alone or in combination. The acid substances in vinegar usually include acetic acid, lactic acid, gluconic acid, and succinic acid. Among them, acetic acid content is usually the most. During storage, organic acids can combine with alcohols to form esters, increasing the flavor of vinegar. Therefore, the total acid content in vinegar is an important indicator of vinegar quality. According to the *National Food Safety Standard for Vinegar* (GB 2719-2018), the total acid (calculated as acetic acid) index of vinegar $\geqslant 3.5$ g·$(100$ mL$)^{-1}$.

Acetic acid is a weak monobasic acid ($K_a = 1.75 \times 10^{-5}$), which can be titrated directly with NaOH standard solution. The reaction equation is as follows:

$$HAc + NaOH == NaAc + H_2O$$

If the initial concentration of vinegar test solution and NaOH standard solution is 0.1 mol·L^{-1}, pH at the stoichiometric point is about 8.7. Hence phenolphthalein can be used as the indicator. The solution changes from colorless to reddish at the end of titration.

Due to the fact that other acids that may exist in vinegar during titration also react with NaOH, the total acidity, $\rho(HAc)[$g·$(100$ mL$)^{-1}]$, can be calculated according to

$$\rho(HAc) = \frac{c(NaOH)\Delta V(NaOH)M(HAc)}{V(sample) \times 10} \tag{5-5-3}$$

Where $c(NaOH)$ is the concentration of NaOH standard solution (mol·L^{-1}), $\Delta V(NaOH)$ is the volume of NaOH standard solution consumed for titration (mL), $M(HAc)$ is the molar mass of acetic acid (60.05 g·mol^{-1}), and $V(sample)$ is the volume of vinegar sample corresponding to each titration (mL), respectively.

【APPARATUS, REAGENTS AND MATERIALS】

Apparatus   Base burette or acid-base universal burette (25 mL), pipet (20 mL, 10 mL), volumetric flask (100 mL), Erlenmeyer flask (250 mL × 3) , burette rack, washing bottle, glass rod, dropper , burette stand

Reagents and Materials   White vinegar, freshly calibrated NaOH standard solution (0.1 mol·L^{-1}), phenolphthalein indicator (2 g·L^{-1}, ethanol solution)

【PROCEDURE】

Take a clean 20 mL pipet and rinse it three times with a small amount of vinegar sample to be tested. Accurately transfer 20.00 mL of vinegar to be tested into a 100 mL volumetric flask, dilute it to the scale line with newly boiled and cooled distilled water, plug the plug and mix the solution thoroughly.

Take a clean 10 mL pipet and rinse 3 times with diluted vinegar test solution. Accurately transfer 10.00 mL of diluted vinegar test solution into a 250 mL Erlenmeyer flask, add 2 drops of phenolphthalein indicator, titrate with the freshly calibrated NaOH standard solution until the solution turns reddish and does not fade within 30 s, which is the end point.

Three parallel titrations should be performed. Record the data in Table 5-5-3, and calculate the total acidity of vinegar [g·(100 mL)$^{-1}$] according to the volume of consumed NaOH standard solution.

【DATA AND RESULTS】

Date:_____   Temperature:_____°C   Relative Humidity:_____

Table 5-5-3   Determination of Total Acidity in Vinegar

Experiment No.	1	2	3
$c(NaOH)/mol·L^{-1}$			
$V_{initial}(NaOH)/mL$			
$V_{final}(NaOH)/mL$			
$\Delta V(NaOH)/mL$			
$\Delta \bar{V}(NaOH)/mL$			
$\bar{\rho}(HAc)/g·(100\ mL)^{-1}$			
$d_r/\%$			
$\bar{d_r}/\%$			

【QUESTIONS】

(1) What type of titration is this experiment? How to choose the indicator in the experiment?

(2) Analyse the sources of errors in this experiment and discuss possible methods for eliminating errors.

(LIN Yi)

4.　Determination of Borax Content

【 OBJECTIVE 】

(1)　Understanding the change of pH during the titration of weak base with strong acid and the principles for selecting indicator.

(2)　Mastering the method for determining borax content.

【 PRE-LAB ASSIGNMENTS 】

Simulated Design Experiment: Present the experimental design as a flowchart, clearly indicating the corresponding precautions and the rationale behind each step.

Preview questions:

(1)　How much sample should be weighed each time in the experiment? Why?

(2)　Why methyl red is selected as the indicator in this experiment?

【 PRINCIPLES 】

Borax (disodium tetraborate decahydrate, $Na_2B_4O_7 \cdot 10H_2O$) is a common chemical material that is widely used for preparing other boron compounds or buffer solutions. Borax can undergo proton transfer reactions with water, making the solution alkaline. Therefore, borax is a monobasic weak base ($K_b = 1.74 \times 10^{-5}$), which can be directly titrated with HCl standard solution. The reaction equation is as follows:

$$Na_2B_4O_7 \cdot 10H_2O + 2HCl = 2NaCl + 4H_3BO_3 + 5H_2O$$

If the initial concentrations of both borax test solution and HCl standard solution are $0.1 \text{ mol} \cdot L^{-1}$, pH at the stoichiometric point is about 5.1. Hence methyl red can be used as the indicator. The solution changes from yellow to light red at the end of titration.

Accordingly, at the stoichiometric point

$$n(HCl) = 2\, n(Na_2B_4O_7 \cdot 10H_2O) \tag{5-5-4}$$

Therefore, the mass fraction of borax

$$w(Na_2B_4O_7 \cdot 10H_2O) = \frac{c(HCl)\Delta V(HCl)M(Na_2B_4O_7 \cdot 10H_2O)}{m(sample) \times 2\,000} \times 100\% \tag{5-5-5}$$

Where, $c(HCl)$ is the concentration of HCl standard solution ($\text{mol} \cdot L^{-1}$), $V(HCl)$ is the volume of HCl standard solution consumed for titration (mL), M(borax) is the molar mass of borax ($381.37 \text{ g} \cdot \text{mol}^{-1}$), and m(sample) is the sample mass corresponding to each titration (g), respectively.

【 APPARATUS, REAGENTS AND MATERIALS 】

Apparatus　Electronic analytical balance, acid burette or acid-base universal burette (25 mL), weighing bottle, Erlenmeyer flask (250 mL × 3), measuring cylinder (100 mL), burette rack, washing bottle, glass rod, burette stand

Reagents and Materials   Borax samples, freshly calibrated HCl standard solution (0.1 mol·L⁻¹), methyl red indicator (2 g·L⁻¹, ethanol solution)

【 PROCEDURE 】

Use the difference method to accurately weigh 0.28-0.38 g (accurate to 0.000 1 g) of sample into a 250 mL Erlenmeyer flask, add about 50.0 mL of distilled water to dissolve it, then add 2 drops of methyl red indicator. Titrate the borax test solution with freshly calibrated HCl standard solution until the solution just turns from yellow to light red and does not fade within 30 s.

Three parallel titrations should be performed. Record the data and calculate the mass fraction of borax $w(Na_2B_4O_7 \cdot 10H_2O)$ in Table 5-5-4.

【 DATA AND RESULTS 】

Date:_____   Temperature:_____℃   Relative Humidity:_____

Table 5-5-4   Determination of Borax Content

Experiment No.	1	2	3
m(Sample)/g			
c(HCl)/mol·L⁻¹			
$V_{Initial}$(HCl)/mL			
V_{Final}(HCl)/mL			
ΔV(HCl)/mL			
w (Na$_2$B$_4$O$_7 \cdot$10H$_2$O)/%			
$\overline{w}$ (Na$_2$B$_4$O$_7 \cdot$10H$_2$O)/%			
d_r/%			
$\overline{d_r}$/%			

【 QUESTIONS 】

Analyse the sources of errors in this experiment and discuss possible methods for eliminating errors.

(LIN Yi)

5. Determination of Acetylsalicylic Acid Content in

Aspirin Tablets by Back Titration

【 OBJECTIVE 】

(1) Mastering the principle and operation of back titration method.

(2) Be familiar with the determination of acetylsalicylic acid in aspirin tablets by acid-base titration.

【PRE-LAB ASSIGNMENTS】

Simulated Design Experiment: Present the experimental design as a flowchart, clearly indicating the corresponding precautions and the rationale behind each step.

Preview questions:

(1) Why direct titration cannot be used to determine the content of acetylsalicylic acid in the tablets?

(2) In the reaction of acetylsalicylic acid with excess NaOH, the sample should be cooled with flowing water quickly after heating in water bath for 15 min. Please explain the reasons for this operation.

【PRINCIPLES】

Aspirin is an antipyretic and analgesic, and its main component is acetylsalicylic acid. Acetylsalicylic acid is an organic weak acid ($K_a = 3.2 \times 10^{-4}$), slightly soluble in water, easily soluble in ethanol and hydrolyse into salicylic acid (o-hydroxybenzoic acid) and acetate in strong alkaline solution. The reaction is

Since a certain amount of excipients such as magnesium stearate, starch, and other insoluble substances are generally added to the tablets, it is not suitable for direct titration, but can be determined by back titration method.

After grinding the tablet into powder, quantitatively add excessive NaOH standard solution, then the acetyl groups can be completely hydrolysed after heating for a period of time. With phenolphthalein as the indicator, titrate the excessive NaOH with HCl standard solution until the pink color just disappeared.

In this reaction, 1 mole of acetylsalicylic acid consumes 2 moles of NaOH. According to the volume of the initially added base, $V(\text{NaOH})$, and the volume of HCl consumed in the titration, $\Delta V(\text{HCl})$, the actual amount of alkali consumed by acetylsalicylic acid in the drug can be known, and the mass fraction of acetylsalicylic acid in the drug can be calculated by

$$w(\text{acetylsalicylic acid}) = \frac{[c(\text{NaOH})V(\text{NaOH}) - c(\text{HCl})\Delta V(\text{HCl})]M(\text{acetylsalicylic acid})}{m(\text{sample}) \times 2} \times 100\% \quad (5\text{-}5\text{-}6)$$

where M (acetylsalicylic acid) is the molar mass of acetylsalicylic acid (180.16 g·mol^{-1}).

【APPARATUS, REAGENTS AND MATERIALS】

Apparatus　Electronic analytical balance, acid burette or acid-base universal burette (25 mL), thermostatic water bath, mortar, weighing bottle, pipet (20 mL), measuring cylinder (100 mL), watch glass, Erlenmeyer flask (250 mL × 3), burette stand, washing bottle, glass rod

Reagents and Materials Aspirin tablets, freshly calibrated NaOH standard solution (0.1 mol·L^{-1}), freshly calibrated HCl standard solution (0.1 mol·L^{-1}), phenolphthalein indicator (2g·L^{-1}, ethanol solution)

【PROCEDURE】

5.1 Determination of acetylsalicylic acid content in aspirin tablets

After grinding aspirin tablets into powder samples with a mortar, accurately weigh 3 portions of 0.10-0.12 g (accurate to 0.000 1 g) powder into 3 clean Erlenmeyer flasks, respectively. Accurately add 20.00 mL of 0.1 mol·L^{-1} NaOH standard solution with a pipet. Then cover with a watch glass and gently shake for a few times. Heat for 15 minutes in a water bath of about 90 °C, then cool it to room temperature quickly with flowing water.

Add about 20.0 mL of distilled water, then add 2-3 drops of phenolphthalein indicator. Titrate with 0.1 mol·L^{-1} HCl standard solution until the red color just disappears. Three parallel titrations should be performed. Calculate the mass fraction of acetylsalicylic acid content in the tablets according to the volume of consumed HCl standard solution Record the data in Table 5-5-5.

5.2 Blank experiment

Accurately transfer 20.00 mL of 0.1 mol·L^{-1} NaOH standard solution into a 250 mL Erlenmeyer flask with a pipet, heat it and cool it under the same experimental conditions as for the aspirin tablets.

Add about 20.0 mL of distilled water, then add 2-3 drops of phenolphthalein indicator. Titrate with 0.1 mol·L^{-1} HCl standard solution until the red color just disappears. Three parallel titrations should be performed. Record the data in Table 5-5-6 and calculate the value of $V(NaOH)/\Delta V(HCl)$ according to the volume of HCl standard solution consumed.

【DATA AND RESULTS】

Date:_____ Temperature:_____°C Relative Humidity:_____

Table 5-5-5   Determination of acetylsalicylic acid content in aspirin content by back titration

Experiment No.	1	2	3
m(Sample)/g			
c(NaOH)/mol·L^{-1}			
V(NaOH)/mL			
c(HCl)/mol·L^{-1}			
$V_{Initial}$(HCl)/mL			
V_{Final}(HCl)/mL			
ΔV(HCl)/mL			
w (Acetylsalicylic acid)/%			
$\overline{w}$ (Acetylsalicylic acid)/%			
d_r/%			
$\overline{d_r}$/%			

Table 5-5-6   Blank experiment

Experiment No.	1	2	3
$c(NaOH)/mol \cdot L^{-1}$			
$V(NaOH)/mL$			
$c(HCl)/mol \cdot L^{-1}$			
$V_{Initial}(HCl)/mL$			
$V_{Final}(HCl)/mL$			
$\Delta V(HCl)/mL$			
$\Delta \overline{V}(HCl)/mL$			
$V(NaOH)/\Delta \overline{V}(HCl)$			
$d_r/\%$			
$\overline{d_r}/\%$			

【QUESTIONS】

(1) Analyse the sources of errors in this experiment and discuss possible methods for eliminating errors.

(2) Please refer to literature to identify alternative methods for determining the content of acetylsalicylic acid in aspirin tablets.

(LIN Yi)

Experiment 6   Oxidation-Reduction Titration

【OBJECTIVES】

(1) To master the principles and methods of preparing a standard solution for potassium permanganate method and iodimetry.

(2) Learn to determine the content of substances by applying the principles of redox titration.

(3) To learn the methods of using self-indicator and chromogenic indicator for indicating the titration endpoint.

【PRINCIPLES】

Oxidation-Reduction titration, also known as Redox titration, is a kind of titration analysis method based on redox reaction. Its essence is the transfer or shift of electrons. The mechanisms of redox reactions are complex. Usually, the reactions proceed slowly and are accompanied by side reactions. In order to ensure that the reaction is quantitative and rapid, conditions such as reactant concentration, reaction temperature, reaction medium, catalyst, etc. are controlled during the titration process to meet the requirements of titrimetric analysis.

According to the types of titrants, redox titration methods can be classified into potassium permanganate method, potassium dichromate method, iodometry, etc. The indicators commonly used in redox titration include self-indicators, chromogenic indicators, and redox indicators. For example, in the permanganate method, $KMnO_4$ acts as its own indicator. In the iodometric method, the starch solution reacts with I_2 to form a blue complex, so starch acts as a chromogenic indicator. Sodium diphenylamine sulfonate in potassium dichromate is originally colorless and turns purple when oxidized by excess potassium dichromate at the titration endpoint, which is a redox indicator.

Redox titration is widely used. Substances with oxidative or reducing properties can be directly determined. For example, the potassium permanganate method is employed to determine the content of hydrogen peroxide; the potassium dichromate method is utilized to measure the total iron content in iron ore; and iodimetry is applied to determine the content of vitamin C, copper ions, and so on. Moreover, redox titration can indirectly determine certain substances that lack oxidizing or reducing properties but can react quantitatively with oxidants or reducing agents. Take the potassium permanganate method as an instance, which can be used to determine the calcium ion content.

The experiments mainly center on the application of potassium permanganate method and iodometric method.

1. Determination of H_2O_2 Content by Permanganometric Titration

【 OBJECTIVES 】

(1) To master the principles and methods of preparing standard solutions of potassium permanganate.

(2) To learn the principles and methods for the determinate content of H_2O_2 with potassium permanganate titration.

(3) To consolidate the normalized operation of analytical balance, burette and pipette.

【 PRE-LAB ASSIGNMENTS 】

Simulated Design Experiment: Based on the principles of redox titration and $KMnO_4$ titration, and with reference to the experimental procedure, present the experimental design in the form of a flowchart. Clearly indicate the titration conditions, operational steps, and the rationale and feasibility of each experimental measure included.

Preview questions:

(1) Can you use filter paper instead of sand core funnel when preparing $KMnO_4$ standard solution? Why?

(2) How to accurately read the volume of colored solution in burette?

(3) How to control reaction conditions during the calibration of $KMnO_4$? Why?

(4) What other substances can be determined by potassium permanganate titration?

(5) Why can't heating be used when determining the content of H_2O_2 in commercial hydrogen peroxide?

【PRINCIPLES】

As a strong oxidant, $KMnO_4$ is frequently used as a standard solution in oxidation-reduction titration methods. In a strongly acidic solution, $KMnO_4$ can be reduced to Mn^{2+}. Its half reaction and standard electrode potential are

$$MnO_4^- + 8H^+ + 5e \Longrightarrow Mn^{2+} + 4H_2O \quad \varphi^\ominus = 1.507 \text{ V}$$

$KMnO_4$ is unstable, and the $KMnO_4$ reagents on the market often contain MnO_2 and other impurities, so $KMnO_4$ standard solution was prepared by indirect method. Additionally, under the catalysis of MnO_2 and light, $KMnO_4$ solution not only undergoes its own decomposition reaction, but also interacts with trace reducing substances in water. Therefore, the MnO_2 in the solution should be removed by filtration before calibration, and the solution should be stored in a brown bottle and placed in a dark place.

The primary reference material $Na_2C_2O_4$ is commonly used to calibrate the $KMnO_4$ ($M_r = 158$ g·mol^{-1}) solution. The reaction between $KMnO_4$ and $Na_2C_2O_4$ in acidic solution is

$$2MnO_4^- + 5C_2O_4^{2-} + 16H^+ \Longrightarrow 2Mn^{2+} + 10CO_2 \uparrow + 8H_2O$$

The reaction is slow at room temperature. Heating can increase the reaction rate. But the reaction temperature should not be too high, otherwise it will lead to the decomposition of $Na_2C_2O_4$. In addition, the Mn^{2+} catalyst can also accelerate the reaction. Therefore, a small amount of $KMnO_4$ solution is added to $Na_2C_2O_4$ before titration and the mixture is slightly heated. At the stoichiometric point, a slight excess of $KMnO_4$ solution makes the solution pink and indicates the end point of titration.

According to the volume of consumed $KMnO_4$ solution and the mass of $Na_2C_2O_4$, the concentration of $KMnO_4$ standard solution can be calculated.

$$c(KMnO_4) = \frac{2 \times m(Na_2C_2O_4) \times 1\,000}{5 \times M(Na_2C_2O_4) \Delta V(KMnO_4)} \text{ mol·L}^{-1} \tag{5-6-1}$$

In equation (5-6-1), $m(Na_2C_2O_4)$ is the mass of $Na_2C_2O_4$ weighed, $M(Na_2C_2O_4)$ is the molar mass of $Na_2C_2O_4$ (134 g·mol^{-1}), and $\Delta V(KMnO_4)$ is the volume of $KMnO_4$ solution consumed during titration (mL).

H_2O_2 is a commonly used medicinal disinfectant. Commercial hydrogen peroxide solutions typically have concentrations of approximately 3% (g·mL^{-1}) or 30% (g·mL^{-1}). In an acidic solution, the reaction of $KMnO_4$ and H_2O_2 is

$$2MnO_4^- + 5H_2O_2 + 6H^+ \Longrightarrow 2Mn^{2+} + 8H_2O + 5O_2 \uparrow$$

Similar to the reactions of $KMnO_4$ and $Na_2C_2O_4$, the reaction starts slowly and gradually accelerates with the increase of Mn^{2+}. When the reaction reaches its stoichiometric point, the addition of a slightly excessive $KMnO_4$ makes the solution pink and indicates the end point of titration. The difference is that H_2O_2 is easy to decompose when heated, so this reaction is carried out at room temperature. According to the volume of the consumed $KMnO_4$ standard solution and the volume of H_2O_2, the content of H_2O_2 in the sample $\rho(H_2O_2)$ can be calculated.

$$\rho(H_2O_2) = \frac{5 \times c(KMnO_4) \Delta V(KMnO_4) M(H_2O_2)}{2 \times V(H_2O_2) \times 1\,000} \text{ g·mL}^{-1} \tag{5-6-2}$$

In formula (5-6-2), $c(KMnO_4)$ is the concentration of $KMnO_4$ standard solution (mol·L^{-1}), $\Delta V(KMnO_4)$ is the volume of $KMnO_4$ standard solution consumed for titration (mL), $M(H_2O_2)$ is the molar mass of hydrogen peroxide (34.01 g·mol^{-1}), and $V(H_2O_2)$ represents the volume of the hydrogen peroxide dilution solution used for titration (mL).

【 APPARATUS, REAGENTS AND MATERIALS 】

Apparatus   0.1 mg-analytical balance, sand core funnel, acid burette (25 mL) or PTFE burette (25 mL), volumetric flask (100 mL × 2), Erlenmeyer flask (250 mL × 3), beakers (250 mL, 100 mL), pipette (20 mL × 2, 1 mL), graduated cylinder (10 mL), pipette bulb, weighing bottle, washing bottle, glass rod, medicine dropper, desiccator, burette stand.

Reagents and Materials $KMnO_4$ (s, A.R.), $Na_2C_2O_4$ (s, A.R.), 6 mol·L^{-1} H_2SO_4, commercial H_2O_2 solution (3%)

【 PROCEDURE 】

1.1   Preparation and standardization of $KMnO_4$ standard solution

(1) Preparation of 0.004 mol·L^{-1} $KMnO_4$ solution: Weigh out about 0.16 g solid $KMnO_4$, dissolve it in a small amount of distilled water in a 250.0 mL beaker, continue to dilute it with water to the 250.0 mL mark. Heat the solution and keep it slightly boiling for 1 h. After storing the solution for 2-3 days, filter it with a sand core funnel. The filtrate should be stored in a brown glass bottle and sealed, then kept in a dark place for future calibration purposes.

(2) Preparation of $Na_2C_2O_4$ standard solution: Weigh precisely 0.13-0.14 g of $Na_2C_2O_4$ (accurate to 0.000 1 g) using an electronic balance and put it in a small beaker. Dissolve it with about 20.0 mL of distilled water, and then transfer it to a 100.00 mL volumetric flask. Add distilled water to the mark, and shake well.

(3) Calibration of $KMnO_4$ solution: Transfer 20.00 mL of $Na_2C_2O_4$ solution to an Erlenmeyer flask, then add 5 mL of 6 mol·L^{-1} H_2SO_4 and 10.00 mL of $KMnO_4$ solution, and heat the mixed solution at about 40 ℃ until the red color disappears. Continuously use $KMnO_4$ solution to titrate the mixed solution till the solution shows a pink color that does not fade within 30 seconds. Perform the titration three times in parallel and record the results in Table 5-6-1.

1.2   Determination of H_2O_2 content in commercial hydrogen peroxide

Using a pipette, transfer 1.00 mL of the commercial hydrogen peroxide solution into a 100.00 mL volumetric flask. Then, dilute the solution to the 100.00 mL mark with distilled water and shake it well. Transfer 20.00 mL of the sample solution to a 250.0 mL conical flask, add 5.0 mL of 6 mol·L^{-1} H_2SO_4. Titrate the sample solution with the standard solution until it turns slightly red, and the titration end point is reached when the slight red color does not fade within 30 seconds. Perform the titration three times in parallel and record the results in Table 5-6-2.

【DATA AND RESULTS】

Date:_____　Temperature:_____℃　Relative Humidity:_____

Table 5-6-1　Calibration of KMnO₄ solution

Experiment No.	1	2	3
$m(Na_2C_2O_4)/g$			
$V_{Initial}(KMnO_4)/mL$			
$V_{Final}(KMnO_4)/mL$			
$\Delta V(KMnO_4)/mL$			
$c(KMnO_4)/mol \cdot L^{-1}$			
$\bar{c}(KMnO_4)/mol \cdot L^{-1}$			
$\bar{d_r}/\%$			

Table 5-6-2　Determination of H₂O₂ content in commercial hydrogen peroxide water

Experiment No.	1	2	3
$V(H_2O_2)/mL$			
$c(KMnO_4)/mol \cdot L^{-1}$			
$V_{Initial}(KMnO_4)/mL$			
$V_{Final}(KMnO_4)/mL$			
$\Delta V(KMnO_4)/mL$			
$\rho(H_2O_2)/g \cdot mL^{-1}$			
$\bar{\rho}(H_2O_2)/g \cdot mL^{-1}$			
$\bar{d_r}/\%$			

【NOTES】

(1) H_2SO_4 is often used as acidic medium when $KMnO_4$ standard solution is used to titrate reducing substances. The suitable acidity of titration system is 0.5-1.0 $mol \cdot L^{-1}$. If the acidity is too high, it will cause the decomposition of $Na_2C_2O_4$.

(2) When calculating $c(KMnO_4)$ by Formula (5-6-1), it is necessary to consider that the volume of $Na_2C_2O_4$ solution in each titration only accounts for 20% of the total volume of $Na_2C_2O_4$ standard solution prepared, and this factor should be considered by dividing the result by 5 during the calculation.

(3) When calculating $\rho(H_2O_2)$ by Formula (5-6-2), the dilution multiple of hydrogen peroxide should be considered and multiplied by 5 during the calculation.

【QUESTIONS】

(1) When determining the content of H_2O_2 by the potassium permanganate method, can the acidity be adjusted using HNO_3, HCl, or HAc? Why?

(2) Why can hydrogen peroxide be used as a disinfectant? What are the hazards of misuse?

(3) What are the other methods for detecting hydrogen peroxide content?

(LV Yajuan)

2. Determination of Vitamin C Content by Iodometric Titration

【OBJECTIVES】

(1) To understand the principle and method for the determination of vitamin C by iodimetry.

(2) To learn the preparation and standardization of iodine standard solution and sodium thiosulfate standard solution.

(3) To learn to determine the endpoints with starch solution.

【PRE-LAB ASSIGNMENTS】

(1) Why add excess KI when preparing iodine solution?

(2) What methods can be used to standardize $Na_2S_2O_3$ solution?

(3) Why should an iodimetric titration be performed in weak acidic condition?

(4) Simulated Design Experiment: Present the experimental design as a flowchart, clearly indicating the corresponding precautions and the rationale behind each step.

【PRINCIPLES】

Iodimetric titrations are based on redox reactions when I_2 is used as oxidizing titrant or I^- is used as reducing agent in titrations. The electrode reaction for iodimetric titration is

$$I_2 + 2e^- \rightleftharpoons 2I^- \qquad \varphi^{\ominus}(I_2/I^-) = 0.535 \text{ V}$$

A reducing agent whose standard electrode potential is lower than 0.535 V can be titrated directly with a standard iodine solution. This method is called "iodimetry". The method can work under acidic, neutral and weak basic condition.

Solid iodine is volatilizable and slightly soluble in water, but it easily dissolves in an aqueous solution of potassium iodide. Usually, standard iodine solution is prepared by dissolving iodine in potassium iodide solution and storing it in a clean brown glass bottle. Iodine solution may be standardized using arsenic trioxide or sodium thiosulfate as the primary standard.

Commercial $Na_2S_2O_3 \cdot 5H_2O$ effloresces or deliquesces when exposed to air. Therefore, it cannot be used as a primary standard substance. For the preparation of standard $Na_2S_2O_3$ solution, freshly boiled distilled water is usually used as solvent. A small amount of sodium carbonate is added to keep pH 9-10. Then the $Na_2S_2O_3$ solution is kept in darkness for 7-10 days and standardized with KIO_3 before use. Briefly, iodine will be generated stoichiometrically by the KIO_3 reacting KI in slightly acidic solution, and then is titrated with standard $Na_2S_2O_3$ solution with starch used as the indicator. The titration reactions are as follows

$$KIO_3 + 5KI + 6HCl \Longrightarrow 3I_2 + 3H_2O + 6KCl$$

$$I_2 + 2Na_2S_2O_3 = 2NaI + Na_2S_4O_6$$

According to the above reactions,

$$n(Na_2S_2O_3) = 6n(KIO_3) \tag{5-6-3}$$

The concentration of the sodium thiosulfate standard solution can be calculated by the following equation

$$c(Na_2S_2O_3) = \frac{6m(KIO_3)}{M(KIO_3) \times V(Na_2S_2O_3) \times 1\ 000}\ (mol \cdot L^{-1}) \tag{5-6-4}$$

In the titration, starch solution as the indicator must be added just before the endpoint (the solution appears light yellow). The endpoint of titration reaches when the blue of the solution disappears.

Vitamin C ($C_6H_8O_6$) ($M_r = 176.12$), also called ascorbic acid, is a water-soluble vitamin that widely exists in both fruits and vegetables.

Vitamin C is a strong reducing agent. It can be oxidized to form dehydroascorbic acid. Thus, its content can be directly determined by iodimetry. The reaction is as follows

where the molar ratio between the reactants is 1 : 1. Vitamin C can be easily oxidized by air, especially in a basic solution due to its strong reducing properties. Therefore the reaction should be carried out in a diluted acetic acid solution (pH 3-4) to prevent side reactions. The endpoint reaches when the solution appears blue by excess iodine reacts with starch. The content of vitamin C can be calculated by the following equation (5-6-5)

$$V_c\% = \frac{c(I_2)V(I_2) \times M(C_6H_8O_6)}{m(sample)}\ (mg \cdot g^{-1}) \tag{5-6-5}$$

where, the $m(sample)$ is the mass of sample containing vitamin C in each titration.

【APPARATUS, REAGENTS AND MATERIALS】

Apparatus　0.1 mg-analytical balance, platform balance, acid burette or PTFE burette (25 mL), volumetric pipette (25 mL × 2), volumetric flask (250 mL), brown reagent bottle (500 mL × 2), measuring cylinder (10 mL, 50 mL, 100 mL), Erlenmeyer flask (250 mL × 3), beakers (100 mL, 250 mL), pipette bulb, burette stand.

Reagents and Materials　Vitamin C tablets, fruits or vegetables (tomato, orange, strawberry, etc.), KIO_3 (A.R.), I_2 (A.R.), $Na_2S_2O_3 \cdot 5H_2O$ (A.R.), Na_2CO_3(A.R.), 0.2% starch aqueous solution (freshly prepared), 2 $mol \cdot L^{-1}$ HAc solution, 1 $mol \cdot L^{-1}$ H_2SO_4 solution, 20% KI solution.

【PROCEDURES】

2.1　Preparation and Standardization of 0.1 $mol \cdot L^{-1}$ Sodium Thiosulfate Solution

Weigh about 12.5 g of $Na_2S_2O_3 \cdot 5H_2O$ ($M_r = 248.17$) with a platform balance. Dissolve it with cold and newly boiled distilled water and add 0.1 g of Na_2CO_3. Dilute to 500.00 mL in a volumetric flask and mix it homogeneously. Then transfer it into a brown reagent bottle. Keep it in darkness for 7-10 days before standardization.

Weigh primary standard substance KIO₃ 0.9-1.0 g (accurate to 0.000 1 g) into a small beaker. Dissolve it with 20.0 mL distilled water, and then transfer it into a 250 mL volumetric flask. Wash the small beaker with distilled water for 2-3 times. Transfer all the rinsing solution to the volumetric flask. Then add distilled water to the mark and homogenize the solution.

Transfer 10.00 mL of standard KIO_3 solution with a volumetric pipette to a 250 mL Erlenmeyer flask, add 5.0 mL of 1 mol·L^{-1} H_2SO_4, 20.0 mL of 20% KI and 50.0 mL of distilled water subsequently with measuring cylinder. Titrate with $Na_2S_2O_3$ solution till the solution appears pale yellow, add 5.0 mL of 0.2% starch solution and titrate till the blue color disappears. Record the data and perform two more titrations in Table 5-6-3. Calculate the concentration of the $Na_2S_2O_3$.

2.2   Preparation and Standardization of 0.05 mol·L^{-1} Iodine Solution

Weigh about 6.6 g of solid iodine (A.R.) and 10.0 g KI into a mortar. Add a small amount of distilled water and grind it in a hood till all the iodine has been dissolved, dilute it with distilled water to 500.00 mL and transfer it to a brown reagent bottle. Keep it in a cool and dark place.

Transfer 10.00 mL of $Na_2S_2O_3$ solution with pipette to a 250 mL Erlenmeyer flask and dilute it with 50.0 mL of water, add 5.0 mL of 0.2% starch solution in it. Then titrate it with iodine standard solution till a blue color persists for at least 30 seconds. Record the data in Table 5-6-4 and perform two more titrations. Then calculate the concentration of the iodine solution.

2.3   Preparation of 0.005 mol·L^{-1} Iodine Solution

Transfer 25.00 mL of 0.05 mol·L^{-1} iodine solution with pipette into a 250 mL volumetric flask and add distilled water to the mark and homogenize the solution.

2.4   Determination of Vitamin C Content in Tablets

Weight 0.150 0 g of vitamin C tablets powder (accurate to 0.000 1 g) in a 250 mL Erlenmeyer flask. Dissolve it with 100.0 mL of freshly boiled distilled water, add 10.0 mL of 2.0 mol·L^{-1} HAc solution and 5.0 mL of 0.2% starch solution, respectively. Titrate the solution with standard iodine solution immediately till a blue color appears and persists for 30 seconds. Record the data in Table 5-6-5 and perform two more titrations and calculate the content of vitamin C in tablets.

2.5   Determination of Vitamin C Content in Fruits or Vegetables

Weight about 25 g (accurate to 0.000 1 g) squeezed fruits or vegetables in a 100 mL dry beaker. Then transfer it entirely into a 250 mL Erlenmeyer flask, add 10.0 mL of 2.0 mol·L^{-1} HAc solution and 5 mL of 0.2% starch solution successively. Titrate the solution immediately with standard iodine solution till the color is changed from red to bluish violet. Record the data in Table 5-6-6 and perform two more titrations. Then calculate the content of vitamin C.

【NOTES】

(1) In the standardization of sodium thiosulfate solution, the starch indicator should be added near the endpoint when the color of I_2 solution almost disappears. Otherwise, the endpoint will be delayed because of the wrapping of I_2 by starch.

(2) Pretreatment of an analyte depends on the kind of fruit or vegetable. For example, for oranges

or grapefruits, only their pulp should be used for squeezing juice. Shell, seed, and fiber must be removed before titration. Furthermore, the color of pulp should be taken into consideration when observing the change of color at the endpoint.

【DATA AND RESULTS】

Date:_____　　Temperature:_____°C　Relative Humidity:_____

Table 5-6-3　Standardization of $0.1 \ mol \cdot L^{-1}$ sodium thiosulfate solution

Experiment No.	1	2	3
$m(KIO_3)/g$			
$c(KIO_3)/mol \cdot L^{-1}$			
$V(KIO_3)/mL$			
$V_{Initial}(Na_2S_2O_3)/mL$			
$V_{Final}(Na_2S_2O_3)/mL$			
$\Delta V(Na_2S_2O_3)/mL$			
$c(Na_2S_2O_3)/mol \cdot L^{-1}$			
$\overline{c}(Na_2S_2O_3)/mol \cdot L^{-1}$			
$d_r/\%$			
$\overline{d_r}/\%$			

Table 5-6-4　Standardization of $0.05 \ mol \cdot L^{-1}$ iodine solution

Experiment No.	1	2	3
$c(Na_2S_2O_3)/mol \cdot L^{-1}$			
$V(Na_2S_2O_3)/mL$			
$V_{Initial}(I_2)/mL$			
$V_{Final}(I_2)/mL$			
$\Delta V(I_2)/mL$			
$c(I_2)/mol \cdot L^{-1}$			
$\overline{c}(I_2)/mol \cdot L^{-1}$			
$d_r/\%$			
$\overline{d_r}/\%$			

Table 5-6-5　Determination of vitamin C content in tablets

Experiment No.	1	2	3
$m(V_C)/g$			
$c(I_2)/mol \cdot L^{-1}$			
$V_{Final}(I_2)/mL$			
$V_{Initial}(I_2)/mL$			

continued

Experiment No.	1	2	3
$\Delta V\,(I_2)/\text{mL}$			
$w\,(V_C)\%/\text{mg}\cdot\text{g}^{-1}$			
$\overline{w}\,(V_C)\%/\text{mg}\cdot\text{g}^{-1}$			
$d_r/\%$			
$\overline{d}_r/\%$			

Table 5-6-6   Determination of vitamin C content in fruits or vegetables

Experiment No.	1	2	3
$m(\text{sample})/\text{g}$			
$c(I_2)/\text{mol}\cdot\text{L}^{-1}$			
$V_{\text{Initial}}\,(I_2)/\text{mL}$			
$V_{\text{Final}}\,(I_2)/\text{mL}$			
$\Delta V\,(I_2)/\text{mL}$			
$w\,(V_C)\%/\text{mg}\cdot\text{g}^{-1}$			
$\overline{w}\,(V_C)\%/\text{mg}\cdot\text{g}^{-1}$			
$d_r/\%$			
$\overline{d}_r/\%$			

【QUESTIONS】

(1) What are the pharmacological functions and clinical applications of vitamin C?

(2) Why is it necessary to add newly distilled cold water in dissolving vitamin C samples?

(3) What factors may cause errors and how to eliminate errors in iodimetry?

(KANG Kai)

Experiment 7   Complexometric Titration

【OBJECTIVES】

(1) Mastering the applications of Eriochrome Black T and Xylenol Orange indicators.

(2) Mastering the preparation and standardization methods of EDTA standard solution.

(3) Mastering the methods of coordination titration to determine the metal ion in samples.

(4) Understanding the procedures of complexometric titration.

【PRINCIPLES】

Ethylenediaminetetraacetic acid (H_4Y) and its disodium salt (Na_2H_2Y) constitute a class of hexadentate chelating ligand, abbreviated as EDTA. EDTA demonstrates exceptional coordination capabilities, forming stable complexes with most metal ions and is often utilized as a standard solution in coordination titrations to determine the concentration of specific metal ions. Due to the limited aqueous solubility of free EDTA (H_4Y), standard solutions are conventionally prepared using its highly water-soluble disodium salt ($Na_2H_2Y \cdot 2H_2O$). The EDTA standard solution was prepared using the indirect method by preparing an approximate concentration and then calibrating it with a primary standard. EDTA standard solution should be stored in polyethylene plastic bottles to prevent metal ion contamination through leaching from glass surfaces.

The primary standard substances for titrating EDTA standard solution include Zn, ZnO, $ZnSO_4$, $CaCO_3$, $MgCO_3$. Among these, Zn, ZnO, and $CaCO_3$ are the most commonly employed. To minimize systematic errors, standardization conditions should closely match those used in subsequent titrations of analyte ions. For example, when titrating ions such as Bi^{3+}, Zn^{2+}, Pb^{2+}, or Al^{3+}, it is advisable to use Zn, ZnO, or $ZnSO_4 \cdot 7H_2O$ as primary standard substances. These titrations are best performed using Xylenol Orange as the indicator at pH 5-6. In contrast, for determining Ca^{2+} and Mg^{2+} in an NH_3-NH_4Cl buffer(pH = 10) with Eriochrome Black T(EBT) as the indicator, $CaCO_3$ is less ideal due to poor endpoint detection for Ca^{2+}. Specifically, EBT exhibits low sensitivity toward Ca^{2+}, resulting in an indistinct color change at the endpoint. Because EBT binds Mg^{2+} with significantly higher sensitivity, $MgCO_3$ is preferred as the primary standard for such determinations.

EBT transitions color with pH: burgundy in acidic media (pH < 6), blue in neutral to weakly alkaline solutions (pH = 7-11), and orange in strongly alkaline environments (pH > 12). The Mg^{2+}-EBT coordination complex is burgundy, requiring titration within pH 7-11 to achieve a sharp endpoint transition from burgundy to blue.

Standard titration protocol for Mg^{2+} determination:

(1) pH adjustment: Buffer the sample solution to pH 10 using an NH_3-NH_4Cl buffer system

(2) Pre-titration reaction: EBT initially binds Mg^{2+}, forming the burgundy Mg-HIn complex

(3) Endpoint detection: EDTA displaces Mg^{2+} from Mg-HIn, releasing free EBT (blue color)

Critical considerations: Avoid pH < 6 (persistent burgundy EBT-Mg complex) or pH > 11 (orange EBT form), as both scenarios obscure endpoint detection. $MgCO_3$ is preferred over $CaCO_3$ as the primary standard due to EBT's higher sensitivity to Mg^{2+}.

$$Mg^{2+} + HIn \Longrightarrow Mg\text{-}HIn$$

blue　　　burgundy

$$H_2Y^{2-} + Mg\text{-}HIn \Longrightarrow MgY^{2-} + HIn$$

burgundy　　　　　blue

The concentration of the EDTA standard solution was determind via the following formula:

$$c(EDTA) = \frac{m(MgCO_3) \times \dfrac{20.00}{250.00}}{M_r(MgCO_3) \times V(EDTA)} \times 1\,000 \ (mol \cdot L^{-1}) \tag{5-7-1}$$

Endpoint determination in EDTA titration: The reaction exhibits slow kinetics, requiring careful monitoring near the endpoint. The color transition originates from the intrinsic pH-dependent chromism of EBT. Post-endpoint (blue), over-titration does not intensify coloration due to EBT's inertness in weakly alkaline media. Near the endpoint, add titrant incrementally (dropwise) with vigorous swirling.

Pause until color stabilizes (about 15–30 s) before subsequent additions.

Back titration: Add excess EDTA to ensure complete chelation of Al^{3+}, then titrate residual EDTA with standardized Mg^{2+}/Zn^{2+} solution. Displacement titration: Introduce a competitive ion (e.g., Mg^{2+}) to displace Al^{3+} from its EDTA complex, thereby enabling indirect quantification.

1. Determination of Water Hardness

【 OBJECTIVE 】

(1) Mastering the titration method of EDTA standard solution.

(2) Mastering the titration method of Ca^{2+} and Mg^{2+} with EDTA standard solution.

(3) Understanding the principles of complexometric titration.

【 PRE-LAB ASSIGNMENTS 】

Simulated Design Experiment: Present the experimental design as a flowchart, clearly indicating the corresponding precautions and the rationale behind each step.

Preview questions：

(1) What is the total hardness of water? According to the GB 5749-2022 standards for drinking water quality, what is the maximum allowable limit for total hardness in drinking water?

(2) What are the primary standard substances that can be used for the standardization of EDTA solution in the determination of water hardness?

(3) Which indicator can be used to determine the total hardness of water? What type of solution is required to regulate the acidity of the water sample?

【 PRINCIPLES 】

Water hardness is defined as the capacity of water to form soap scum, primarily caused by dissolved Ca^{2+} and Mg^{2+}. It comprises two categories: Temporary hardness (carbonate hardness): Caused by bicarbonate salts (HCO_3^-) of Ca^{2+} and Mg^{2+}, which precipitate as carbonates upon heating. Permanent hardness (non-carbonate hardness): Attributable to chloride, sulfate, or nitrate salts of Ca^{2+} and Mg^{2+}, which remain soluble even after boiling.

The standard unit for water hardness is $mg \cdot L^{-1}$. According to GB 5749-2022, the maximum allowable total hardness in drinking water is $450 \ mg \cdot L^{-1} \ CaCO_3$.

Water hardness is quantified through titration with a standardized EDTA solution in a NH_3-NH_4Cl buffer system (pH 10), using Eriochrome Black T (EBT) as a metallochromic indicator. The endpoint is visually identified by a sharp color transition from burgundy to blue, corresponding to the release of EBT from the metal-EDTA complex.

Pre-titration：
$$Mg^{2+} + HIn \Longrightarrow Mg\text{-}HIn$$
$$\qquad\qquad\quad \text{blue} \qquad \text{burgundy}$$

During titration：
$$H_2Y^{2-} + Ca^{2+} \Longrightarrow CaY^{2-} + 2H^+$$
$$H_2Y^{2-} + Mg^{2+} \Longrightarrow MgY^{2-} + 2H^+$$

At the end of the titration： $H_2Y^{2-} + Mg\text{-}HIn \Longrightarrow MgY^{2-} + HIn + 2H^+$

burgundy　　　　　blue

Traceamounts of metal ions-including Fe^{3+}, Al^{3+}, Cu^{2+}, Zn^{2+}, Pb^{2+} may interfere with the determination of Ca^{2+}, Mg^{2+}, or total water hardness when EBT is used as the indicator. To suppress these interferences: Triethanolamine is added to mask Fe^{3+} and Al^{3+} by forming stable, water-soluble complexes. Na_2S is introduced to precipitate Cu^{2+}, Zn^{2+}, and Pb^{2+} as insoluble sulfide salts, effectively removing them from solution.

To determine Ca^{2+} and Mg^{2+} concentrations in water, adjust the solution to pH 12 by adding NaOH. At this pH, Mg^{2+} precipitates as $Mg(OH)_2$, leaving Ca^{2+} in solution. A calcium-specific indicator (e.g., calcon or murexide) is then added, forming a red complex with free Ca^{2+}. During titration with a standardized EDTA solution, EDTA preferentially binds free Ca^{2+} until it is fully sequestered. Subsequently, EDTA displaces Ca^{2+} from the indicator complex, releasing the indicator and causing a sharp color transition from burgundy to blue, marking the endpoint. Mg^{2+} concentration is calculated by subtracting the titrated Ca^{2+} content from the previously determined total hardness ($Ca^{2+} + Mg^{2+}$).

Based on the amount of EDTA $V_1(EDTA)$, the total hardness c (total hardness) of the water sample can be calculated according to equation (5-7-2).

$$c(\text{total hardness})=\frac{c(EDTA)\times V(EDTA)\times M(CaCO_3)}{V(\text{Water Sample})}\times1\,000\,(mg\cdot L^{-1}) \tag{5-7-2}$$

Based on the amount of EDTA $V_2(EDTA)$, the concentrations of Ca^{2+} and Mg^{2+} can be calculated according to equation (5-7-3) and equation (5-7-4), respectively.

$$c(Ca^{2+})=\frac{c(EDTA)\times V_2(EDTA)\times M(Ca^{2+})}{V(\text{Water Sample})}\times1\,000\,(mg\cdot L^{-1}) \tag{5-7-3}$$

$$c(Mg^{2+})=\frac{c(EDTA)\times\{V_1(EDTA)-V_2(EDTA)\}\times M(Mg^{2+})}{V(\text{Wate Sample})}\times1\,000\,(mg\cdot L^{-1}) \tag{5-7-4}$$

or $$c(Mg^{2+})=c(\text{total hardness})-c(Ca^{2+})\,(mg\cdot L^{-1}) \tag{5-7-5}$$

To minimize systematic errors, the EDTA standard solution was standardized against a high-purity $MgCO_3$ primary standard prior to use.

【APPARATUS, REAGENTS AND MATERIALS】

Apparatus　Balance, electronic analytical balance (0.1mg precision), platform, acid or PTFE burette (25 mL), conical flasks (250 mL × 3), volumetric pipette (20 mL, 50 mL), volumetric flask (250 mL, 1 000 mL), beaker (150 mL, 250 mL), polyethylene bottle (1 000 mL), graduated cylinder (5 mL, 10 mL × 2, 50 mL, 1 000 mL), stirring rod, burette stand.

Reagents and Materials　$Na_2H_2Y\cdot2H_2O$ (s, A.R.), 3 $mol\cdot L^{-1}$ HCl solution, $MgCO_3$ Reference Material, 6 $mol\cdot L^{-1}$ NaOH solution, 1.5 $mol\cdot L^{-1}$ triethanolamine solution, NH_3-NH_4Cl buffer solution (pH 10), 0.25 $mol\cdot L^{-1}$ Na_2S solution, Eriochrome Black T, calcium indicator [2-Hydroxy-1-(2-hydroxy-4-sulfo-1-naphthylazo)-3-naphthoic acid], universal pH test paper.

【 PROCEDURE 】

1.1   Preparation of 0.01 mol·L^{-1} EDTA solution

Accurately measure 3.8 g of $Na_2H_2Y\text{-}2H_2O$ ($M_r = 372.26$) using an analytical a balance. Transfer the weighed EDTA to a 250 mL beaker. Add 50 mL of distilled water and stir vigorously with a magnetic stirrer until complete dissolution. Quantitatively transfer the solution to a 1.0 L volumetric flask. Rinse the beaker three times with distilled water to ensure full transfer. Dilute to the mark with distilled water and homogenize by inverting the flask 10–15 times. Store the standardized EDTA solution in a clean polyethylene bottle to minimize leaching of metal ions from glass containers.

1.2   Titration of standard EDTA solution

Accurately weigh 0.15 g-0.20 g (accurate to 0.000 1 g) of the primary standard substance $MgCO_3$ ($M_r = 84.32$) (pre- dried at 110 ℃ for 2 hours to constant mass) using an analytical balance (± 0.000 1 g precision). Transfer the sample to a 150 mL beaker. Add 5 drops of water to hydrate the $MgCO_3$. Cover the beaker with a watch glass, then slowly add 3.0 mL of 3 mol·L^{-1} HCl through its lip to dissolve the $MgCO_3$. Gently boil the solution for 3–5 minutes to expel CO_2. Rinsing the watch glass with deionized water, collecting the rinseate into the beaker. Then transfer the solution to a 250 mL volumetric flask. Rinse the beaker 2–3 times with small portions of deionized water, combining all the rinses into the flask. Dilute to the mark with deionized water and homogenize by inversion.

Transfer 20.00 mL of $MgCO_3$ standard solution in a 250 mL conical flasks. Add 10 mL of NH_3-NH_4Cl buffer solution (pH 10) and 2-3 drops of EBT indicator. Titrate with standard EDTA solution until the color of the solution changes from burgundy to blue. Record the data in Table 5-7-1 and repeat the titration three times to ensure reproducibility.

1.3   Determination of water hardness

(1) Determination of total hardness in water samples: Transfer 50.00 mL of water sample in a 250 mL conical flask, and add 1-2 drops of 3 mol·L^{-1} HCl to acidify the solution ensuring all carbonates are converted to CO_2. Heat the solution to a gentle boil for a few minutes to expel dissolved CO_2 which could interfere with subsequent pH adjustments. Allow the solution to cool to room temperature. Add 2.0 mL of triethanolamine to mask interfering metal ions (e.g., Fe^{3+}, Al^{3+}) . Introduce   5.0 mL of NH_3-NH_4Cl buffer solution (pH = 10) to stabilize Mg^{2+} and Ca^{2+} ions for complexation. Add 5 drops of Na_2S solution o precipitate sulfide-forming metals (e.g., Pb^{2+}, Cu^{2+}). Then add 2-3 drops of EBT indicator, and titrate with EDTA standard solution until the the color transitions from burgundy to blue, persisting for 30 seconds without reversion. Record the data in Table 5-7-2 and repeat the titration three times to ensure precision.

(2) Determination of Ca^{2+} and Mg^{2+} concentration individually: Transfer 50.00 mL of a water sample into a 250 mL conical flask, and add 1–2 drops of 3 mol·L^{-1} HCl to acidify the solution. Heat the solution to a gentle boil for a few minutes to expel dissolved CO_2. Allow the solution to cool to room temperature. Add 2.0 mL of triethanolamine, 5.0 mL of 6 mol·L^{-1} NaOH, and a suitable amount of calcium indicator (typically 0.1 g). Titrate slowly with standard EDTA solution while vigorously swirling the flask to ensure uniform mixing. Stop when the solution transitions from burgundy to blue, persisting for 30 seconds without reversion. and shake vigorously until the colour changes from burgundy to blue,

and the colour stays for 30 seconds without fading as the endpoint. Record the data in Table 5-7-3 and repeat the titration three times to ensure precision.

【DATA AND RESULTS】

Date:_____   Temperature:_____°C   Relative Humidity:_____

Table 5-7-1   Standardization of EDTA solution

Experiment No.	1	2	3
m (mass of MgCO$_3$)/g			
Indicator			
The change of color at the endpoint of the titration NH$_3$-NH$_4$Cl buffer solution/mL			
V(MgCO$_3$)/mL			
$V_{Initial}$(EDTA)/mL			
V_{Final}(EDTA)/mL			
ΔV(EDTA)/mL			
c(EDTA)/mol·L^{-1}			
$\bar{c}$(EDTA)/mol·L^{-1}			
Relative mean deviation $\overline{d_r}$/%			

Table 5-7-2   Determination of water hardness

Experiment No.		1	2	3
Indicator				
The change of color at the endpoint of the titration				
V(water sample)/mL				
Preparation of water sample	3 mol·L^{-1} HCl/drop			
	Boil gently to expel CO$_2$/min			
	Triethanolamine/mL			
	NH$_3$-NH$_4$Cl buffer solution/mL			
	Na$_2$S/drop			
Determination	$V_{Initial}$(EDTA)/mL			
	V_{Final}(EDTA)/mL			
	ΔV(EDTA)/mL			
	c(Total hardness)/mg·L^{-1}			
	$\bar{c}$(Total hardness)/mg·L^{-1}			
Relative mean deviation $\overline{d_r}$/%				

Table 5-7-3   Determination of Ca^{2+} and Mg^{2+} concentration individually

Experiment No.		1	2	3
Indicator				
The change of color at the endpoint of the titration				
V(water sample)/mL				
Preparation of water sample	$3\ mol\cdot L^{-1}$ HCl/drop			
	Boil gently to expel CO_2/min			
	Triethanolamine/mL			
	$6\ mol\cdot L^{-1}$NaOH solution/mL			
	Calcium indicator/g			
$V_{Initial}$(EDTA)/mL				
V_{Final}(EDTA)/mL				
ΔV(EDTA)/mL				
$c(Ca^{2+})/mg\cdot L^{-1}$				
$c(Mg^{2+})/mg\cdot L^{-1}$				
$\overline{c}(Ca^{2+})/mg\cdot L^{-1}$				
$\overline{c}(Mg^{2+})/mg\cdot L^{-1}$				
Relative mean deviation $\overline{d}_r$/%				

【QUESTIONS】

(1) Why is it necessary to add a buffer solution with a pH of 10 to the sample solution when determining the total hardness of water?

(2) What interference occurs with the titration if the solution contains Fe^{3+}, Al^{3+}, Cu^{2+}, Zn^{2+}, and Pb^{2+} ions? What methods can be used to eliminate the interference caused by the ions above?

(3) Why is it necessary to add 1-2 drops of $3\ mol\cdot L^{-1}$ HCl to the water sample? Why should triethanolamine and Na_2S be added?

(WANG Yingji)

2. Determination of $KAl(SO_4)_2\cdot 12H_2O$ in Alum

【OBJECTIVES】

(1) To know the general process of back titration.

(2) To learn the standardization method of EDTA solution.

(3) To master the method and conditions of xylenol orange indicator.

(4) To learn the determination principle and method of $KAl(SO_4)_2\cdot 12H_2O$ in alum.

【PRE-LAB ASSIGNMENTS】

Simulated Design Experiment: Present the experimental design as a flowchart, clearly indicating the corresponding precautions and the rationale behind each step.

Preview questions：

(1) In experiment, how to determine $KAl(SO_4)_2 \cdot 12H_2O$ in Alum?

(2) When shall back titration be adopted in the titration?

(3) Why is the back titration adopted in the determination of $KAl(SO_4)_2 \cdot 12H_2O$ in alum?

(4) How to apply xylenol orange indicator in the complex titration?

【PRINCIPLES】

Alum is commonly called as white alum, which is extracted from alumstone. In the determination of Al^{3+} content in a sample by EDTA titration, a difficulty is that the complexation of Al^{3+} with EDTA takes place very slowly, especially when Al^{3+} is present in the form of hydroxide complex. Furthermore, the xylenol orange indicator would be blocked by Al^{3+}. Thus Al^{3+} is often determined by back titration instead of direct titration. The procedures can be described as follows: add a measured excess of standard EDTA solution into the sample solution containing Al^{3+}, then boil to ensure the complete formation of Al-EDTA complex. Cool the solution to room temperature and add HAc-NaAc buffer solution to adjust the solution pH 5-6. Using xylenol orange as the indicator (the xylenol orange indicator would not be blocked by Al^{3+} because of the formation of complex AlY^-), titrate the excess of EDTA with standard Zn^{2+} solution. When the excessive EDTA has been coordinated with Zn^{2+}, the xylenol orange indicator will react with Zn^{2+} to produce purplish red ZnH_3In^{2-}, so the color of solution changes from yellow (the color of xylenol orange) to orange (the combination color of yellow and purplish red). That is, the orange is just the color of the end point of titration. Then the content of Al^{3+} can be determined according to the concentration and consumed volume of the two standard solutions. The reactions are as follows

$$Al^{3+} + H_2Y^{2-}(excess) + 2H_2O \Longrightarrow AlY^- + 2H_3O^+$$

$$H_2Y^{2-}(rest) + Zn^{2+} + 2H_2O \Longrightarrow ZnY^{2-} + 2H_3O^+$$

$$Zn^{2+} + H_3In^{4-} \Longrightarrow ZnH_3In^{2-}$$

$$\text{(yellow)} \qquad \text{(purplish red)}$$

The stability order of complex ions during the titration is: $AlY^- > ZnY^{2-} > ZnH_3In^{2-}$.

【APPARATUS, REAGENTS AND MATERIALS】

Apparatus Electronic balance, acid or amphotericity burette (25 mL), conical flask (250 mL × 3), volumetric pipette (25 mL × 3), volumetric flask (100 mL, 250 mL), beaker (100 mL × 2), reagent bottle (250 mL), cylinder (10 mL × 3, 100 mL), glass rod, burette stand, washing bottle, ear washing bulb.

Reagents and Materials 0.05 mol·L^{-1} EDTA solution, $ZnSO_4 \cdot 7H_2O$ (A.R. or C.P.), 2 mol·L^{-1} HCl, HAc-NaAc buffer solution (pH 4.5), 0.5% xylenol orange indicator solution, alum sample.

【PROCEDURES】

2.1 Preparation of 0.05 mol·L⁻¹ Zn²⁺ standard solution

Weigh 3.6-3.8 g (accurate to ±0.000 1 g) primary standard $ZnSO_4 \cdot 7H_2O$ ($M_r = 287.56$) into a 100 mL beaker, add 2.0 mL of 2 mol·L⁻¹ HCl solution with cylinder and a little distilled water, dissolve it and transfer quantitatively into a 250 mL volumetric flask, dilute it to the mark, and mix well. Calculate the concentration of Zn^{2+} by the equation (5-7-6)

$$c(ZnSO_4 \cdot 7H_2O) = \frac{m(ZnSO_4 \cdot 7H_2O)}{M_r(ZnSO_4 \cdot 7H_2O) \times \dfrac{250.00}{1\,000}} (mol \cdot L^{-1}) \tag{5-7-6}$$

2.2 Determination of the concentration of EDTA solution

Transfer 25.00 mL EDTA solution into a 250 mL volumetric flask, then add 100.0 mL of distilled water, 5.00 mL of HAc-NaAc buffer solution and 1.00 mL of xylenol orange indicator. Titrate with Zn^{2+} standard solution until the color of the solution changes from yellow to orange. Record the date in Table 5-7-4. Repeat the titration twice and calculate the concentration of EDTA solution by the equation (5-7-7).

$$c(EDTA) = \frac{c(ZnSO_4) \times V(ZnSO_4)}{V(EDTA)} (mol \cdot L^{-1}) \tag{5-7-7}$$

2.3 Determination of $KAl(SO_4)_2 \cdot 12H_2O$ content in alum

Weigh precisely 1.3-1.4 g ground alum into a 100 mL beaker, dissolve it with distilled water and transfer quantitatively to a 100 mL volumetric flask, dilute to the mark and mix thoroughly. Transfer 25.00 mL of the solution and 25.00 mL of standardized EDTA solution into a conical flask, and warm the solution in a boiling water bath for 10 minutes. Cool to room temperature; add 100.0 mL of distilled water and 5.00 mL of HAc-NaAc buffer solution and 1.00 mL of xylenol orange indicator. Titrate with the Zn^{2+} standard solution until the color changes from yellow to orange. Record the date in Table 5-7-5. Repeat the titration twice and calculate the mass fraction of $KAl(SO_4)_2 \cdot 12H_2O$ in the alum by the following equation (5-7-8)

$$\omega[KAl(SO_4)_2 \cdot 12H_2O] =$$

$$\frac{[c(EDTA)V(EDTA) - c(ZnSO_4)V(ZnSO_4)] \times M_r[KAl(SO_4)_2 \cdot 12H_2O] \times 10^{-3}}{m(sample) \times \dfrac{25.00}{100.00}} (g \cdot g^{-1}) \tag{5-7-8}$$

【NOTES】

(1) In order to accelerate the reaction between the Al^{3+} and EDTA, the mixture must be boiled after the addition of excess EDTA into the Al^{3+} sample solution.

(2) After cooling, adjust the pH of the reaction solution to 5-6 to ensure the quantitative coordination between Al^{3+} and EDTA.

(3) After the reaction of Al^{3+} with EDTA was completed, xylenol orange was added as an indicator, and excessive EDTA was titrated with Zn^{2+} standard solution.

【DATA AND RESULTS】

Date:_____   Temperature:_____°C   Relative Humidity:_____

Table 5-7-4   Concentration determination of EDTA solution

Experiment No.	1	2	3
$m_{\text{Weighing}}(\text{ZnSO}_4 \cdot 7\text{H}_2\text{O}) / \text{g}$			
$m_{\text{Determine}}(\text{ZnSO}_4 \cdot 7\text{H}_2\text{O}) / \text{g}$			
Indicator			
The change of color at the end point of titration			
$V_{\text{Initial}}(\text{ZnSO}_4) / \text{mL}$			
$V_{\text{Final}}(\text{ZnSO}_4) / \text{mL}$			
$\Delta V_{\text{Consume}}(\text{ZnSO}_4) / \text{mL}$			
$c(\text{EDTA}) / \text{mol} \cdot \text{L}^{-1}$			
$\overline{c}(\text{EDTA}) / \text{mol} \cdot \text{L}^{-1}$			
Relative mean deviation $\overline{d_r} / \%$			

Table 5-7-5   Determination of $\text{KAl(SO}_4)_2 \cdot 12\text{H}_2\text{O}$ in alum

Experiment No.	1	2	3
$m_{\text{Weighing}}(\text{Alum}) / \text{g}$			
$m_{\text{Determine}}(\text{Alum}) / \text{g}$			
$V(\text{Alum}) / \text{mL}$			
Indicator			
The change of color at the end point of titration			
$V_{\text{Initial}}(\text{ZnSO}_4) / \text{mL}$			
$V_{\text{Final}}(\text{ZnSO}_4) / \text{mL}$			
$\Delta V_{\text{Consume}}(\text{ZnSO}_4) / \text{mL}$			
$\omega [\text{KAl(SO}_4)_2 \cdot 12\text{H}_2\text{O}] / \text{g} \cdot \text{g}^{-1}$			
$[\text{KAl(SO}_4)_2 \cdot 12\text{H}_2\text{O}] / \text{g} \cdot \text{g}^{-1}$			
$\overline{\omega} / \%$			

【QUESTIONS】

(1) Can direct titration be adopted in the determination of Al^{3+} with EDTA? Why or why not?

(2) Can eriochrome black T be used as the indicator in the Al^{3+} determination? Why or why not?

(3) Why can xylenol orange be used as the indicator in the Al^{3+} determination, although Al^{3+} will block it?

(Liang Hongwen)

3. Determination of Calcium Gluconate

【OBJECTIVES】

(1) To learn the preparation and standardization method of EDTA solution.

(2) To master the method and conditions of eriochrome black T indicator.

(3) To learn the determination principle and method of calcium gluconate.

【 PRE-LAB ASSIGNMENTS 】

Simulated Design Experiment: Present the experimental design as a flowchart, clearly indicating the corresponding precautions and the rationale behind each step.

Preview questions:

(1) How to prepare EDTA standard solution?

(2) What's the principle of the calcium gluconate determination?

(3) Which indicator will be used in the calcium gluconate determination?

(4) How to apply eriochrome black T in the coordination titration? Why should an assistant indicator be added in this experiment?

【 PRINCIPLES 】

Calcium gluconate is commonly used as tablets or injections in clinic. Usually, the content of calcium gluconate is determined by coordination titration as follows: adjust the acidity of the calcium gluconate solution with NH_3-NH_4Cl buffer solution (pH10), add eriochrome black T as the indicator, then titrate with standard EDTA solution until the color of solution changes from purplish-red to pure blue at the end point. In this experiment, however, no sharp color variation can be observed without the presence of Mg^{2+}. A common procedure is to add a small amount of Mg^{2+} to the buffer solution. In that case, the additional Mg^{2+} must be determined with EDTA solution first. After this additional procedure, the sample of calcium gluconate can be added in the solution, and then continue the titration to get the consumption of EDTA solution for the calcium gluconate sample. Thus, the percentage of calcium gluconate can be calculated by the molarity of the standard EDTA solution and the volume of EDTA solution required for titration from the first to the second end point. Hence the steps and the reactions of this experiment are as follows:

(1) Add a small amount of $MgSO_4$ solution and some drops of eriochrome black T indicator into the NH_3-NH_4Cl buffer solution (pH10). Titrate with standard EDTA solution until the color changes from purplish-red to pure blue at the first end point.

(2) Add sample solution of calcium gluconate in the above solution (1). Then continuously titrate with the same EDTA solution until the color changes from purplish-red to pure blue again as the second end point.

The titration for the calcium gluconate needs only the volume of EDTA solution from the first end point to the second.

【 APPARATUS, REAGENTS AND MATERIALS 】

Apparatus   Electronic analytical balance, base or PTFE burette (25 mL), conical flask (250 mL × 3), volumetric pipette (10 mL, 20 mL), volumetric flask (250 mL × 3), beaker (250 mL × 2), measuring cylinder (10 mL × 2, 50 mL), washing bottle, burette stand, ear washing bulb.

Reagents and Materials $Na_2H_2Y \cdot 2H_2O$ (s, A.R.), $MgSO_4$ (1%), NH_3-NH_4Cl buffer solution (pH10), eriochrome black T indicator (0.5%), calcium gluconate (tablets or injections).

【PROCEDURES】

3.1　Preparation of 0.01 mol·L⁻¹ standard EDTA solution

Weigh 1.0-1.1 g (accurate to ± 0.000 1 g) primary standard substance $Na_2H_2Y·2H_2O$ (M_r=372.26) into a 250 mL beaker. Dissolve it with 50.0 mL of distilled water, then transfer quantitatively to a 250 mL volumetric flask, dilute it to the mark and mix well.

$$c(EDTA) = \frac{m(EDTA)\times 1\,000}{M_r(EDTA)\times 250.00}(mol·L^{-1}) \tag{5-7-9}$$

3.2　Preparation of the calcium gluconate sample

For tablets Weigh precisely 1.0-1.1 g powder of calcium gluconate (from the tablet). Put it into a 250 mL beaker, dissolve it with 50.0 mL distilled water and transfer quantitatively into a 250 mL volumetric flask. Dilute it to the mark with distilled water, and mix well.

For injections Transfer 10.00 mL of injection solution with a pipette into a 250 mL volumetric flask. Dilute it to the mark and mix well.

3.3　Determination of calcium gluconate content

Add 10.0 mL of distilled water and 10.0 mL of NH_3-NH_4Cl buffer solution (pH10) into a 250 mL conical flask. Add 1-2 drops of 1% $MgSO_4$ and 2-3 drops of eriochrome black T indicator and mix well. Titrate with standard EDTA solution until a color changes from purplish-red to pure blue. Record the first end point, reading of EDTA in the burette as V_1. Transfer 20.00 mL of sample solution into the above conical flask. Continue the titration with the same EDTA solution until the color changes from purplish-red to pure blue again. Record the second end point, reading of EDTA in the burette as V_2. in Table 5-7-6 Repeat the titration twice. Calculate the mass fraction (ω) for tablets by the equation (5-7-10) and mass concentration (ρ) for injections of the calcium gluconate by the equation (5-7-11).

For tablets

$$\omega(calcium\ gluconate)=\frac{c(EDTA)[V_2(EDTA)-V_1(EDTA)]\times M_r(calcium\ gluconate)}{m(calcium\ gluconate)\times \frac{20.00}{250.00}}(mg·g^{-1}) \tag{5-7-10}$$

where m is the mass of calcium gluconate tablet.

For injections

$$\rho(calcium\ gluconate)=\frac{c(EDTA)[V_2(EDTA)-V_1(EDTA)]\times M_r(calcium\ gluconate)}{10.00\times \frac{20.00}{250.00}}(g·L^{-1}) \tag{5-7-11}$$

【NOTES】

(1) Eriochrome black T indicator must be used in the solution of pH 10.

(2) A small amount of $MgSO_4$ is added into the solution to avoid the advance of the titration end point owing to the instability of calcium eriochrome black T complex.

(3) There are two titration end points in the titration. Hence the volume of EDTA solution consumed by the calcium gluconate is recorded from the first end point to the second.

【DATA AND RESULTS】

Date:_____   Temperature:_____℃   Relative Humidity:_____

Table 5-7-6   Determination of the calcium gluconate in injections or tablets

Experiment No.	1	2	3
$m(Na_2H_2Y \cdot 2H_2O)/g$			
$c(EDTA)/mol \cdot L^{-1}$			
Indicator			
The change of solution color at the first end point of titration			
The change of solution color at the second end point of titration			
V(diluted injection solution)$/mL$			
$V_{End\ point\ 1}(EDTA)/mL$			
$V_{End\ point\ 2}(EDTA)/mL$			
$[V_{End\ point\ 2} - V_{End\ point\ 1}(EDTA)]/mL$			
$V_{Consumed}(EDTA\ for\ calcium\ gluconate)/mL$			
ω(calcium gluconate)$/mg \cdot g^{-1}$			
$\bar{\omega}$ (calcium gluconate)$/mg \cdot g^{-1}$			
ρ(calcium gluconate)$/g \cdot L^{-1}$			
$\bar{\rho}$ (calcium gluconate)$/g \cdot L^{-1}$			
$\bar{d_r}/\%$			

【QUESTIONS】

(1) Why can a small amount of Mg^{2+} be added into the calcium gluconate sample solution? Does it influence the result of the determination?

(2) Can Mg^{2+} be added into the solution as an assistant indicator when the EDTA standard solution is being prepared?

(Liang Hongwen)

Chapter 6 | Spectrophotometry

Experiment 8 Determination of Fe^{3+} (Fe^{2+}) Content in Water Sample with Visible Spectrophotometry

【OBJECTIVES】

(1) To understand the principles and methods for the determination of Fe^{3+} (Fe^{2+}) content in a water sample with visible spectrophotometry.

(2) To learn the operation of a spectrophotometer.

【PRE-LAB ASSIGNMENTS】

Simulation Design Experiment: With reference to this experimental procedure, illustrate the steps using a flowchart. Describe how to determine the Fe^{3+} (or Fe^{2+}) content in a water sample. Clearly label the experimental conditions and explain the rationale for each step in the flowchart.Preview questions:

(1) What is the basic content of Lambert-Beer's law? How to express it with two different expressions?

(2) What are the most common quantitative analysis methods with spectrophotometry?

(3) How to obtain an absorption spectrum? What is the maximum absorption wavelength?

(4) What are the basic components of a spectrophotometer? What can they be used for, respectively?

(5) What are the basic principles for the determination of Fe^{3+} (Fe^{2+}) content in water sample with O-phenanthroline method, sulfocyanate method, and sulfosalicylic acid method, respectively? Summarize the similarities and differences among them.

【PRINCIPLES】

Spectrophotometry is a modern instrumental analysis method. It is based on the absorption spectrum of matter and the absorption law of light. According to a light source, spectrophotometry can be divided into visible spectrophotometry (380-760 nm), ultraviolet spectrophotometry (200-380 nm), and infrared spectrophotometry (780-3 × 10^5 nm). Lambert-Beer law is the basic law of absorption, which describes the relationship between the absorbance of a substance and its concentration (c) and thickness of the cell (b). Lambert-Beer law provides the mathematical correlation between absorbance and concentration as following

$$A = \varepsilon bc \tag{6-8-1}$$

where A is the absorbance, ε is the analyte's molar absorptivity or extinction coefficient (L·mol^{-1}·cm^{-1}) that characterizes the medium. When the concentration of the light-absorbing medium is expressed in mass concentration with units of $g \cdot L^{-1}$, $A = ab\rho_B$. Here a is the mass absorptivity ($L \cdot g^{-1} \cdot cm^{-1}$), and b is the path length of the radiation that is identical with thickness of the absorption cell.

When the light-absorbing materials, the wavelength of incident light, the temperature and the solvent are all fixed, ε is a constant. Then the absorbance A is proportional to the concentration of the absorbing species (c) and the thickness of the cell (b). The Lambert-Beer law can be used as the basis for the quantitative analysis and to determine the content of the absorbing species.

However, since the Lambert-Beer law can be applied only for the monochromatic light, an optimum wavelength of incident radiation should be chosen by absorption spectrum of the light-absorbing species in experiments. A plot of absorbance *versus* wavelength is called absorption spectrum. The maximum absorption wavelength, λ_{max}, can be located in absorption spectrum and used as the incident radiation in spectrophotometry.

The spectrophotometry method is only suitable for the analysis of microcomponents. Generally, A within 0.2–0.7 is the best.

The quantitative analysis methods commonly used in spectrophotometry include standard comparison method and standard curve method.

For the comparison method, standard solution of absorbent species and sample solution of absorbent species are prepared. Then absorbance is determined under the same conditions.

$$A(\text{Standard}) = abc(\text{Standard}) \tag{6-8-2}$$

$$A(\text{Sample}) = abc(\text{Sample}) \tag{6-8-3}$$

When cuvettes in the spectrophotometer have the same thickness with b, and absorbent species of standard solution and sample solution are the same, they have the same constant of a. Thus, the following equations can be used for the determination of the sample concentration.

$$\frac{A(\text{Standard})}{A(\text{Sample})} = \frac{abc(\text{Standard})}{abc(\text{Sample})} \tag{6-8-4}$$

$$c(\text{Sample}) = \frac{A(\text{Sample})}{A(\text{Standard})} \times c(\text{Standard}) \tag{6-8-5}$$

In practice, in order to simplify the calculation and increase the accuracy of the determination, a standard curve (working curve) of absorbance versus concentration is plotted by determining the absorbance of a series of standard solutions with known concentration. Then the concentration of sample solution containing the same absorbent substance as standard species can be obtained by determining its absorbance under the same conditions and locating its value on the working curve. This way is called the working curve method. This plot can be represented by the regression equation $y = ax + b$.

1. Determination of Fe^{2+} Content with O-phenanthroline Method

In spectrophotometric determination of trace Fe^{2+}, o-phenanthroline is a sensitive color-developing agent, with which a complex of Fe^{2+} is formed to give orange red color ($\lg K_s = 21.3$). The colored solution can be measured with a spectrophotometer, maximum absorbance is observed at 510 nm. Molar absorption coefficient is equal to $1.1 \times 10^4 \, L \cdot mol^{-1} \cdot cm^{-1}$. In the range of pH 3 to 9, the complex is very stable. Iron must be in ferrous state and hence a reducing agent is added before the color is developed. Hydroxylamine hydrochloride can be used to reduce Fe^{3+} to Fe^{2+}. These reactions are given below:

$$2\,Fe^{3+} + 2\,NH_2OH \cdot HCl + 2\,H_2O \Longrightarrow 2\,Fe^{2+} + N_2 \uparrow + 4\,H_3O^+ + 2Cl^-$$

【 APPARATUS, REAGENTS AND MATERIALS 】

Apparatus　Spectrophotometer, 0.1 mg-electronic analytical balance, volumetric flask (50 mL × 7, 1 000 mL), measuring pipette (1 mL, 2 mL × 2, 5 mL, 10 mL), dropper, adjustable transfer gun(5 mL, 10 mL).

Material and Reagents　8 mmol·L^{-1} o-Phenanthroline solution (freshly prepared), 1.5 mol·L^{-1} hydroxylamine hydrochloride solution (freshly prepared), 1 mol·L^{-1} sodium acetate solution, 2.000 mmol·L^{-1} Fe^{2+} standard solution.

【 PROCEDURES 】

1.1　Preparation of Standard Solutions and the Sample Solution

Prepare seven 50 mL volumetric flasks. Using a measuring pipette, accurately dispense the volumes of each solution specified in Table 6-8-1 into the respective flasks. Dilute each solution to the calibration mark with distilled water, ensuring thorough mixing to homogenize the contents. This procedure yields a blank solution, a series of standard solutions spanning defined concentration gradients, and the test solution for subsequent analysis.

Table 6-8-1　Preparation of Fe^{2+} standard solutions and the sample solution

Experiment No.	1 (Blank)	2	3	4	5	6	7
2.000 mmol·L^{-1} Fe^{2+}(Standard solution)/mL	0	0.40	0.80	1.20	1.60	2.00	—
Fe^{2+}(Water sample)/mL	—	—	—	—	—	—	10.00
1.5 mol·L^{-1} Hydroxylamine hydrochloride/mL	1.00	1.00	1.00	1.00	1.00	1.00	1.00
8 mmol·L^{-1} o-Phenanthroline solution/mL	2.00	2.00	2.00	2.00	2.00	2.00	2.00
1 mol·L^{-1} NaAc/mL	5.00	5.00	5.00	5.00	5.00	5.00	5.00
V_{Total}(diluted)/mL	50.00	50.00	50.00	50.00	50.00	50.00	50.00
c(Fe^{2+} diluted)/μmol·L^{-1}							

1.2   Determination of Absorption Spectrum

Before starting the experiment, read the operation manual of spectrophotometer carefully.

The absorption spectrum of the complex of Fe^{2+} can be obtained by measuring the absorbance of standard solution No.4 in Table 6-8-1. According to the method of the spectrophotometer, in the wavelength range of 450-560 nm, with the reagent blank as the reference solution, the absorbance of the solution is measured every 10 nm, and the absorbance can be measured every 5 nm near the wavelength of the maximum absorbance. The experimental data is recorded in Table 6-8-2.

1.3   Plotting the Standard Curve

Select λ_{max} as the wavelength of the incident light, use the blank solution of No.1 as the reference solution, measure the absorbance of the series of standard solutions, and record the experimental data in Table 6-8-3. Draw a working curve,which can be expressed by the regression equation y = ax + b.The abscissa is the concentration of Fe^{2+} in standard solutions, and the ordinate is the absorbance of the standard solutions.

1.4   Determination of Fe^{2+} Content in a Water Sample

Under the same conditions as determination of the working curve, determine the A of the water sample. Record the reading of the absorbance, A, into Table 6-8-3.

【 DATA AND RESULTS 】

Date:_____   Temperature:_____°C   Relative Humidity:_____

(1) Plot the absorption spectrum: According to Table 6-8-2, plot the absorption spectrum(Figure 1). Determine the maximum absorption wavelength λ_{max}.

Table 6-8-2   Determination of absorption spectrum

λ / nm	
A	
λ_{max} / nm	

(2) Plotting the curve: According to Table 6-8-3, plot the working curve(Figure 2).

Table 6-8-3   Absorbance of Fe^{2+} standard solutions and the water sample

Experiment No.	1 (Blank)	2	3	4	5	6	7 (Sample)
$c(Fe^{2+}$ diluted) / $\mu mol \cdot L^{-1}$							
A							

Please attach Figure 2 (the working curve) to the lab report, and include the regression equation and correlation coefficient

(3) Determination of Fe^{2+} Content in the Water Sample

1) Standard curve method: The concentration of the sample solution from the working curve is_____ $\mu mol \cdot L^{-1}$ .The concentration of the Fe^{2+} in sample solution is _____ $\mu mol \cdot L^{-1}$.

2) Standard comparison method: $c_{Standard}$ = _____ $\mu mol \cdot L^{-1}$, $A_{Standard}$ = _____, A_{Sample} = _____, c_{Sample} = _____ $\mu mol \cdot L^{-1}$.

【QUESTIONS】

(1) Why is it better for controlling the absorbance of the solution in the A range of 0.2-0.7? How can it be controlled?

(2) Is the Fe^{2+} determined by the working curve equal to the Fe^{2+} in the original sample solution?

(3) According to this experimental result, identify the advantages and disadvantages of comparison method and working curve method.

2.　Determination of Fe^{2+} Content with Sulfocyanate Method

【PRINCIPLES】

Visible spectrophotometry only applies to colored materials. But dilute solution of Fe^{3+} is almost colorless. KSCN is used as a color developing reagent in the experiment. Fe^{3+} can react with SCN^- and produce red $[Fe(SCN)_6]^{3-}$ ($lgK_s = 6.4$):

$$Fe^{3+} + 6 SCN^- \Longrightarrow [Fe(SCN)_6]^{3-}$$

According to the Lambert Beer law, the color depth of the solution is in proportion to the concentration of Fe^{3+}. Thus, in this experiment SCN^- must excess so that it can react with Fe^{3+}. HNO_3 should be added into the sample solution to prevent Fe^{3+} from hydrolysis. Furthermore, Fe^{3+} can be slowly reduced to Fe^{2+} by SCN^-, $(NH_4)_2S_2O_8$ should also be added as a strong oxidant to prevent Fe^{3+} from being reduced.

【APPARATUS, REAGENTS AND MATERIALS】

Apparatus　Spectrophotometer, volumetric flasks (50 mL × 7, 1 000 mL), measuring pipettes (1 mL, 5 mL, 10 mL), dropper.

Material and Reagents　0.2 mol·L^{-1} KSCN solution, 2 mol·L^{-1} HNO$_3$ solution, concentrated H$_2$SO$_4$ solution, 0.100 0 g·L^{-1} Fe^{3+} standard solution, 25 g·L^{-1} (NH$_4$)$_2$S$_2$O$_8$ solution.

【PROCEDURES】

2.1　Preparation of Standard Solutions and the Sample Solution

Prepare seven 50 mL volumetric flasks. Using a measuring pipette, accurately dispense the volumes of each solution specified in Table 6-8-4 into the respective flasks. Dilute each solution to the calibration mark with distilled water, ensuring thorough mixing to homogenize the contents. This procedure yields a blank solution, a series of standard solutions spanning defined concentration gradients, and the test solution for subsequent analysis.

Table 6-8-4　Preparation of Fe^{3+} standard solutions and the sample solution

Experiment No.	1 (Blank)	2	3	4	5	6	7
0.100 0 g·L^{-1} Fe^{3+}(Standard solution)/mL	0	0.50	1.00	1.50	2.00	2.50	—

continued

Experiment No.	1 (Blank)	2	3	4	5	6	7
Fe^{2+}(Water sample)/mL	—	—	—	—	—	—	10.00
2 mol·L^{-1} HNO_3/mL	1.00	1.00	1.00	1.00	1.00	1.00	1.00
0.2 mol·L^{-1} KSCN/mL	5.00	5.00	5.00	5.00	5.00	5.00	5.00
25 g·L^{-1} $NH_4Fe(SO_4)_2$/drop	1	1	1	1	1	1	1
V_{total}/mL	50.00	50.00	50.00	50.00	50.00	50.00	50.00
$\rho(Fe^{3+})$/mg·L^{-1}							

2.2 Determination of Absorption Spectrum

Before starting the experiment, read the operation manual of spectrophotometer carefully.

The absorption spectrum of the complex of Fe^{3+} can be obtained by measuring the absorbance of standard solution No.4 in Table 6-8-4. According to the method of the spectrophotometer, in the wavelength range of 450-520 nm, with the reagent blank as the reference solution, the absorbance of the solution is measured every 10 nm, and the absorbance can be measured every 5 nm near the wavelength of the maximum absorbance. The experimental data is recorded in Table 6-8-5.

2.3 Plotting the Standard Curve

Select λ_{max} as the wavelength of the incident light, use the blank solution of No.1 as the reference solution, measure the absorbance of the series of standard solutions, and record the experimental data in Table 6-8-6. Draw a working curve,which can be expressed by the regression equation y = ax + b. The abscissa is the concentration of Fe^{3+} in standard solutions, and the ordinate is the absorbance of the standard solutions(The literature-reported absorption is λ_{max} = 480 nm).

2.4 Determination of Fe^{3+} Content in a Water Sample

Under the same conditions as determination of the working curve, determine the A of the water sample. Record the reading of the absorbance, A, into Table 6-8-6.

【DATA AND RESULTS】

Date:_____ Temperature:_____°C Relative Humidity:_____

(1) Plot the absorption spectrum: According to Table 6-8-5, plot the absorption spectrum(Figure 1). Determine the maximum absorption wavelength λ_{max}.

Table 6-8-5   Determination of absorption spectrum

λ/nm	
A	
λ_{max}/nm	

(2) Plotting the curve: According to Table 6-8-6, plot the working curve (Figure 2).

Table 6-8-6　Absorbance of Fe^{3+} standard solutions and the water sample

Experiment No.	1 (Blank)	2	3	4	5	6	7 (Sample)
$\rho(Fe^{3+})/mg \cdot L^{-1}$							
A							

Please attach Figure 2 (the working curve) to the lab report, and include the regression equation and correlation coefficient

(3) Determination of Fe^{3+} Content in a Water Sample

1) Standard curve method: The concentration of the sample solution from the working curve is _____mg $\cdot L^{-1}$. The concentration of the Fe^{3+} in sample solution is _____mg $\cdot L^{-1}$.(List regression equations and correlation coefficients)

2) Standard comparison method: $\rho_{Standard}$ = _____mg $\cdot L^{-1}$, $A_{Standard}$ = _____, A_{Sample} = _____, ρ_{Sample} = _____mg $\cdot L^{-1}$.

【QUESTION】

Why should excess KSCN be added to the solution?

3. Determination of Fe^{3+} Content with Sulfosalicylic Acid Method

【PRINCIPLES】

Sulfosalicylic acid (H_2Ssal) is the color developing reagent in this experiment. Fe^{3+} can react with H_2Ssal to produce many kinds of complex ions, with different colors under different pHs. For example, violet red $[FeSsal]^+$ forms under pH 1.8-2.5, brown $[Fe(Ssal)_2]^-$ is forms under pH 4-8, and stable yellow $[Fe(Ssal)_3]^{3-}$ forms under pH 8.0-11.5. Fe^{3+} is easy to hydrolyze and produce precipitation $Fe(OH)_3$ when pH > 12. Therefore, this method can only be used when pH < 12 and pH remains a constant.

In the experiment, brown complex of $[Fe(Ssal)_2]^-$ forms in HAc-NaAc buffer solution (pH5). Determine the absorbance at 466 nm. This reaction is given below

In the experiment, absorption spectrum first should be plotted to determine λ_{max} in a range of 420-490 nm. The concentration of an unknown solution can be determined by comparison method or the working curve method.

【APPARATUS REAGENTS AND MATERIALS】

Apparatus　Spectrophotometer, volumetric flasks (25 mL × 7), pipette (2 mL × 2, 1 mL), dropper.

Reagents and Materials $0.1 \text{ g} \cdot \text{L}^{-1}$ Fe^{3+} standard solution, $100 \text{ g} \cdot \text{L}^{-1}$ sulfosalicylic acid solution, HAc-NaAc buffer solution (pH5), Fe^{3+} sample solution, coordinate paper.

【PROCEDURES】

3.1   Preparation of Standard Solutions and the Sample Solution

Transfer each solution into 7 of 50 mL volumetric flasks respectively according to Table 6-8-7. Add HAc-NaAc buffer solution (pH 5) until the meniscus descends to the ring mark and homogenize.

Table 6-8-7   Preparation of Fe^{3+} standard solutions and the sample solution

Experiment No .	1 (Blank)	2	3	4	5	6	7 (Sample)
$0.1 \text{ g} \cdot \text{L}^{-1}$ Fe^{3+} standard solution / mL	0.00	0.40	0.60	0.80	1.00	1.20	—
Fe^{2+} (Water sample) / mL	—	—	—	—	—	—	1.00
$100 \text{ g} \cdot \text{L}^{-1}$ H_2Ssal solution / mL	2.00	2.00	2.00	2.00	2.00	2.00	2.00
V_{Total} / mL	25.00	25.00	25.00	25.00	25.00	25.00	25.00
$\rho(Fe^{3+})$ / $mg \cdot L^{-1}$							

3.2   Determination of Absorption Spectrum

Before starting the experiment, read the operation manual of spectrophotometer carefully.

The absorption spectrum of the complex of Fe^{3+} can be obtained by measuring the absorbance of standard solution No.4 in Table 6-8-7. According to the method of the spectrophotometer, in the wavelength range of 420-490 nm, with the reagent blank as the reference solution, the absorbance of the solution is measured every 10 nm, and the absorbance can be measured every 5 nm near the wavelength of the maximum absorbance. The experimental data is recorded in Table 6-8-8.

3.3   Plotting the Standard Curve

Select λ_{max} as the wavelength of the incident light, use the blank solution of No.1 as the reference solution, measure the absorbance of the series of standard solutions, and record the experimental data in Table 6-8-9. Draw a working curve,which can be expressed by the regression equation $y = ax + b$.The abscissa is the concentration of Fe^{3+} in standard solutions, and the ordinate is the absorbance of the standard solutions(The literature-reported absorption is $\lambda_{max} = 466$ nm).

3.4   Determination of Content in Sample Solution

The concentration of trace Fe^{3+} ($mg \cdot L^{-1}$) in the sample solution can be calculated with the comparison method or the standard curve method.

【DATA AND RESULTS】

Date:_____   Temperature:_____°C   Relative Humidity:_____

(1) Plot the absorption spectrum: According to Table 6-8-8, plot the absorption spectrum(Figure 1). Determine the maximum absorption wavelength λ_{max}.

Table 6-8-8   Determination of absorption spectrum

λ/nm	
A	
$\lambda_{\max}/\text{nm}$	

(2) Plotting the curve: According to Table 6-8-9, plot the working curve(Figure 2).

Table 6-8-9   Absorbance of Fe^{3+} standard solutions and the water sample

Experiment No.	1 (Blank)	2	3	4	5	6	7(Sample)
$\rho(Fe^{3+})/\text{mg}\cdot\text{L}^{-1}$							
A							

(3) Determination of Fe^{3+} content in a water sample

1) Standard curve method: The concentration of the sample solution from the working curve is _____ $\text{mg}\cdot\text{L}^{-1}$. The concentration of the Fe^{3+} in sample solution is _____ $\text{mg}\cdot\text{L}^{-1}$. Please attach Figure 2 (the working curve) to the lab report, and include the regression equation and correlation coefficient.

2) Standard comparison method: $\rho_{\text{Standard}} =$ _____ $\text{mg}\cdot\text{L}^{-1}$, $A_{\text{Standard}} =$ _____, $A_{\text{Sample}} =$ _____, $\rho_{\text{Sample}} =$ _____ $\text{mg}\cdot\text{L}^{-1}$.

【QUESTIONS】

(1) Why are buffer solutions used for volumetric preparation in the experiment?

(2) How to prepare the blank solution for the experiment?

(WANG Jinling)

Experiment 9   Determination of Acetylsalicylic Acid Content in Aspirin Tablets by Visible Spectrophotometry

【OBJECTIVES】

(1) To learn and be able to apply the method for the determination of the content of aspirin in the tablets by visible spectrophotometry.

(2) To learn and be able to apply proficiently the operation of 722(721) spectrophotometer.

【PRE-LAB ASSIGNMENTS】

Simulated Design Experiment: Present the experimental design as a flowchart, clearly indicating the corresponding precautions and the rationale behind each step.

Preview questions:

(1) Can we use distilled water instead of alcohol as solvent in this experiment?

(2) Why must the order of reagent addition be strictly followed in this experiment?

(3) What factors affect the accuracy of the experiment?

【PRINCIPLES】

Aspirin ($CH_3COOC_6H_4COOH$) is a white and crystalline compound, which can be synthesized from salicylic acid. Aspirin is powerful in the relief of pain and in reducing fever and inflammation. It is commonly used in medicine in the form of tablet.

The major composition of aspirin tablet is acetylsalicylic acid, and its ethoxycarbonyl structure can react with hydroxylamine to form hydroxamic acid in alkaline condition, the latter with ferric chloride to form a red hydroxamic acid iron complex in acidic solution. The wavelength of maximum absorbance for the complex is $\lambda_{max} = 520$ nm. Lambert-Beer's law can be applied to determine the content of aspirin within a certain range of concentration of aspirin by the standard curve method.

【APPARATUS REAGENTS AND MATERIALS】

Apparatus   722(or 721)-Spectrophotometer, volumetric flask (25 mL × 6), measuring pipets (1 mL × 5, 5 mL), dropper, beaker (100 mL).

Reagents and Materials   2.00 mol·L^{-1} NaOH, 4.00 mol·L^{-1} HCl, 10% $FeCl_3$, 0.500 g·L^{-1} standard ethanol solution of acetylsalicylic acid, 7% hydroxylamine hydrochloride ethanol solution, aspirin samples solution (aspirin tablet 20 tablets·L^{-1} ethanol solution).

【PROCEDURES】

1. Preparation of Standard Solutions and a Sample Solution

According to Table 6-9-1, prepare the blank solution, a series of standard solutions and a sample solution.

Please pay attention to 2 points: (1) After the addition of 2.00 mol·L^{-1} NaOH to the solution, you need to allow the solution to settle down for 3 minutes. Then you can continue to add 4.00 mol·L^{-1} HCl and 10% $FeCl_3$ solution. (2) After the preparation of the solutions, you need to allow them to settle down for 10 minutes before the measurement of their absorbance.

Table 6-9-1   Preparation of the standard solution and the sample solution

Experiment No.	1(Blank)	2	3	4	5	6	7(Sample)
0.500 g·L^{-1} Standard Aspirin / mL	0.00	0.50	1.00	1.50	2.00	2.50	—
Aspirin samples / mL	—	—	—	—	—	—	1.00
7% Hydroxylamine / mL	1.00	1.00	1.00	1.00	1.00	1.00	1.00
2.00 mol·L^{-1} NaOH / mL	1.00	1.00	1.00	1.00	1.00	1.00	1.00
4.00 mol·L^{-1} HCl / mL	1.00	1.00	1.00	1.00	1.00	1.00	1.00
10% $FeCl_3$ / mL	1.00	1.00	1.00	1.00	1.00	1.00	1.00
V_{Total}(solution diluted) / mL	25.00	25.00	25.00	25.00	25.00	25.00	25.00
c(solution diluted) / mg·L^{-1}							

2. Determination of Absorbance (*A*) of the Standard Solution and the Sample Solution

According to the manual of 722(721) type spectrophotometer (refer to Part I of Chapter 2: Ordinary Instruments in Basic Chemistry Experiments), select wavelength of 520 nm as incident radiation and suitable sensitivity of the spectrophotometer, use blank solution as reference solution to determine absorbance of each of the five standard solutions and the sample solution. Record the results in Table 6-9-2.

【DATA AND RESULTS】

Date:_____　Temperature:_____℃　Relative Humidity:_____

1. Absorbance (*A*) of the standard solutions and the sample solution

Table 6-9-2　Determination of absorbance of standard solution and sample solution

Experiment No.	1 (blank)	2	3	4	5	6	7(sample)
c(solution diluted) / mg·L^{-1}							
A							

2. Draw standard curve of the acetylsalicylic acid

According to the results (Table 6-9-2), draw a standard curve, the abscissa is concentration of aspirin standard solutions; the ordinate is absorbance of the standard solution. Linear regression equation and correlation coefficient should be given.

3. Determine the content of aspirin in tablets

The concentration of the aspirin sample solution from the standard working curve is: $\rho_1 =$ _____mg·L^{-1}.

The original concentration of aspirin in the initial sample solution is: $\rho_2 = \rho_1 \times 25 =$ _____mg·L^{-1}.

The content of the aspirin in commercial aspirin tablets:　_____mg / Tablet.

【QUESTIONS】

(1) Why does the acidity of the test solution change during the determination procedure?

(2) How to eliminate the influence of the purple color formed by the salicylic acid and ferric chloride?

(3) Please give the structure formula of aspirin and its properties based on the literatures search.

(4) Through a literature search, review the ways that may be used to determine the content of aspirin in tablets.

(YIN Jiqiu)

Experiment 10　Determination of the Formula and the Stability Constant of Sulfosalicylate Iron (III) by Spectrophotometry

【OBJECTIVES】

(1) To understand the basic principles of spectrophotometry.

(2) To learn the operation of spectrophotometer.

(3) To learn the principles and methods of determining the formula and the stability constant of the complex by spectrophotometry.

【PRE-LAB ASSIGNMENTS】

Simulated Design Experiment: Present the experimental design as a flowchart, clearly indicating the corresponding precautions to determine the wavelength of maximum absorption, the composition and the stability constant of the complex and the rationale behind each step.

Preview questions:

(1) How to select color developing reagent in spectrophotometry?

(2) How to control the composition of Sulfosalicylate Iron (Ⅲ) in this experiment?

(3) Why is perchloric acid chosen to control the acidity of the solution in this experiment? Can perchloric acid be replaced with other acids?

(4) How to select the measurement wavelength? How to select a blank solution? What is the blank solution in this experiment?

(5) What methods can be used to determine the formula and the stability constant of the complex? Which method is selected in this experiment?

(6) The composition of the complex is measured by equimolar series method. And why does the complex have the maximum concentration when the ratio of metal ions and ligands in the solution and that in complex are the same?

【PRINCIPLES】

A complex can be yielded by a metal ion reacting with a ligand as follows.

$$M + nL \rightleftharpoons ML_n$$

$$K_s = \frac{[ML_n]}{[M][L]^n} \tag{6-10-1}$$

where n is the coordination number of the complex and K_s is the stability constant of the complex.

If M and L are colorless and ML_n is colored, the absorbance of the solution is proportional to the concentration of the complex according to Lambert-Beer law, $A = \varepsilon bc$. The experiment is carried out with an equimolar series method.

The equimolar series method is also called the continuous variation method or the concentration ratio variation method. In this method, the same concentration solutions of metal ions and ligands are prepared. Under the conditions of total volumes unchanged, the absorbance of the serial mixtures with different volume ratios (molarity ratios) is determined under the wavelength of maximum absorption. When the concentration of the complex reaches the maximum, the coordination number n can be obtained according to the following equation

$$n = \frac{c(L)}{c(M)} = \frac{1-f}{f} \tag{6-10-2}$$

where $c(M)$ and the $c(L)$ are the concentrations of the metal ions and the ligands, respectively. f is fraction of the metal ions in the total concentration.

$$c(M) + c(L) = c = \text{constant} \tag{6-10-3}$$

$$f = \frac{c(M)}{c} \tag{6-10-4}$$

As can be seen in Figure 6-10-1, if $f = 0$ or $f = 1$, no metal ion or ligand exists, so no complex forms with its zero concentration. When the molar ratio of metal ions and ligands in the solutions is the same as that of the composition of the complexes, the concentration of the complexes is maximum. The absorbance and the corresponding f all reach their maximal value in the figure. For example, in a $1 : 1$ type complex, the value of f is 0.5 at the maximum absorbance. For the $1 : 2$ type complex, $f = 0.34$.

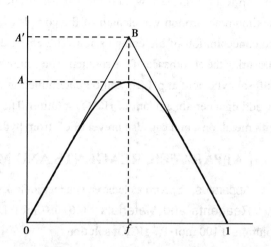

Figure 6-10-1　The plot of complex absorbance with metal ions concentration gradient

For complex ML in Figure 6-10-1, its maximum absorbance A is somewhat lower than the absorbance A' at the junction B of elongation lines as the complex slightly dissociates in the solutions. A' refers to absorbance when the complex does not thoroughly dissociate. The smaller difference between the A and A' there is, the more stable the complex is. So, the stability constant of the complex can be calculated as following

$$K_s = \frac{[ML]}{[M][L]} \tag{6-10-5}$$

Because the absorbance of the complex solution is proportional to the concentration of the complex, we have

$$\frac{A}{A'} = \frac{[ML]}{c'} \tag{6-10-6}$$

where c' is the concentration of the complex when it does not dissociate completely.

$$c' = c(M) = c(L) \tag{6-10-7}$$

and

$$[M] = [L] = c' - c'\frac{A}{A'} = c'\left[1 - \frac{A}{A'}\right] \tag{6-10-8}$$

Taking equations of (6-10-6) and (6-10-8) into (6-10-5), the formula of the calculation of the stability constant of the complex is as follows

$$K_s = \frac{\dfrac{A}{A'}}{\left[1 - \dfrac{A}{A'}\right]^2 c'} \tag{6-10-9}$$

The composition of Fe^{3+} complex with sulfosalicylic acid varies with pH. Under pH 1.8-2.5, a fuchsia complex with one ligand is formed; under pH 4-8, the complex contains two ligands forms. Under pH 8-11.5, the yellow complex containing three ligands forms; When pH > 12, $Fe(OH)_3$ will precipitate by the destruction of the colored complex. In the solution, sulfosalicylic acid is colorless, Fe^{3+} appears light yellow, and the sulfosalicylic acid-iron(III) complex ion is purplish red. At the maximum absorption wavelength of the complex ion, the absorbance of the solution is proportional to the concentration of the complex ion. Therefore, the composition of the complex can be determined by measuring the absorbance of the solution. The composition and stability constant of the complex of Fe^{3+} and sulfosalicylic acid at pH 2-3 can be determined in the experiment. pH of the solution can be controlled by adding a certain amount of $HClO_4$ solution. The main advantage is that ClO_4^- is not really coordinate with metal ions, and can also prevent Fe^{3+} from hydrolysis and from being reduced to Fe^{2+}.

【APPARATUS, REAGENTS AND MATERIALS】

Apparatus   Spectrophotometer, volumetric flask (50 mL × 7), measuring pipette (10 mL × 2), pipette bulb.

Reagents and Materials   0.010 0 mol·L^{-1} H_2Ssal solution, 0.010 0 mol·L^{-1} $Fe(NH_4)SO_4$ solution, 0.100 mol·L^{-1} $HClO_4$ solution.

【PROCEDURES】

1. Preparation of a Series of Solutions

According to Table 6-10-1, transfer freshly prepared 0.010 0 mol·L^{-1} ferric sulfate and 0.010 0 mol·L^{-1} sulfosalicylic acid to seven 50 mL volumetric flasks, respectively. Dilute these solutions with 0.100 mol·L^{-1} $HClO_4$ to the marks and homogenize. The solutions of sulfosalicylate iron (III) complex with different concentrations were obtained and let them stand for about 10 minutes.

2. Plot of the Absorption Spectrum of Complex

The absorbance of the No. 4 solution is determined over a range of 400-700 nm with an interval of 10 nm, taking distilled water as the blank solution. In the vicinity of maximum absorbance, the wavelength interval is 5 nm. Record the absorbance in Table 6-10-1. Plot the absorption spectrum and locate the peaks to determine the maximum wavelength (λ_{max}).

3. Determination of Absorbance of the Series Solutions

Determine the absorbances of the series solutions in the first procedure at the maximum absorption wavelength of the complex. Record the absorbances in Table 6-10-2.

【DATA AND RESULTS】

1. Plot the absorption spectrum to find out measurement wavelength

Date:_____   Temperature:_____°C   Relative Humidity:_____

Table 6-10-1   Determination of the absorption spectrum of complex

λ / nm	
A	
λ_{max} / nm	

Plot the absorption spectrum of the complex.

Measurement wavelength: $\lambda_{max} = $ _____ nm

2. The composition of the complex

According to the determined data in Table 6-10-2, plot A-f graph of the complex in which the abscissa is f and the ordinate is the absorbance, determine the composition of the complex and give the formula of the complex under 2-3 of pH aqueous solution.

Table 6-10-2　Preparation and determination of sulfosalicylate iron(III) complex solution

Experiment No.	1	2	3	4	5	6	7
$0.010\,0\ mol \cdot L^{-1}$ sulfosalicylic /mL	1.00	2.00	3.00	5.00	7.00	8.00	9.00
$0.010\,0\ mol \cdot L^{-1}$ $NH_4Fe(SO_4)_2$ /mL	9.00	8.00	7.00	5.00	3.00	2.00	1.00
$0.100\ mol \cdot L^{-1}$ $HClO_4$ /mL				40			
A							
$f = \dfrac{c(M)}{c}$							

3. The stability constant of sulfosalicylate iron(III) complex

Get maximum absorbance A from A-f graph, and then extend the straight lines on both sides of the curve at one point. This point is absorbance A' when the complex does not completely dissociate. The stability constant of sulfosalicylate iron (III) was obtained by taking the c' to the formula (6-10-9).

【QUESTIONS】

(1) What are the conditions in the determination of the stability constant of the complex by the equimolar series method?

(2) What is the effect of acidity on the composition of sulfosalicylate iron (III)?

(Qin Xiangyang)

Experiment 11　Identification and Determination of Vitamin B$_{12}$
Content by Ultraviolet Spectrophotometry

【OBJECTIVES】

(1) To learn the application of ultraviolet (UV) spectrophotometer.

(2) To master the method for qualitative analysis of vitamin B$_{12}$ by UV spectrophotometry.

【PRE-LAB ASSIGNMENTS】

Simulated Design Experiment: Present the experimental design as a flowchart, clearly indicating the corresponding precautions for measuring the content of vitamin B$_{12}$ and the rationale behind each step. Preview Questions

(1) What's the structure of vitamin B_{12}? Briefly introduce the main functions of vitamin B_{12} in the body?

(2) Briefly describe the basic principles of UV spectrophotometry.

(3) Consult the relevant literature, and analyse what factors affect the accuracy of the determination of vitamin B_{12} content by UV spectrophotometry.

(4) Refer to Chinese Pharmacopoeia (2020 edition), point out the identification and detection methods of vitamin B_{12}, and the requirements of UV spectrophotometer.

【PRINCIPLES】

UV spectrophotometry is an analytical technique used for the qualitative and quantitative determination of substances based on their absorption of ultraviolet (UV) light in the wavelength range of 200–400 nm. This method involves measuring the absorbance of a sample at specific wavelengths or over a defined spectral range where the analyte exhibits characteristic absorption. The relationship between absorbance and substance concentration is described by the Lambert-Beer law, which states that absorbance is directly proportional to the concentration of the absorbing species in the sample.

Vitamin B_{12} is a cobalt coordination polymer, with porphyrin as the ligand (molecular formula: $C_{63}H_{88}CoN_{14}O_{14}P$, $M_r = 1\ 355.38$). It is a deep-red, hydroscopic crystal. The labelling quantities of the vitamin B_{12} injection solution are 500 $\mu g \cdot mL^{-1}$, 250 $\mu g \cdot mL^{-1}$, 100 $\mu g \cdot mL^{-1}$, and 50 $\mu g \cdot mL^{-1}$, respectively. The water solution of vitamin B_{12} absorb at wavelength of 278 nm, 361 nm, and 550 nm. The ratio of the absorbance at the three wavelengths is the basis for qualitative identification of vitamin B_{12}. The ranges of the ratios are

$$A_{361\ nm}/A_{278\ nm} = 1.70\text{-}1.88 \qquad A_{361\ nm}/A_{550\ nm} = 3.15\text{-}3.45$$

The absorption rate of vitamin B_{12} solution at 361 nm is strongest and minimal interference, so it can be used to calculate the concentration of vitamin B_{12}. The absorption coefficient of vitamin B_{12} is $E_{1\ cm}^{1\%} = 207$.

$$A_{361nm} = E_{1\ cm}^{1\%} \cdot b \cdot c \tag{6-11-1}$$

where, A is the absorbance, b is the path length, and c is the analyte concentration, $E_{1\ cm}^{1\%}$ is equal to the absorbance at a specific wavelength when $1\%\ [g \cdot (100\ mL)^{-1}]$ concentration of the solution and 1 cm of liquid layer thickness are adopted.

To determine the content of vitamin B_{12} injection, the unit of concentration should be expressed as $\mu g \cdot mL^{-1}$. In the calculation, it is necessary to change the unit of the absorption coefficient $E_{1\ cm}^{1\%}$ 361 nm = 270 $[1\ g \cdot (100\ mL)^{-1}]$ into $\mu g \cdot mL^{-1}$.

$$E_{1\ cm}^{1\ \mu g \cdot L^{-1}}\ 361\ nm = \frac{207 \times 100}{10^6} = 207 \times 10^{-4} \tag{6-11-2}$$

【APPARATUS, MATERIAL AND REAGENTS】

Apparatus   UV-visible spectrophotometer, volumetric flask (10 mL), pipette (1 mL), beaker (100 mL), dropper

Material and Reagents   Vitamin B_{12} injection (500 $\mu g \cdot mL^{-1}$)

【PROCEDURES】

1. Preparation Sample Solution

Transfer 0.50 mL of vitamin B_{12} injection solutions by pipette from 3 ampoules, respectively into 3 of 10 mL volumetric flasks and add distilled water to the mark and homogenize the solution, respectively.

2. Identification and Content Determination of Vitamin B_{12}

Transfer a certain volume of the above solution into a 1 cm quartz cell carefully, distilled water as the blank solution. Take the quartz cells in the UV-visible spectrophotometer. Next, find out the absorption peak at 278 nm, 361 nm, and 550 nm with the UV-visible spectrophotometer. Measure the absorbance of sample solution at three wavelengths, respectively. Then repeat this operation three times. Record the data in Table 6-11-1 and take the average as the results.

【NOTES】

(1) The test solution must be settled to clarify.

(2) Usually, the absorbance reading of the test solution should be between 0.3 and 0.7 to ensure a small error.

(3) The absorption cell should be rinsed for 3-4 times by the test solutions, respectively. Wipe the outside of absorption cell surface with a lens cleaning paper.

(4) Don't open the cover of sample chamber during the measuring.

【DATA AND RESULTS】

1. Identification of vitamin B_{12}

Calculate the ratios of absorbance at three wavelengths ($A_{361\ nm}/A_{278\ nm}$ = 1.70-1.88; $A_{361\ nm}/A_{550\ nm}$ = 3.15-3.45) and compare with values from *Chinese Pharmacopoeia* (2020 edition).

Table 6-11-1　Absorption Spectral Determination of Vitamin B_{12}

λ/nm	361	278	550
A			
$A_{361\ nm}/A_{278\ nm}$:		$A_{361\ nm}/A_{550\ nm}$:	

2. Determining the content of vitamin B_{12}

Calculate the content of vitamin B_{12} injection solution ($\mu g \cdot mL^{-1}$) according to the absorbance at 361 nm, the absorption coefficient of vitamin B_{12} ($\mu g \cdot mL^{-1}$), and the diluted times of injection sample.

$$\rho = \frac{A}{E_{1\ cm}^{1\ \mu g \cdot L^{-1}}} = \frac{A}{207 \times 10^{-4}} = A \times 48.31\ (\mu g \cdot mL^{-1}) \tag{6-11-3}$$

Injection solution of vitamin B_{12}

$$\rho_{injection} = A \times 48.31 \times 20\ (\text{diluted times})\ (\mu g \cdot mL^{-1}).$$

The injection can be considered qualified when measured value is certificated as between 90% and 110% of the given value according to *Chinese Pharmacopoeia*.

【QUESTIONS】

(1) Why it is necessary to find out the absorption peak from the three wavelengths on the UV-visible spectrophotometer before determination?

(2) If 2 mL of injection solution is diluted to 15 times with water, the absorbance (A) is 0.698 at a wavelength of 361 nm, calculate the content of vitamin B_{12}.

(3) What are the prerequisites for direct determination of sample content by absorption coefficient method?

(WU Shikui)

Experiment 12   Determination of Vitamin B_2 Content by Fluorescence Spectrophotometry

【OBJECTIVES】

(1) To master the principles and methods of fluorometry.

(2) To understand the basic structure of a fluorescence photometer.

(3) To learn the operation of a 930-fluorometer.

【PRE-LAB ASSIGNMENTS】

Simulated Design Experiment: Present the experimental design as a flowchart, clearly indicating the corresponding precautions and the rationale behind each step.

Preview questions:

(1) In fluorescence measurements, why is the excitation wavelength shorter than the emission wavelength? Is it possible for the excitation and emission wavelengths to be the same in fluorescence analysis?

(2) What is the prerequisite for a molecule to produce fluorescence?

(3) Can spectrophotometry be used to measure the concentration of riboflavin in a multivitamin?

【PRINCIPLES】

When a substance is excited by a beam of light, usually ultraviolet light excites the electrons in the molecules of the substances causing them to emit a certain frequency of light that is called fluorescence. The method for the qualitative or quantitative analysis based on the fluorescence is called fluorometry.

Different fluorescent substances have different characteristic excitation wavelength and emission wavelength.

If the concentration of fluorescent substance is very low, the intensity of fluorescence (F) and the solution mass concentration (ρ) correlate with each other

$$F = 2.3\Phi I_0 ab\rho \tag{6-12-1}$$

where Φ is the fluorescence efficiency, I_0 is the intensity of incidence, a is the mass absorptivity, and b is the thickness of sample cell.

For a fluorescent substance, when I_0 and b are fixed, the intensity of fluorescence is proportional to the mass concentration of the substance. Therefore,

$$F = K'\rho \tag{6-12-2}$$

Vitamin B_2, $C_{17}H_{20}N_4O_6$ ($M_r = 376.37$) also known as riboflavin, is an orange-yellow crystal powder. Its structure formula is as following

Vitamin B_2 molecular formula: $C_{17}H_{20}N_4O_6$ ($M_r = 376.37$)

Vitamin B_2 in 0.1 mol $\cdot$ L^{-1} HAc solution can be excited by ultraviolet and quantitatively determined by its emitting of yellow-green florescence. The excitation light wavelengths may be 360 nm, 400 nm or 420 nm, with an emission wavelength of 530 nm.

【 APPARATUS, REAGENTS AND MATERIALS 】

Apparatus　930 fluorometer, 0.1 mg-analytic balance, volumetric flask (25 mL × 6, 50 mL, 1 000 mL), pipette (1 mL, 5 mL), beaker (100 mL), dropper (25 mL), stirring rod

Reagents and Materials　Vitamin B_2 (biochemistry reagent), vitamin B_2 tablet, 0.1 mol $\cdot$ L^{-1} HAc solution

【 PROCEDURES 】

1. Preparation of Standard Solution of Vitamin B_2

Weigh approximately 10.0 mg of vitamin B_2 into a small beaker, then dissolve it with a small amount 0.1 mol $\cdot$ L^{-1} HAc solution. Transfer the solution quantitatively to a 1 000 mL volumetric flask. Dilute to the mark with 0.1 mol $\cdot$ L^{-1} HAc solution and mix thoroughly. Store the vitamin B_2 standard solution at a low temperature in darkness.

Label six 25 mL volumetric flasks and add 0.00 mL (blank), 0.50 mL, 1.00 mL, 1.50 mL, 2.00 mL, and 2.50 mL of the vitamin B_2 standard solution to each flask, respectively. Dilute each flask to the mark of 0.1 mol $\cdot$ L^{-1} of HAc solution and mix thoroughly to obtain a series of standard solutions.

2. Plotting the Standard Curve

Turn on the power button to pre-heat the instrument for 10 minutes before the determination. Select 360 nm or 400 nm as the excitation wavelength and 530 nm as the emission wavelength. Use 0.1 mol $\cdot$ L^{-1} of HAc solution as a reference to calibrate the instrument. Then use the standard solution with the highest concentration to adjust the scale to maximum reading. Fix the conditions, following the order from diluted solution to concentrated solution to determine the intensity of fluorescence for the series of standard solutions. Record the data in Table 6-12-1. According to the data, plot the standard curve.

3. Determination of Vitamin B₂ in Tablet Sample

Take one vitamin B₂ tablet and weigh it (accurate to 0.1 mg). The powder was prepared by mortar, dissolve it in 0.1 mol·L^{-1} HAc solution, then transfer and dilute it to 1 000 mL, store in a brown reagent bottle.

Transfer 2.50 mL of the solution into a 50 mL volumetric flask and diluted with 0.1 mol·L^{-1} HAc solution. Fluorescence intensity of the sample can be determined under the same conditions as for the standard solution. Find out the corresponding concentration $c_{determined}$ from the standard curve. Then the concentration of the sample solution and in the tablets can be calculated. Record the data in Table 6-12-1.

【DATA AND RESULTS】

(1) The Standard Curve of Vitamin B₂

Date:_____   Temperature:_____°C   Relative Humidity:_____

Table 6-12-1   Standard curve and measuring sample of vitamin B₂

Volumetric flask No.	0	1	2	3	4	5	Sample
m (vitamin B₂)/mg			10.0				—
ρ_{Stock} (vitamin B₂)/μg·mL^{-1}			10.0				—
$V_{Standard}$ (stock vitamin B₂)/mL	0	0.50	1.00	1.50	2.00	2.50	—
V_{Total} (diluted by 0.1 mol·L^{-1} of HAc)/mL			25.00				50.00
$\rho_{Standard}$ (vitamin B₂)/μg·mL^{-1}	0	0.20	0.40	0.60	0.80	1.00	—
F							
m (sample of vitamin B₂)/mg			—				

According to the results in Table 6-12-1, plot a working curve.

The regression equation of the standard curve is _____.

The correlation coefficient is _____.

The concentration of the vitamin B₂ sample solution from the working curve is _____ μg·mL^{-1}.

(2) The Concentration of Vitamin B₂ in Tablets

$$\omega(\text{Vitamin B}_2)\% = \frac{\rho_{determined}(\mu g \cdot mL^{-1}) \times 20(\text{dilution multiple}) \times 1\,000\,mL \times 10^{-3}}{m(\text{sample of vitamin B}_2)} (mg \cdot mg^{-1}) \quad (6\text{-}12\text{-}3)$$

【QUESTIONS】

(1) What is the excitation spectrum? What is the emission spectrum?

(2) Why is 0.1 mol·L^{-1} HAc solution used to prepare the vitamin B₂ solution in this experiment?

(3) If light with wavelengths of 420 nm or 440 nm is selected as the excitation wavelength, will this affect the determination results?

(ZHOU Haofei)

Chapter 7 | Chemical Principles Experiment

Experiment 13   Colligative Properties of Dilute Solution
and Their Application

【 OBJECTIVES 】

(1) To master the principles and methods and to determine the molecular mass of solute by freezing point depression.

(2) Learn to use a freezing point osmometer and to determine the molecular mass of solute from osmotic concentration of solution.

(3) Learn to use a common microscope and to observe the shape of red blood cell in solutions with different osmolarity.

(4) Learn to use 0.10 °C indexing thermometer.

【 PRE-LAB ASSIGNMENTS 】

Simulated Design Experiment: Present the experimental design as a flowchart, clearly indicating the corresponding precautions for determining the molar mass of the solute and the rationale behind each step

Preview questions:

(1) What are the general methods to measure the molecular mass of solute? Which one is the usual method in the common tests? Why?

(2) What is the condition for a solution about "$c_{os} \approx b(B)$" ?

(3) Why the cooling curves of solvent are different from the dilute solution? What does the cooling curve look like in the ideal condition?

(4) Why does the more NaCl solid must be added in the ice-water bath in freezing point depression experiment?

(5) Why is there the supercooling phenomenon in determining the osmotic concentration test? How to resolve them?

(6) We can't stir glucose solution with a glass rod in the test tube when we prepare it. Why?

【 PRINCIPLES 】

Some physical properties of the solvent such as the freezing point and osmotic pressure etc. will be altered quantitatively when a non-volatile and non-electrolyte solute is dissolved in the solvent. The magnitude of the alteration is directly proportional to amount of solute dissolved but not the kind of the solute. These properties are collectively called colligative properties. They provide the useful ways to determine the molar mass of solute experimentally.

The freezing point T_f of a solution is lower than that T_f^0 of its solvent. For a non-volatile and non-electrolyte dilute solution, the relationship between the freezing point depression and molality of solution is

$$\Delta T_f^0 = T_f^0 - T_f = K_f b(B) \qquad (7\text{-}13\text{-}1)$$

$$b(B) = \frac{m(B)\big/M(B)}{m(A)} \times 1\,000 \qquad (7\text{-}13\text{-}2)$$

$b(B)$ is the molality of the solution $(mol \cdot kg^{-1})$; $M(B)$ is the molar mass of the solute$(g \cdot mol^{-1})$; $m(B)$ is the mass of solute dissolved in solution in gram (g); $m(A)$ is the mass of solvent in gram(g); K_f is the molar freezing point depression constant $(K \cdot kg \cdot mol^{-1})$ of solution; ΔT_f is the freezing point depression in Kelvin temperature (K) of this dilute solution.

So that

$$M(B) = \frac{K_f m(B)}{m_A \Delta T_f} \times 1\,000 \qquad (7\text{-}13\text{-}3)$$

We can calculate the relative molar mass M_B of solute from the Equations (7-13-3) by test due to every date in this equation can be determined experimentally. The relative error E_r of experiment is

$$E_r(\%) = \frac{M(B) - M(B)_T}{M(B)_T} \times 100\% \qquad (7\text{-}13\text{-}4)$$

where, $M(B)_T$ is the true molar mass of solute.

You can find how to determine the freezing point T_f of dilute solution and freezing point T_f^0 of solvent (distilled water normally) by Figure 7-13-1. The cooling curve (b) of dilute solution is different from the cooling curve (a) of the solvent.

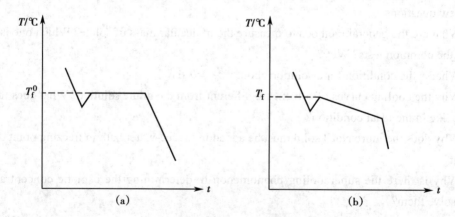

Figure 7-13-1   Cooling curve
(a) Solvent; (b) Solution.

Freezing point osmometer is often used to determine the osmolarity of solution because of principle determining the osmolarity c_{os} $(mol \cdot L^{-1})$ is by the freezing point depression in the osmometer. The relationship between the freezing point depression ΔT_f, osmolarity of a solution c_{os} and molality $b(B)$ of solution is expressed by

$$c_{os} \approx b(B) = \frac{\Delta T_f}{K_f} \tag{7-13-5}$$

Generally, the density of dilute solution d is $1 g \cdot cm^{-3}$ nearly. So

$$M(B) = \frac{m(B)}{m(A)c_{os}} \times 1\,000 \tag{7-13-6}$$

When a certain mass of non-electrolyte substance is dissolved in a certain mass of solvent, Osmolarity of the solution can be determined by osmometer. The molar mass of the solute in dilute solution can be calculated by Equation (7-13-6). The osmotic pressure at a given temperature for the dilute solution is known by the following equation, that is

$$\Pi = c_{os} R T \tag{7-13-7}$$

where Π is the osmotic pressure of solution (kPa); R is the ideal gas constant ($8.314\ J \cdot mol^{-1} \cdot K^{-1}$); T is the Kelvin temperature of solution (K).

The osmotic pressures of different solutions can be known by comparing their osmolarity directly if the temperature is unchanged. The solution with higher osmolarity is called hypertonic solution and hypotonic solution with lower osmolarity in the same way. If a semi-permeable membrane is used to separate two solutions with different osmolarity, the osmosis would occur. The solvent will pass though the semi-permeable from hypotonic solution to hypertonic solution.

The osmolarity of normal plasma ($280\text{-}320\ mmol \cdot L^{-1}$) is used as a reference standard to compare the osmolarity with the other solutions clinically. If the osmolarity of a solution is more than or equal to $320\ mmol \cdot L^{-1}$, it is called hypertonic solution. On the contrary, be called hypotonic solution if it's less than $280\ mmol \cdot L^{-1}$. The red blood cell would not keep its normal case in the non-isotonic solutions. We can observe the shape of cell to judge the osmolarity of a solution roughly. To know the osmolarity has a abroad range of applications in medicinal and other fields.

1. Determination of Molar Mass of Glucose by Freezing Point Depression

【 APPARATUS, REAGENTS AND MATERIALS 】

Apparatus   Electronic analytical balance, thermometer(0.10 ℃), dry test tube(40 mm × 150 mm), large beaker (500 mL), pipette (50 mL), rubber suction bulb, magnifying glass, graduated cylinder (100 mL)

Reagents and Materials   Ice, salt, glucose (A. R.), distilled water

【 PROCEDURES 】

1.1   Determination of the freezing point for glucose solution

Weigh out 4.2-5.1 g (0.000 1 g) of glucose solid by an electronic analytical balance and put it into a dry test tube, add 50.00 mL of distilled water (solvent) into it by pipette and make the glucose to dissolve completely. Be sure not to take the glass rod to stir glucose solution when you dissolve it.

Put the test tube with the solution into a large beaker which contains the mixture of ice, salt and a little of tap water as shown in Figure 7-13-2.

Keep the temperature of ice-salt-water system below −5 °C. Keep going to stir the solution and observe the thermometer carefully until some pieces of ice appear.

Record the temperature many times until the temperature rises no longer, you finish the first group of tests. Take out the test tube and make the ice in it to be melt by rinsing the outside of it with running tap water, don't drain the solution from the test tube! Use this test tube with the original solution to repeat the above step and measurement the temperature three times, the highest rebound temperature is just the freezing point of solution T_f. The difference between any two data among the three data does not exceed 0.05 °C. Take the average value and record it in Table 7-13-1.

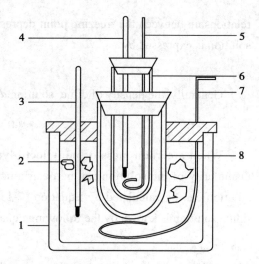

Figure 7-13-2   Apparatus of determining the freezing point

1. Beaker; 2. Ice; 3,4. Thermometer; 5,7. Stirrer; 6,8. Test tube.

1.2   Determination of the freezing point of solvent

Clean the test tube carefully with the distilled water of preparing the solution, and then add about 50 mL of it into the test tube. Repeat measurement operation three times as above steps. Similarly, record the freezing point of distilled water T_f^0 in Table 7-13-1.

【DATA AND RESULTS】

Calculate the freezing point depression ΔT_f of solution, the molar mass of glucose $M(B)$ and the relative error E_r by Equation (7-13-1), Equation (7-13-3) and Equation (7-13-4), respectively. Fill the data and results in Table 7-13-1.

Date:_____   Temperature:_____°C   Relative Humidity:_____

Table 7-13-1   Determination of Molar Mass of Glucose by Freezing Point Depression

Experiment No.	1	2	3
$m(A)/g$			
$m(B)/g$			
$T_f/°C$			
$T_f^0/°C$			
$\Delta T_f/°C$			
$M(B)/g·mol^{-1}$			
$E_r/\%$			

【NOTES】

You should use the thermometer very carefully because the relatively low temperature makes the glass instruments to be broken easily when you operate.

【QUESTIONS】

(1) Freezing point of biological sample solution such as blood serum and urine can be determined by this test? Which kinds of substances can be determined about their molar mass by the freezing point depression of solution?

(2) If the boiling point elevation of solution can be used to determine the molar mass of glucose?

2. Determination of the Molar Mass of Glucose by Determining Osmolarity

【APPARATUS, REAGENTS AND MATERIALS】

Apparatus　Electronic analytical balance, freezing point osmometer, small dry test tube (2 mL), dry beaker (100 mL), pipette (50 mL), pipette (1 mL), rubber suction bulb.

Reagent and Materials　Glucose (A.R.), standard NaCl solutions ($c_{os}=0.300$ mol·kg^{-1} and $c_{os}=0.800$ mol·kg^{-1}).

【PROCEDURES】

2.1　Preparation of glucose solution

Weigh out 9.1-9.5 g (0.000 1 g) of glucose solid by an electronic analytical balance and put it into a dry beaker, add 50.00 mL of distilled water into it by pipette, make all the glucose dissolve completely.

2.2　Calibrate the freezing point osmometer

Read the technical manual of freezing point osmometer before the experiment. Start the freezing point osmometer and keep cool cell in a proper temperature range (usually between −8 ℃ and −10 ℃). Take 0.50 mL of standard NaCl solution ($c_{os}=0.300$ mol·kg^{-1}) by pipette into a small dry test tube and measure the osmolarity on the freezing point osmometer. Adjust the scale and make osmolarity value just at $c_{os}=0.300$ mol·kg^{-1}. And then transfer 0.50 mL of another standard NaCl solution ($c_{os}=0.800$ mol·kg^{-1}) by pipette into another small dry test tube, measure the osmolarity of it on the freezing point osmometer again. Adjust the scale and make osmolarity value just at $c_{os}=0.800$ mol·kg^{-1}. Repeat the above step several times until the measured values are equal to the value of standard solution exactly.

2.3　Osmolarity determination of glucose solution

Transfer 0.50 mL of glucose solution into a small dry test tube with a volumetric pipette. Measure the osmolarity of it on the freezing point osmometer and record the data. Measure it twice again and take the average value as the last osmolarity of this glucose solution.

【DATA AND RESULTS】

Calculate the molar mass of glucose by Equation (7-13-6) and relative error by Equation (7-13-4) respectively (True molar mass of glucose is 180 $g \cdot mol^{-1}$). Fill the data and results in Table 7-13-2.

Date:_____ Temperature:_____°C   Relative Humidity:_____

Table 7-13-2   Determination of Molar Mass of Glucose by Determining Osmolarity

Experiment No.	1	2	3
$m(A)/g$			
$m(B)/g$			
$c_{os}/mol \cdot L^{-1}$			
$M(B)/g \cdot mol^{-1}$			
$E_r/\%$			

【QUESTIONS】

(1) How to know the osmotic pressure of a solution at room temperature after getting the osmolarity of it by freezing point osmometer?

(2) What do you need to pay attention to when you determine the osmolarity of a solution by freezing point osmometer?

(FU Ying)

3. Application of Freezing Point Osmometer

【APPARATUS, REAGENTS AND MATERIALS】

Apparatus   Microscope, glass slides × 5, freezing point osmometer, small dry test tube (2 mL), dry beaker (100 mL), test tube (20 mL), graduated pipette (1.00 mL), measuring cylinder, rubber suction bulb, droppers × 5, stirring rod.

Reagents and Materials   Standard NaCl solution ($c_{os} = 0.30$ mol $\cdot L^{-1}$, $c_{os} = 0.80$ mol $\cdot L^{-1}$), 0.35 mol $\cdot L^{-1}$ NaCl, 0.050 mol $\cdot L^{-1}$ NaCl, 9.0 g $\cdot L^{-1}$ NaCl, 54 g $\cdot L^{-1}$ glucose solutions, polyvinyl alcohol eyedrops, animal blood, anti-coagulator.

【PROCEDURES】

3.1   Calibration of the freezing point osmometer

Calibrate the freezing point osmometer refer to Part I of Chapter 2: Ordinary Instruments in Basic Chemistry Experiments.

3.2   Determination of osmotic concentrations

Transfer 0.50 mL of 0.35 mol $\cdot L^{-1}$ NaCl solution with graduated pipette into a small dry test tube. Measure the osmotic concentration on the freezing point osmometer and record the data. Repeat twice again and take the average value as the osmotic concentration of this solution. Similarly, measure $0.050 \ mol \cdot L^{-1}$ NaCl, $9.0 \ g \cdot L^{-1}$ NaCl, $54 \ g \cdot L^{-1}$ glucose and polyvinyl alcohol eyedrops one by one. Record their osmotic concentrations in Table 7-13-3.

3.3　Observation of red blood cell morphology under microscope

(1) Preparation of red blood cell suspension: Transfer 1.00 mL of fresh animal blood (from mice or rabbit) and add 20.0 mL isotonic solution containing anti-coagulator (10 drops of $0.050 \ mol \cdot L^{-1}$ sodium citrate or Na_2EDTA solution) into a beaker, stir it slightly until it is homogenous.

(2) Add 1.00 mL $0.35 \ mol \cdot L^{-1}$ NaCl, $0.050 \ mol \cdot L^{-1}$ NaCl, $9.0 \ g \cdot L^{-1}$ NaCl, $54 \ g \cdot L^{-1}$ glucose and polyvinyl alcohol eyedrops into five test tubes respectively. Add 0.10 mL of red blood cell suspension solution into each of five test tubes respectively. Stir the mixture in test tubes slightly until they are uniformity. Wait for 15-20 min.

(3) Read the technical manual of microscope carefully before the experiment and be sure to observe the morphology of red blood cell under the microscope. Take out one drop of mixture from five test tubes respectively and drop the mixture on the five different glass slides. Remove superfluous liquid with another glass slides. Put the glass slides with red blood cell under a microscope and observe the morphology of red blood cells. Record the results in Table 7-13-4.

【DATA AND RESULTS】

Date:＿＿＿＿＿＿＿　Temperature:＿＿＿＿＿＿℃　Relative Humidity:＿＿＿＿＿＿

Table 7-13-3　Determination of osmotic concentration of solutions

Experiment No.	1	2	3
$0.35 \ mol \cdot L^{-1}$ NaCl			
$0.050 \ mol \cdot L^{-1}$ NaCl			
$9.0 \ g \cdot L^{-1}$ NaCl			
$54 \ g \cdot L^{-1}$ Glucose			
Polyvinyl alcohol eyedrops			

Table 7-13-4　The morphology of red blood cell in different osmotic concentration solutions

Solutions	$0.35 \ mol \cdot L^{-1}$ NaCl	$0.050 \ mol \cdot L^{-1}$ NaCl	$9.0 \ g \cdot L^{-1}$ NaCl	$54 \ g \cdot L^{-1}$ Glucose	Polyvinyl alcohol eyedrops
Morphology of red blood cell					

【QUESTIONS】

(1) What's the morphologies when the red blood cell is in hypertonic solution, hypotonic solution and isotonic solution respectively? Explain the reason.

(2) Why would our eyes feel pain when we swim in fresh water, but better in sea water?

(BAI Tianyu)

Experiment 14　Determination of the Relative Atomic Mass of Magnesium by a Displacement Reaction

【OBJECTIVE】

(1) To master the operation method of an analytical balance

(2) To learn gas collection techniques and volume determination methods

(3) To understand the principles and methods for determining the relative atomic mass of Mg

【PRE-LAB ASSIGNMENTS】

Simulated Design Experiment: Present the experimental design as a flowchart, clearly indicating the corresponding precautions for determining the relative atomic mass of magnesium through a displacement reaction, as well as the rationale behind each step.

Preview questions:

(1) What is the principle of determining the relative atomic mass of Mg by the displacement method?

(2) What is the principle for checking whether the system is sealed?

(3) If the gas bubbles in water are not removed completely, how will this affect the experimental results?

(4) If the oxide film on the magnesium ribbon surface is not removed completely, how will it affect the results of this experiment?

(5) How does incomplete cooling of the reaction system to room temperature affect the direct measurement of the volume of hydrogen gas (H_2) in this experiment?

(6) Why must the liquid level in the eudiometer be the same as that in the funnel when recording the gas volume?

【PRINCIPLES】

Magnesium is an active metal, which can displace hydrogen from diluted sulphuric acid to produce H_2 and magnesium sulphate. The reaction is given as follows:

$$H_2SO_4 + Mg \rightleftharpoons H_2 \uparrow + MgSO_4$$

According to the stoichiometric ratio, when the magnesium ribbon is completely consumed, the molar amount of substance of Mg equals that of H_2. By collecting the hydrogen gas and measuring its volume, pressure and temperature, the amount of H_2 can be calculated according to the ideal gas equation of state.

$$n(\text{Mg}) = n(\text{H}_2) = \frac{p(\text{H}_2) \times V(\text{H}_2)}{R \times T} \tag{7-14-1}$$

where p (H_2)/kPa is the partial pressure of hydrogen gas, $V(H_2)$ is the volume of gas collected, R is gas constant with $8.314 \text{ J} \cdot \text{mol}^{-1} \cdot \text{K}^{-1}$, and T is absolute temperature.

$$p_{\text{Total}} = p(H_2) + p_{\text{Saturaed}}(H_2O) \tag{7-14-2}$$

$$p(H_2) = p_{\text{Total}} - p_{\text{Saturated}}(H_2O) \tag{7-14-3}$$

If magnesium ribbon is weighed before reaction and the mass is $m(Mg)$ in grams, the relative atomic mass of Magnesium can be determined by the following equation

$$A_r(Mg) = \frac{m(Mg)}{n(Mg)} = \frac{m(Mg) \times R \times T}{\left[p_{\text{Total}} - p_{\text{Saturated}}(H_2O) \right] \times V(H_2)} \tag{7-14-4}$$

【APPARATUS, REAGENTS AND MATERIALS】

Apparatus   0.1 mg-electronic analytical balance, thermometer, barometer, eudiometer (50 mL base burette), big test tube (20 mL), long-stem funnel (× 2), graduated cylinder (10 mL).

Reagents and Materials   2.0 mol·L^{-1} H$_2$SO$_4$, magnesium ribbon (about 25-35 mg), glycerol, stand and clamp; pipe with stopper, rubber pipe, sandpaper.

【PROCEDURE】

(1) Magnesium ribbon must be treated with sandpaper until there is no black substance (MgO) on its surface before the experiment. Weigh three pieces of Mg ribbons with an electronic analytical balance one by one, each piece is about 0.030 0 g and no more than 0.035 0 g (± 0.000 1 g precisely). Record the mass of each magnesium ribbon.

(2) Set up the apparatus as shown in Figure 7-14-1, pour some water into the eudiometer connected with a funnel until the liquid level is slightly below the "0" mark. Move the funnel up and down repeatedly to expel the gas bubbles in the liquid completely.

(3) Check whether this system is sealed by the following procedure. Connect the eudiometer and the big test tube with a rubber pipe, stop them with a stopper. Move the funnel down to a proper position, the liquid level will move down at the beginning, 3 min later, it will maintain at a certain position that means this system is sealed. If not, you must check all joints and repeat this test mentioned above until this system is sealed.

(4) Remove the test tube and pour 5.0 mL of 2 mol·L^{-1} H$_2$SO$_4$ into it with a funnel (avoid letting H$_2$SO$_4$ adhere to the inner wall of test tube), rinse the magnesium ribbon with a small amount of glycerol or water and attach it to the inner wall of test tube, ensure the magnesium ribbon does not come into contact with the solution of H$_2$SO$_4$, reassemble the test tube, recheck the system's airtightness, and confirm it is properly sealed.

(5) Adjust the funnel to the right side of the eudiometer and keep the liquid surfaces of the funnel and eudiometer at the same level, record the initial eudiometer reading (V_{Initial}).

(6) Gently tilt the iron stand and make the magnesium ribbon connect with a solution of diluted H$_2$SO$_4$, the reaction-

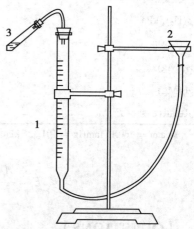

Figure 7-14-1 Determination of the atomic mass of magnesium

1. Eudiometer; 2. Funnel; 3. Test tube.

generate gases (hydrogen and water vapor) will enter the eudiometer ,displacing water into the funnel. As the liquid level decreases, gradually lower the funnel to maintain approximately equal liquid levels in both the eudiometer and funnel throughout the process.

(7) After the magnesium ribbon is completely consumed, cool the system to room temperature, make both liquid levels at the same level completely, and record the position of liquid level of the eudiometer. 1-2 min later, record the final reading (V_{Final}) if the position keeps consistently, it states that the temperature of the system reaches room temperature. Record the room temperature and atmosphere pressure. After the procedure is completed, remove the test tube and pour the acid solution out. Rinse the tube with running tap water.

(8) The experiment needs to be repeated two more times using magnesium ribbon samples of varying mass. Record the data in Table 7-14-1. Calculate the relative atomic mass of magnesium and the relative error using experimental data.

【DATA AND RESULTS】

Date:_____ Temperature:_____°C   Relative Humidity:_____

Table 7-14-1   Determination of the atomic mass of magnesium

Experiment No.	1	2	3
$m(Mg)/g$			
$V(H_2SO_4)/mL$			
$V_{Initial}/mL$			
V_{Final}/mL			
$V(H_2)/mL$			
T/K			
p_{Total}/kPa			
$p_{Saturated}(H_2O)/kPa$			
$p(H_2)/kPa$			
$A_r(Mg)_{Determination}$			
$A_r(Mg)_{Average}$			
$A_r(Mg)_{Theory}$			
Relative error $E_r/\%$			

(1 atm = 760.15 mmHg = 101.325 kPa, $p(H_2O)$ can be obtained from appendix)

$$E_r = \frac{A_r(Mg)_{Determination} - A_r(Mg)_{Theory}}{A_r(Mg)_{Theory}} \times 100\% \qquad (7\text{-}14\text{-}5)$$

【QUESTIONS】

(1) Which factors may lead to the errors in this experiment?

(2) If dilute sulfuric acid enters the eudiometer during the reaction, how would this affect

experimental results?

(SONG Hui)

Experiment 15   Determination of the Rate and Activation Energy of Chemical Reaction

【 OBJECTIVE 】

(1) To understand the effects of the concentration, temperature, and catalyst on the rate of chemical reaction.

(2) To determinate the rate of chemical reaction in which $(NH_4)_2S_2O_8$ oxidizes KI, for calculating the reaction order, rate constant and activation energy of the reaction.

(3) To master the graphing method to deal with experimental data.

【 PRE-LAB ASSIGNMENT 】

Simulated Design Experiment: Present the experimental design as a flowchart, clearly indicating the corresponding precautions and the rationale behind each step.

Preview questions:

(1) Which factors affect the rate of the chemical reaction? How do they affect?

(2) For $(NH_4)_2S_2O_8 + 3KI = (NH_4)_2SO_4 + K_2SO_4 + KI_3$, how to determine the reaction rate?

(3) How to determine the reaction order of each reactant in a chemical reaction?

(4) Why will the reaction rate increase as the temperature rises?

(5) How to determine the activation energy of the chemical reaction?

(6) Why does the reaction rate change after adding the catalyst?

【 PRINCIPLES 】

In a mixed solution of $(NH_4)_2S_2O_8$ and KI, the following redox reaction take place

$$(NH_4)_2S_2O_8 + 3KI \Longrightarrow (NH_4)_2SO_4 + K_2SO_4 + KI_3$$

or

$$S_2O_8^{2-} + 3I^- \Longrightarrow 2SO_4^{2-} + I_3^- \tag{7-15-1}$$

The rate of this reaction is

$$v = k\,c(S_2O_8^{2-})^m c(I^-)^n \tag{7-15-2}$$

here, v is the rate of the reaction. $c(S_2O_8^{2-})$ and $c(I^-)$ indicate the original concentration, k is rate constant, the sum of m and n is the reaction order.

In order to determine v, we should determine the change of the concentration of $S_2O_8^{2-}$ in an interval time Δt. The average rate of this reaction is:

$$\overline{v} = -\frac{\Delta c(S_2O_8^{2-})}{\Delta t} \tag{7-15-3}$$

Here, the average rate can instead of instantaneous rate approximatively:

$$v = -\frac{\Delta c(S_2O_8^{2-})}{\Delta t} \approx k\,c(S_2O_8^{2-})^m c(I^-)^n \tag{7-15-4}$$

The starch solution is used as an indicator. A certain volume starch solution and $Na_2S_2O_3$ solution with accurately known concentration are added into the KI solution before the KI solution mixed with $(NH_4)_2S_2O_8$ solution. Then I_3^- will be released from the reaction (1) immediately and reacts with $Na_2S_2O_3$ to form the colorless $S_4O_6^{2-}$ and I^-:

$$I_3^- + 2S_2O_3^{2-} \Longrightarrow S_4O_6^{2-} + 3I^- \tag{7-15-5}$$

The rate of reaction (2) is much faster than that of reaction (1). As the $Na_2S_2O_3$ is consumed completely, the I_3^- will be released from the reaction (1) immediately and reacts with the starch to turn the color of the solution into blue.

Comparing reaction (1) with (2), 1 mol of $S_2O_8^{2-}$ must be consumed 2 mol of $S_2O_3^{2-}$, so

$$\Delta c(S_2O_8^{2-}) = \frac{\Delta c(S_2O_3^{2-})}{2} \tag{7-15-6}$$

$\Delta c(S_2O_3^{2-})$ was the concentration of $Na_2S_2O_3$ because the $Na_2S_2O_3$ was consumed completely during the Δt. We record the time interval Δt from the beginning of the reaction to the moment that the color of the solution turns into blue. From the above, the rate of the reaction (1) can be written as follows

$$v = -\frac{\Delta c(S_2O_3^{2-})}{2\Delta t} = \frac{c(S_2O_3^{2-})}{2\Delta t} \tag{7-15-7}$$

or

$$v = -\frac{\Delta c(S_2O_8^{2-})}{\Delta t} = \frac{c(S_2O_3^{2-})}{2\Delta t} = k c(S_2O_8^{2-})^m c(I^-)^n \tag{7-15-8}$$

Take logarithm to both sides of formula (7-15-6), then

$$\lg v = \lg k + m \lg c(S_2O_8^{2-}) + n \lg c(I^-) \tag{7-15-9}$$

When $c(I^-)$ is kept constant and $c(S_2O_8^{2-})$ is changed, we can obtain different rate of the reaction under different condition, the plot of $\lg v$ versus $\lg c(S_2O_8^{2-})$ is a straight line. The slope of the line m is the reaction order of $S_2O_8^{2-}$. Similarly when $c(S_2O_8^{2-})$ is kept constant, the plot of $\lg v$ versus $\lg c(I^-)$ is also a straight line and its slope n is the reaction order of I^-. The total reaction order $(m + n)$ can be calculated from m and n. When we know m and n, the reaction rate constant k at a given temperature can be calculate from reaction rate equation.

According to the Arrhenius equation, the effect of temperature on reaction rate constant can be determined.

$$\lg k = -\frac{E_a}{2.303\,RT} + \lg A \tag{7-15-10}$$

In the equation, A is a unique constant to the reaction, R is the gas constant, T is the absolute temperature, and E_a is the activation energy of the reaction.

We can calculate different values of k under different temperatures. Based on the equation $\lg k = -\frac{E_a}{2.303\,RT} + \lg A$, plot $\lg k$ versus $\frac{1}{T}$ yields a straight line. The activation energy of the reaction can be determined from the slope $(-\frac{E_a}{2.303\,R})$ of the line.

【APPARATUS, REAGENTS AND MATERIALS】

Apparatus   Erlenmeyer flask (100 mL × 8), test tube(10 mL × 1), graduated cylinder(10 mL × 6), thermometer, stopwatch, thermostat water bath, stirrer.

Reagents and Materials   0.2 mol·L^{-1} (NH$_4$)$_2$S$_2$O$_8$ solution, 0.2 mol·L^{-1} KI solution, 0.01 mol·L^{-1} Na$_2$S$_2$O$_3$ solution, 0.2 mol·L^{-1} KNO$_3$ solution, 0.02 mol·L^{-1} Cu(NO$_3$)$_2$ solution, 0.2 mol·L^{-1} (NH$_4$)$_2$SO$_4$ solution, 0.2% starch solution.

【PROCEDURE】

1. The Effects of Concentration on the Rate of the Reaction

At room temperature, KI, (NH$_4$)$_2$SO$_4$, Na$_2$S$_2$O$_3$, KNO$_3$ and starch solution are added to 100 mL Erlenmeyer flask by graduated cylinder according to the amount of experiment No.1-5 in Table 7-15-1. The mixed solutions are then stirred uniformly. Then, the certain volume (NH$_4$)$_2$S$_2$O$_8$ solutions are measured out by graduated cylinder and added into the corresponding Erlenmeyer flask. At the same time, the stopwatch is started and the Erlenmeyer flask is stirred continuously. Finally, the stopwatch is stopped immediately when the color of the solution turns into blue, then the Δt and room temperature is recorded.

To keep the ionic strength and total volume constant, the insufficient amounts of KI and (NH$_4$)$_2$S$_2$O$_8$ are supplemented by KNO$_3$ and (NH$_4$)$_2$SO$_4$.

Table 7-15-1   The effect of concentration and temperature on the rate of the reaction

	Experiment No.	1	2	3	4	5	6	7	8
Reagent Volume/mL	0.01 mol·L^{-1} Na$_2$S$_2$O$_3$	4.0	4.0	4.0	4.0	4.0	4.0	4.0	4.0
	0.2% starch solution	2.0	2.0	2.0	2.0	2.0	2.0	2.0	2.0
	0.2 mol·L^{-1} KI	10.0	10.0	10.0	5.0	2.5	10.0	10.0	10.0
	0.2 mol·L^{-1} KNO$_3$	—	—	—	5.00	7.50	—	—	—
	0.2 mol·L^{-1} (NH$_4$)$_2$SO$_4$	7.5	5.0	—	—	—	5.0	5.0	5.0
	0.2 mol·L^{-1} (NH$_4$)$_2$S$_2$O$_8$	2.5	5.0	10.0	10.0	10.0	5.0	5.0	5.0
$c\{(NH_4)_2S_2O_8\}$/mol·L^{-1}									
$c(KI)$/mol·L^{-1}									
$c(Na_2S_2O_3)$/mol·L^{-1}									
Reation temperature/K									
Δt/s									
v/mol·L^{-1}·s^{-1}									

According to the data of experiment No.1-3 in the Table 7-15-1, the results can reflect the influence of S$_2$O$_8^{2-}$ concentration on the chemical reaction rate. According to the data of experiment No.3-5 in the Table 7-15-1, the results can reflect the influence of I$^-$ concentration on the chemical reaction rate.

2. The Effects of Temperature on the Rate of Reaction

According to the experiment No.6 in Table 7-15-1, KI, (NH$_4$)$_2$SO$_4$, Na$_2$S$_2$O$_3$, and starch solution are added to a 100 mL Erlenmeyer flask and mixed together. 5.00 mL 0.2 mol·L^{-1} (NH$_4$)$_2$S$_2$O$_8$ is measured out by a 10 mL graduated cylinder and added into a test tube. Then the Erlenmeyer flask and the test tube are heated in the thermostat water bath(room temperature $+10\ ^{\circ}\text{C}$) about 5 minutes. The $(NH_4)_2S_2O_8$ solution is put into the Erlenmeyer flask, the solution is stirred and the stopwatch is started at the same time. Stop the stopwatch immediately when the color of the solution turns into blue, the Δt and the reaction temperature are recorded.

Repeat other experiment in the same way when the temperature is $0\ ^{\circ}\text{C}$ (in the ice water mixture) or $20\ ^{\circ}\text{C}$ higher than the room temperature and record the Δt and the reaction temperature for experiment No.7.

According to the data of experiment No.2, 6 and 7 in the Table 7-15-1, the results can reflect the influence of temperature on the chemical reaction rate.

3. The Effect of the Catalyst on the Rate of the Reaction

Cu^{2+} can catalyze the reaction (1) mentioned above. The rate of the reaction (1) can increase rapidly with the addition of trace Cu^{2+}. The experiment was conducted according to the experiment No.8 in Table 7-15-1. Here, add 2 drops $0.02\ \text{mol}\cdot\text{L}^{-1}\ Cu(NO_3)_2$ as catalyst before adding $(NH_4)_2S_2O_8$ to the Erlenmeyer flask. After comparing the results of experiment No.8 with No.2, please discuss the effects of $Cu(NO_3)_2$ catalyst on the rate of the reaction.

【DATA AND RESULTS】

Date:_____ Temperature:_____℃ Relative Humidity:_____

1. Calculate reaction order and rate constant

According to experimental data of Table 7-15-1, the rate of reaction can be calculated. m can be got from the slope of the diagrams of $\lg v$ versus $\lg c(S_2O_8^{2-})$ using the data of experiment No.1-3 in the Table 7-15-1. n also can be got from the slope of the diagrams of $\lg v$ versus $\lg c(I^-)$ using the data of experiment No. 3-5 in Table 7-15-1. The reaction rate constant k can be calculated after putting m and n into the equation and record the results in Table 7-15-2.

Table 7-15-2   Reaction order and reaction constant

Experiment No.	1	2	3	4	5
$\lg v$					
$\lg c(S_2O_8^{2-})$					
$\lg c(I^-)$					
m					
n					
k					
$\bar{k}$ (mean)					

2. Calculate activation energy of the reaction

Using the data of experiment No.2, 6 and 7 in Table 7-15-1, plotting $\lg k$ versus $\dfrac{1}{T}$ ields a straight line. The activation energy of the reaction can be calculated from the slope of the line and record the results in Table 7-15-3.

Table 7-15-3   Activation energy of the reaction

Experiment No.	2	6	7
k			
$\lg k$			
$\dfrac{1}{T}/\mathrm{K}^{-1}$			
$E_{\mathrm{a}}/\mathrm{kJ\cdot mol^{-1}}$			

Based on the above experimental results, please discuss the influence of concentration, temperature and catalyst on the reaction rate respectively.

【NOTES】

It is necessary to use the fresh $(NH_4)_2S_2O_8$ solution, because the solution of $(NH_4)_2S_2O_8$ is easy to decompose.

【QUESTIONS】

(1) Why $(NH_4)_2SO_4$ and KNO_3 solutions are added in the experiments No.1-5 in Table 7-15-1?

(2) What is the purpose of adding certain amount of $Na_2S_2O_3$ and starch? How does the amount of the $Na_2S_2O_3$ solution influence on the result of experiment?

(3) Does the reaction stop when the color of solution turns blue? Why?

(LI Zhenquan)

Experiment 16   Determination of the surface tension of ethanol solutions by maximum bubble pressure method

【OBJECTIVE】

(1) To grasp the principle and methods for measuring the surface tension of solutions using the maximum bubble pressure method.

(2) To understand the relationships between the concentration and the surface tension as well as the concentration and the surface excess concentration.

(3) To learn how to calculate the saturated surface excess concentration and the cross-sectional area of surface-active substances.

【PRE-LAB ASSIGNMENTS】

Simulated Design Experiment: Present the experimental design as a flowchart, clearly indicating the corresponding precautions and the rationale behind each step.

Preview questions:

(1) What is the definition of surface tension? And what are the main factors that influence the surface tension of a liquid?

(2) What are the consequences of air leakage in the system during the experiment? How can you ensure the system is sealed?

(3) Why should the capillary orifice need to be tangent to the water surface?

(4) Why should the ethanol solutions be measured from low to high concentration when determinating surface tension?

(5) Does this experiment need to be conducted under isothermal conditions? Why?

【PRINCIPLES】

As liquid molecules at the interface experience unbalanced attractive forces, the liquid surface tends to contract spontaneously. Surface tension can be regarded as the contraction force acting on per unit length of the interface between two phases, the direction of which is along the tangent line of the interface and points to the direction of the surface contraction.

Factors affecting surface tension include temperature, pressure, solution composition, solution concentration and so on. For example, at a given temperature and pressure, the surface tension of water is influenced by the chemical nature and the concentration of the solute. Compounds that lower the surface tension of the solvent are called surface-active substances. Increasing the concentration of a surface-active substance usually decreases the surface tension of the solution, while the concentration of the solute at the solution surface is typically higher than that in the bulk solution. The gap between the two concentrations is called the surface excess concentration. The relationship of the surface tension, concentration and the surface excess concentration can be described by the Gibbs adsorption isotherm equation

$$\Gamma = -\frac{c}{RT} \times \frac{\mathrm{d}\sigma}{\mathrm{d}c} \tag{7-16-1}$$

where Γ is the surface excess concentration $(\mathrm{mol}/\mathrm{m}^2)$, σ is the surface tension $(\mathrm{N}\cdot\mathrm{m}^{-1})$, T is the absolute temperature (K), c is the concentration $(\mathrm{mol}\cdot\mathrm{L}^{-1})$, R is the gas constant $(8.314\ \mathrm{J}\cdot\mathrm{mol}^{-1}\cdot\mathrm{K}^{-1})$, $\frac{\mathrm{d}\sigma}{\mathrm{d}c}$ is the gradient of $\sigma = f(c)$ function under constant temperature. The $\sigma = f(c)$ curve under isothermal condition is shown in Figure 7-16-1. By drawing a tangent line at any concentration, $\frac{\mathrm{d}\sigma}{\mathrm{d}c}$ can be calculated from the slope of the tangent line. The surface excess concentration can then be calculated using equation (7-16-1) and the resulting $\Gamma = f(c)$ curve is shown as Figure 7-16-2.

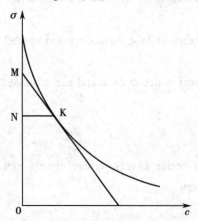

Figure 7-16-1   Relationship between surface tension(σ) and concentration(c)

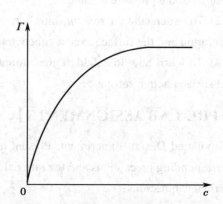

Figure 7-16-2   Relationship between surface excess concentration (Γ) and concentration(c)

Surface-active substance molecules typically have both hydrophilic and hydrophobic groups. When dissolved in the water, the hydrophilic groups tend to point inward the bulk solution, and the hydrophobic groups tend to point toward the air. As a result, the molecules are adsorbed at the solution surface, reducing the surface tension. When the concentration of the surface-active substance is low, the molecules randomly distribute at the surface, as shown in Figure 7-16-3(a). When the concentration increases, the surface-active substance occupies more area. When the concentration reaches a certain level, all the surface area is occupied by the surface-active substance, forming a monolayer of the molecules, as shown in Figure 7-16-3(b). Once the adsorption of surface-active substance at the surface reaches saturation, the surface concentration of adsorbed molecules per unit area is defined as the saturated surface excess concentration Γ_∞. Further increases in concentration lead to the formation of micelles, with no additional increase in the number of molecules at the surface, as shown in Figure 7-16-3(c).

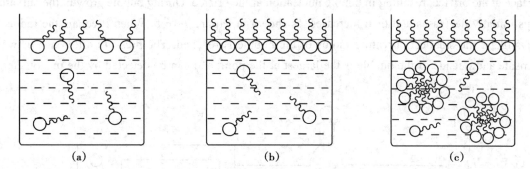

(a)   (b)   (c)

Figure 7-16-3   The distribution state of the surface-active substance molecules at different concentrations in solution

(a) $c < \Gamma_\infty$; (b) $c = \Gamma_\infty$; (c) $c > \Gamma_\infty$.

The relationship of surface tension, concentration and saturated surface excess concentration is described by the Langmuir adsorption isotherm equation

$$\Gamma = \Gamma_\infty \times \frac{Kc}{1 + Kc} \ (\text{mol} \cdot \text{m}^{-2}) \tag{7-16-2}$$

where K is a constant, Γ_∞ is saturated surface excess concentration. This equation can also be written as

$$\frac{c}{\Gamma} = \frac{c}{\Gamma_\infty} + \frac{1}{K\Gamma_\infty} \tag{7-16-3}$$

Taking $\dfrac{c}{\Gamma}$ as the ordinate and c as the abscissa, a straight line is obtained, the slope of this line is the reciprocal of saturated surface excess concentration.

Upon achieving monolayer coverage of surfactant adsorption at the surface, the cross-sectional area of individual surface-active substance molecules can be determined through the saturated surface excess concentration

$$S = \frac{1}{\Gamma_\infty N_A} \ (\text{m}^2) \tag{7-16-4}$$

where N_A is the Avogadro constant (6.02×10^{23}), S is the cross-sectional area of individual surface-active substance molecules.

Since the cross-sectional area of molecules is typically small, nm^2 is often used as the unit. Therefore, the following equation is commonly used to calculate the cross-sectional area

$$S = \frac{10^{18}}{\Gamma_\infty N_A} \ (nm^2) \tag{7-16-5}$$

In this experiment, the surface tension of ethanol solution at different concentrations is determined by the maximum bubble pressure method, and the surface excess concentration, saturated surface excess concentration and the cross-sectional area of ethanol are calculated.

The apparatus of maximum bubble method is shown in Figure 7-16-4. During the experiment, the orifice of the capillary b should be tangent to the liquid surface in the dropping funnel a. Open the stopcock on the dropping funnel c to initiate water flow, thereby lowering the system pressure. Atmospheric pressure compresses the gas in the capillary (open to the atmosphere) down to the liquid interface at the orifice, resulting in bubble nucleation at the orifice. During bubble growth, the curvature radius initially decreases and then increases, as shown in Figure 7-16-5. When it equals the radius of the capillary, the smallest curvature radius of the bubble is reached. The pressure difference between the inside and outside of the bubble is the largest at the point and can be detected by the manometer d.

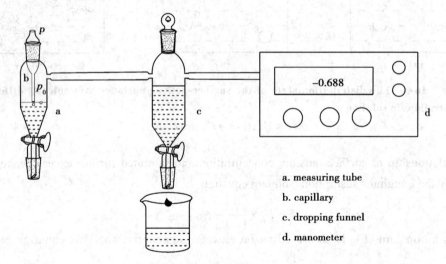

a. measuring tube

b. capillary

c. dropping funnel

d. manometer

Figure 7-16-4   The apparatus for determining the surface tension by the maximum bubble pressure method

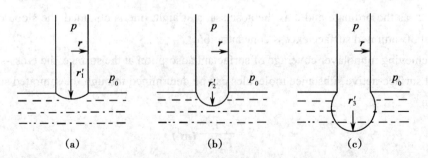

Figure 7-16-5   The curvature radius of the growing bubble

(a)$r_1' > r$; (b)$r_2' = r$; (c)$r_3' > r$.

Finally, the bubble is extruded from the capillary orifice, and the pressure difference returns to a relative low value. During this course, the relationship of the maximum pressure difference Δp, curvature radius r'_2 of the bubble(equals to the radius of the capillary r) and the surface tension σ is described by the Young-Laplace equation

$$\Delta p = p - p_0 = \frac{2\sigma}{r} \tag{7-16-6}$$

As the radius of the bubble is difficult to be determine, a standard solution with a known surface tension is used. Using the same capillary to determine the maximum pressure difference of each solution and applying the Young-Laplace equation (equation 7-16-6), the following formula (7-16-7) is obtained and the surface tension of the sample solution can be calculated.

$$\frac{\sigma}{\sigma'} = \frac{\Delta p}{\Delta p'} \tag{7-16-7}$$

Where σ and σ' are the surface tensions of the standard solution and the sample solution ($N \cdot m^{-1}$), Δp and $\Delta p'$ are the maximum pressure differences of the standard solution and the sample solution (kPa).

【APPARATUS, REAGENTS AND MATERIALS】

Apparatus   Surface tension measuring apparatus, beaker (500 mL × 2), volumetric flasks (50 mL × 8), measuring pipets (5 mL, 10 mL, 20 mL), medicine dropper.

Reagents and Materials   Anhydrous ethanol (A. R.), pure water.

【PROCEDURE】

1. Preparation of ethanol solution

Prepare a series of ethanol solutions according to Table 7-16-1 for the following experiments.

2. Determination of the surface tension

(1) Add water to dropping funnel c (with side arm) to two thirds of its volume, rinse the dropping funnel a and the capillary b for three to four times with the measured solution. Then add the measured solution into dropping funnel a and insert the capillary b into it. Adjust the volume of the solution in the dropping funnel a, making the capillary orifice be tangent to the water surface.

(2) Open the top cock of the dropping funnel c, turn on the manometer d and correct the pressure difference to zero. Close the top cock to create a sealed system. Open the stopcock of dropping funnel c and let the water drop, lowering the system pressure. Close the stopcock again and wait for one to two minutes. If the pressure difference remains unchanged, the system is sealed.

(3) Open the stopcock of dropping funnel c again and generate bubbles at a rate of eight to ten seconds per bubble. Record the maximum pressure difference three times, ensuring the values are closed to each other.

(4) Measure the surface tension of the ethanol solution from low to high concentration. Rinse the dropping funnel a and the capillary b with measured solution for each measurement.

【NOTES】

(1) The temperature should remain constant during the experiment.

(2) While rinsing the dropping funnel a, water should not enter the side arm, as this would affect the pressure reading.

(3) All the data should be obtained using the same capillary.

【DATA AND RESULTS】

Date:＿＿＿＿＿＿   Temperature:＿＿＿＿＿＿℃   Relative Humidity:＿＿＿＿＿＿

Table 7-16-1   Determination of surface tension of ethanol solution

Number	1	2	3	4	5	6	7	8
V(ethanol)/mL	0.00	0.50	1.00	2.00	4.00	8.00	12.00	16.00
V_{total}/mL	50.00	50.00	50.00	50.00	50.00	50.00	50.00	50.00
Δp_1/kPa								
Δp_2/kPa								
Δp_3/kPa								
$\overline{\Delta p}$/kPa								
c(ethanol)/mol·L^{-1}								
σ/N·m^{-1}	—							
$b = c \times \dfrac{\mathrm{d}\sigma}{\mathrm{d}c}$	—							
Γ/mol·m^{-2}	—							
c/Γ	—							
Γ_{∞}/mol·m^{-2}	—							
S/nm^2	—							

(1) Taking the surface tension σ of the ethanol solution as the ordinate, and the concentration c as the abscissa, the $\sigma = f(c)$ curve is obtained. Summarize the relationship between σ and c.

(2) Construct the tangent line and the parallel line of the horizontal x-axis at point K simultaneously. Assuming that the two lines intersect the y-coordinate at point M and point N (as shown in Figure 7-16-1), measure the distance b between M and N on the plotting paper ($b = c \times \dfrac{\mathrm{d}\sigma}{\mathrm{d}c}$). Substitute the value into the Gibbs adsorption isotherm equation (7-16-1) to calculate the surface excess concentration Γ under different concentrations.

(3) Taking the surface excess concentration Γ as the ordinate, and the concentration c as the abscissa, the $\Gamma = f(c)$ curve is obtained. Summarize the relationship between the surface excess concentration and the concentration.

(4) Taking $\dfrac{c}{\Gamma}$ as the ordinate, and the concentration c as the abscissa, the $\dfrac{c}{\Gamma} = f(c)$ curve is obtained. Calculate the saturated surface excess concentration and the cross-sectional area of single ethanol molecule.

【QUESTIONS】

(1) Besides the maximum bubble pressure method, list at least two other methods for determining the surface tension of a liquid, and make a comparison of all these methods.

(2) What is a surface-active substance? What indices are commonly used to evaluate the performance of surface-active substances?

(3) List at least three applications of surface-active substances in daily life.

(LIAO Chuan'an)

Chapter 8 | Preparation of Compounds

Experiment 17　Purifying Sodium Chloride

【OBJECTIVES】

(1) To practice basic operations such as dissolving, filtration, evaporation, concentration, crystallization and drying.

(2) To master the principle and method of purifying salt and test its purity.

(3) To understand the application of precipitation-dissolution balance in purification of inorganic matter.

【PRE-LAB ASSIGNMENTS】

Simulated Design Experiment: Present the experimental design as a flowchart, clearly indicating the corresponding precautions for purifying sodium chloride and the rationale behind each step. Preview questions:

(1) What are the clinic applications of NaCl?

(2) What is the purification method of solid substances?

(3) What is recrystallization , and can NaCl be purified using this method?

(4) What are the common methods for solid-liquid separation? How to choose in experiment? What problems should be paid attention to in vacuum filtration?

(5) In this experiment, why is SO_4^{2-} removed first, followed by Ca^{2+}, Mg^{2+} and Fe^{3+}? Can the order of precipitants be changed?

(6) Why shouldn't the water in the solution be evaporated completely during the concentrating step?

【PRINCIPLES】

NaCl and other salines are all derived from crude salt that usually contains ions such as K^+, Ca^{2+}, Mg^{2+}, Fe^{3+}, SO_4^{2-}, etc., and some other insoluble impurities including silt, sand, and organic matter, etc., are also included. The insoluble material can be removed by filtering the solution of crude salt, while soluble ones can be eliminated by adding the appropriate reagent ($BaCl_2$, Na_2CO_3, HCl, etc.) to the solution to form precipitates so that precipitates can form. The general method is to add the $BaCl_2$ solution into the NaCl solution to remove SO_4^{2-}:

$$Ba^{2+} + SO_4^{2-} =\!=\!= BaSO_4 \downarrow$$

Filter the precipitate of $BaSO_4$, then add Na_2CO_3 solution to remove Ca^{2+}, Mg^{2+}, Fe^{3+} and the excessive Ba^{2+}, respectively:

$$Mg^{2+} + 2OH^- = Mg(OH)_2 \downarrow$$

$$2Mg^{2+} + 2OH^- + CO_3^{2-} = Mg_2(OH)_2CO_3 \downarrow$$

$$Ca^{2+} + CO_3^{2-} = CaCO_3 \downarrow$$

$$Fe^{3+} + 3OH^- = Fe(OH)_3 \downarrow$$

$$Ba^{2+} + CO_3^{2-} = BaCO_3 \downarrow$$

Filter the precipitates, the excessive NaOH and Na_2CO_3 can be neutralized by hydrochloric acid:

$$H_3O^+ + OH^- = 2H_2O$$

$$2H_3O^+ + CO_3^{2-} = 3H_2O + CO_2 \uparrow$$

Finally, purified salt can be obtained through several steps including evaporation crystallization, filtration and drying.

【 APPARATUS, REAGENTS AND MATERIALS 】

Apparatus　Platform balance, beaker(50 mL × 2, 100 mL), cylinder(10 mL, 50 mL), test tube(10 mL × 6), glass funnel, suction instrument, evaporating dish, burner, tripod, spatula, stirring rod, dropper.

Reagent and Materials　Crude salt, 6 mol·L^{-1} HCl solution, 6 mol·L^{-1} HAc solution, 6 mol·L^{-1} NaOH solution, 1 mol·L^{-1} $BaCl_2$ solution, saturated Na_2CO_3 solution, saturated $(NH_4)_2C_2O_4$ solution, magnesium agent, filter paper, universal pH paper, 95% ethanol.

【 PRINCIPLES 】

1. Purifyingsodium chloride

1.1　Weighing and dissolving

Weigh out approximately 5.0 g of crude salt and place it into a 100 mL beaker. Add 25 mL of distilled water and stir to dissolve. Heat the beaker over a burner until the solution reaches boiling to ensure complete dissolution of the salt.

1.2　Removal of SO_4^{2-}

Add 1 mol·L^{-1} $BaCl_2$ solution dropwise (about 2 mL) with stirring, and continue heating for 5 minutes until the $BaSO_4$ precipitate has completely formed (Caution: Do not ingest $BaCl_2$ solution, as it is toxic). Remove the heater and cool the solution to room temperature. Then filter the solution and collect the filtrate in another beaker.

1.3　Removal of Ca^{2+}, Mg^{2+}, Fe^{3+} and the excessive Ba^{2+}

Add 1 mL of 6 mol·L^{-1} NaOH solution and 2 mL of saturated Na_2CO_3 solution in the filtrate. Boil gently for 5 minutes. After cooling, take a small amount of supernatant and put it in the test tube. Drop a few drops of Na_2CO_3 solution into the test tube to check if there is any precipitation. If there is no precipitation, filtrate and collect the filtrate in the evaporating dish.

1.4　Removal of the excessive OH^- and CO_3^{2-}

Add 6 mol·L^{-1} HCl solution dropwise in the filtrate and test the acidity with universal pH paper, until pH is 2-3.

1.5   Evaporating and drying

Decant the filtrate into an evaporating dish, heat the solution to the boiling point. (Be careful not to dry up). Allow to settle down and cool, transfer the crystal to the Buchner funnel with a filter paper and use a suction instrument to remove the excess liquid containing K^+, then let it remain on the filter paper until to be the dried crystal as much as possible. Washing the crystal 2-3 times with 95% ethanol. Transfer the crystal to the evaporating dish and heat it with gentle flame to dry up. Weigh the purified crystal and calculate the yield.

2. Test the purity of the purified salt

Take 1.0 g crude salt and purified salt in two 50 mL beakers respectively. Dissolve them with 5 mL of distilled water, respectively (if the crude salt is muddy, then filter it.) Put the clear solution of crude salt and purified salt in three pairs of small tubes respectively (each with 1.0 mL) to form control groups to test and compare their purities.

2.1   Test of SO_4^{2-}

Add two drops of 6 mol·L^{-1} HCl solution and 3-5 drops of 1 mol·L^{-1} $BaCl_2$ solution to test tubes respectively. It implies that SO_4^{2-} exist if white precipitate forms. Observe and compare the results in the two tubes and record them in Table 8-17-1.

2.2   Test of Ca^{2+}

To another set of test tubes containing the same solutions, add two drops of 6 mol·L^{-1} HAc and 3-5 drops of saturated $(NH_4)_2C_2O_4$ solution. It is indicated that Ca^{2+} exist if the white precipitate forms. Observe and compare the results in the two tubes and record them in Table 8-17-1.

2.3   Test of Mg^{2+}

To a third set of solutions in test tubes, add 3-5 drops of 6 mol·L^{-1} NaOH solution and 1 drop of magnesium reagent. It is shown that Mg^{2+} exists if blue precipitate forms. Observe and compare the results in the two tubes and record them in Table 8-17-1.

【NOTES】

(1) Additional water should be added to avoid the loss of NaCl during removing impurity by precipitation.

(2) Boiling the solution after each adding of precipitating agents, and then wait for the solution to cool down.

【DATA AND RESULTS】

Date:_____   Temperature:_____°C   Relative Humidity:_____

(1) Purifying the sodium chloride

Crude salt $m(NaCl)$ = _____ g, purified salt $m(NaCl)$ = _____ g

$$\text{Yield of product}(\%) = \frac{\text{weight of purified salt}}{\text{weight of crude salt}} \times 100\% = \underline{\qquad}$$

(2) Test the purity of purified salt

Table 8-17-1   The result of testing the purity of the purified salt

Item	Way of performance	Crude salt solution	Purified salt solution
Test SO_4^{2-}	Add $BaCl_2$ solution	Phenomenon: Conclusion:	Phenomenon: Conclusion:
Test Ca^{2+}	Add saturated $(NH_4)_2C_2O_4$ solution	Phenomenon: Conclusion:	Phenomenon: Conclusion:
Test Mg^{2+}	Add magnesium agent	Phenomenon: Conclusion:	Phenomenon: Conclusion:

【QUESTIONS】

(1) Can we use other acids to remove CO_3^{2-} in the experiment?

(2) Why is the hydrochloric solution added in during testing SO_4^{2-}?

(QIAO Xiuwen)

Experiment 18   Preparation of Ammonium Ferrous Sulfate

【OBJECTIVES】

(1) To understand the principle of preparing double salt.

(2) To practice the basic operations of water bath heating, filtration, evaporation, concentration, crystallization, and drying.

(3) To learn the method to inspect the quality of products with visual colorimetry.

【PRE-LAB ASSIGNMENTS】

Simulated Design Experiment: Present the experimental design as a flowchart, clearly indicating the corresponding precautions and the rationale behind each step.

Preview questions:

(1) What are the basic principles for the preparation of inorganic compounds?

(2) How to deal with the oil contamination of iron filings?

(3) How to deal with the evaporation of the solution during the reaction process?

(4) To what extent should ammonium ferrous sulfate solutions evaporate and why?

(5) What is the principle of optical colorimetry? How should grades be determined?

【PRINCIPLES】

The Mohr's salt, ammonium ferrous sulfate $[(NH_4)SO_4 \cdot FeSO_4 \cdot 6H_2O]$, a bluish transparent crystal, is a water soluble salt (insoluble in alcohol). Because it is more stable than the other ferrous salts in the air, it can often be used as a primary standard substance in a quantitative inorganic analysis.

Like most other double salts, the solubility of $(NH_4)_2SO_4 \cdot FeSO_4$ in water is less than that of

$(NH_4)_2SO_4$ or $FeSO_4$. Thus, the crystal of $(NH_4)_2SO_4 \cdot FeSO_4 \cdot 6H_2O$ can be obtained by mixing the two highly concentrated solutions of $FeSO_4$ and $(NH_4)_2SO_4$.

In this experiment, $FeSO_4$ solution is firstly obtained by dissolving iron metal in diluted H_2SO_4 solution. Then add the solid $(NH_4)_2SO_4$ and heat to dissolve. After concentrating and cooling, the slightly soluble crystal of $(NH_4)_2SO_4 \cdot FeSO_4$ can be obtained.

$$Fe + H_2SO_4 \Longrightarrow FeSO_4 + H_2 \uparrow$$

$$FeSO_4 + (NH_4)_2SO_4 + 6H_2O \Longrightarrow (NH_4)_2SO_4 \cdot FeSO_4 \cdot 6H_2O$$

As Fe^{2+} is easy to be oxidized to Fe^{3+}, therefore it needs to be added strong acid to prevent Fe^{2+} from being oxidized to Fe^{3+} during the experiment.

Since the Fe^{3+} ion reacts with excess SCN^- to give an intensely red-colored compound of $[Fe(SCN)_6]^{3-}$, it is therefore possible to determine the content of Fe^{3+}, the impurity, present in the product by visual colorimetry as follow.

With the addition of excess KSCN in the same way, a series of Fe^{3+} standard solutions and a sample product solution are prepared into the same colorimetric tubes. Comparing the red color of the standard solution with that of $[Fe(SCN)_6]^{3-}$ to find the standard solution with the same depth, the content of Fe^{3+} in the standard solution is similar to that of impurity Fe^{3+} in the product. Thus, the grade of the product can be determined accordingly. The limit of detection standard of Fe^{3+} for 1 g ammonium ferrous sulfate for grade I, II, and III are 0.05 mg, 0.10 mg and 0.20 mg, respectively.

【APPARATUS, MATERIAL AND REAGENTS】

Apparatus　Scale platform, analytical balance, conical flask (250 mL), beaker (50 mL), water bath (inner diameter 16 cm), graduated cylinder (20 mL × 2, 25 mL), volumetric flask (250 mL), pipet (1.0 mL × 2, 2.0 mL), colorimetric tube (25.0 mL × 4), suction instrument, evaporating dish, filter papers.

Material and Reagents　Iron filings, $(NH_4)_2SO_4$ (s), 10%Na_2CO_3 solution, 3 mol·L^{-1} H_2SO_4 solution, 3 mol·L^{-1} HCl solution, 25% alcohol solution, 25% KSCN solution, Fe^{3+} standard solution: Grade I (containing 0.05 mg Fe^{3+}), Grade II (containing 0.10 mg Fe^{3+}), Grade III (containing 0.20 mg Fe^{3+}).

【PROCEDURES】

1. Cleanse the Iron Filings

Weigh 4.0 g of iron filings into a conical flask. Add 20.0 mL of 10% Na_2CO_3 solution and heat it in a water bath for 10 minutes. Discard the solution and rinse the iron filings with distilled water.

2. Preparation of $FeSO_4$

Add 25.0 mL 3.0 mol·L^{-1} H_2SO_4 into the previous conical flask containing the iron filings. Heat it in a water bath for 30 minutes. During the reaction, the conical flask should be shaken frequently to accelerate the reaction, and a small amount of water should be added as needed. When the bubbling nearly ceases, filter the hot solution through a Büchner funnel. Transfer the solution to an evaporating dish, and rinse the residues in conical flask with 1.0 mL 3.0 mol·L^{-1} H_2SO_4 and some of distilled water in order. Add the rinse together to above evaporating dish (Note: since Fe^{2+} is stable in the strongly acidic solution, the addition of H_2SO_4 is to avoid the Fe^{2+} inverting to Fe^{3+}). Collect the residue of iron filings and dry it with filter paper. Weigh the residue and calculate the consumption of the iron in the reaction and the mass of ammonium sulfate required.

3. Preparation of $(NH_4)_2SO_4 \cdot FeSO_4 \cdot 6H_2O$

Weigh the ammonium sulfate according to the above calculated values and add it into evaporating dish containing the $FeSO_4$ solution. Place the evaporating dish above the water bath and heat it while stirring until all of the $(NH_4)_2SO_4$ has dissolved. Continue the heating and evaporating until the crystal films appear on the surface of the solution. Remove the evaporating dish from the heat and allow to settle down and cool to the room temperature, the $(NH_4)_2SO_4 \cdot FeSO_4 \cdot 6H_2O$ can be obtained. Filter it through the Büchner funnel and rinse with a small amount of alcohol twice with suction on. Transfer the solid to a dry piece of filter paper. Press dry with another sheet of filter paper. Weigh it and calculate the yield of the product.

4. Test the Product

Protocols for preparing Fe^{3+} standard solution of different grades are as follows.

The preparation of Fe^{3+} standard solution: The standard solution of 8.95×10^{-3} mol·L^{-1} Fe^{3+} was obtained by accurately weighing 0.431 7 g $NH_4Fe(SO_4)_2 \cdot 12H_2O$ and dissolving it at 250.00 mL conical flask, dilute to 250.00 mL.

Grade I (containing 0.05 mg Fe^{3+}): Add 0.25 mL Fe^{3+} standard solution, 2.0 mL 2.0 mol·L^{-1} HCl solution and 1.0 mL 1 mol·L^{-1} KSCN solution in a colorimetric tube. Then dilute to 25.00 mL.

Grade II (containing 0.10 mg Fe^{3+}): Add 0.50 mL Fe^{3+} standard solution, 2.0 mL 2.0 mol·L^{-1} HCl solution and 1.0 mL 1 mol·L^{-1} KSCN solution in a colorimetric tube. Then dilute to 25.00 mL.

Grade III (containing 0.20 mg Fe^{3+}): Add 1.00 mL of Fe^{3+} standard solution, 2.0 mL 2.0 mol·L^{-1} HCl solution and 1.0 mL 1 mol·L^{-1} KSCN solution in a colorimetric tube. Then dilute to 25.00 mL.

Weigh out 1.0 g of solid product into a 25 mL colorimetric tube, dissolve it with 15.0 mL of distilled water, add 2.0 mL 3.0 mol·L^{-1} HCl and 1 mL 25% KSCN, and finally dilute with distilled water to the mark of colorimetric tube. Homogenize and compare with the Fe^{3+} standard solutions to give the grade of the product.

【NOTES】

(1) It is necessary to cleanse the iron filings before use.

(2) The reaction between iron filings and sulfuric acid must be in the ventilating cabinet.

(3) To prevent the transformation of Fe^{2+} to Fe^{3+} in filtrate, 1.0 mL 3.0 mol·L^{-1} H_2SO_4 and oxygen-free distilled water are used to wash the conical beaker and ion residue.

【DATA AND RESULTS】

Date:_____ Temperature:_____°C   Relative Humidity:_____

(1) Preparation of ammonium ferrous sulfate

Weight of iron filings $m_{initial}(Fe) = $ _____ g;

The residue of iron filings $m_{final}(Fe) = $ _____ g;

Involved in the reaction $m[(NH_4)_2SO_4 \cdot FeSO_4 \cdot 6H_2O] = $ _____ g.

Yield of $(NH_4)_2SO_4 \cdot FeSO_4 \cdot 6H_2O(\%) =$

$$\frac{m[(NH_4)_2 SO_4 \cdot FeSO_4 \cdot 6H_2O] \times M(Fe)}{[m_{initial}(Fe) - m_{final}(Fe)] \times M[(NH_4)_2 SO_4 \cdot FeSO_4 \cdot 6H_2O]} \times 100\% = \underline{\qquad}.$$

(2) Test the purity of the product

Fe^{3+} standard solution	Grade I (Fe^{3+} 0.05 mg)	Grade II (Fe^{3+} 0.10 mg)	Grade III (Fe^{3+} 0.20 mg)
Grade of the product			

【QUESTIONS】

(1) What is double salt? What is the difference between simple and double salt?

(2) Why does the color of solution change to yellow during the evaporation and concentration? How to deal with it?

(3) How do we calculate the yield of ammonium ferrous sulfate — based on the amount of iron ions or ammonium sulfate?

(YU Kun)

Experiment 19   Preparation of Potassium Nitrate by Conversion Method

【OBJECTIVES】

(1) To learn the method for preparing the salt by double decomposition reaction and separating the substance by the effect of temperature on the solubility.

(2) To master the method and the principle of the recrystallization.

(3) To strengthen and improve basic operations such as dissolving, evaporating, crystallizing and filtrating.

【PRE-LAB ASSIGNMENTS】

Simulated Design Experiment: Present the experimental design as a flowchart, clearly indicating the corresponding precautions for the preparation of potassium nitrate by the conversion method, and the rationale behind each step.

Preview question:

(1) What are the common preparation methods for inorganic substances?

(2) What are the preparation methods for KNO_3? Please point out the advantages and disadvantages of each method.

(3) What is recrystallization? What problems should be paid attention to during recrystallization?

(4) How to determine the amount of raw material added in this experiment? What is the theoretical yield of KNO_3?

【 PRINCIPLES 】

The method based on the conversion of potassium chloride with sodium nitrate is carried out in industrial measurements. The reaction is as follows:

$$NaNO_3 + KCl \Longrightarrow NaCl + KNO_3$$

The solubility of four salts at different temperatures is shown in Table 8-19-1. This reaction is a reversible reaction. The effect of solubility at different temperatures stimulates the forward reaction and shift of the equilibrium condition to the right. In addition, when vaporizing a large amount of NaCl will crystallize, which will improve the yield and purity of KNO_3.

The solubility of KNO_3 is much more temperature dependent than that of NaCl (Table 8-19-1). These solubilities indicate the probability of a fractional crystallization process in which KNO_3 is crystallized from a solution containing both NaCl and KNO_3 by evaporating, concentrating and cooling the solution. At about 120 ℃, KNO_3 is unsaturated at a high temperature due to its high solubility. The filtrate is evaporated and filtered while hot in order to remove NaCl. Meanwhile, when cooled down to room temperature, less soluble KNO_3 will start to crystallize. Then the crude product can be purified by recrystallization.

Table 8-19-1　Solubility of KNO_3, NaCl, KCl and $NaNO_3$ at different temperature [g · $(100 \text{ g})^{-1}$ H_2O]

$T/℃$	0	10	20	30	40	60	80	100
KNO_3	13.3	20.9	31.6	45.8	63.9	110.0	169.0	246.0
KCl	27.6	31.0	34.0	37.0	40.0	45.5	51.1	56.7
$NaNO_3$	73.0	80.0	88.0	96.0	104.0	124.0	148.0	180.0
NaCl	35.7	35.8	36.0	36.3	36.6	37.3	38.4	39.8

【 APPARATUS, REAGENTS, MATERIALS 】

Apparatus　Hard test tube (300 mL), test tube (10 mL × 2), cylinder (50 mL), beaker (500 mL, 100 mL), thermometer (200 ℃), ring stand, plat form balance, glass rod, glass sand funnel, filter flask, vacuum pump, radiant-cooker, evaporating dish, watch glass.

Reagents and Materials　Sodium nitrate (Chemically Pure, C.P.), potassium chloride (Chemically Pure, C.P.), $AgNO_3$ solution (0.1 mol · L^{-1}), HNO_3 solution (5 mol · L^{-1}), dimethyl silicone oil.

【 PROCEDURES 】

1. Preparation of Potassium Nitrate

Firstly, 22.0 g of sodium nitrate is mixed with 15.0 g of potassium chloride and 35.0 mL of deionized water in a 300 mL boiling tube. Boil the mixture in dimethyl silicone oil at 140-160 ℃. Mark at the liquid level outside the oil bath beaker and inside the test tube. Stir until the solid can be thoroughly dissolved. Boil and stir until nearly two thirds of the solution left, then amounts of crystal is formed. While still hot, the solution is rapidly filtered through a glass sand funnel under diminished pressure. Cool down the filtrate to room temperature while shaking. The KNO_3 crystals start to form. Vacuum filter the concentrated solution containing the crystal by the glass sand funnel. Weigh the crude crystal. Calculate the theoretical yield and the crude yield of product.

2. Recrystallization of Potassium Nitrate

Reserve a small amount of the crude product for purity, take the remainder and the deionized water into the evaporating dish. The ratio of crude product and deionized water is 2 : 1 (the mass ratio). Boil and stir it until dissolved, then remove from heat. Settle down and cool to the room temperature, then filter it through the glass sand funnel under diminished pressure. Transfer the solid to a watch glass and dry in an oven at 120 °C. Weigh the purified crystal and calculate the theoretical yield of the product. Record the data in Table 8-19-2.

3. Test of the Purity

Take 0.03 g of crude product and purified product into two test tubes, respectively. Dissolve them individually with 3.0 mL deionized water. Add one drop of 5 $mol \cdot L^{-1}$ HNO_3 solution and two drops of 0.1 $mol \cdot L^{-1}$ $AgNO_3$ solution to individual test tubes. Record your observations and compare the results in the two tubes in Table 8-19-2.

【NOTES】

(1) When heating the reactants, water cannot hang outside the hard test tube because the temperature of the oil bath exceeds 100 °C. Otherwise, it is easy to cause explosive boiling.

(2) Do not rapidly freeze the filtrate after heating in case the crystals are super-small.

(3) If the solution is boiling and the crystal is still not completely dissolved during the recrystallization, add a small amount of deionized water and stir until the solid is thoroughly dissolved.

【DATA AND RESULTS】

Date:_____   Temperature:_____°C   Relative Humidity:_____

Table 8-19-2   Result of the yield and purity of the product

Substance	Mass / g	Yield / %	Phenomenon of the test for the purity
NaNO₃	—		—
KCl	—		—
KNO₃(Theoretical yield)	—		—
KNO₃(Crude product)			
KNO₃(Purified product)			

【QUESTIONS】

(1) In the preparation of KNO_3, why is the crystal obtained after the second vacuum filtration of the crude product?

(2) According to the solubility, how much NaCl and KNO_3 crystals in this experiment can be obtained?

(3) Why can NaCl crystals be removed by immediate filtration in the experiment at a low temperature?

(4) How to determine the proportion of crude products and water when the crude products are recrystallized?

(5) When KNO_3 is mixed with KCl and $NaNO_3$, how should it be purified?

(HUANG Jing)

Chapter 9 | Comprehensive Experiments

Experiment 20   Determination of HAc Concentration and Its Dissociation Equilibrium Constant in Vinegar

【OBJECTIVES】

(1) To study and comprehend the procedure for measuring the dissociation degree and the dissociation equilibrium constant.

(2) To understand and implement pH meter techniques.

(3) To understand how to use acid-base titration to determine the concentration of acetic acid in vinegar.

【PRE-LAB ASSIGNMENTS】

Simulated Design Experiment: Present the experimental design as a flowchart, clearly indicating the corresponding precautions for determining the dissociation equilibrium constant and the concentration of HAc in vinegar, as well as the rationale behind each step.

Preview question:

(1) Explain the concept of equilibrium dissociation constant of acid.

(2) By what methods can you determine the dissociation equilibrium constant of acetic acid?

(3) When preparing HAc solutions at different concentrations, is it necessary to dry the volumetric flask in advance? Is it necessary to dry the beaker in which the pH value of HAc is measured?

(4) Why should the pH of HAc solutions of varying concentrations be tested from low to high concentration?

【PRINCIPLES】

Acetic acid is a weak monoprotic acid. Its dissociation equilibrium in water solution is as follows

$$HAc + H_2O \rightleftharpoons H_3O^+ + Ac^-$$

Its dissociation equilibrium expression is given

$$K_a = \frac{[H_3O^+][Ac^-]}{[H_2O][HAc]} \approx \frac{[H_3O^+]^2}{c} \tag{9-20-1}$$

where K_a is dissociation equilibrium constant, α is degree of dissociation.

$$\alpha = \frac{[H_3O^+]}{c} \tag{9-20-2}$$

$[H_3O^+]$, $[Ac^-]$ and $[HAc]$ are the concentrations of H_3O^+, Ac^- and HAc in equation 9-20-1 and 9-20-2 respectively. c is the initial concentration of HAc. c can be determined by titration with NaOH standard solution, and $[H_3O^+]$ can be obtained by determining the pH of HAc solution. Thus, K_a and α can be calculated by the equations listed above.

Acetic acid (HAc) is the main composition in vinegar. Its content is in the range of 3.5-5.0 g $\cdot(100\ \text{mL})^{-1}$. Its K_a is 1.76×10^{-5} at 25℃. So it can be titrated by NaOH standard solution directly. In this titration, phenophthalein is used as the indicator.

【APPARATUS, REAGENTS AND MATERIALS】

Apparatus   pH meter , base burette (25 mL) or PTFE burette (25 mL) , conical flask (250 mL × 3) , volumetric flask (50 mL × 4, 100 mL), transfer pipette (10 mL, 25 mL), measuring pipette (15 mL), beaker (100 mL × 4), thermometer, burette stand.

Reagents and Materials   0.100 0 mol·L⁻¹ NaOH standard solution, 0.1 mol·L⁻¹ HAc solution, commercial vinegar, phenolphthalein indicator, standard buffer solution (pH = 6.86, pH = 4.00).

【PROCEDURES】

1. Determination of the dissociation degree and dissociation equilibrium constant of HAc solution

1.1   Determination of the concentration of HAc solution

Transfer 25.00 mL 0.1 mol·L⁻¹ HAc solution to a conical flask with a transfer pipette. Add 2 drops of phenolphthalein to the solution. Titrate the solution with 0.1 mol·L⁻¹ NaOH standard solution. When the pink appears and remains for at least 30 seconds, the end point is reached. Repeat the experiment twice more. Record the data into Table 9-20-1 and determine the HAc solution concentration.

1.2   Preparation of HAc solution with different concentrations

Transfer varied volumes of known concentration HAc solution to four 50 mL volumetric flasks, as shown in Table 9-20-2. Carefully pour distilled water into each volumetric flask until the meniscus touches the mark, then thoroughly mix the solution. Determine the exact concentrations of HAc solutions in four flasks.

1.3   Measuring pH of the HAc solutions

Transfer 40.0 mL of the prepared HAc solutions into four dry 50 mL beakers. Using a pH meter, determine their pH as they progress from diluted to concentrated solution. Keep track of the pH and temperature. Determine the dissociation degree and dissociation equilibrium constant, respectively. Enter the data into Table 9-20-2. (For the use of the pH meter, refer to Part I of Chapter 2: Ordinary Instruments in Basic Chemistry Experiments)

2. Determination of the concentration of HAc in vinegar

2.1   Preparation of Acid Solutions

According to Table 9-20-3, transfer 10.00 mL of vinegar to 100 mL volumetric flask. Dilute it to 100.00 mL with distilled water, and then mix thoroughly.

2.2   Titration of the Acid Solutions with NaOH Standard Solution

Transfer 25.00 mL of the sample solution into a conical flask and add 2 drops of phenolphthalein indicator in it, titrate it with NaOH standard solution until the pink appear and keep for 30 seconds, the endpoint of titration is reached. Write down the readings of the volume of NaOH standard solution consumed. Repeat the titration three times. The parallel measurements should be repeated three times using the same titration methods and the data is recorded in Table 9-20-3.

According to the following equation, calculate the content of HAc in vinegar.

$$\rho(HAc) = \frac{c(NaOH) \times V(NaOH) \times M(HAc)}{25.00 \times \dfrac{10.00}{100.00} \times 1\,000} \times 100 \ [g \cdot (100\ mL)^{-1}]$$ 　(9-20-3)

$$M(HAc) = 60.05 \ g \cdot mol^{-1}$$

【DATA AND RESULTS】

Date:_____   Temperature:_____℃   Relative Humidity:_____

Table 9-20-1　Determination of the concentration of HAc solution

Experiment NO.	1	2	3
Indicator			
Change of end point color			
$V(HAc)/mL$			
$V_{Initial}(NaOH)/mL$			
$V_{Final}(NaOH)/mL$			
$\Delta V(NaOH)/mL$			
$c(NaOH)/mol \cdot L^{-1}$			
$c(HAc)/mol \cdot L^{-1}$			
$\bar{c}(HAc)/mol \cdot L^{-1}$			
Relative mean deviation $\bar{d_r}/\%$			

Table 9-20-2　Determination of the dissociation degree and dissociation constant of HAc solution

Experiment No	1	2	3	4
$c_{Original}(HAc)/mol \cdot L^{-1}$				
$V_{Original}(HAc)/mL$	2.50	5.00	25.00	50.00
$V_{Total}(HAc\ diluted)/mL$	50.00	50.00	50.00	50.00
$c(HAc\ diluted)/mol \cdot L^{-1}$				
pH				
$[H_3O^+]$				
α				
K_a				
$\bar{K_a}$				
Relative mean deviation $\bar{d_r}/\%$				

Table 9-20-3   Determination of the content of HAc in vinegar

Experiment NO	1	2	3
Indicator			
Change of end point color			
$V_{Original}(HAc)/mL$			
$V_{Total}(HAc\ diluted)/mL$			
$V_{Determined}(HAc\ diluted)/mL$			
$V_{Initial}(NaOH)/mL$			
$V_{Final}(NaOH)/mL$			
$\Delta V(NaOH)/mL$			
$c(NaOH)/mol \cdot L^{-1}$			
$\rho(HAc)/g \cdot (100\ mL)^{-1}$			
Relative mean deviation $\overline{d_r}/\%$			

【 QUESTIONS 】

(1) What are the differences and similarities between dissociation degree and dissociation constant in expressing electrolyte nature? Are the dissociation degrees or dissociation constants of different concentrations of HAc solution at a given temperature the same?

(2) Does the temperature affect the dissociation degree or dissociation constant of HAc solution?

(3) Is it possible to utilize methyl red as an indicator in the titration of HAc with NaOH solution? Is the result higher or lower than the true concentration if it is used as the indicator?

(LI Rong)

Experiment 21   Determination of the Content of Calcium, Magnesium, and Iron in Tea

【 OBJECTIVES 】

(1) To master the method and the principle for determining calcium and magnesium content using complexometric titration.

(2) To master the method and the principle for determining trace iron content using a visible spectrophotometer.

(3) To learn the dry ashing method for natural product pretreatment.

【 PRE-LAB ASSIGNMENTS 】

Simulated Design Experiment: Present the experimental design as a flowchart, clearly indicating the precautions for determining calcium and magnesium in tea by coordination titration, and iron by visible spectrophotometry. Include the rationale behind each step.

Preview questions:

(1) Draw the structure of EDTA and describe its key physical and chemical properties.

(2) How does the pH of the solution effect the stability of coordination compounds?

(3) How can interference from other metal ions be minimized during measurements?

(4) Explain how calcium and magnesium are quantified separately in this experiment.

(5) Why Fe^{2+} can be determined with o-phenanthroline?

【 PRINCIPLES 】

Tea is an organic substance primarily composed of elements such as carbon, hydrogen, oxygen, and nitrogen. Additionally, it contains essential minerals like calcium (Ca), magnesium (Mg), and iron (Fe), which are vital for the human body. To analyse these minerals, dry ashing can be performed by heating tea in an open evaporation vessel or crucible, oxidizing it into ashes. The resulting ashes can then be dissolved in acid, and the solution can be used for analytical determination of Ca, Mg, and Fe.

At pH 10.0, Ca^{2+} and Mg^{2+} can be determined via complexometric titration using an EDTA standard solution, with Eriochrome Black T (EBT) as the indicator. To eliminate interference from Fe^{3+} and Al^{3+}, triethanolamine is added as a masking agent.

The iron content in tea is typically very low and can be quantified using spectrophotometry. To prepare the sample, hydroxylamine hydrochloride is added to reduce Fe^{3+} to Fe^{2+}, as shown in the following reaction:

$$2Fe^{3+} + 2NH_2OH \cdot HCl = 2Fe^{2+} + 4H^+ + N_2\uparrow + 2Cl^- + 2H_2O$$

Under pH conditions of 2–9, Fe^{2+} reacts with o-phenanthroline to form an orange-red complex:

The $[Fe(phen)_3]^{2+}$ complex exhibits a high molar absorptivity ($\varepsilon = 1.10 \times 10^4$ L·mol^{-1}·cm^{-1} at 508 nm) and an extreme stability ($lgK_s = 21.3$ at 20°C), making it ideal for spectrophotometric detection. However, the formation of the $[Fe(phen)_3]^{2+}$ complex is pH-dependent: at pH < 2, protonation of o-phenanthroline's nitrogen donors reduces their chelating ability, significantly slowing complexation kinetics; at pH > 9, Fe^{2+} undergoes hydrolysis, leading to precipitation of $Fe(OH)_2$ and preventing complex formation.

【APPARATUS, REAGENTS AND MATERIALS】

Apparatus visible spectrophotometer, analytical balance with a readability of 0.1 mg, volumetric flask (50 mL × 8, 250 mL × 2), volumetric pipette (25 mL, 10 mL), graduated cylinder (10 mL, 25 mL), burette, Erlenmeyer flask, beaker, evaporating dish or crucible, funnel, qualitative filter paper, stirring rod, burette stand.

Reagent and Materials 6 mol·L^{-1} NH$_3$·H$_2$O solution, 6 mol·L^{-1} HCl solution, 0.010 0 mol·L^{-1} EDTA standard solution, 0.010 g·L^{-1} Fe^{2+} standard solution, 25% triethanolamine solution, NH$_3$-NH$_4$Cl buffer solution (pH = 10), HAc-NaAc buffer solution (pH = 4.6), 0.1% *o*-phenanthroline solution, 1% hydroxylamine hydrochloride solution, 1% Eriochrome Black T, tea, deionized water.

【PROCEDURES】

1. Tea Ashing and Reagent Preparation

Weigh out 6–8 g of the tea sample (accurate to 0.000 1 g) and transfer it to an evaporation vessel or crucible. Heat the sample until complete ashing occurs. After cooling, dissolve the ash with 10.0 mL of 6 mol·L^{-1} HCl.

Transfer the solution to a small beaker, rinse the evaporation vessel three times with 20.0 mL deionized water, combining all washings with the primary solution. Adjust pH to 6–7 using 6 mol·L^{-1} NH$_3$·H$_2$O to induce precipitation. Heat the mixture in a boiling water bath for 30 minutes, then filter it. Thoroughly rinse the beaker and filter paper with deionized water. Transfer the filtrate directly into a 250 mL volumetric flask and add deionized water until the meniscus reaches the 250 mL mark, cap and shake thoroughly. Label the solution as Ca^{2+} and Mg^{2+} sample solution 1$^{\#}$.

Place a 250 mL volumetric flask beneath a glass funnel to collect the filtrate. Slowly pass 10.0 mL of 6 mol·L^{-1} HCl through the filter paper to completely redissolve the precipitate. Rinse the filter paper twice with deionized water, ensuring all material transfers into the flask. Add deionized water until the meniscus reaches the 250 mL mark, cap and shake thoroughly. Label the solution as Fe^{2+} sample solution 2$^{\#}$.

2. Determination of the Total Content of Calcium and Magnesium in Tea

Pipette 25.00 mL of sample solution 1$^{\#}$ into a 250 mL Erlenmeyer flask. Add sequentially 5.0 mL of triethanolamine solution and 15.0 mL of NH$_3$-NH$_4$Cl buffer solution, then swirl gently to homogenize the solution. After adding 2 drops of Eriochrome Black T indicator, titrate immediately with 0.010 0 mol·L^{-1} EDTA standard solution until the endpoint is reached. Repeat the titration in triplicate to ensure statistical reliability, and record the consumed EDTA volume in Table 9-21-1. Calculate the total content of calcium and magnesium, expressed as the mass fraction of CaO.

3. Determination of the Iron Content in Tea

3.1 Plotting the Standard Curve

Pipette 0.00 mL, 1.00 mL, 2.00 mL, 3.00 mL, 4.00 mL, 5.00 mL, and 6.00 mL of Fe^{2+} standard solution into seven labelled 50 mL volumetric flasks. To each flask, add sequentially 5.0 mL of hydroxylamine hydrochloride solution, 5.0 mL of HAc-NaAc buffer, and 5.00 mL of *o*-phenanthroline solution to each flask. Add deionized water until the meniscus reaches the 50 mL mark, cap and shake thoroughly. Then let stand for 10 minutes for full colour development. Using a 1 cm cuvette, measure the absorbance of each solution at 508 nm, and record all absorbance values in Table 9-21-2. Plot Fe^{2+} concentration $(g \cdot L^{-1})$ on the x-axis *versus* absorbance (A) on the y-axis. Perform linear regression to determine the best-fit equation and R^2 value.

3.2   Determination of the Iron Content in Tea

Pipette 2.50 mL of the $2^{\#}$ sample solution into a 50 mL volumetric flask. Follow the same procedure as above to measure the absorbance, and record all absorbance values in Table 9-21-3. Using the standard curve equation, calculate the Fe^{2+} concentration (x) by substituting the measured absorbance for y. Convert the Fe^{2+} concentration to the total iron content in the original tea sample, expressed as the mass fraction of Fe_2O_3.

【DATA AND RESULTS】

(1) Determination of the total content of calcium and magnesium in tea

Date:_____   Temperature:_____°C   Relative Humidity:_____

m (tea sample) =_____g

Table 9-21-1   Determination of the content of calcium and magnesium in tea

Experiment No.	1	2	3
sample solution $1^{\#}$/mL	25.00	25.00	25.00
Triethanolamine /mL	5.0	5.0	5.0
NH_3-NH_4Cl/mL	15.0	15.0	15.0
Indicator			
Color change at the end point $V_{Initial}$ (EDTA)/mL			
V_{Final} (EDTA)/mL			
$\Delta V_{Consume}$ (EDTA)/mL			
$c(Ca^{2+}$ and $Mg^{2+})$/mol·L^{-1}			
$\bar{c}$ $(Ca^{2+}$ and $Mg^{2+})$/mol·L^{-1}			
$\omega(CaO)$/g·g^{-1}			
$\bar{\omega}(CaO)$/g·g^{-1}			
$\bar{d_r}$			

Calculate the total content of calcium and magnesium based on the provided formulas, and express the combined content as the mass fraction of CaO.

$$\omega(CaO) = \frac{c(EDTA) \times \Delta V_{Consume}(EDTA) \times M_r(CaO)}{m(Sample) \times \dfrac{25.00}{250.00} \times 1\,000} \times 100\% \ (g \cdot g^{-1})$$

(9-21-1)

$$M_r(CaO) = 56.077\,4$$

(2) Determination of iron content in tea

Table 9-21-2   Determination of the standard curve

Experiment No.	1	2	3	4	5	6	7
Fe^{2+} standard solution/mL	0	1.00	2.00	3.00	4.00	5.00	6.00
hydroxylamine solution/mL	5.0	5.0	5.0	5.0	5.0	5.0	5.0
HAc-NaAc/mL	5.0	5.0	5.0	5.0	5.0	5.0	5.0
o-Phenanthroline solution/mL	5.00	5.00	5.00	5.00	5.00	5.00	5.00
V_{Total}/mL	50.00	50.00	50.00	50.00	50.00	50.00	50.00
c (Fe^{2+})/g·L^{-1}							
A							
Linear equation							
R^2							

Plot the standard curve and fit the linear regression equation.

Table 9-21-3   Determination of the iron content in tea

Experiment No.	1	2	3
sample solution 2$^{\#}$/mL	2.50	2.50	2.50
hydroxylamine solution/mL	5.0	5.0	5.0
HAc-NaAc/mL	5.0	5.0	5.0
o-Phenanthroline solution/mL	5.00	5.00	5.00
V_{Total}/mL	50.00	50.00	50.00
A			
$\rho(Fe^{2+})$/g·L^{-1}			
$\bar{\rho}$ (Fe^{2+})/g·L^{-1}			
$\omega(Fe_2O_3)$/g·g^{-1}			
$\bar{\omega}(Fe_2O_3)$/g·g^{-1}			
$\bar{d_r}$			

Calculate the total content of iron based on the provided formulas, and express the combined content as the mass fraction of Fe_2O_3.

$$\omega(Fe_2O_3) = \frac{\rho(Fe^{2+})\times 50.00}{m(\text{sample})\times \dfrac{2.50}{250.00}\times 1\,000}\times \frac{M_r(Fe_2O_3)}{2\times M_r(Fe)}\times 100\% \ (g\cdot g^{-1}) \tag{9-21-2}$$

$$M_r(Fe_2O_3) = 159.688, \ M_r(Fe_2O_3) = 55.845$$

【QUESTIONS】

(1) Briefly describe the principle of spectrophotometric determination of iron. Does this method

measure only the Fe^{2+} content in tea sample? Provide the rationale.

(2) Why can Fe^{3+} be separated completely from Ca^{2+} and Mg^{2+} in the pH range 6–7?

(3) What is the function of triethanolamine in the determination of Ca^{2+} and Mg^{2+}? Why is hydroxylamine hydrochloride solution added during Fe^{2+} measurement?

(GOU Baodi)

Chapter 10 | Open-ended Design Experiment

Experiment 22   Open-ended design experiment

【SUBJECTS】

(1) Determination of dissociation equilibrium K_b constant of NH_3.

(2) Determination of the content of $NaHCO_3$ in the sample of saleratus.

(3) Determination of the content of Al^{3+} in the sample of alum.

(4) Determination of the content of Cu^{2+} in the sample of copper salt.

(5) Determination of the content of Ca^{2+} in eggshell.

【OBJECTIVES】

(1) To search for information and independently develop and experimental design. Thereby cultivate the comprehensive experimental skills.

(2) To be familiar with the application of analytical methods for quantitative determination of the content of certain substances.

(3) To learn to process the experimental data.

(4) To master the general experimental operation and the use of appropriate equipments.

【APPARATUS, REAGENTS AND MATERIALS】

Apparatus   Electronic analytical balance (accurate to 0.001 g), platform balance, Visible spectrophotometer, pH meter, electric cooker (hot plate), water bath heating pot, gauze with asbestos, rubber suction bulb, alcohol burner, transfer pipette (10 mL × 2, 25 mL × 2), measuring pipette (1 mL, 2 mL, 5 mL, 10 mL, 20 mL), graduated cylinder (5 mL, 10 mL, 25 mL), acid burette (25 mL), base burette (25 mL) or PTFE burette (25 mL), colorimetric tube (25 mL × 6), beaker (50 mL × 6, 100 mL, 250 mL), Erlenmeyer flask (250 mL × 3), volumetric flask (50 mL × 3, 100 mL × 3), stirring rod dropper, burette stand, trivet, and weighing bottle, funnel, filter paper.

Material and Reagents

(1) Samples: $NH_3 \cdot H_2O$ solution (1.0 mol·L⁻¹), alum, saleratus, bluestone, eggshell samples.

(2) Primary standard substance: Anhydrous Na_2CO_3 (A.R.), $KHC_8H_4O_4$ (A.R.), $CuSO_4 \cdot 5H_2O$ (A.R.), $MgSO_4 \cdot 7H_2O$ (A.R.), $ZnSO_4 \cdot 7H_2O$ (A.R.).

(3) Reagents: 6 mol·L⁻¹ H_2SO_4 solution, 6 mol·L⁻¹ HCl solution, 0.1 mol·L⁻¹ HCl solution, 6 mol·L⁻¹ HNO_3 solution, distilled water, buffer solution of pH = 10 NH_3-NH_4Cl, 0.1 mol·L⁻¹ NaOH solution, buffer solution of 1.0 mol·L⁻¹ HAc-NaAc, 6.0 mol·L⁻¹ $NH_3 \cdot H_2O$ solution, 0.01 mol·L⁻¹ EDTA

solution, 0.05 mol·L^{-1} EDTA solution, 95% ethanol, triethanolamine, etc.

(4) Indicator: Phenolphthalein, methyl orange, eriochrome black T (s), xylenol orange, cal-red indicator (s), universal pH indicator paper and so on.

【REQUIREMENTS】

1. Design of experimental scheme

(1) Group Formation: Each group should consist of 4–5 students, who are expected to form teams independently 1–2 weeks before the assessment.

(2) Project Design and Submission: Each group is required to design and submit five experimental projects.

After the group is formed, team members should design the experimental methods, instruments, equipment, dosage, reagent concentrations, and other relevant details for each project. This should be done by consulting the literature and referring to the gauges, materials, and reagents listed under 【APPARATUS, REAGENTS AND MATERIALS】, as well as the sample dosage ranges provided in Table 10-22-1.

Each project must be accompanied by a written proposal, which should include the experimental objective, principle, instruments, reagents, detailed procedure, and a data recording table.

2. Operation assessment and result of experimental scheme

(1) Review of Experimental Schemes: After the assessment begins, the instructor will evaluate, provide feedback on, and grade the five projects submitted by each team.

(2) Selection of Assessment Item: The instructor will randomly select one of the five submitted projects to serve as the team's designated assessment item.

(3) Operational Assessment: Based on the number of team members, the instructor will divide the selected project into 4–5 sequential yet relatively independent operational tasks.

Each team member must independently complete the assigned task according to the project plan within the allotted time. The instructor will observe and record each member's performance and assign individual grades.

(4) Completion of the Project Report: After the operational assessment, the team must process the experimental data within the designated time and complete the written project report.

(5) Presentation and Defense: One team member will present the project, including experimental phenomena, data, results, conclusions, discussions, and references. After the presentation, all team members must respond to questions from the instructor or other teams. The instructor will assess the team based on the completeness, fluency, and accuracy of both the presentation and the defense.

(6) Submission of the Final Report: Teams should revise their project report based on feedback from the defense and submit the final version.

Table 10-22-1   Experimental projects

Projects	Quantity of samples and requirements
Determination of Dissociation Equilibrium Constant K_b of Ammonia	10.00 mL

continued

Projects	Quantity of samples and requirements
Determination of the Content of $NaHCO_3$ in the Sample of Saleratus	1.000 0–1.200 0 g
Determination of the Content of Al^{3+} Ions in the Sample of Alum	1.300 0–1.400 0 g
Determination of the Content of Cu^{2+} in the Sample of Copper Salt.	0.700 0–0.800 0 g
Determination of the Content of Ca^{2+} in Eggshell	0.150 0–0.200 0 g

3. Grade composition

The score consists of four parts Five Project schemes, operation, project presentation and defence, as shown in Table 10-22-2.

Table 10-22-2   Score sheet of the experimental test

Date: _____   Week:_____   Lesson:_____

Subject					Teacher	
Grade					Major	
Project number					Laboratory	
Test number	1	2	3	4	5	
Name						
Group						
Student ID						
Operating contents						
Time limited						
Non-standard operations						
Operation(50 points)						
Project (25 points)						
Experiment report (20 points)						
Thesis defense (5 points)						
Total score						

【HINTS】

(1) At the appropriate absorption wavelength, the relationship between the concentration of $[Cu(NH_3)_4]^{2+}$ and absorbance value is shown in Table 10-22-3.

Table 10-22-3   Relationship between the concentration of $[Cu(NH_3)_4]^{2+}$ and absorbance

Concentration of $[Cu(NH_3)_4]^{2+}$, $c/mol \cdot L^{-1}$	0.002–0.01
Absorbance (A)	0.1–0.5

(2) While preparing the solution of $[Cu(NH_3)_4]^{2+}$, ratio of concentrations of Cu^{2+} and NH_3 is 1∶200-1∶40.

(3) To dissolve the 0.15-0.20 g of eggshell, you can use 3.0-4.0 mL of 6 mol·L^{-1} HNO$_3$ and heat the solution slightly.

(4) Weighing range of primary standard substance is X ± 10%, X is calculation value.

(5) The volume of titrated solution in a conical flask is generally about 20.00 mL, and the consumed volume of the titrant is generally about 20.00 mL when using a 25.00 mL burette.

(6) When designing the experimental program, it is recommended that the solids be sampled into 100.00 mL solution, and 20.00 mL of sample solution is taken each time for determination.

【QUESTIONS】

(1) Why do we have to determine the pH of solutions with various concentrations from low to high when using a pH meter?

(2) Why should the solution be shaken violently near the end point when the content of NaHCO$_3$ in baking soda is determined by titration?

(3) Why is direct titration unsuitable for the determination of Al^{3+} ion content in alum samples?

(4) When conducting tests using a visible spectrophotometer, is it necessary to determine the maximum absorption wavelength of the sample? Can the determination range be narrowed down during the process of identifying the maximum absorption wavelength based on the principle of complementary light?

(5) How can the concentration of Mg^{2+} in eggshell be quantified?

(LI Fusen)

附录 I | 国际相对原子量表

1	氢	H	1.007 94	27	钴	Co	58.933 194
2	氦	He	4.002 602	28	镍	Ni	58.693 4
3	锂	Li	6.941	29	铜	Cu	63.546
4	铍	Be	9.012 183 1	30	锌	Zn	65.38
5	硼	B	10.811	31	镓	Ga	69.723
6	碳	C	12.010 7	32	锗	Ge	72.630
7	氮	N	14.006 7	33	砷	As	74.921 595
8	氧	O	15.999 4	34	硒	Se	78.971
9	氟	F	18.998 403 163	35	溴	Br	79.904
10	氖	Ne	20.179 7	36	氪	Kr	83.798
11	钠	Na	22.989 769 28	37	铷	Rb	85.467 8
12	镁	Mg	24.305 0	38	锶	Sr	87.62
13	铝	Al	26.981 538 4	39	钇	Y	88.905 84
14	硅	Si	28.085 5	40	锆	Zr	91.224
15	磷	P	30.973 761 998	41	铌	Nb	92.906 37
16	硫	S	32.065	42	钼	Mo	95.95
17	氯	Cl	35.453	43	锝	Tc	(98)
18	氩	Ar	39.948	44	钌	Ru	101.07
19	钾	K	39.098 3	45	铑	Rh	102.905 49
20	钙	Ca	40.078	46	钯	Pd	106.42
21	钪	Sc	44.955 908	47	银	Ag	107.868 2
22	钛	Ti	47.867	48	镉	Cd	112.414
23	钒	V	50.941 5	49	铟	In	114.818
24	铬	Cr	51.996 1	50	锡	Sn	118.710
25	锰	Mn	54.938 045	51	锑	Sb	121.760
26	铁	Fe	55.845	52	碲	Te	127.60

53	碘	I	126.904 47	86	氡	Rn	(222)
54	氙	Xe	131.293	87	钫	Fr	(223)
55	铯	Cs	132.905 451 96	88	镭	Ra	(226)
56	钡	Ba	137.327	89	锕	Ac	(227)
57	镧	La	138.905 47	90	钍	Th	232.037 7
58	铈	Ce	140.116	91	镤	Pa	231.035 88
59	镨	Pr	140.907 66	92	铀	U	238.028 91
60	钕	Nd	144.242	93	镎	Np	(237)
61	钷	Pm	(145)	94	钚	Pu	(244)
62	钐	Sm	150.36	95	镅	Am	(243)
63	铕	Eu	151.964	96	锔	Cm	(247)
64	钆	Gd	157.25	97	锫	Bk	(247)
65	铽	Tb	158.925 354	98	锎	Cf	(251)
66	镝	Dy	162.500	99	锿	Es	(252)
67	钬	Ho	164.930 328	100	镄	Fm	(257)
68	铒	Er	167.259	101	钔	Md	(258)
69	铥	Tm	168.934 218	102	锘	No	(259)
70	镱	Yb	173.045	103	铹	Lr	(262)
71	镥	Lu	174.966 8	104	𬬻	Rf	(265)
72	铪	Hf	178.486	105	𬭊	Db	(268)
73	钽	Ta	180.947 88	106	𬭳	Sg	(271)
74	钨	W	183.84	107	𬭛	Bh	(270)
75	铼	Re	186.207	108	𬭶	Hs	(277)
76	锇	Os	190.23	109	鿏	Mt	(276)
77	铱	Ir	192.217	110	𫟼	Da	(281)
78	铂	Pt	195.084	111	𬬭	Rg	(280)
79	金	Au	196.966 570	112	鿔	Cn	(285)
80	汞	Hg	200.592	113	鉨	Nh	(284)
81	铊	Tl	204.383 3	114	鈇	Fl	(289)
82	铅	Pb	207.2	115	镆	Mc	(289)
83	铋	Bi	208.980 40	116	𫟷	Lv	(293)
84	钋	Po	(209)	117	鿬	Ts	(294)
85	砹	At	(210)	118	鿫	Og	(294)

附录 II | 不同温度下水的饱和蒸气压

$t/℃$	p/kPa	$t/℃$	p/kPa	$t/℃$	p/kPa
0.01	0.611 65	34	5.325 1	70	31.201
2	0.705 99	36	5.947 9	72	34.000
4	0.813 55	38	6.632 8	74	37.009
6	0.935 36	40	7.384 9	76	40.239
8	1.073 0	42	8.209 6	78	43.703
10	1.228 2	44	9.112 4	80	47.414
12	1.402 8	46	10.099	82	51.387
14	1.599 0	48	11.177	84	55.635
16	1.818 8	50	12.352	86	60.173
18	2.064 7	52	13.631	88	65.017
20	2.339 3	54	15.022	90	70.182
22	2.645 3	56	16.533	92	75.684
24	2.985 8	58	18.171	94	81.541
25	3.169 9	60	19.946	96	87.771
26	3.363 9	62	21.867	98	94.390
28	3.783 1	64	23.943	100	101.42
30	4.247 0	66	26.183		
32	4.759 6	68	28.599		

附录Ⅲ 危险药品的分类、性质和管理

一、危险药品

危险药品是指受光、热、空气、水或撞击等外界因素的影响,可能引起燃烧、爆炸的药品,或具有强腐蚀性、剧毒性的药品。常用危险药品按危害性可分为以下几类来管理,见表1。

表1 危险药品的分类、性质和注意事项

类别	举例	性质	注意事项
易燃液体	汽油、丙酮、乙醚、甲醇、乙醇、苯	沸点低、易挥发,遇水则燃烧,甚至引起爆炸	存放阴凉处,远离热源。使用时注意通风,不得有明火
易燃固体	赤磷、硫、萘、硝化纤维	燃点低,受热、摩擦、撞击或遇氧化剂,可引起剧烈连续燃烧、爆炸	同上
易燃气体	氢气、乙炔、甲烷	因撞击、受热引起燃烧。与空气按一定比例混合,则会爆炸	使用时注意通风。如为钢瓶气,不得在实验室存放
遇水易燃品	钠、钾	遇水剧烈反应,产生可燃气体并放出热量,此反应热会引起燃烧	保存于煤油中切勿与水接触
自燃物品	白磷	在适当温度下被空气氧化、放热,达到燃点而引起自燃	保存于水中
易爆炸品	硝酸铵、苦味酸、三硝基甲苯	遇高热摩擦、撞击时会产生猛烈爆炸放出大量气体和热量	存放于阴凉、低下处。轻拿、轻放
氧化剂	硝酸钾、氯酸钾、过氧化氢、过氧化钠、高锰酸钾	具强氧化性,遇酸、受热、与有机物、易燃品、还原剂等混合时,因反应引起燃烧或爆炸	不得与易燃品、爆炸品、还原剂等一起存放
剧毒药品	氰化钾、三氧化二砷、升汞、氯化钡、六六六	剧毒,少量侵入人体(误食或接触伤口)引起中毒,甚至死亡	专人、专柜保管,并应设有使用登记制度。现用现领,用剩的剩余物都应交回保管人
腐蚀性药品	强酸、氟化氢、强碱、溴、酚	强腐蚀性,触及物品造成腐蚀、破坏,触及人体皮肤,引起化学烧伤	不要与氧化剂、易燃品、爆炸品放在一起

二、剧毒物品

中华人民共和国公安部1993年发布并实施中华人民共和国公共安全行业标准GA58—1993。将剧毒药品分为A、B两级,见表2和表3。

表 2　A 级无机剧毒药品名表

品名	别名	品名
白磷	黄磷	氟
液化二氧化硫	亚硫酸酐	一氧化氮
氟化氢（无水）	无水氢氟酸	二氟化氧
磷化镁	二磷化三镁	二氧化氮
磷化氢	磷化三氢,膦	磷化钾
液化氯	液氯	磷化铝
氯化汞	氧化高汞,二氯化汞	磷化铝农药
氯化氰	氰化氯,氯甲腈	磷化钠
氰化汞	氰化高汞	六氟化钨
氰化汞钾	氰化钾汞,汞氰化钾	六氟化硒
氰化钴钾	钴氰化钾	氯化溴
氰化钠	山奈	氢氰酸
氰化镍	氰化亚镍	氰
氰化镍钾	氰化钾镍	氰化钡
液化氰化氢	无水氢氰酸	氰化钙
氰化铜	氰化高铜	氰化镉
氰化溴	溴化氰	氰化钴
氰化银钾	银氰化钾	氰化钾
三氯化砷	氯化亚砷	氰化金钾
三氧化二砷	白砒、砒霜、亚砷酸酐	氰化铅
砷化氢	砷化三氢,胂	氰化铈
四氟化硅	氟化硅	氰化锌
液化四氧化二氮	二氧化氮	氰化亚钴
羰基镍	四羰基镍,四碳酰镍	氰化亚铜
锑化氢	锑化三氢	氰化银
五羰基铁	羰基铁	三氟化氯
五氧化二砷	砷酸酐	三氟化氯
溴化羰	溴光气	四氟化硫
亚砷酸钠	偏亚砷酸钠	五氟化磷
氧氯化硒	氯化亚硒酰,二氯氧化硒	硒化氢
氧氰化汞	氰氧化汞	硒酸钾
迭氯化钠		硒酸钠
叠氮化钡		亚砷酸钾
叠氮酸		亚硒酸钾
氧化镉		亚硒酸钠
五铌化氯		

表3　剧毒物品急性毒性分级标准和半致死量

中毒途径	A 级	B 级
口服	$\leq 5\ mg\cdot kg^{-1}$	$5\sim 50\ mg\cdot kg^{-1}$
皮肤接触	$\leq 40\ mg\cdot kg^{-1}$	$40\sim 200\ mg\cdot kg^{-1}$
吸入粉尘或烟雾	$\leq 0.5\ mg\cdot L^{-1}$	$0.5\sim 2\ mg\cdot L^{-1}$
吸入蒸气或气体	$\leq 1\,000\ mg\cdot L^{-1}$	$\leq 3\,000\ mg\cdot L^{-1}$

三、化学实验室毒品管理规定

1. 实验室使用毒品和剧毒品(无论 A 或 B 类毒品)应预先计算使用量,按用量到毒品库领取,尽量做到用多少领多少。使用后剩余毒品应送回毒品库统一管理。毒品库对领出和退回毒品要详细登记。

2. 实验室在领用毒品和剧毒品后,由两位教师(教辅人员)共同负责保证领用毒品的安全管理,实验室建立毒品使用账目。账目包括:

药品名称,领用日期,领用量,使用日期,使用量,剩余量,使用人签名,两位管理人签名。

3. 实验室使用毒品时,如剩余量较少且近期仍需使用须存放实验室内,此药品必须放于实验室毒品保险柜内,钥匙由两位管理人员掌管,保险柜上锁和开启均须两人同时在场。实验室配制有毒药品溶液时也应按用量配制,该溶液的使用,归还和存放也必须履行使用账目登记制度。

附录Ⅳ | 标准缓冲溶液

标准缓冲溶液名称	标准缓冲溶液配制	pH(25℃)
$0.05\ mol \cdot L^{-1}$ 四草酸氢钾溶液	称取(54±3)℃下烘干4~5 h的四草酸氢钾12.61 g,溶于蒸馏水,稀释至1 L	1.679
$0.05\ mol \cdot L^{-1}$ 邻苯二甲酸氢钾溶液	称取已在(115±5)℃下烘干2~3 h的邻苯二甲酸氢钾10.12 g,溶于蒸馏水,稀释至1 L	4.008
约$0.034\ mol \cdot L^{-1}$ 25 ℃饱和酒石酸氢钾溶液	在玻璃磨口瓶中装入蒸馏水和过量的酒石酸氢钾粉末(约20 g·L⁻¹),温度控制在(25±5)℃下,剧烈摇动20~30 min,溶液澄清后,用倾泻法取其清液备用(如用0.02级的仪器,饱和温度应控制在(25±3)℃	3.557
$0.025\ mol \cdot L^{-1}$磷酸二氢钾 $-0.025\ mol \cdot L^{-1}$磷酸氢二钠混合溶液	分别称取已在(115±5)℃下烘干2~3 h的磷酸氢二钠3.53 g和磷酸二氢钾3.39 g溶于蒸馏水,稀释至1 L(如用0.02级的仪器,蒸馏水应预先煮沸15~30 min)	6.865
$0.008665\ mol \cdot L^{-1}$磷酸二氢钾 $-0.03032\ mol \cdot L^{-1}$磷酸氢二钠混合溶液	分别称取已在(115±5)℃下烘干2~3 h的磷酸二氢钾1.179 g和磷酸氢二钠4.30 g溶于蒸馏水,稀释至1 L(如用0.02级的仪器,蒸馏水应预先煮沸15~30 min)	7.413
$0.01\ mol \cdot L^{-1}$ 硼砂溶液	称取硼砂3.80 g(注意不能烘),溶于蒸馏水,稀释至1 L(如用0.02级的仪器,蒸馏水应预先煮沸15~30 min)	9.180
$0.025\ mol \cdot L^{-1}$碳酸氢钠 $-0.025\ mol \cdot L^{-1}$碳酸钠混合溶液	分别称取已在270~300 ℃干燥至恒重的碳酸钠2.65 g和在硫酸干燥器中干燥约4 h的碳酸氢钠2.10 g,溶于蒸馏水,稀释至1 L(如用0.02级的仪器,蒸馏水应预先煮沸15~30 min)	10.012
约$0.020\ mol \cdot L^{-1}$ 25 ℃饱和氢氧化钙溶液	在玻璃磨口瓶或聚乙烯塑料瓶中装入蒸馏水和过量的氢氧化钙粉末(约5~10 g·L⁻¹),温度控制在(25±5)℃下,剧烈摇动20~30 min,迅速用抽滤法滤取清液备用[如用0.02级的仪器,饱和温度应控制在(25±1)℃]	12.454

附录Ⅴ | 参考书目

［1］北京大学化学与分子工程学院分析化学教学组.基础分析化学实验.北京:北京大学出版社,2010.

［2］北京大学化学系物理化学教研室.物理化学实验.4版.北京:北京大学出版社,2002.

［3］北京师范大学无机化学教研室.无机化学实验.4版.北京:高等教育出版社,2014.

［4］曹凤歧,刘静.无机化学实验与指导.南京:东南大学出版社,2013.

［5］陈虹锦.实验化学(上册).北京:科学出版社,2007.

［6］陈焕光.分析化学实验.广州:中山大学出版社,2003.

［7］复旦大学.物理化学实验.3版.北京:高等教育出版社,2004.

［8］郭伟强.大学化学基础实验.2版.北京:科学出版社,2010.

［9］国家药典委员会.中华人民共和国药典(四部).北京:中国医药科技出版社,2015.

［10］李雪华,籍雪平.基础化学实验.4版.北京:人民卫生出版社,2019.

［11］吕苏琴,张春荣,揭念芹,等.基础化学实验(Ⅰ).北京:科学出版社,2001.

［12］孟凡德.医用基础化学实验.北京:科学出版社,2001.

［13］钱可萍.无机及分析化学实验.北京:高等教育出版社,1989.

［14］清华大学化学系物理化学实验组.物理化学实验.北京:清华大学出版社,1991.

［15］南京大学无机及分析化学实验组.无机及分析化学实验.4版.北京:高等教育出版社,2006.

［16］刘春丽.物理化学实验.北京:化学工业出版社,2017.

［17］中南民族大学分析化学实验组.分析化学实验.北京:化学工业出版社,2017.

［18］王少云.分析化学与药物分析实验.济南:山东大学出版社,2004.

［19］魏祖期,李雪华.基础化学实验.北京:人民卫生出版社,2005.

［20］无机及分析化学实验编写组.无机及分析化学实验.武汉:武汉大学出版社,2001.

［21］武汉大学化学分子科学中心编写组.无机及分析化学实验.武汉:武汉大学出版社,2005.

［22］曾慧慧.现代实验化学(上册).北京:北京大学医学出版社,2004.

［23］周锦兰,张开诚.实验化学.武汉:华中科技大学出版社,2005.

［24］冯清.医学基础化学实验(双语版).武汉:华中科技大学出版社,2007.

［25］徐伟亮.基础化学实验.北京:科学出版社,2010.

［26］中山大学.无机化学实验.3版.北京:高等教育出版社,2015.

［27］Gershon J. Shugar. Chemical technician's ready reference handbook. 5th ed. New York: McGraw-Hill Book Company,2011.

［28］Stanley Marcus. Experimental General Chemistry. New York: McGraw-Hill Education,1999.